Rent, Resources, Technologies

Springer
Berlin
Heidelberg
New York
Barcelona
Hong Kong
London
Milan
Paris
Singapore
Tokyo

Alberto Quadrio Curzio
Fausta Pellizzari

Rent, Resources, Technologies

With 39 Figures
and 15 Tables

Springer

Alberto Quadrio Curzio
Professor of Economics
and Dean of the Faculty of Political Science
Catholic University
Milan

Fausta Pellizzari
Professor of Development Economics
Faculty of Political Science
Catholic University
Milan

Originally published in Italian by
Società editrice Il Mulino, 1996

ISBN 3-540-66007-0 Springer-Verlag Berlin Heidelberg New York

Library of Congress Cataloging-in-Publication Data
Die Deutsche Bibliothek – CIP-Einheitsaufnahme
Quadrio Curzio, Alberto: Rent, resources, technologies: with 15 tables / Alberto Quadrio Curzio; Fausta Pellizzari. – Berlin; Heidelberg; New York; Barcelona; Hong Kong; London; Milan; Paris; Singapore; Tokyo: Springer, 1999
ISBN 3-540-66007-0

Printed in Germany

Hardcover-Design: Erich Kirchner, Heidelberg

SPIN 10656366 43/2202-5 4 3 2 1 0 – Printed on acid-free paper

Preface

This volume deals with problems of resources, technology, and rent from a theoretical perspective. These are significant issues for both history and economics, and it is widely acknowledged that extraordinary and ever-accelerating technological progress is by no means assurance of eliminating the natural and environmental scarcities. On the contrary, as several scarcities disappear or diminish, such as those related to agricultural land and its products, new, more complex and ever-changing scarcities emerge, such as those associated with environmental factors.

Analogously, technological progress has by no means eliminated the category of rent, by concentrating the distribution of national income only to profits and salaries. The simultaneous existence of technologies with different degrees of efficiency has kept rents and quasi-rents alive, in forms that are linked to production processes, and are considerably more complex then the old form of land rent.

More generally, it is evident that in the economic system there are means of production that may be or may become scarce and thus, at first, slow down, and subsequently, as a reaction, contribute to stimulating technical progress. Altogether with such productive scarcities, rent and quasi-rent still affect the price relations and the distribution of income —they appear with the scarcities, disappear when the latter are eliminated, only to reappear again when new scarcities emerge.

This volume deals with these problems from an analytical and formal theoretical standpoint. With the sole exception of the first Chapter which contains some introductory considerations, readers will not find here historical-quantitative analysis, nor descriptive references to reality.

We are aware —and we wish to remind it both to ourselves and to the reader—, that each contribution of economic science inherently brings about a dilemma between analytical and formal rigor on the one hand and interpretative significance on the other. Often this dilemma does not have an equilibrium point and thus there appears to be the risk of becoming too abstract or too descriptive. Whoever endeavors into formalized economic theory (which some call "pure") knows the running risk of abstraction. Nevertheless, the risk becomes acceptable, if one is aware of the broader boundaries of economic science —it encompasses theory with empirical analysis, formal rigor with interpretative vision of reality, analytical knowledge with policy and institutional oriented goals.

Perhaps a helpful classification consists of dividing economic theory into at least three components: analytical and formal economic theory, historical and quantitative economic theory, and quantitative economic theory. They should all be considered "theories" only to the extent that they formulate, even by means of different methods, propositions of general character.

The combination of these elements is characteristic only of the contributions of great Scholars, of whom there have been many since the Classics and who still exist today, and to whom one must continually refer in order to understand the breadth of economic science. Each economist can give a personal —more or less significant— contribution to economics only to the extent there exists awareness that such own contribution cannot but be of limited nature.

The authors of this volume are aware of having conducted a study of analytical and formal economic theory that is specific and partial. Within the field and the method chosen, however, it is the authors' hope that this volume can be a contribution of some relevance, the extent of which shall be judged by the readers.

The volume is divided among its two authors as follows. Chapters I - VI and chapter XIV have been written by Alberto Quadrio Curzio, and they also include previously published works. Chapters VII - X have been jointly written by Alberto Quadrio Curzio and Fausta Pellizzari. Chapters XI, XII, and XIII have been written by Fausta Pellizzari.

In this English version we have not presented the Appendixes, published in the Italian version (from page 355 to page 406), which contain in details all the mathematical proofs and a remarkable set of numerical simulations. The more demanding readers, however, are referred to those Appendixes.

For the translation from the Italian edition thanks are due to Fausta Pellizzari, Gianpaolo Mariutti, Giulio Cainelli, Riccardo Leoncini.

The authors point out that Chapter I as well as Chapters VII - XIV were elaborated within projects (89.00810.ct10, 92.01943.ct10, 93.00951.ct10) during the years 1989-1994, of the CNR (National Research Council), Comitato Nazionale per le Scienze Economiche, Sociologiche, e Statistiche (National Committee for Economic, Sociological, and Statistical Sciences). Instead, Chapter IV is a new version of an essay published in 1987 and supported by the Ministry of Education (MPI 40% - 1987). The revision and the translation of the Italian version have been partially carried out within a research project financed by CNR 1996 (96.01611.CT10). Here, we wish to acknowledge these two Institutions.

The authors greatly thank those who, in different stages, provided suggestions: Siro Lombardini; Carlo Felice Manara; Luigi Pasinetti; Mario Faliva and Pier Carlo Nicola; Salvatore Baldone; Enrico Bellino; Marco Fortis; Roberto Zoboli and Gianpaolo Mariutti. Of course, the authors share all responsibilities.

An acknowledgement must also be made to Il Mulino Publishers, in particular to Giovanni Evangelisti, and to the Centro di Ricerche in Analisi Economica e Sviluppo Economico Internazionale-CRANEC (International Centre for Economic Analysis and Development Research) of the Faculty of Political Science of the Catholic University, Milan where all of the research was carried out.

A.Q.C. - F.P.

Catholic University, Milan
March 1999

Contents

Chapter I – Historical and theoretical introduction to rent, resources and technologies

1. Introduction

It is useful to introduce this theoretical study with some propositions from the history of economic thought. The review will focus on some general categories later recalled in the analytical part of the book. In so doing, we avoid a superficial survey of issues that would by themselves require monographic studies. Since a selection has to be made, it will be based upon the analytical and intellectual framework followed over several years by the authors in their research on this topic.

Concerning resources -usually, though not exclusively, natural resources- we shall refer to categories such as relative and absolute scarcity, static and dynamic scarcity, innovative and technological scarcity.

Concerning technology we shall refer to categories such as the antagonism-synergy between scarcity and technical innovation, the choice of techniques and technical progress, the relationship between scarcity and circular process of production, and between efficiency and scarcity.

Concerning rent we shall refer to categories such as extensive and intensive rent, surplus rent, differential rent, marginal rent, quasi-rent, structural rent, and technological rent.

The recognition of all these "past" concepts is important. A study of economic theory, when it is not intended exclusively as a formal exercise, is always grounded in the history of economic thought which helps to assess the precise scientific locus where the research at stake lays -or one thinks it lays.

In the preface to this volume we argued that each contribution to economics is marked by an intrinsic dilemma of being analytical rigorous or rather interpretative meaningful, and we put forward the need of identifying at least three components in the economic theory: (i) the analytical-formal; (ii) the historical-quantitative; and (iii) the analytical-quantitative.

Though such individual components emphasize quite different methods, they can still be reckoned theory as far as they are able to formulate general propositions. In fact, when this does not occur, the first approach ends up in a tautological exercise, the second approach in simple description without interpretation, and the third approach in estimation without explanation.

In the history of economic theory many scholars have been capable of combining analytic rigor with interpretative meaningfulness, starting, of course, from the Classical economists, who may be considered for the time they wrote authors of "complete economic theories".

In the most recent experience, with the exception of few masters, the effect of specialization has led the majority of scholars to focus only on one of these components —either analytic formal, or historical-quantitative, or, finally, quantitative and econometric.

In the following survey we refer to contributions of economic theory in its whole spectrum: analytical-formal, historical-quantitative, and analytical-quantitative.

In particular we adopt a restrictive criterion of selection. The starting reference is the Classical Theory (Smith, Malthus, Ricardo) and the Marginal Theory (Wicksteed, Marshall). By 1890 the main categories, with which we are concerned, were already established.

From those bases, three specific lines of theoretical analysis were developed during the 1930s and survived up until today. We will briefly consider them in turn: (i) the line of researches on resources and specific scarcities (initiated by Hotelling); (ii) the line on growth without scarcity (initiated by Harrod and von Neumann); and (iii) the line on complex growth and relative scarcity (initiated by Kuznets). We will also take into account a fourth line (initiated by Leontief in the 1970s) based on dynamics with natural resources and relative scarcity.

In short, these are complementary lines of research that considered alone remain incomplete, but nevertheless fundamental. They have older reference that for the sake of simplicity we omit. None of them however appears entirely committed, adequate, or sufficiently general in re-establishing in modern terms the concepts of resources, technology, and rent, which find their historical-theoretical roots in the contributions of Ricardo and Marshall. It was Sraffa who moved along this tradition at the beginning of the 1960s. Using a static multi-sectoral model, he developed a very original concept of structural rent, yet unable in many ways in coupling with the interdependence between changes in production and distribution and the dynamic processes. Such issues were later tackled, among others, by Quadrio Curzio with contributions on complex and dynamic scarcity and technological rent. It is from these contributions that we will depart.

Therefore, from Chapter II our theoretical analysis will offer a general model on resources, technologies, and rent.

Before starting the theoretical analysis, we recall here some concepts from economic history and stylized empirical evidence with the aim of making clear our awareness of the complexity of this topic in the past and present economic context. The fact that we make reference to many of our previous works on natural resources and technology in historical and applied perspectives is not due to a self-indulgent behavior. Rather, it aims to safeguard the following analysis and to demonstrate that we consider the analytical-formal approach discussed in this volume only as one component of an exhaustive treatment of these issues.

2. Historical and empirical stylized facts

a) A proposition of common sense: resources are scarce. Our starting point refers to natural resources, primary commodities derived from natural resources, and their scarcity. Indeed, economic history and economic theory have deserved to them a long lasting interest.

Usually, the attention has focused on quantitative scarcities, with an emphasis that has moved alternatively from the concept of absolute scarcity to the concept of relative scarcity. The former deals with scarcities that cannot be modified whatsoever, while the latter deals with scarcities that can be tackled and, in many cases, eliminated by means of technical progress and technical substitution. There have been also cases that deny the existence of any kind of scarcity.

It is well known that natural resources can be either renewable (such as agricultural and forest resources) or non-renewable (such as mines). All of them, however, can be depleted if over-utilized. Sometimes the renewable resources — think the agro-forest resources— require a very long time indeed to be fully restored. On the other hand, the non-renewable resources can be renovated by means of recycling and increased through process of expansion (new mines) or substitution.

Until recently, those natural resources that did not directly constitute a consumption or production constraint were, with few exceptions, disregarded from the analysis since they were neither scarce nor did they generate scarce primary commodities. In other words, environmental natural resources have been underestimated as it has been the case with air and, in some cases, water which were considered as free goods.

Nowadays, it is commonly held that environmental resources are, or are becoming, scarce due to both production and consumption. In many cases their scarcity appears to be even more severe than that faced in the past by those resources directly employed in production and consumption. Furthermore, the chain which links primary commodities, natural resources, and the environment is more complex than the shorter chain which connects primary commodities to natural resources. Let us look, for example, to timber, a primary commodity derived from forest which is a renewable resource, even though characterized often by a very slow process of regeneration. The deforestation, however, affects also air and climate, that is, other environmental natural resources whose qualitative recovery is highly uncertain. Phenomena of environmental pollution, that affect natural resources such as water and air, are also the indirect result of production (industrial pollution) and consumption (civil pollution) processes.

Therefore, it is necessary to distinguish between two types of natural resources (though they obviously overlap): (i) those directly productive with their primary commodities, and (ii) those which are environmental, and enter only indirectly in the process of production and consumption and which are not part of market transactions.

Our analysis will be concerned primarily with natural resources and primary commodities that enter directly in the production process. We will take also into account those scarce means of production that can be indirectly referred to natural resources, both renewable and non-renewable natural resources.

b) A historical proposition: scarcity is relative. Even a superficial overview of the past and present economic history reveals continuous references to quantitative and qualitative scarcities of natural resources. They have usually resulted in a slowdown of the process of economic growth and in the rate of innovation —both innovation induced by economic growth or autonomous innovation. (Quadrio Curzio 1982; Quadrio Curzio, and Antonelli 1988; Quadrio Curzio, Fortis and Zoboli, 1994; Quadrio Curzio, Fortis, and Zoboli 1994 (eds.)).

Undoubtedly, throughout the centuries circumstances characterized by severe scarcities of natural resources and primary commodities did occur. The choice of different techniques and the adoption of technological innovation that removed or shifted upwards the original constraint, however, have subsequently overcome such scarcities. Indeed, there is ground to believe that at least part of the innovations has been promoted by the scarcity of the natural resources. Therefore, among the multitude of causes that might explain the dynamics and the long-run economic growth of the nowadays developed countries there is also the antagonism-coexistence-synergy between the scarcity of natural resources and primary commodities on the one hand, and the producibility of commodities on the other.

The existence of scarce natural resources provoked the reaction of technological and economic progress, so that what was initially an antagonism between the scarcity of natural resources and the producibility of commodities has eventually become a synergic process.

The ways in which this occurred were many. First, by extending progressively the boundaries of the locations were the resources were exploited, i.e. by increasing the endowment of a given category of natural resources. Second, by substituting scarce resources with either other abundant natural resources that were not previously utilized for the lack of technological know-how, or with some produced means of production or other commodities. Third, by reducing the use of natural resources and primary commodities per unit of production, or, in other words, by increasing their productivity.

From a historical perspective, one may argue that technological and economic progress raised an increasing "distance" between natural resources and primary commodities, on the one hand, and the demand for final goods and means of production on the other. The difference that for example exists between industrialized and developing economies can be interpreted in this view. In the industrialized countries technical progress has constantly, though irregularly, moved the natural resources apart from the demand for goods and primary commodities, thus reducing the direct pressure of the latter upon the former. On the contrary, in the developing countries the pressure exerted on natural resources is always quite strong due to the combined effects of economic growth and relative backwardness of the technological systems.

To put it differently, technical progress has created a widening gap between two distinct productive apparatuses. On the one hand the "structural industrial apparatus", which is able to implement flexible substitution processes and in so doing it reduces the pressure that the final demand exerts on natural resources and primary commodities. On the other hand the "apparatus of transformation", which is able to convert, with only some qualitative changes, the required primary commodities to final consumption, but without any significant substitution processes between resources and productive capacities (Quadrio Curzio and Scazzieri, 1983, 1986).

The previous considerations could be discussed with reference to both specific and broad historical evidence. Take, for example, the three economic revolutions of the past 500 years: the geographic-mercantile revolution, the industrial revolution, and the scientific-technological revolution (see quoted works in Quadrio Curzio, 1993b). The first revolution did find new natural resources but it did not create a technological distance between natural resources and final demand. By obtaining energy from machinery, the second revolution introduced a new "force" which was different from that produced by human beings and natural agents (wind and water). In terms of natural resources, however, the overall result was contradictory. On the one hand, there were high advantages with the exploitation of "new" raw materials and with important substitution in the use of the old ones. On the other hand, the industrial-technological revolution brought about an increased demand for primary commodities to feed the growth of production. The third revolution finds its stimuli in the industrial-technological revolution, which produced a new abundance of processes and products, on the one hand, and at least two scarcities on the other: the first relates to the environment and natural resources; the second relates to time.

In the attempt of removing the first scarcity, one may refer to the developments of new materials, atomic energy, biology and genetics in agriculture, and the list may go on.

In the attempt of removing the second scarcity, i.e. the "time" scarcity, one may mention the introduction of informatics, telematics, multimedia systems, and faster means of transportation. In brief, science —intended as the refined elaboration of the "human intellectual power"— becomes increasingly concerned with technology. In the economic context it has become a substitute for natural and human resources, a new synonym of wealth and productive capacity.

There is already a massive amount of literature that has tackled these issues (to mention only some essential references: Cipolla, 1966; Deane, 1967; Landes, 1969; Usher, 1982; Ray, 1983; Rosenberg, 1982; Forester, 1988; Gille, 1986; Mokyr, 1990). From these studies, we infer the conclusion that in economic history there is a component of "innovative scarcity", that is, scarcity that generates innovation. In turn this innovation brings about other new scarcities, but until the present day, these scarcities have always been proved relative and not absolute.

All this authorizes to continue the analysis on scarce resources. If the scientific and technological innovation seem capable of overcoming many obstacles, this neither means that they will do so in sufficiently brief time-spans to prevent the formation of new scarcities, nor that the productive application of innovations is always institutionally and economically feasible.

For example, if the old fear of the conflict between agro-food scarcity and size of population seems a past heritage, although with some cautions (see Bairoch, 1969; Wolman and Fournier, 1987; Antonelli and Quadrio Curzio, 1988; Quadrio Curzio and Antonelli, 1988 (eds.); Alexandratos, 1993), another scarcity is making its way through: the environmental scarcity. Acknowledged for long time, such a scarcity never became of central concern as the agro-food scarcity did. Yet, now everyone is conscious that the environmental scarcity is in various cases even more harmful than the agro-food scarcity. This is because it is less manageable, it overrides the national borders and it is less detectable, at least until the scarcity itself does not appear particularly threatening and with irreversible consequences

(Quadrio Curzio, 1987b; World Bank, 1992; Quadrio Curzio, Fortis, and Zoboli, 1994; Quadrio Curzio and Zoboli 1995 (eds.)).

Because of the many different ways with which environmental resources are consumed (direct ways, such as the utilization of land, forests, water, air, etc. and indirect ways, such as the disposal of urban industrial wastes and pollution), it is difficult to assess the emergence and the size of the problem. In other words, it is difficult to understand whether we are facing with an absolute scarcity —which should bring about an overall slowdown of economic growth— or a relative scarcity —which can be overcome thanks to the scientific and technical progress and a more civilized development. Whether one case or the other will prevail, it is a complex matter that depends on the overall planetary accumulated effects such as the exploitation of resources, pollution, demographic dynamics, geographic distribution and concentration, the degree of awareness of the problem at different levels (political, legal, institutional, economic, and civil level), and depends also on the scientific and technological research (Quadrio Curzio, Fortis, Zoboli, 1994).

To conclude: a world without constraints of natural resources does not yet exist, and one may realize this by referring to a widely popular publication such as the *World Bank Atlas* (1995), where international data on the main socio-economic variables are collected: population, the economy, the environment.

In its economic section, the *Atlas*, along with data concerning per-capita income, exports and investments, shows also figures on agriculture. This is the ancient and well established consciousness that agriculture remains always crucial to economic development, especially in a world that is still largely underdeveloped and in which billions of people live at the edge of the subsistence level. Concerning environmental and natural resources, the publication reports the following data: consumption of energy, water, and forest acreage. What appears is then a connection between economic development and quality of the environment in the sense that a certain type of environmental degradation has at its roots a lack of development, as well as in that some environmental problems are emphasized by the process of economic growth.

In conclusion: it is true that scarcity has been relative, but it still exists and the future gives no guarantees of growth without constraints.

c) *A synthesizing proposition: the scarcity is technological.* If it remains true that the stylized evidence from economic history shows the scarcity of natural resources as to be considered a "relative scarcity" thanks to the intervention of technological innovation, then it is no less true that there exists also a "technological scarcity".

A "relative" scarcity remains nevertheless a kind of 'scarcity' which sometimes can impose heavy constraints. The relaxation of such constraints takes often a long time and the qualitative contents that has to be resolved appears of growing importance. What appears a relative scarcity for a single economic system could become historically an absolute scarcity for the planet as a whole. Furthermore, the reduction of some scarcities is often matched with the raise of other different scarcities.

Therefore, the technological scarcity maintains in existence the relative scarcity and only a sufficient pace of technical progress can remove both. Their reduction will depend upon the developments of both science and technology just as their current management will be the result of legal norms as well as the presence of national and international institutions.

What marks the difference between the current historical period and the past is the degree to which these scientific and institutional factors of progress and civilization can be "translated" into economic and productive terms. The result could potentially be that of having markets respectful of the stocks of natural and environmental resources. Sometimes the logic of markets drives to a non-sustainable exploitation of both resources and environment. This bias can be prevented by imposing additional cost on resources and using research and better technologies. Therefore a form of correction of these market tendencies is the use of norms and institutions that, in accordance with the situation, may impose restrictions on human activity to prevent the emerge of irreversible scarcities.

Yet, in our formal analysis we will not deal with normative and institutional factors whose importance in the past and present economic and social development remains certainly fundamental.

Instead, we will deal with technology, choice of techniques, and technological progress. It is for this reason that the previous concepts of technological scarcity, natural scarcity and technological innovation will be used as the starting conceptual point of our theoretical analysis.

Of course, we are full aware of the empirical problems regarding natural resources and primary commodities, which we have studied since long (Quadrio Curzio, 1983; 1985a; 1992a; 1992b; 1993a; 1993b; Quadrio Curzio and Antonelli, 1988; Quadrio Curzio and Fortis, 1985; 1986; Quadrio Curzio, Fortis, Zoboli, 1991; see also the following journals, edited by Quadrio Curzio, Fortis, and Zoboli, "Materie Prime" [Primary Commodities] 1982-1990 and "Innovazione e Materie Prime" [Innovation and Primary Commodities] 1991-1993). They affect current and historical aspects of reality that cannot be fully highlighted by the analytical synthesis we propose in this volume.

We are also aware of the enormous complexity of the process of economic development which cannot be reduced to a mere positive role played by technology and by substitutive factors of scarce natural resources. In general, the concept of technological scarcity carries in itself both elements of optimism and pessimism. On the one hand, it potentially allows to overcome the existence of scarcity through innovation; on the other hand, the innovation itself comes to be perceived as scarce and eventually the same can be said for the degree with which it is applied to the economic and social context. All this calls for a prudent attitude in dealing with studies of economic dynamics without constraints, and it legitimates an analysis focused on scarce natural resources.

3. Classical dynamics, scarcity, and surplus rent

The arguments, which is put forward in succinct terms in the previous sections, have been studied by economic theory with the use of many different methodologies.

Economic theory has frequently inquired into the problems raised from the scarcity of natural resources. Yet, it also showed limitations in the analysis of those aspects of scarcity concerning both physical and technological variables — which have been object instead of our stylized introduction— as well as those concerning the distribution of income in relationship to rent. While economics shares the analysis of resources, technologies, and scarcities with other sciences, it does not so for the analysis concerning income distribution, price, and accumulation, whose study remains of its exclusive domain.

In examining these aspects, we will not embark of course on a complete review of the history of economic theory. We shall instead concentrate our attention on few elements and authors that are connected with our analytical-intellectual framework. As a result we are forced to make substantial restrictive choices. Particular attention will be paid to the role of scarce resources in a context of economic dynamics and technological dynamics, the changes in the distribution of income, and to the various categories of rents (for previous surveys on these topics, see Quadrio Curzio and Pellizzari, 1981; Quadrio Curzio, 1987a; 1988; 1994).

a) Smith, Malthus, Ricardo and the different concepts of scarcity. The starting point, even today, is the analysis of the Classical economists, in particular Adam Smith (1776), Robert Malthus (1798; 1814; 1815a; 1815b), and especially David Ricardo (1815; 1817). Despite some limitations, their analysis should be considered as "complete economic theory".

An initial mention, however, deserves the Physiocratic School, established in the period that stretches approximately from 1700 to 1770. Particularly relevant it appears the notion put forward by François Quesnay (1758) that agriculture represents the only source of the net product and farmers the only productive social class. The net product is made up by the difference between "corn" produced and "corn" used as means of production. The manufacturers are a sterile class, but not a worthless class —it does not generate a net product but it does transform goods originating from land. Therefore land —a synonym of natural resources— is the source of all wealth, whereas industry and commerce are not. The economic system conceived by Quesnay is in a stationary state, not because it is constrained by the scarcity of natural resources, but rather because of the absence of an accumulation process.

For the Classical economists (1776-1870), land, natural resources, and primary commodities assume a very different role. According to these economists (for an excellent review see Cannan, 1893) the utmost important problem is the creation of the net product, its distribution, accumulation, and dynamics. The framework that they built, even if incomplete, is in many respects still fundamental.

According to Adam Smith (1776), the creativity of human capabilities places the economic system in the condition of "absolute" productiveness in terms of commodities and means of production. Scarcity takes on a secondary role in his framework, though Smith did not overlook agricultural resources and rent. He elaborated a concept of surplus rent by analyzing its dynamic behavior as a consequence of a more rapid technical progress in manufacturing than in agriculture. However, according to Smith, the wealth of a nation depends on skills and division of labor, which are more intensively developed in manufacturing sector.

Instead, for Robert Malthus (1798; 1814; 1815a; 1815b) there exists a structural incompatibility between the dynamics of population and food production. While the former grows according to a geometric progression, the latter grows according to an arithmetic one. From this divergence, he derives the principle of absolute scarcity of natural agricultural resources with its well-known dramatic consequences. Malthus made many efforts in analyzing the problems related to rent, receiving both positive and negative evaluations from Ricardo. He conceptualized rent as surplus that affects all lands, with little consideration for differences in fertility.

Finally, David Ricardo (omitting other authors, among whom J.S. Mill (1848) is very important) developed a dynamic theory with natural resources that, in our opinion, is halfway between Smith's and Malthus' analysis. His theory states clearly the principle that the process of accumulation of the net product occurs in the presence of scarce natural resources, —and it states also the principle that the economic growth occurs at decreasing productive rates until the stationary state is reached. This dynamic theory is at least as relevant as his theory of rent.

Therefore, it is true that the Ricardian economic dynamics leads with the arrest of growth to the stationary state. Yet, it is also true that the Ricardian theory takes into account the presence of technical progress which converts, at least temporarily, the absolute scarcity into a form of relative scarcity.

This mechanism, which was not thoroughly utilized by Ricardo, places his analysis even nowadays at the starting point of those studies concerned with economic dynamics, scarce (natural) resources and rent.

b) Ricardo: relative dynamic scarcity and rent surplus. Ricardo builds up a theory of production and distribution that we will briefly review by focusing primarily upon rent and relative scarcity (Quadrio Curzio, 1972; 1987a; 1994).

The theory of surplus rent elaborated by Ricardo finds several premises in the period that spans from the contribution of William Petty (1662) to that of Adam Smith (1776). The overall concept that emerges from these premises —though punctuated by many contradictions and some confusion— is that of rent as surplus over the cost of production —cost which includes farmers' maintenance. The level of this surplus depends upon the demand for agricultural products and upon the supply costs, which in turn depends on fertility and land location. The beneficiaries of this surplus are the landowners.

Taking advantage of the preceding and contemporary contributions of James Anderson (1777), Robert Malthus (1814; 1815a; 1815b), Edward West (1815), Robert Torrens (1815), the final formulation of surplus rent is given by David Ricardo in his *Essay on Profits* (1815) and in his *Principles* (1817-1823), notably Chapter II, *On Rent,* but also Chapter III, *On the Rent of Mines*, Chapter X, *Taxes on Rent*, Chapter XXIV, *Doctrine of Adam Smith concerning the Rent of Land*, and Chapter XXXII, *Mr. Malthus's Opinions on Rent.*

The vast literature which followed his work cannot be reviewed even briefly in our study. To describe some propositions that concern our analysis, the best way of recalling Ricardo's thoughts is by quoting himself. Let us begin from the Preface of his *Principles,* where Ricardo states that without a theory of rent, it becomes impossible to understand the effects of economic growth on profits and wages.

b. 1) Rent, distribution, and accumulation

"...in different stages of society, the proportions of the whole produce of the earth which will be allotted to each of these classes [namely, the proprietors of the land, the owners of capital, and the labourers (Authors' note)], under the names of rent, profit and wages, will be essentially different; depending mainly on the actual fertility of the soil, on the accumulation of capital and population, and on the skill, ingenuity, and instruments employed in agriculture." (Ricardo, 1819, p. 5)

b. 2) Rent, productivity, and economic dynamics

"Rent is that portion of the produce of the earth, which is paid to the landlord for the use of the original and indestructible powers of the soil." *(ibid., p. 67).*

"It is only [...] because land is not unlimited in quantity and uniform in quality, and because in the progress of population, land of an inferior quality, or less advantageously situated, is called into cultivation, that rent is ever paid for the use of it. When in the progress of society, land of the second degree of fertility is taken into cultivation, rent immediately commences on that of the first quality, and the amount of that rent will depend on the difference in the quality of these two portions of land." (*ibid., p. 70*)

"With every step in the progress of population, which shall oblige a country to have recourse to land of a worse quality, to enable it to raise its supply of food, rent on all the more fertile land, will rise." (*ibid., p. 70*)

"The rise of rent is always the effect of the increasing wealth of the country, and of the difficulty of providing food for its augmented population. It is a symptom but it is never a cause of wealth; for wealth often increases most rapidly while rent is either stationary, or even falling. Rent increases most rapidly, as the disposable land decreases in its productive powers. Wealth increases most rapidly in those countries where the disposable land is most fertile, where importation is least restricted, and where through agricultural improvements, productions can be multiplied without any increase in the proportional quantity of labour, and where consequently the progress of rent is slow." (*ibid., p. 77*).

"...whatever diminishes the inequality in the produce obtained from successive portions of capital employed on the same or on new land, tends to lower rent; and [...] whatever increases that inequality, necessarily produces an opposite effect, and tend to raise it." (*ibid., p. 83*).

b. 3) Rent and prices

"The reason then, why raw produce rises in comparative value, is because more labour is employed in the production of the last portion obtained, and not because a rent is paid to the landlord. The value of corn is regulated by the quantity of labour bestowed on its production on that quality of land, or with that portion of capital, which pays no rent. Corn is not high because a rent is paid, but a rent is paid because corn is high." (*ibid., p. 74*).

"Raw material enters into the composition of most commodities, but the value of that raw material, as well as corn, is regulated by the productiveness of the portion of capital last employed on the land, paying no rent; and therefore rent is not a component part of the price of commodities." (*ibid., p. 78*).

Rent, therefore, derives from the increasing costs in agriculture, as a result of the decreasing productivity as the scale of production rises. Its explanation is based on the qualitative property of the land factor which shows diminishing fertility. This property generates two kinds of decreasing returns: the extensive decreasing returns and the intensive decreasing returns. Therefore there exist also two type of rents, the extensive and the intensive rent. The first appears when higher quantities of land are used for agricultural purposes. The second appears when a unit of land employs increasing quantities of labor and capital.

Since the system displays a uniform rate of profit due to competition and a fixed unit wage, decreasing returns generate differential input costs per unit of output. In particular, the last unit of output has, among all the other units, the highest cost and this latter cost determines the price of corn. The existence of a unique price and differential costs, in turn, gives rise to the category of rent as surplus at the advantage of those lands and processes (and owners) with better fertility and lower cost. Therefore, rent emerges as the consequence and not as the cause of the high price of corn. For this reason, it does not enter into the theory of value. When, however, an increase of prices is not the result of some change in the conditions of production, such as an increase in demand, rents will remain unaffected, while it will increase the level of profits.

b. 4) Relative scarcity and stationary state

The other important concept, which emerges from the former quotations, is that of relative scarcity. In fact, in Ricardian theory, scarcity is relative until the system reaches the stationary state. At this point without technical progress, the scarcity becomes absolute, profits fall to zero and rent reaches its maximum level.

Briefly, rent emerges from the existence of relative scarcity, grows with the dynamic economic process, and, without technical progress, it does not have an effect on prices, but rather on the distribution of the net product and the level of profits, with which it conflicts to.

Our opinion is that in dealing with economic dynamics and natural resources, Ricardo's framework is intermediate between the Malthusian pessimism (absolute scarcity) and the Smithian optimism (absolute productiveness). His vision of economic dynamics with natural resources embodies the principle of relative scarcity, because different types of land do not constitute an absolute scarcity until some form of growth exists.

During the process of economic growth, rent continues to increase if there is no technical progress that contrasts the law of extensive and intensive decreasing returns. However, with the presence of technical progress, that reduces the different unit costs of production on the different lands, the level of rent will eventually diminish.

Unfortunately, Ricardo does not thoroughly utilize the principle of relative scarcity. Having underestimated technical progress, he arrives at the conclusion that the rate of profit will fall, the process of accumulation will end, and, hence, the stationary state will be established. All this implies a principle of absolute scarcity.

After Ricardo and the Classical economists, economic theory followed many directions as far as scarce natural resources are concerned. The Ricardian theory, however, remained at the foundation of many of these new approaches, at least in their first stages of development.

4. General static scarcity and marginal rent

The marginal —or neoclassical— theory of income distribution and rent (Quadrio Curzio, 1972; 1987a; 1994) was founded and established in the period between 1871 and 1936. Many economists contributed to its elaboration (see Stigler, 1941 for an always interesting review). Concerning rent, two economists seem particularly important for our purposes: Wicksteed and Marshall. In this context, they are the only two authors quoted by Sraffa (1960) who —as we shall see— adopts in his work the Ricardian theory of rent.

a) Wicksteed: the marginal productivity. The most concise, elegant, and clear formulation of the marginal theory of distribution is found in the work entitled *Coordination* (1894) by Philip H. Wicksteed —"the purist of marginal theory" according to Sraffa (1960, VI).

The theory of marginal productivity has been interpreted as a "consequence" of the Ricardian theory of intensive rent and intensive decreasing returns. Based on the assumption of perfect factor substitution of the means of production, perfect competition, and 'well-behaved' production functions (homogeneous of degree one), this theory shows three key points worth stressing: static scarcity, marginal productivity ad rent based on marginal productivity.

a.1) Static scarcity

The static and general scarcity of inputs implies that all factors (land, labour, capital) are treated with the same analytical apparatus. Natural resources and primary commodities are not distinguished from other factors of production for any peculiar kind of scarcity. The general problem that economic theory has to resolve concerns only the efficient utilization of scarce factors and the calculation of the marginal productivity of these factors gives the solution.

a.2) Marginal productivity

In the theory of distribution, the unified element that makes the three production factors analytically equivalent is the entity of their contribution to production. The level of the marginal productivity in fact determines the remuneration of each factor.

To elaborate his theory of distribution based on marginal productivity, Wicksteed refers back to the Ricardian theory of intensive rent with this interpretation:

> "In investigating the laws of distribution it has been usual to take each of the great factors of production such as Land, Capital and Labour, severally, to enquire into the special circumstances under which that factor co-operates in production [...] to deduce a special law regulating the share of the product that will fall in distribution to that particular factor.
>
> Now as long as this method is pursued it seems impossible to co-ordinate the laws of distribution [...] in order that this may be possible it seems essential that all the

laws should be expressed in common terms. As long as the law of rent, for example, is based on the objective standard of fertility of land, while the law of interest is based on the subjective standard of estimate of the future as compared with the present, it is difficult even to conceive any calculus by which the share of land and the share of capital could be added together and an investigation then instituted as to whether the residual share will coincide with what the theory assigns as the share of wages [...] The basis of those laws is being sought not in the special nature of the services rendered by the several factors but in the common fact of service rendered. If an objective measure of the service rendered by each factor in its marginal application can be discovered there will seem to be at any rate a possibility of co-ordinating the claims based thereon." (Wicksteed, 1894, p. 1)

The marginal productivity law of land determines the level of rent. This same law, applied to all other factors of production for a 'well-behaved' production function, guarantees, according to Euler's theorem, the exhaustion of the product.

a.3) Rent based on marginal productivity

The consequence of this theory is the uselessness of considering rent as surplus. It is in fact possible to show that, given certain assumptions, surplus rent equals the rent derived from a much more general law: the law of marginal productivity.

b) Marshall: generalizations concerning rent and quasi-rent. The other author —usually classified as a Neoclassical but whose theory holds a much broader perspectives— is Alfred Marshall. We would like to consider his contribution to the theory of rent on "land" and the theory of quasi-rent. He is also the second Neoclassical-marginalist economist quoted by Sraffa (1960), in this case for the concept of quasi-rent. In his *Principles* (1890-1920) —whose contents were also widely quoted by Wicksteed— Marshall tries to maintain a sort of continuity with the Classical School, while, on the other hand, he contributes to the development of the new marginal explanation of income distribution and elaborates original ideas on rent. In particular, much of the attention devoted to rent and land follows a complex approach that compared to Wicksteed's comes difficult to assimilate *tout court* to the marginal theory. There are three Marshallian propositions on rent that deserve our interest. We shall recall them by means of the following quotations.

b.1) Rent as producer surplus

This first proposition concerns the definition of rent as surplus and as a particular category of the more general one of the producer's surplus:

"...the rent of land is no unique fact, but simply the chief species of a large genus of economic phenomena; and [...] the theory of the rent of land is no isolated economic doctrine, but merely one of the chief applications of a particular corollary from the general theory of demand and supply; [...] there is a continuous gradation from the true rent of those free gifts which have been appropriated by man, through the income derived from permanent improvements of the soil, to those yielded by farm and factory buildings, steam-engines and less durable goods. [It is necessary] to make a special study of the net income of land [in] two parts. One part relates to the total quantity of the net income, or producer's surplus from land: the other to the way in which this income is distributed between those who have the interest in the land." (Marshall, 1890, p. 523).

b.2) Quasi-rent

The second proposition concerns the definition of quasi-rent:

> "That which is rightly regarded as interest on "free" or "floating" capital, or on new investments of capital, is more properly treated as a sort of rent - a quasi-rent [...] -on old investments of capital. And there is no sharp line of division between floating capital and that which has been "sunk" for a special branch of production, nor between new and old investments of capital; each group shades into the other gradually. And thus even the rent of land is seen, not as a thing by itself, but as the leading species of a large genus; though indeed it has peculiarities of its own which are of vital importance from the point of view of theory as well as of practice." (Marshall, 1890, p. vii)

Time is of utmost importance to the distinction between rent and quasi-rent because the former —in contrast to the latter— is obtained when the supply of a limited productive factor cannot be increased, no matter what is the length of time involved.

b. 3) Scarcity rent and differential rent

The third proposition concerns the distinction between scarcity rent and differential rent, a distinction that Marshall finds to be very subtle as is shown in how he expresses himself:

> "Finally a little may be said on a distinction that is sometimes made between "scarcity rents" and "differential rents". In a sense all rents are scarcity rents, and all rents are differential rents. But in some cases it is convenient to estimate the rent of a particular agent by comparing its yield to that of an inferior (perhaps a marginal) agent, when similarly worked with appropriate appliances. And in other cases it is best to go straight to the fundamental relations of demand to the scarcity or abundance of the means for the production of those commodities for making which the agent is serviceable." (Marshall, 1890, p. 351).

5. Dynamic and static scarcity, surplus and marginal rent: comparisons and developments

As already said, the previous sections did not attempt to provide a review of the literature on distribution and rent. (For this see among others Cannan, 1893; Sensini, 1912; Fetter, 1932; Stigler, 1941; Valassina, 1976; Quadrio Curzio, 1987a; 1994.) Rather, they aimed to stress some of the main concepts upon which we will ground our future analysis.

Let us further examine the difference between surplus rent and marginal-rent, or, in other words, between Ricardo and Wicksteed. This question was incidentally risen by Sraffa (1960) who emphasized the neglect by the Marginalists of the concept of extensive rent and extensive diminishing returns — the focal point of Ricardo's theory. This occurred because extensive diminishing returns do not implicate changes in the proportions of productive factors so essential for the marginal theory, since without them "there can be neither marginal product nor marginal cost". (Sraffa, 1960, p. v).

The extensive rent is differential rent, because different lands have different rents per acreage. In such an extensive case, no adjustment can be considered to be satisfactory according to the marginal theory because of

> "[...] the absence of the requisite kind of change [i.e. in the proportions between productive factors, (Authors' note)]. The most familiar case is that of the product of the 'marginal land' in agriculture, when lands of different qualities are cultivated side by side: on this, one need only refer to P. H. Wicksteed, the purist of marginal theory, who condemns such a use of the term 'marginal' as a source of 'dire confusion'". (Sraffa, 1960, pp. v-vi)

Classical surplus rent, therefore, appears to be typically extensive differential rent. Wicksteed's marginal-rent appears, instead, to be intensive rent —and not differential— because homogeneous lands do not have here the same rent per acreage.

Wicksteed's contribution was certainly important, but it led to a theory of rent which is different from that based on Ricardian theory. They both derive from the existence of "scarcity", but one must not confuse between different types of scarcity. Marginalist scarcity, in particular, which is static and general, has nothing to do with Ricardian dynamic scarcity. Still, one could argue that the marginalist framework is similar to the Ricardian one because both emphasize the concept of efficiency.

However, the real difference with respect to Ricardo lies in the fact that for many Marginalists there is no place in their general theory of distribution centered around the marginal productivity principle for an autonomous treatment of rent and natural resources.

An assessment of Marshall's concept of rent and quasi-rent is much more complex. More precisely, by characterizing quasi-rent as result of temporary scarcities, Marshall made an important contribution. The category of quasi-rent allows economists to explain very general phenomena in which the degree of scarcity of the resources can be manipulated by means of both technical substitution and technical progress. (An excellent comment to this theory of rent and quasi-rent is still found in J.A. Schumpeter, 1954; pp. 440-448.).

In other words, since any scarce means of production can generate quasi-rent, this frees the category of scarcity from the limited analysis of natural resources. In our theoretical work, we shall follow this line of research rather extensively.

We are aware of the fact that within the history of thought and economic analysis simplifications cannot be drawn easily and specifically that between Ricardo and Marshall there exist differences in the conceptualization of rent. Nonetheless, we shall attempt to bridge them and place our theoretical basis upon both.

By 1890, the foundations of the theories concerning scarcities, economic dynamics, and rent —i.e. the theories with which we are concerned— had been established. From that date we shall jump directly to the 1930s, not because during this "interval" of 40 years there were no contributions in the field, but rather because our review has a more limited scope. From the 1930s, at least three lines of analysis took off. In one way or the other, all of them show links with either the Classical or the Marginalist approach: *(i)* the line of research on specific scarcity of natural resources, initiated by Hotelling, which is in many ways connected to the Marginalist theory; *(ii)* the theory of growth without scarcity, initiated by Harrod and von Neumann, and which is connected —depending on the different contributions— to the Classical or the Marginalist analysis; and *(iii)* the line on complex growth initiated by Kuznets. Moreover, there is finally Leontief's contribution on relative scarcity that —though formulated in the 1970s— is based upon the input-output analysis of the 1930s.

Each one of these different lines of analysis deserves a brief account in order to explain where our theoretical contribution has to be placed with respect to them. In particular, we shall concentrate our attention upon Harrod-von Neumann's and Kuznets' line of research.

6. Specific natural scarcities

As already stated, the marginalist theory leads to the formulation of a general theory of static scarcity that concerns all productive factors: land, labor, and capital. In such a theory, scarce natural resources and rent cannot take on an autonomous identity, since they are included in the more general theory of marginal productivity, prices and income distribution. However, in the 1930s within the marginal theory started a line of research that took into consideration natural resources as an autonomous element. This theoretical development considers natural resources as a specific scarcity to be analyzed independently from the effects that they exerts upon the entire economic system.

a) Hotelling and the regulations in the use of resources. H. Hotelling (1931) is the first to contribute to this new line of research devoted to the specific problems of primary commodities and natural resources. His work, in our opinion, has to be considered a pioneer contribution because after its publication many other works on exhaustible resources followed, utilizing similar techniques and addressing the same problems.

This does not imply that previous studies completely ignored the specific problems of natural resources. One needs only to recall Jevons (1865) who in his work on coal shows many concerns about the implication for the national wealth of the exploitation of an exhaustible natural resource. In particular, he argues that the rapid exploitation of coalmines will result in their depletion and this could damage Great Britain's industry by making it less competitive than other nations still well endowed with natural resources. In such an analysis Jevons underestimates the role of technical progress and the processes of substitution. Nonetheless, the stance displayed for the problem is interesting, and the concept here developed will return many years later under the heading of "energy constraints".

In his works, also Hotelling points out that many non-renewable resources —or renewable only in the long-term— are exploited too rapidly and that some control over their utilization is required. He aims, thus, to determine what are the optimal exploitation rates that maximize the social welfare, what market structure best guarantees it, and what regulations appear the most efficient.

According to Hotelling, the market structure that maximizes social welfare is perfect competition, but he recognizes that it is impossible to find perfect competitive markets for natural resources.

In the following years, a broad debate has sprung from this framework in the attempt of defining social welfare in relation to the use of natural resources. In this debate were introduced other concepts such as the consumption utility function of overlapping generations, the per capita consumption, and the consumer rent.

b) Later analyses. Hotelling's contribution was followed by many others that can find their reference point in the Neoclassic models of growth. They focused along two lines: one concerning renewable resources and the other concerning non-renewable resources (Clark, 1976; Dasgupta and Heal, 1979; Fisher, 1981; Quadrio Curzio and Pellizzari, 1981; Dasgupta, 1982; Pellizzari, 1985; Pearce and Turner, 1990).

Concerning renewable resources (such as those in vegetable and animal's kingdoms), the first issue to be studied was their law of growth, as a net combination between birth and death rates. Growth depends on many factors, among them the dimension of the species, their biological characteristics, age and gender structure, and the environmental conditions where they live. A hypothesis widely accepted and utilized is that the process of growth follows a logistic pattern, where the rate of change depends on the size of population, but according to a non-linear relationship. There are two population boundaries that correspond to the minimum and the maximum self-sustainable level. Therefore, the renewable resource may come to an end because its dimension is either too scarce or too abundant with respect to the environment's sustainability. If the resource is kept in the sustainable levels, the population develops at the beginning with growing rates until it reaches some size; beyond that size, growth occurs with decreasing rates due to less favorable environmental conditions as precisely resulted by the greater pressure exercised by the growing population.

Given the overall natural rate of growth of a given resource, its chances of conservation or extinction depend on the interaction between the rate of reproduction and the rate of exploitation. To determine the optimal rate of exploitation the theoretical models, almost without exception, make use of techniques of dynamic programming and dynamic control. Yet they differ in the choice of the objective function: for some it is social welfare; for others private welfare, that is the maximization of profits (or rents) pursued by the resource owner.

The choice of the optimal rate for exploitation differs also according to whether the resource has public or private property rights. If the resource is common property, this may imply significant external diseconomies in the decision-making and, thus, regulations to avoid an excessive exploitation or even the extinction appear more necessary.

The models concerning renewable resources have been utilized in the analysis of numerous kind of animal and vegetable resources, in order to establish optimal management criteria, and to determine whether it is possible to predict —and prevent— the extinction of some species. However, the possibilities of drawing valid operative indications have been, up until now, scarce, and improvements of the models would surely require more collaboration between economists and naturalists.

In the case of non-renewable resources the above arguments are even more important. The attempt of understanding what is the acceptable rate of exploitation that does not threat the extinction of the resource is obviously essential. As a general rule, if non-renewable resources are an input of production, then at some point they will become extinct. This "natural" law may in practice not occur because technical progress, processes of substitution, consumption patterns, and recycling are able to transform what is, fundamentally, an absolute scarcity into a relative one. Also in this case, starting with different concepts of welfare, the models have attempt to determine the optimal exploitation rate as well as the determination of price and rent for resource owners. In practice, however, the determination of an optimal exploitation policy for an exhaustible resource is subjected to uncertainties —mainly estimation uncertainties. For instance, it is very difficult to forecast correctly the dimension of the available reserves and the impact that technical progress will have on the rates of both extraction, substitution and recycling.

7. Growth without natural scarcities

a) Back to dynamics. In the recent history of economic analysis, we must now consider theories in which scarcity and natural resources play no role. The classification of these theories and their common denominator is difficult to find. Some of them have however a post-Classical flavor for the attention deserved to dynamic global phenomena of production and accumulation.

The reasons for this Classical revival, which began in the 1930s and 1940s, are numerous. One reason is the recurrence of topics in the evolution of economic science. After having privileged problems linked to the static scarcity and optimization, economics returned to the long neglect problems of dynamic nature. That this approach was left for long time at the border of economic theory found, however, exception in some masters, notably Joseph Schumpeter (1912). He pioneered a fundamental line of analysis on dynamics and innovation that later overspread almost to all economic analysis.

Another reason is the revolution brought about by John Maynard Keynes (1936), who re-focused attention upon the macroeconomic aspects of productive capacity and effective demand. There was finally, the emerging factual perception that technical progress and economic growth increasingly dominate the dynamics of industrialized countries.

Among the lines of dynamic analysis, re-established in the 1930s, two are of particular interest for our study. One is the macroeconomic approach, pioneered by Roy Harrod (1939; 1948), which links to the Keynesian theory and examines capital accumulation, the dynamics of labor, and technical progress. The other one is the multi-sectoral approach of John von Neumann (1937), which deals with the problem of maximum growth. Although some elements of diversity exist, von Neumann's multi-sectoral approach can be linked to Leontief's (1941) scheme of industrial interdependencies and his dynamic version (Leontief 1953).

We shall not review here the stream of contributions on economic dynamics that followed these works. Rather our attempt is that of demonstrating the similarities of these approaches in dealing in a dynamic context with natural resources, primary commodities, and rent: dimensions that in almost all cases were either neglected, excluded, or underestimated.

As regards, it is probably worth recalling some passages from the macroeconomic approach *à la* Harrod and the multi-sectoral approach *à la* von Neumann-Leontief.

b) Harrod: the quantitatively negligible importance of "land". Roy Harrod, after having synthetically re-explained Ricardo, writes:

> "The [Classical] dynamic theory was crude, in part untenable as universal law, and in part untenable altogether. But nothing has been put in the place of this theory [...], and the corpus of theoretical economics that we teach to-day right up to and including Keynesian doctrine remains almost exclusively static. [...] This old dynamic theory had two aspects. There was (1) the theory of motive power, and (2) the theory of progressive redistribution. [...] accumulation was the motive power. [...] In this approach there are two propositions in the classical system which can be tentatively discarded. One is the population doctrine [according to which] changes in it may be regarded as exogenous changes.
> Secondly, I propose to discard the law of diminishing returns from the land as a primary determinant in a progressive economy. Not that there was any fallacy in the classical treatment of this subject. I discard it only because in our particular context it appears that its influence may be quantitatively unimportant." (Harrod, 1948, pp. 18 and ff.)

Therefore with some caution, Harrod excludes, by hypothesis, scarce natural resources from the analysis on the rather questionable ground that they have a negligible quantitative impact.

c) Von Neumann: no constraints from the natural factors. Let us now consider the multi-sectoral theories beginning with von Neumann, who writes: "...goods are produced not only from 'natural factors of production', but in the first place from each other" (von Neumann, 1937, p. 1); "...natural factors of production, including labour, can be expanded in unlimited quantities" (*ibid*, p. 3). Therefore, von Neumann excludes the existence of scale constraints from the natural factors of production, though he recognizes that they play an important role in the production process.

d) Leontief: greater caution. In our opinion Leontief (1941; 1953) is more cautious in excluding natural resources. His theory takes into account all sectors that transform primary commodities. Yet, he does not examine the scale constraints that natural resources impose upon the productive system. Apart the quotation reported in the following § 9, the central proposition concerning natural resources in all Leontief's work is in our opinion the following:

> "Invisible in all these tables but ever present as a third factor or rather as a whole additional set of factors determining [US] productive capacity and, in particular, its comparative advantage vis-a-vis the rest of the world, are natural resources: agricultural land, forests, rivers, and our rich mineral deposits. Absence of systematic quantitative information, similar to that which has been collected,

organized, and used in this paper with respect to capital and labor, prevents us as yet from introducing this important element explicitly into this preliminary analysis." (Leontief, 1953, p. 96).

e) The others. The majority of studies that followed from these pioneering contributions confirms the underestimation of natural resources and rent, or more generally, of scarce resources and rent. One needs only examine two significant reviews on the theory of growth of the period pre-1970 (Hahn and Matthews, 1965; Sen, 1970) in order to realize that almost all the referred contributions neglect scarce natural resources and rent. This is not perceived as a limit even by the authors of the surveys, so much so that the argument —when not completely ignored— is resolved in few words. (See, for example, Hahn and Matthews, 1965.)

In short, an overview of the contributions in the theory of growth, developed from the "Harrod-Domar model" (a mention should be deserved also to the second author: Domar, 1946) and usually classified in the two camps of Neo-Keynesian and Neoclassical theory (Sen 1970), offers the clearest proof of our proposition. By referring to the "archetypes" of the Neo-Keynesian approach, we end up with the conclusion that Kaldor (1955-1956) says nothing about scarce resources and rent and Robinson (1956) discusses them only in specific terms. Her approach, though contains many original elements, is seriously baffled by the historical conception of land and rent in agriculture. Among the "archetypes" of the Neoclassical approach, Solow (1956) excludes the existence of those scarce resources that cannot be increased by arguing that the introduction of a scarce "land" factor would reestablish the Ricardian diminishing returns. In a different position among the Neoclassical approach is Meade (1961). He considers land and rent in an original fashion but in our opinion still with a quite heavy historical legacy.

In other words, in dealing with land and rent it seems as though Robinson and Meade look backward rather than forward. This is not to undermine the exception they represent. The general climate of indifference that surrounds the themes can be, at best, summed up by the following proposition of Hicks (1965) who writes:

> "Growth equilibrium has other difficulties to face which are quite serious. One, it is very well known, is the matter of land, it is only when land is in abundant supply that an economy can maintain itself in growth equilibrium with an unchanged technology. If one overrides this objection, one is following Smith, not Ricardo; to go back to a state of innocence before diminishing returns is not a thing which one feels comfortable in doing. Nevertheless, for the time being, that is what we shall do here." (Hicks, 1965, pp. 133 and ff.)

f) Pasinetti: dynamics without scarcity. Though other economists in later works came across with scarce resources and rent we will not include them in this review (see for instance the study of Kurz and Salvadori, 1995). Rather, we will immediately refer to Pasinetti, one of the original scholars on the theory of growth. In particular, he was able to combine the post-Classical with the Neo-Keynesian approach and, in the end, with the Sraffian approach too. In other words, he integrates the macroeconomic theories of growth and distribution with the multi-sectoral theories of production, prices, and technical progress. It is for this reason, and for the appreciation we owe to his multi-sectoral analysis, that Pasinetti appears as a primary reference for those theories of production, distribution, and growth that neglect scarce resources and rent.

Pasinetti builds:

> "... a theoretical model for an industrial economic system [which] against the pure exchange model of marginal economics [...] might well be called a pure production model. All commodities considered are produced, and can be made in practically whatever quantity may be wanted, provided that they are devoted that amount of effort they technically require.
>
> To avoid unnecessary complications, scarce resources will not be considered. This does not imply any disregard of the problems of rationality. [...] Also, the procedure does not mean that natural resources are assumed to be homogeneous and non-scarce. Not to consider a problem does not mean assuming that it does not exist. What it means is that the basic theory will be developed *independently* of the problems of optimum allocation of the scarce resources." (Pasinetti, 1981, pp. 23-24)

These propositions by Pasinetti form the premises of a model of pure production where the hypotheses are clearly spelled out. They have the important quality of being transparent —as opposed to what one may find in other more unclear authors— and thus open to the possibility of critique. We raise two observations. The first is that his writings seem to suggest that scarce resources can be easily included into a model of production; the second is that the problem of scarce resources —included natural resources of course— seems to coincide with the problem of their optimal allocation. On this latter aspect Pasinetti states that: "... the marginalist economists [...] have developed a theory of optimum allocation of scarce resources to begin with, independently of the problems concerning production" (*ibid.*, p. 24).

Such an interpretation identifies the role of scarcity and natural resources with the Marginalist approach, which instead is only one of the several ways of dealing with the problem. Further, the Marginalist approach of the static general scarcity generally denies any specific role to natural resources and rent as we saw in Wicksteed.

Pasinetti maintains his interpretative framework by linking it to the Classical economists:

> "The economists who have taken the production approach to economic reality have always claimed that production can in fact be investigated independently of the problems concerning the scarce resources. This claim goes back to Ricardo, who 'eliminated' land from his analysis of value and distribution by referring his arguments to the 'marginal' land (that piece of land that yields no rent)." (*ibid.*, p. 24)

This thesis —which Pasinetti reinforces by quoting a passage from Sraffa to whom we are concerned later— is valid with regards to the Ricardian theory of value. However, it must be qualified when referred to other aspects. The fact that Ricardo determines prices on the basis of the production conditions in the less fertile land (which cannot be called "marginal' in the extensive case, as Wicksteed and Sraffa remind us) by no means signifies that land is eliminated from the theory of production and growth. In fact, it is the scarcity of land that eventually constraints the economy to the stationary state, imposes a dynamic fall of profits, and a rise of the price of corn and rent.

The above macroeconomic and multi-sectoral theories are very important contributions in order to understand economic dynamics, technologies, technical progress, accumulation, and the dynamics of quantities, prices, and distribution. From a theoretical point of view, they do explain a large portion of economic dynamics —but not all.

It seems that these scholars place economic analysis at the opposite extreme of the Marginalist theory by jumping from static general scarcity to absolute dynamic productiveness. In so doing, however they forget the existence of a relative dynamic scarcity, where natural resources play a relevant role. Given the "specialization" of the profession, the choice of camp of these analytical-formal theories is understandable and somewhat justified. Yet, it would become unacceptable as an interpretive general framework of the actual economic reality even in its stylized form.

8. Complex development and relative scarcities

a) The complexity of growth in Kuznets' analysis. The third line of research of our interest concerns the historical-quantitative theory of growth and development. It started —or more precisely regained strength— in the 1930s due to the fundamental contributions of Simon Kuznets (see the well-organized collection of papers and the introduction of Castellino in Kuznets 1990). Methodologically, these historical-quantitative theories show the influence of the economic measurement approach started by Mitchell (1913). Kuznets states that "theory consists in the constant investigation of empirically identifiable variables and their relations examined under a wide variety of conditions, those which are necessary in order to demonstrate the available and ensured evidence" (Kuznets, 1955, p. 77).

"This theory necessitates variables that are empirically identifiable and verifiable and which move according to a model that is relatively invariable in time, in spite of important variations with respect to conditions" (*ibid.*, p. 78).

Kuznets, since his first fundamental work (1930), always combined quantitative analyses —preferably historical long-time series— and research of regularities and stylized facts on economic growth of various nations.

Kuznets intends to focus the attention of economics on long-run dynamics, as the Classical economists did, and on secular movements with their shorter business cycles. His analysis —applied for the United States and other four countries with hundreds of time-series data on production and prices— identifies secular trends of long cycles, shorter cycles, and intermediate "secondary secular movements" of about 15-25 years, now commonly known as "Kuznets cycles".

Furthermore, Kuznets examines in different historical phases the importance of the role of the national state and the various economic sectors that lead to development:

> "If we take the world from the end of the eighteenth century, there unrolls before us a process of uninterrupted and seemingly unslackened growth. [...] But if we single out the various nations or the separate branches of industry, the picture becomes less uniform. Some nations seem to have led the world at one time, others at another. [...] As we observe the various industries within a given national system,

> we see that the lead in development shifts from one branch to another. [...] Within any country we observe a succession of different branches of activity leading the process of development, and in each mature industry we notice a conspicuous slackening in the rate of increase." (Kuznets, 1930, pp. 3 and ff.)

In his numerous later works (for example, Kuznets, 1955; 1965; 1966; 1972; 1990), Kuznets extended the historical-quantitative approach to other focal themes of development. It is worth mentioning the relations between demographic trends and economic growth; the influence of technical innovations; the existence of structural transformations; the historical tendencies of income distribution and its inequalities; the accumulation of capital; and the limited international diffusion of economic development.

Therefore, the complexity of economic growth emerges from this historical-quantitative theory, whose references to natural resources and environment we shall now look at. Kuznets deals with these problems in particular when he studies the following economic issues:

- the structural transformations of the economy and in particular agriculture;
- capital accumulation;
- technological innovations and the impact of those innovations concerned with energy and industrial materials;
- the environmental effects of innovations.

Let us consider briefly each of these points in turn.

a. 1) Agriculture

In analyzing Colin Clark's "law" (1940) of the historical decline of the share of agriculture output, Kuznets advances two explicative hypotheses: first, the substitution of agricultural products with other goods from different sectors (coal for wood, nylon for cotton, etc.); second, and more significantly, the rate of growth of labour productivity in agriculture is greater than the growth of per-capita demand of its products. This increase in labor productivity is due to both the extension of agriculture to new lands and —primarily- to the revolutionary technological and organizational changes experienced by the sector "in some old countries" (Kuznets, 1973).

a.2) Natural resources

On natural resources, Kuznets argues that "the factors that induce formation of reproducible capital adequate as the basis of economic growth are unlikely to be inhibited by an absolute lack of natural resources" (Kuznets, 1965, p. 31). The availability of natural resources is an important factor, however, since it influences "... the *direction* of growth, the distribution of its emphasis among various industrial sectors of the economy" (*ibid.*, p. 31n), though it does not suffice to assure the process of development:

> "...in the sense that growth can be attained despite poverty in resources (as in Japan and some smaller countries); that in the underdeveloped countries even known natural resources are exploited at a much lower rate than in the developed; and that many countries, with a wealth of valuable natural resources, such as Brazil through much of the nineteenth century and Venezuela today, are still underdeveloped." (Kuznets, 1965, p.31n.).

a.3) Technical progress

Concerning technical progress and innovation, Kuznets (who quotes with emphasis also several economists concerned with technological change) analyzes in detail the different types of innovation, and in particular those in the field of energy and industrial materials. He argues that:

> "An innovation involving a new type of power, or a new type of industrial material, or a new type of mechanism for transmitting power is a basic component in the production system of many industrial branches, either already or soon to be operating. It is obviously of much greater magnitude than an innovation affecting a relatively limited, specialized branch of production, with a rather specialized type of process." (*ibid.*, p. 191).

a. 4) Environment

The interest on technological innovation brings Kuznets to deal also with the environmental problems and to keep into account the sense of worry reminiscent of the Malthusian approach to the limits of natural resources. In his words:

> "Since technology [...] is manipulation of the natural environment for the benefit of man [...] there has always been a concern as to the limits of the finite environment, the supply of irreproducible natural resources" (ibid., p. 205).
>
> "It persisted through the decades of the Classical and Marxian schools to the second half of the nineteenth century but became muted because experience showed that the initial assumption that technological progress could not compensate for possible exhaustion of natural resources was unrealistic. But this fear of the natural limits has always been present, while dormant at times; and has grown recently with the observation of negative effects of economic growth —not on the supply of natural resources necessary for direct economic goods (such as productive land, mineral deposits, water, etc), but on the general environment in the way of pollution, crowding, noise and the like." (*ibid.*, p. 205)

But Kuznets shows an optimistic outlook about the capability of technology, with its adaptive mechanisms, to challenge the negative environmental effects that technology itself originally produces. On this issue his point of view is articulated in four points:

> "First [...] resources are a function of technology, and technological advance can, for example, move to oil from coal or to atomic energy from oil long before the supplies of coal and oil are exhausted. [...]Second, the long time involved in major technological innovations and their novelty make it almost impossible to predict and prepare for the ultimate effects, both positive and negative. [...] Third, economic growth in the past and the technological innovations that underlay it involved major deteriorations in the broader environment, which were eventually overcome even if with difficulty. Thus, as recently as the middle of the nineteenth century, when industrialization and urbanization proceeded at a high rate in many Western European countries, the movement into the cities meant, under the existing conditions of medical and public health services, that an increasing proportion of the population was subject to much higher rates of mortality and morbility than those prevailing in the countryside. It took a revolution in our understanding of infectious diseases and a half century of struggle to reform sanitation and health conditions in the cities as well as a program of substantial capital investment to adjust to, and offset, this deterioration of the environment for the population of the developed countries. [...] Fourth, we can assume from past experience that, with the knowledge and technology at our disposal, adjustments will be made to the negative

effects of technological innovation in the way of depletion of resources and deterioration of the environment. [...] It is the social and political obstacles that are likely to be more serious that our technological capacity. Assuming that the growing impact of pollution and other negative effects force a needed social and political consensus, the adjustment is likely to come and prove as effective as past adjustments to far more critical cases of such deterioration and depletion." (*ibid.*, pp. 206-208)

b) Rostow and others. A second important line of historical-quantitative theory was initiated by Hoffmann (1931; 1958) and Rostow (1960), who elaborated a theory of the "stages of economic growth" sketched around the different importance in economic history of certain industrial sectors and dominant organizations.

In particular, Rostow elaborates an articulated theory that identifies five stylized stages of growth: (i) traditional society; (ii) preconditions for take-off; (iii) take-off; (iv) drive to maturity; and (v) high-mass consumption. The last three stages coincide with what can be broadly defined as modern economic growth.

In these theories, natural resources do not bear a relevant role, even if Rostow devotes some attention to agriculture in the phases of "preconditions for take-off" and "take off".

Moving along similar lines of research, Fortis (1994) is able to show the progressive shift in the last 150 years of the center of the world manufacturing production from Europe to North America, and recently from North America to Asia. As proxy to capture these changes he uses the national consumption of raw materials as evolved during the various phases of economic development and industrial and technological competition.

c) Abramovitz and Fuà. There are many other contributions in the tradition of historical-quantitative theories; of particular importance is that of Abramovitz (1950; 1956; 1961). Among other things, he precisely reviewed the literature of the historical-quantitative theories of growth (Abramovitz, 1952), an article which is considered the twin of Hahn and Matthews' review of the analytical-formal theories.

Within the more recent historical-quantitative contributions to economic theory, Fuà deserves a special mention. His research is one of the most interesting and complete and deals with the economies of late development (Fuà 1980; 1992), the economic consequences of demographic dynamics (Fuà 1986), and the discussion on economic growth (Fuà 1993). In this latter work, Fuà summarizes and reinterprets various historical-quantitative aspects, and concludes with the following question: to what extent are national income and its growth rates indicators of the "progress" of an economy? Conversely, to what extent are qualitative components of growth neglected? We shall evaluate his theory at the end of the volume but, for now, we shall anticipate one of his conclusions: the qualitative variables have been largely neglected.

In this framework, Fuà also deals with the situation of advantage that certain countries can benefit from their endowment of natural resources; the environmental damages provoked by growth and the frequent lack of commitment in evaluating and eliminating them.

In short, he strongly emphasizes the qualitative factors that in the works of Kuznets, Abramovitz, and Rostow —though mentioned— have been rather overlooked.

Our conclusion is that the historical-quantitative theory, which deals extensively with primary commodities but little with natural resources, remains for its long-term perspectives a fundamental indirect contribution in tackling the concept of relative scarcity.

9. Relative and absolute scarcities

The last theoretical approach of our concern is the quantitative line or, to be more precise, the analytical-quantitative line of Leontief (Leontief et al., 1977). We have already referred to the works of Leontief in terms of industrial interdependencies. We shall now consider an application of this theory to natural resources.

As a premise it should be noted that some authors have classified this contribution among the family of forecasting "global models" which came about in the 1970s. This identification does not seem convincing: first, Leontief bases his analysis on economic theory, whereas the global models are predictions without theory (for a review, see Fortis, 1981); second, Leontief, in a certain extent, criticizes those global models that advance very pessimistic predictions such as the complete depletion of natural resources and the risk of a global economic collapse. These global models, in fact, conceive natural resources as an absolute scarcity and offer the ground for proposals of general static equilibrium of the ecological and economic conditions, a sort of stationary state (Forrester, 1971; Meadows *et al.*, 1972).

Despite the serious limitations and criticisms, these models —recently reconsidered in the light of an enlarged environmental scarcity (Meadows *et al.*, 1992)— would require some further reflections though they are not directly connected to the theories of central interest in our analysis.

On the contrary, Leontief's work is a global economic model built upon a firm conception of input-output theory. The conclusion that it reaches is that natural resources-primary commodities face a problem of relative scarcity. The model is the composition of various input-output sub-models which are mutual dependent, and refer to the continental regions of the world. In each of these regional sub-models, the analysis takes into account the interrelations between production, consumption of goods and services and natural resources.

Three propositions are of particular interest to our study:

a) Limits to growth

> "The principal limits to sustained growth and accelerated development are political, social and institutional in character rather than physical. No insurmountable physical barriers exist within the twentieth century to the accelerated development of the developing regions [...] The most pressing problem of feeding the rapidly increasing population of the developing regions can be solved by bringing under cultivation large areas of currently unexploited arable land and by doubling and trebling land productivity." (Leontief *et al.*, 1977, pp. 10-11)

b) Availability of mining and energy resources. Concerning the availability of these resources and, most of all, the compatibility between known reserves and global needs, Leontief predicts that the natural reserves of only two raw materials (lead and zinc), as estimated in 1970, could be depleted before the year 2000. Even according to the most cautious scenario, coal is relatively abundant, whereas the available estimate of worldwide oil reserves is a multiple of the estimated total demand for the year 2000. Prudently, nonetheless, he notes that: "...the adequacy of the world endowment does not necessarily ensure against regional shortages and high prices, nor does it guarantee smooth economic transitions to dependence on shale oil, gasified coal and other "new" energy sources." (*ibid.*, p. 6).

c) Pollutant emissions. For the developed regions of the world, Leontief predicts the technical feasibility of maintaining at the current level the net emission of pollutants. Furthermore, the overall economic cost of the strict implementation of similar technological standards in the developing countries should not constitute an insurmountable obstacle to their economic growth either.

The falling prices of primary commodities and energy in the late 1980s and in the 1990s, both in nominal and real terms, seems to confirm, up till now, the validity of the Leontief 's approach. At the same time this phenomenon has dissolved the wide interest for the first vintage of both the Meadowian "global models" and what we call the "intercontinental Leontievian models". However, some further models at sectoral level have been elaborated since then for the sectors: forestry (Kallio *et al.*, 1987; Zoboli, 1994); agriculture (Parikh *et al.*, 1988); water (Shiklomanov, 1994); energy (Colombo, 1992).

In the last few years, however, models with a global approach have shown an afresh attention due to the perception that the environmental problems have global systemic features and planetary dimensions. There is not only an increasing elaboration of global ecological models —in particular those on climate, and multidisciplinary projects with broad scale interactions between ecological and social systems (see also, for example, Clark and Munn, 1986)— but also a renaissance of more traditional global models in the light of the 1970s tradition.

Thus, the contrast between the Meadows approach (Meadows, 1992) and the Leontief approach (Duchin and Lange, 1994), or in other words, between absolute and relative scarcity, has been revived also in more recent times with works that, starting from the two lines of analysis of the 1970s, focus on an "enlarged" resource and environmental scarcity.

The studies *à la* Leontief, for example, insist that those sectors with higher environmental impact are now open to considerable opportunities of technological innovation, and these opportunities must be stimulated through policy intervention.

To conclude, even in these most recent environment-oriented versions, the evaluation of the rate and the impact of innovation still remains the main element of division between the two approaches.

10. Scarce resources and structural rent in static conditions

All these works that followed the Classics and Marginalists are very interesting, but they neglect a specific analysis on production and distribution where scarce resources and rent show a sufficient degree of generality.

It is Sraffa with *Production of commodities by means of commodities* (1960), who elaborated in an analytical-formal theory, a multi-sectoral model of production, distribution, and prices that partially rehabilitates the Ricardian approach on "land", "natural resources", and "rent".

Frequently, and for many reasons, Sraffa's theory has been labelled as "neo-Ricardian" thereby being attributed with impenetrable ideological attributes that have nothing to do with the economic analysis to which we are exclusively concerned. Curiously enough, in the attempt to justify their label, economists have very rarely mentioned the role Sraffa assigns to "land". Let us deal with those aspects of Sraffa's theory which directly concern our study, although the reader can find further references in the vast literature that surrounds this author. (Among others, see Roncaglia, 1975; Samuelson, 1987; Kurz and Salvadori, 1995.)

a) Natural resources and non-basic commodities in Sraffa's theory. The first aspect of the theory of Sraffa we shall look at is the link between the *scarcity* of natural resources and the *circularity* of productive processes. "Land" — synonymous of a particular type of natural resource— enters into a multi-sectoral and circular representation of production. This appearance, by and large, could seem incompatible with the principle of circularity as implicitly or explicitly many economists pointed out. In fact, some of these economists consider Chapter XI, "Land", of Sraffa's work, as secondary or even incoherent compared to the central theme of the book: the production of commodities.

There is some truth in this opinion: despite the originality of his approach, one has the impression that Sraffa attributes a rather limited role to "land". The conclusion is fueled by Sraffa himself who considers the non-produced means of production a break in the circularity process of commodity production. This occurs with the comparison he made between two formally symmetrical entities of his model: natural resources and non-basic products.

Sraffa writes:

> "Natural resources which are used in production, such as land and mineral deposits, and which being in short supply enable their owners to obtain rent, can be said to occupy among means of production a position equivalent to that of 'nonbasic' among products. Being employed in production, but not themselves produced, they are the converse of commodities which, although produced, are not used in production. They are, in fact, already included under the wider definition of non-basic [already] given [...].
> The similarity of rent-earning natural resources with non-basic products shows itself at once in the impossibility of their being counted among the components of the Standard product, since they appear on one side only of the production process." (Sraffa, 1960, p. 74)

Though we refer the reader to Chapter XI for a complete and essential reading, we also suggest that there is a substantial ambiguity in this proposition. Consider for example the use —in certain respects possible- that Pasinetti makes of it, to support Sraffa's view that natural resources:

> "...do not affect the rest of the analysis, and can therefore be left aside and when they are introduced they bring with them the required necessary information about their rents and prices. [...] This gives a powerful analytical justification to the approach which is taken here [i.e. which does not consider natural resources, (Authors' note)]. It means effectively that the model, though not explicitly dealing with the problems concerning the scarce resources, will be kept open to their introduction." (Pasinetti, 1981, pp. 24-25).

Pasinetti's interpretation of Sraffa differs from the interpretation given by Quadrio Curzio (1967; 1975 and thereafter). For the latter, natural resources do influence distribution, prices, and quantities; this occurs because the economic system needs primary commodities. It is useful to remind that Sraffa elaborated a static theory, and in such a framework his argument is partially acceptable. In a general context, however, the importance of natural resources cannot be excluded from those comparative or dynamic models with changes of production and distribution conditions. We shall see that a full introduction of natural resources into multi-sectoral models is by no means easy.

Returning to Sraffa, it should be noted that the symmetry between natural resources and non-basic commodities is useful from a formal perspective, but it can also be misleading from a more comprehensive analysis, because natural resources, by means of primary commodities, significantly affect the standard system. As a matter of fact, for causes that we shall see later, those changes in the productive process that, without paying rent, uses "land" as input and produces "corn" as output (in other words a process not yet bound by the scarcity of land, but that it is part of the standard system), affects the whole economy, so that the circularity of production is constrained by natural resources.

Furthermore, in a general perspective it is difficult to associate consumer goods expressed by non-basic commodities with means of production such as land, whose role is so central in the process of production and growth.

What justifies —and qualifies— this association is that Sraffa treats scarcity and circularity in a stationary state, or in a comparative static setting but without any changes of quantities —changes that instead are essential for a true comparative static and dynamic analysis. So if on one hand Sraffa comes close to Ricardo for the role of "land" in a static context, on the other hand he moves away from Ricardo with the neglect of changes in production, growth, and economic dynamics.

b) Structural rent in Sraffa's theory. The second aspect of Sraffa concerns structural rent, even though this terminology does not appear in Sraffa's work.

It must be said from the outset that for Sraffa the importance of scarcity resides in its influence of prices, distribution and rent determination and not for its effects on growth.

There is structural rent because the economic structure and the level of production are based on at least two productive processes that utilize different qualities of land to produce the same primary commodity. The existence of different lands gives rise to differential rents at the advantage of the more productive lands. Instead, the less productive and rent-free land is central, through the links with the other economic processes, for the determination of commodity prices, the rate of profit, or alternatively the unit wage. Sraffa writes:

> "...if n different qualities of land are in use, they will give rise to an equal number of different methods of producing. corn [...]. There will therefore be n production equations, to which must be added the condition that one of the lands pays no rent." (Sraffa, 1960, p. 74)

In the case of intensive rent:

> "...if land is all of the same quality and is in short supply, this by itself makes it possible for two different processes or methods of cultivation to be used consistently side by side on similar lands determining a uniform rent per acre." (*ibid.*, p. 75)

In other words, if the level of production requires the activation of two or more land-based processes, then the rent in each of these processes is determined by the structure and the relative efficiency of all other productive processes, once the profit rate or the unit wage is fixed exogenously.

c) The order of fertility in Sraffa's theory. The third aspect deals with the problems of the order of fertility of different lands. Sraffa points out that a natural ordering of land fertility does not exist. Let us consider a case of extensive farming in which different processes are in place, each with its quality of land in order to produce the same commodity. Side by side with this land-based processes there are other sectors of the economy that do not utilize land. The fertility of each land could be identified, unambiguously, in physical terms, only if for each land the productive process could be ordered in physical inputs and physical outputs. This, however, is by no means realistic: "...the order of fertility [...] is not defined independently of the rents [and thus of prices, (Authors' note)]; may vary with the variation of profit and unit wage" *(ibid.*, p. 75).

By means of these propositions, Sraffa concludes that a unique "order of fertility" does not exist, and therefore he attempts to study the changes of order between processes. However, he does not resolve these problems. It is at this point that the theory of Sraffa shows its weakness. Sraffa does not take into account:

-the analytic distinction between fertility of lands and efficiency of the methods of production that make use of them. Such efficiency depends on the technology of the whole economic system;

-the distinction between the order of efficiency that should be followed while activating lands and the order of rents;

-the effects that quantitative variations of commodities exercise upon rents;

-the effects that variations in the exogenous distributive variables (unit wage or rate of profit) have upon the order of efficiency of land-based processes and rents;

-the effects of accumulation and technological change on quantity, prices, distribution, and above all on rents.

For these reasons the approach of Sraffa on resources, scarcity, and rents remains incomplete, though for originality, it represents the starting point of the modern theory of rent from which also our contribution departs.

To sum up, since Sraffa's model is based on fixed quantities, the relationship between variations in the prices-distribution-rent system and those in the "land"-production-"corn" system never emerge.

d) Quasi-rent in Sraffa's theory. Our final interest in Sraffa's theory concerns the aspect of quasi-rent:

> "Machines of an obsolete type which are still in use are similar to land in so far as they are employed as means of production, although not currently produced. The quasi-rent (if we may apply Marshall's term in a more restricted sense than he gave it) which is received for those fixed capital items which, having been in active use in the past, have now been superseded but are worth employing for what they can get, is determined precisely in the same way as the rent of land. And like such obsolescent instruments have the properties of non-basics and are excluded from the composition of the Standard commodity." (*ibid.*, p. 78).

This proposition on quasi-rent opens up many possibilities of applying the theory of structural rent to all non-produced means of production that are scarce compared to the scale of production —no matter what the origin of this scarcity is. It allows an analysis of the effects of this scarcity when there are employed also other means of production and the economy operates with processes of different efficiency. But it also opens up the possibility of examining how this category may arise from processes of technological innovation.

11. Resources, complex and dynamic scarcities, technological rent

With the sole exception of Sraffa's fundamental contribution, the overall picture at the beginning of the 1960s is discouraging. The attention given by theoretical models to natural resources, their scarcity, rent, non-produced and scarce means of production, and their quasi-rent was negligible. Basically, almost all postwar economic theory considered these problems irrelevant, or at least secondary.

Against this tendency, and starting with the approach of Sraffa on "land" (from which an abundant literature is now developed. For an important review see Kurz and Salvadori, 1995) and more in general with von Neumann-Leontief's multi-sectoral approach, Alberto Quadrio Curzio began constructing a new multi-sectoral model of production. His intention was to put at the center of the analysis categories such as "natural resources" (emblematically summarized by "land"), and more in general "scarce resources", non-produced (or non-reproduced) means of production and the (primary) commodities generated from them (emblematically summarized by "corn"), and finally "rent".

With two volumes (1967) and (1975), Quadrio Curzio elaborated two complementary and consecutive models that later were improved and partially generalized in numerous papers. Since these works are elaborated in several Chapters of this volume, we shall limit ourselves to some general concepts that we shall connect to the analysis carried out until now.

a) Technological rent, order of efficiency and rentability. Stemming from a broadly modified version of Sraffa's theory, the first model concerns a static and comparative static analysis. In the Preface to *Rendita e distribuzione in un modello economico plurisettoriale* (1967), Quadrio Curzio writes:

> "The following analysis has two general and connected objectives [...]. It aims at: (i) introducing, in a general way, the category of rent into a residual theory of income distribution; (ii) introducing primary productive factors (different from labor), or more generally non-reproducible or non-produced scarce productive factors into a general model of production [...] The study analyzes the interrelations between the price-distribution system and the quantity system of different produced commodities, when [...] scarce factors are taken into account [...] To give full account of all these interdependencies we need to build a system that, starting from those of Leontief, Sraffa, and von Neumann, develops the analysis —to our knowledge— in a yet unexplored direction. [...] Our model[...] shows [...] a brand new type of causal dependence between the price-distribution system and the quantity system, a feature that is derived from the particular treatment of scarce factors and the associated rents." (Quadrio Curzio, 1967, p. 9 and ff.)

This model has been further elaborated and generalized in Quadrio Curzio (1980, It. ed. 1977), Quadrio Curzio, Manara, and Faliva (1987), and Quadrio Curzio (1996b).

Let us look at the two focal points of these works:

i) They identify the orders of efficiency and profitability of those processes that use different scarce resources and how the autonomous variations in the distribution of income and the level of activity affect these orders. Rent, therefore, becomes the central factor of income distribution with a significant change in the well-known relationship between wages and profits.

ii) They put forward the concept of "global technologies" that include, by means of shared technical coefficients, more processes that produce the same commodity, and processes that individually produce a distinct commodity. In this way, it becomes possible to examine the variations of efficiency, structure, and scale of production of one technology, due to the progressive full utilization of scarce resources during the process of growth.

In conclusion, while surplus rent and structural rent depend respectively on different fertility of lands, and the existence of two simultaneous processes that produce the same commodity, "technological rent" —a concept that we are now introducing, but whose essence is already evident in the cited works of Quadrio Curzio— takes into consideration broader dynamic aspects of technology. These latter aspects emerge as effect of some scarcities generated by either increased levels of production or changes in income distribution or movements in the order of efficiency between processes that make use of scarce resources. Though it is not our aim of following closely past legacies, the precursors of the concept of "technological rent" may be identified in Ricardo, Marshall and Sraffa.

b) Relative scarcities and non proportional dynamics. The second model elaborated by Quadrio Curzio concerns dynamics and growth in presence of scarce resources. He writes, in the initial pages of *Accumulazione del capitale e rendita* (1975):

> "One of the clearest aspects shown by the dynamic process of the economies is the antagonism among means of production (and commodities) which are reproducible without limits and those which are not so, either forever or for very long periods of

time. This antagonism can give rise to a particular form of dynamics: periods of growth can be followed by periods of stagnation or recession". (Quadrio Curzio, 1975, p. 1)
"One of the cornerstones of the production schemes à la von Neumann, à la Leontief, or à la Sraffa is that, with the accumulation of the entire surplus, the rate of growth of production and surplus coincide and remain constant [...] One of the cornerstones of the economic dynamics with non-produced means of production is [...] the absence of the above identities, and the change over time of the rates of growth." (ibid., p. 2).

This model was then further elaborated and generalized in Quadrio Curzio (1986) and in Quadrio Curzio and Pellizzari (1991).

The central point consists of the concept of "compound technologies", that involves techniques of production with fixed coefficients, each one being characterized by a scarce resource and connected dynamically in the process of accumulation to other techniques. The dynamic process, therefore, occurs at variable rates over time and uneven across commodities. This raises complex problems of structural compatibility between techniques and it generates some residuals, that is, net products which cannot be utilized in the process of accumulation.

In conclusion, the analysis points out the importance of "technological scarcity", which is scarcity not only of scarce resources, but also of those techniques bounded in scale and structure by scarce resources.

12. Conclusions and further lines of analysis

a) Towards a more general model. The previous accounts aimed at clarifying some stylized propositions of economic history and economic theory, and introducing the past Quadrio Curzio's theoretical analysis which serves as framework and foundation of the present study. What this study does now is an attempt to go beyond such references with a more general model of resources, technologies, and rent.

The latter statement should not be misunderstood; however we do not support any claim that our theoretical scheme is "the" answer to the limits shown by some literature on economic dynamics, production, and distribution in dealing with scarce resources. Rather, we hope —and it is not a little thing— that our contribution is deemed as being innovative for the adoption of the concepts of technological rent and technological scarcity. They are regarded in this volume as more general categories than those of surplus rent, structural rent and natural scarcities so emblematically rooted in the history of economics in explaining the different fertility and scarcity of "land".

More ambitiously, we also hope that our study could be considered as an evolution of the multi-sectoral models of production, distribution, and growth that have their reference point in the contributions of von Neumann, Leontief, and Sraffa —models that, in some other respects, have found a development in Pasinetti's formulation (1981; 1993).

To all these models we shall refer frequently. A certain familiarity with them therefore is a required condition for our readers. In particular the volume of Sraffa

(1960), and, to a certain extent, also the works of von Neumann and Leontief, are assumed known even through some clear textbooks, such as Pasinetti (1975). This familiarity combined with the assumption of some knowledge of linear algebra, will exempt us from further references in the rest of the volume.

b) The structure of this volume.. In an attempt to ease the reading, we shall conventionally divide the volume into five parts, excluding this introductory chapter.

The first part consists of chapters II, III, IV, and V; it deals with static and comparative static analysis of prices, distribution of income, level of production and techniques. We identify the order of efficiency and rentability of techniques, and analyze how changes in income distribution (in particular rent) follow from changes in one of the exogenous distributive variable (either unit wage or rate of profit), or in the level of activity. Finally, we study the effects produced on technology by changes in the income distribution and the level of activity.

The second part consists of chapters VI, VII, VIII, and IX; it deals with dynamic analysis involving both the quantity system and the problems concerned to the order of efficiency between techniques and technologies. Crucial in this respect is the existence of accumulated residuals and uneven intertemporal growth rates. The latter are the result of different technologies, the quantity available of scarce resources, the intensity of accumulation, and the dimension of the accumulated residuals. This implies the reexamination of the orders of efficiency as identified in the static and comparative static analysis. What emerges is the existence of three orders of efficiency among those techniques that use scarce resources: physical dynamics, value dynamics, and price-distribution dynamics.

The third part consists of chapters X and XI; it deals with the analysis of income distribution in an entirely dynamic context. The investigation is carried out with reference to movements of total wages, total profits, total rents and their individual shares. The complexity of the outcomes with the potential existence of conflict or concordance among the three major economic categories (earners of wages, profits, and rents) profoundly modifies the traditional analysis of profits and wages. This has convinced us that rent represents a pivotal element, also in the dynamic analysis of income distribution.

The fourth part consists of chapters XII and XIII; it deals with technological progress, technical change, the distribution of income, and rent. The analysis identifies a wide range of possible dynamic paths, all of which relate to the presence of scarce resources. We then made the necessary distinction between technical and technological progress. Once again, scarce resources greatly modify the behavior of technical progress, as described by the usual linear production models. Analogously important appears to be the effects of technical and technological progress on income distribution and in particular rent, which being a measure of scarcity-efficiency, is highly affected by technological variations.

The fifth part consists of chapter XIV where we draw our conclusions and some lines of possible extension concerning the *numeraire*, the reintegration of natural resources, and the environment. This further analysis indirectly suggests the potentialities of our approach for other important issues. In concluding this volume, we also broaden our perspective, in very general terms, with a cross-reference to some recent dynamic analyses that highlight the complexity and vastness of the problems put forward in this volume.

c) Cross-references and acknowledgements. This last section regards the works that are either reprinted or largely reproduced in this volume, the attribution of the various Chapters to each of the two authors, the acknowledgements and the financial help received for research projects involved in this work.

Chapters I, II, III, IV, V, VI, and XIV have been written by Alberto Quadrio Curzio. Chapter I refers, sums up, and broadens previous works by Quadrio Curzio. Chapters II, III, and V refer to *Rendita, distribuzione del reddito, ordine di efficienza e di redditivita'* (1977; english version 1980) and Chapter IV refers to *Produzione ed efficienza con tecnologie globali* (1987; english version 1996b). Chapter VI refers to *Technological Scarcity: An Essay on Production and Structural Change* (1986). An English collected version of Quadrio Curzio's works (1977, 1986, and 1987) can be found in *Rent, Distribution, and Economic Structure. A Collection of Essays* (1990).

Chapters VII through X are written by both authors. Chapters VII and VIII sum up and extend *Structural Rigidities and Dynamic Choice of Technologies* (Quadrio Curzio and Pellizzari 1991), whereas Chapters IX and X are completely new.

Chapters XI XII, and XIII are written by Fausta Pellizzari and are completely new too.

All our past works have been substantially modified and reorganized in the attempt to coherently integrate them in the structure of the volume and unify their mathematical notation.

The Authors acknowledge Il Mulino, MPI, CNR.

Chapter II - Production and distribution: data, hypothesis and problems

1. Introduction

We represent a disaggregate and interdependent economic system characterized by sectors producing primary commodities and sectors producing non-primary commodities.

Whenever possible in our analysis we shall limit the use of formal methods, but nevertheless the reader should be familiar with linear algebra and linear production theory.

We shall start this formal analysis by defining data, hypotheses, notations and some basic concepts about production, distribution and also techniques and prices that will be used throughout the book.

2. Basic products and primary commodities (Pcc1)

In the economic system there exist m + 1 basic commodities which are produced and used as means of production. Basic commodities are of two different types: *(i)* commodity 1 (Pcc1, Primary commodity or commodity 1, an abbreviation that we shall adopt), is a primary commodity which is produced in quantity q_1 using also non-produced means of production in number, quantity, and quality to be determined; *(ii)* the other m commodities which are produced in quantities q_j, for $j = 2, \ldots, m+1$, but without any direct use of non-produced means of production.

3. Non-produced means of production (NPMP) and the processes directly using them

The non-produced means of production (NPMP) is a general category that includes "natural resources" and "land" and, therefore, involves production processes that are upper-bounded in their scale of activity.

The Pcc1 is produced by NPMP of different qualities. We assume that the number of processes producing Pcc1 ranges from 1 to k. These processes are represented by the vector of technical coefficients as follows:

[2.1] $[\mathbf{a}_1(h)'; l_1(h); \tau_1(h)]$, $h = 1, 2, \ldots, k$,

where

$$\mathbf{a}_1(h)' = [a_{11}(h), \ldots, a_{m+1,1}(h)], \qquad h = 1, \ldots, k.$$

The vector $\mathbf{a}_1(h)$ represents the inputs of the m + 1 commodities necessary for producing the PCC1 by means of NPMP of type h. The technical coefficients also include the quantities of "necessary consumption" for each commodity (see below, §5); l_1 (h) are the labor technical coefficients and τ_1 (h) the coefficients of the NPMP of type h. Each vector $\mathbf{a}_1(h)$ is such as to allow the viability of technique [2.5] (see below). T(h) is the available fund of the NPMP of type h, therefore the PCC1 quantity that can be produced by process h is subject to the following constraint:

[2.2] $q_1(h)\, \tau_1(h) \leq T(h)$.

From [2.2] it follows that the maximum quantity of $q_1(h)$ that can be produced is equal to:

[2.3] $\bar{q}_1(h) = T(h)/\tau_1(h)$.

4. Commodities and processes not directly using NPMP

The commodities that do not require directly the NPMP input are the commodities j. Each one of them is produced by a single process:

$$[\mathbf{a}_j'; l_j],$$

with

[2.4] $\mathbf{a}_j' = [a_{1j}, \ldots, a_{m+1,j}]$, $j = 2, \ldots, m+1$,

where the latter is the vector of the standard input-output coefficients. These processes give rise to viable techniques.

5. Technical coefficients and shares of necessary consumption

Every coefficient of vectors $\mathbf{a}_1(h)$ and $\mathbf{a}_j$ is augmented, compared to the Leontief ones, by the shares of necessary consumption: that is, by the amount of each commodity which is included in the conventional consumption bundle. In so doing, the analysis of the process of maximum growth may avoid the reference to final consumption demand.

6. Production techniques

In order to produce the m + 1 basic commodities, the system must employ all the processes [2.4] and at least one process [2.1]. Since the viable processes of type [2.1] are k, it is possible to identify k distinct production techniques which differ only for the process which produces commodity 1. Each technique is formally represented by the matrix:

[2.5] $$\mathbf{A}(h) = [\mathbf{a}_1(h); \mathbf{a}_2; \ldots; \mathbf{a}_{m+1}] \geq \mathbf{0}$$

together with the vector

$$\mathbf{l}(h)' = [l_1(h); l_2; \ldots; l_{m+1}] \geq \mathbf{o}$$

and the constraint given by

$$q_1(h) \leq T(h)/\,\tau_1(h),$$

where h = 1, …, k.

7. The viability of the techniques

Every matrix **A**(h) is non-negative, non-decomposable and viable. It allows, therefore, a positive uniform rate of net product (or, in other words, an eigenvalue which is maximum, real, positive, non-repeated, and less than 1).

8. Scale constraints of the techniques and technological scarcity

Because of the limited availability of each NPMP of type h and, thus, because of the constraint [2.3] on quantity $q_1(h)$, each technique [2.5] cannot produce more than a given quantity of all the m + 1 commodities.

The scale constraints can be reinterpreted to take into consideration a great variety of technical and institutional cases. Hence, the analysis must not be necessarily confined to natural resources, but rather it should be considered within the more general heading of technological scarcity. In fact, we can argue that there is technological scarcity every time a production factor, different from labor, constrains the scale of activity of a technique.

9. Production technologies

The scale constraints of each technique, due to the limited availability of NPMP of type h, may require that more techniques **A**(h) are activated in order to satisfy certain production levels. The simultaneous use of many techniques **A**(h) can be studied by means of two different analytical methods or —better— theoretical frameworks: that of "global technologies" where techniques **A**(h) are "joined" together following specific rules; and that of "compound technologies" where techniques **A**(h) remain "disjoined", though interconnected.

10. Dimension of the economic system

The dimension of an economic system can be identified in different ways and by means of different criteria. One of these is the dimension of the technology: that is, the number of technological active processes employing NPMP. In this way, one may state that an economic system with only one active process NPMP-based is "smaller" than an economic system with two or more active process employing NPMP.

11. Some problems: new interdependence between production and distribution

To examine the problems that we will shortly outline, it is necessary at first to consider the relationships between the two systems that depend on the production techniques **A**(h) —the price-distribution system and the physical-quantity system.

The introduction in our analysis of NPMP involves the lost of independence between these two systems as it is typically found in the linear production models where labor is the only original factor.

From the previous analysis emerges that the economic system is composed of two main and interconnected "parts". The first includes a certain number of sectors, up to a maximum of k, which produce one single primary commodity using non-produced and produced means of production. The second includes m sectors, each one producing a different commodity, by means of the primary commodity and the produced commodities. Obviously, both parts of the economic system employ labor. Among the k independent processes, which produce the primary commodity, at least one must be active, because the primary commodity is directly or indirectly a means of production for all the other sectors of the economic system. When the level of economic activity reaches a certain level, the system to keep up with the production activity requires an increasing number of processes producing the primary commodity. Such activation of further processes, of course, should follow an order of efficiency.

This is the starting point from which we shall depart in our strictly economic analysis and from these premises we shall analyze the issues at stake in the next Chapters.

12. The order of efficiency (OE)

The order of efficiency (OE) refers to both techniques and non-produced means of production. Techniques [2.5] differ among themselves only for the process that produces PCC1. Establishing an OE among the [2.5], therefore, means establishing also an OE among the k non-produced means of production. In fact, the latter cannot be compared in terms of their individual productivity because the NPMP processes cannot generally be classified on the basis of a direct comparison of the technical coefficients. In activating the k processes with NPMP one must follow therefore the OE.

13. The levels of activity of the economic system

The levels of activity of the economic system refers to the determination of the following set of variables: the number of NPMP in operation, the production, and the employment.

14. The technology of the economic system

The technology of an economic system is strictly related to both the OE and the level of activity. If the latter changes, this affects the means of production, the quantity produced, the net products and the employment and may vary also the number of active processes and the structural composition of the means of production.

When more than one process with NPMP is used, the technology becomes a complex entity, being composed of many techniques of the type [2.5].

The changes in technology is determined by three broad factors: changes in the level of activity, the choice of techniques based on prices and income distribution, and the technical progress that affects the single techniques.

15. The order of rentability

The order of rentability (OR) is determined by the rent per unit of NPMP. This order, as well as the absolute level of rent, may vary when the level of activity of the economy grows and when, in line with the OE, there is a rise in the number of active processes utilizing NPMP.

At this point, rent can be defined as the income gained by a NPMP factor as a result of both its scarcity and the relative level of efficiency of its transformation process, compared to the other processes producing the same commodity. Thus, the rent includes both scarcity and technological elements.

16. Induced changes in the distribution of income

Induced changes in the distribution of income are generated by variations in the level of activity of the economy. These changes come about because of the existence of NPMP and, thus, they are totally absent in the traditional linear models of production and distribution.

17. Autonomous changes in the distribution of income

Autonomous changes in the distribution of income are generated by variations in the rate of profit or in the unit wage, and they give rise to complex effects on the OE and OR, as well as the quantity system.

18. Static analysis and dynamic analysis

All these problems will be analyzed at two levels: first within a static (one-period) or comparative statics context, and second, within a dynamical context, with and without the presence of technical progress.

19. Conclusions

The above variables represent our study's concern. As the analysis unfolds, they will be subsequently re-examined and explained —this will hopefully clarify what now still appears difficult to grasp.

Chapter III - Order of efficiency

1. Introduction

We have already noticed (Chapter II, § 12) that the determination of the OE is of primary concern. It rises from the fact that there are more processes that employ the NPMP to produce the same basic primary commodity. The choice of the order to activate these processes has fundamental effects on both the price-distribution system and the physical system.

According to which analysis we are pursuing —respectively static or dynamic analysis— it is possible to distinguish different types of orders of efficiency. In both cases we will define an order either dependent on the "price-distribution" system or on the "physical" system. In this Chapter we consider the OE with reference to the static (one-period) analysis, whereas the dynamic OE will be analyzed in Chapters VII, VIII and IX.

2. The general system price-distribution

To determine the static price-distribution OE it is necessary to construct for each technique [2.5] an "economic sub-system" (so defined because the denomination of economic system regards technologies that embody several processes utilizing NPMP). Specifically, we consider the general system of price-distribution as represented by the following system of equations *à la* Sraffa:

[3.1] $\mathbf{a}_1(h)'\,\mathbf{p}(h)\,[1+\pi(h)] + l_1(h)w(h) + \tau_1(h)\,\rho(h) = p_1(h), \qquad h = 1,\ldots,k.$

[3.2] $\mathbf{a}_j'\,\mathbf{p}(h)\,[1+\pi(h)] + l_j\,w(h) = p_j(h), \qquad j = 2,\ldots,m+1.$

[3.3] $p_1(h) = 1,$

[3.4] $\prod_{h=1}^{k} \rho(h) = 0,$

[3.5] $w(h) = \bar{w} \geq 0, \text{ or } \pi(h) = \bar{\pi} \geq 0.$

The known data are the vectors of technical coefficients $\mathbf{a}_1(h)' = [a_{11}(h), \ldots, a_{m+1,1}(h)]$; $\mathbf{a}_j' = [a_{1j}, \ldots, a_{m+1,j}]$ which are formed by the Leontievian coefficients augmented by the coefficients of necessary consumption. These coefficients concern the commodities required to produce commodities, and all of them are supposed to be basic. On the other hand, $l_1(h)$ and l_j are the technical coefficients of labor and $\tau_1(h)$ the technical coefficients of NPMP.

The unknowns are $\mathbf{p}(h)' = [p_1(h), \ldots, p_{m+1}(h)]$, the prices of commodities; $\pi(h)$, the profit rate; $w(h)$, the unit wage; $\rho(h)$, the unit rents.

Let us consider the meaning of the above equations. Each of the [3.1] equations concerns the price of commodity 1 produced by that particular production process that utilizes NPMP of quality h. Since commodity 1 is basic, at least one process producing the PCC1 must be active, otherwise the economic system cannot work. What remains to be determined is the number of active processes among the k available.

The active processes will have $\rho(h^*) \geq 0$, with the exception of the least efficient process h* for which $\rho(h^*) = 0$. This is due to the differential nature of rents —rent is the measure of the relative efficiency of a process compared to the least efficient still in activity that obviously will not have rent.

The different efficiency of the processes will also depend on labor and circulating capital inputs, represented by vectors $[\mathbf{a}_1(h)'; l_1(h)]$. We assume that these vectors cannot be ordered directly in real terms but only on the basis of their prices.

Each equation [3.2] concerns the price of commodity j produced by employing labor and circulating capital. The equation [3.3] shows that the Pcc1 is chosen as *numeraire*. From equation [3.5] turns out that either π or w must be set out exogenously. We still recall the fact that w is the "surplus wage" since the "conventional subsistence wage" is included into the technical coefficients by means of the component of necessary consumption.

To sum up, we have a well-known open theory of income distribution, where one of the distributive variables is determined by external factors. Reflecting on choice of which variable between w and π should be set exogenously and perceiving the factors that affect its level is of fundamental importance if we want to link this theory to specific historical, economic and institutional contexts.

3. The sub-system prices-wage-profit

The solutions of the system [3.1]-[3.5] are straightforward. Given w or π the results change according to which process yields zero rent. Therefore there are k potential solutions, even though the effective price-distribution system is eventually only one. In order to find these solutions we substitute the [3.4] with the following

$$[3.6] \qquad \rho(h^*) = 0,$$

taking separately one after the other all the h processes.

Equation [3.1] —for which [3.6] has been formulated— is thus the "solution" of the whole system. In fact, this equation, altogether with [3.2], forms the following system of equations:

[3.7] $$[1 + \pi(h^*)]\, \mathbf{A}(h^*)'\mathbf{p}(h^*) + \mathbf{l}(h^*)w(h^*) = \mathbf{p}(h^*),$$

where $\mathbf{A}(h^*)$ is the matrix of technical coefficients, and $\mathbf{l}(h^*)$ is the vector of labor coefficients. All the quantities have h* as argument, because process h* represents the only difference between the [3.7] equations.

The equations [3.7], [3.3], [3.5] represent an "economic sub-system prices-wage-profit" that henceforth we shall quote for short as "sub-system pwπ". It is a sub-system compared to the equations [3.1]-[3.5] and therefore the terminology has a quite different meaning of that given by Sraffa.

Instead, each sub-system pwπ coincides with Sraffa's single products system, and has economically significant solutions $\mathbf{p}(h^*) > \mathbf{o}$, $\pi(h^*) \geq 0$, $w(h^*) \geq 0$. In fact $\mathbf{A}(h^*)$ is non decomposable, since products are basics, and its maximum eigenvalue is bounded within the interval $0 < \lambda(h^*) < 1$. This means that for a range of values of the exogenous distributive variable the economic system is viable.

4. The rent sub-system and types of rent

Now let us consider the other k–1 equations, named "rent sub-system" or "R sub-system". Each equation has only one unknown: rent. In fact given $\mathbf{p}(h^*)$, $\pi(h^*)$, $w(h^*)$ we have:

[3.8] $$\rho(h; h^*) = \{p_1(h^*) - \mathbf{a}_1(h)'\mathbf{p}(h)\, [1 + \pi(h^*)] - l_1(h)w(h^*)\}\, [\tau_1(h)]^{-1},$$

being h* exogenously given and h = 1, 2, ..., k, with h different from h*.

Let us focus on the nature of rent, a topic we have already mentioned in Chapter I. Our theory concerns differential rent, which is, in our opinion, the more general category. Someone could add that it would be better to define this rent as extensive since the case taken into account concerns "lands" of different qualities limited in extension. However, this specification seems to us not necessary.

Firstly, also intensive rent can be treated as differential rent. In the intensive case two processes are in operation on a "land" of uniform quality. The first process has a unit cost of production lower than the second one because its production per acreage is greater.

To determine production prices it is sufficient that the price of corn be high enough to cover the production cost of the least efficient process: that is, the second one. This is the only condition of efficiency required to have production in the second "land" and positive rent in the first. But this is precisely a simplified case of differential rent.

Yet, if we refer to a context of competition, the extensive and intensive rent will have a quite different result. Competition requires a uniform rent per acreage, and hence the price of "corn" should result higher than in the case of differential rent already considered.

Secondly, if the reader decides to stick with the idea of extensive rent, he or she should acknowledge the fact that omitting the intensive rent does not mean that the intensive cultivation is not taken into account. Even when the intensive rent disappears, the effects of intensive cultivation persist in the different productive processes applied to the different lands, which affect the extensive differential rents.

Thirdly, we have decide to focus the attention on differential-technological rent which can be extended from land to other resources —both natural and non natural resources— such as mines, or old machines, no longer produced but still in activity. Even more efforts will be deserved to those rents generated by the introduction of new techniques, when they do not involve the elimination of the old ones. In order to recall these and other possible developments, we analyze again the role of NPMP in the following section.

5. The central role of NPMP

NPMP are fundamental for the determination of prices and distribution. There will be different **p**, π, w and ρ, depending on which process has zero rent. Process h* is determined by two elements that we will consider in turn: the first is the order of efficiency; the second is the level of activity of the economy. We know that each NPMP is available in a given "extension" T(h). Therefore the maximum quantity of the commodity 1 that can be produced with that NPMP is given by:

$$[3.9] \qquad q_1(h) \leq \bar{q}_1(h) = T(h)/\tau_1(h).$$

Since commodity 1 is basic, only the further activation of the k processes with NPMP allows economic production to grow continuously.

6. Static price-distribution order of efficiency

The order of efficiency cannot be derived from the production per unit of T(h). This measure is not significant in itself since the processes [$\mathbf{a}_1(h)$; $l_1(h)$] cannot be ordered in physical terms, that is, in terms of "corn per acreage". As we shall see in Chapter V, it cannot even be derived by the order of $\rho(h)$ related to any $\rho(h^*) = 0$. In fact changes of the $\rho(h^*)$ —i.e. the process with zero rent— will affect the order of the other $\rho(h)$ because of the simultaneous changes of prices and the endogenous distributive variable. Once fixed π or w exogenously we must thus find an order among the k processes which does not change whatever is the $\rho(h^*)$ set equal to zero, otherwise, we would face problems of circularity. It is possible to show that only when the OE remains stable with different numbers of active processes, then the activation of the processes itself depends on the OE and the [3.9] constraints.

To determine the OE we consider the sub-systems pwπ [3.7]. Since the difference between equations [3.7] depends only on the process h*, then it follows that the order of efficiency among the NPMP depends on the sequence of values assumed by π, when w is exogenously given. Conversely, the sequence of values of w determines the order of efficiency when π is exogenously given.

7. The order of efficiency with zero wage and maximum rate of profit

Let us consider in detail all possible cases. We start by the case

[3.10] $$w = 0,$$

for which [3.7] becomes

[3.11] $$\{[1 + \max \pi(h^*)]\, \mathbf{A}(h^*)' - \mathbf{I}\}\, \mathbf{p}(h^*) = \mathbf{o}$$

that is

$$[\mathbf{A}(h^*)' - \lambda(h^*)\mathbf{I}]\, \mathbf{p}(h^*) = \mathbf{o}$$

since $\lambda(h^*) = [1 + \max \pi(h^*)]^{-1}$.

By the properties of $\mathbf{A}(h^*)$ and by the theorems of Perron-Frobenius, we know that there is a unique maximum eigenvalue $\lambda(h^*)$ which guarantees the maximum rate of profit, $\max \pi(h^*)$, to which is associated an eigenvector $\mathbf{p}(h^*) > \mathbf{o}$.

On the basis of the values of $\max \pi(h^*)$ and $\mathbf{p}(h^*)$, it is possible to order the k sub-systems pwπ, that is, to order the k processes employing NPMP, on the basis of the following property

[3.12] $$\max \pi(1) > \max \pi(2) > \ldots > \max \pi(k)$$

$$\mathbf{p}(1) \geq \mathbf{p}(2) \geq \ldots \geq \mathbf{p}(k),$$

This is obtained by appropriate permutations of the h indices, which were initially randomly attributed, and taking into account that the only equality across the various $\mathbf{p}(h)$ is $p_1 = 1$.

The order, established on the basis of the maximum profit rate, is obviously equal to that established on the basis of the vector of prices. This is so, because the difference between the vector of prices is determined by the h* process included in the sub-system pwπ. The production cost of commodity 1 grows, as the activation of the process continues following the order established by [3.12]. Consequently the price of the other commodities decreases in terms of commodity 1, which represents the *numeraire*.

The OE achieved depends on the cost of the circulating capital and labor used in each production process. Given w, the lower is the cost of the circulating capital and total labor, the higher is the rate of profit.

The identification of the most and least efficient process can be carried out also on the basis of the rent attached to each NPMP. The process associated to a NPMP with zero rent is the most efficient, if all the other processes have negative rents. On the contrary, the process with zero rent is the least efficient, if the others have positive rents.

Let us consider the R sub-system. When h* = 1, namely $\rho(1) = 0$, the prices and rate of profit of the economy are respectively **p**(1) and max $\pi(1)$. They are plugged into [3.8] to determine $\rho(h; 1)$ for h = 2, ... , k. These rents are necessarily negative because **p**(1) and max $\pi(1)$ are greater than those values that would equal them to zero. In general:

[3.13] $$\rho(h; h^*) > 0 \text{ for } h < h^*; \rho(h; h^*) < 0 \text{ for } h > h^*.$$

In raising the activity from one to k processes with NPMP, it can never occur that, an already active process becomes non-economic, that is, it yields negative rent.

The order [3.12] allows us to identify also the "absolute maximum", max $\pi(1)$, and the "relative maximum", max $\pi(k)$, of the rate of profit. These maxima acquire meaning for their boundary lines when π is set exogenously.

If $0 \leq \pi = \bar{\pi} \leq \max \pi(k)$, all the existing processes with NPMP can operate, if the level of activity of the economy requires them.

If $\max \pi(k) < \pi = \bar{\pi} \leq \max \pi(1)$, one or more processes with NPMP become non-economic at the given level of π and cannot be activated.

Finally if $\pi = \bar{\pi} > \max \pi(1)$, no one process with NPMP will be activated and therefore also the economic system will be unable to operate.

8. The order of efficiency with zero profit and maximum unit wage

Now let us consider the choice of the variable opposite to [3.10], that is:

[3.14] $$\pi = 0.$$

Then [3.7] becomes:

[3.15] $$[\mathbf{I} - \mathbf{A}(h^*)'] \, \mathbf{p}(h^*) = \mathbf{l}(h^*) \max w(h^*),$$

That is

$$\mathbf{p}(h^*) = [\mathbf{I} - \mathbf{A}(h^*)']^{-1} \, \mathbf{l}(h^*) \max w(h^*).$$

Since $\mathbf{l}(h^*)$ and $[\mathbf{I} - \mathbf{A}(h^*)']^{-1}$ are both positive (the latter for well known theorems of linear algebra), the previous relation shows $\mathbf{p}(h^*) > \mathbf{o}$.

We now have the following OE:

[3.16] $$\max w(1) > \max w(2) > \ldots > \max w(k)$$

$$\mathbf{p}(1) \geq \mathbf{p}(2) \geq \ldots \geq \mathbf{p}(k),$$

where the sign of equality has been introduced for reasons already explained in [3.12], and once having permuted the indices h. The OE [3.16] can be different from [3.12] due to the different proportions of means of production and labor.

Therefore changes in π or w will affect the OE, and [3.12] and [3.16] can have a different process h* and sub-system pwπ of type h*.

This analysis gives us also the "absolute maximum" unit wage, max w(1), and the "relative maximum", max w(k). Their meaning is equivalent to that of max $\pi(1)$ and max $\pi(k)$.

9. The order of efficiency with unit wage and rate of profit different from zero

Let us consider the OE when [3.7] becomes

[3.17] $$\pi = \bar{\pi} > 0 \quad 0 < \bar{\pi} \leq \max \pi(k) < \max \pi(1),$$

then [3.7] becomes

[3.18] $$[\mathbf{I} - (1 + \bar{\pi})\, \mathbf{A}(h^*)']^{-1}\, \mathbf{l}(h^*)\, w(h^*) = \mathbf{p}(h^*).$$

Since the inverse matrix is positive, being the matrix $\mathbf{A}(h^*)$ non-negative, non decomposable and with maximum eigenvalue less than one, from [3.18] it follows $\mathbf{p}(h^*) > \mathbf{o}$.

As usual, we identify the OE

[3.19] $$w(1) > w(2) > \ldots > w(k)$$

$$\mathbf{p}(1) \geq \mathbf{p}(2) \geq \ldots \geq \mathbf{p}(k).$$

Since the number of processes is higher than two, the OE [3.19] can be different from both [3.12] and [3.16], even though partial similarities may occur.

Since for every sub-system there exists a unique inverse relation between w(h) and $\pi(h)$, these conclusions can be extended to the case in which w is exogenously given such that $0 < w = \bar{w} \leq \max w(h^*)$.

10. The order of physical efficiency

The OE previously determined, which is unique for every level of w and π, can be defined as the static price-distribution order of efficiency. As already stated, it is possible to define a second type of static OE: the "physical" one, which is determined independently from the system pwπ.

The matrices $\mathbf{A}(h) = [\mathbf{a}_1(h); \mathbf{a}_2; \ldots ; \mathbf{a}_{m+1}]$ can be ordered according to the value of the uniform rate of net product s(h), which is determined by solving, for each h, the following system

[3.20] $$[(1 + s(h))\, \mathbf{A}(h) - \mathbf{I}]\, \mathbf{q}(h) = \mathbf{o},$$

where $\mathbf{q}(h)$ denotes the vector of productions.

In this case the OE is determined by the sequence

[3.21] $$s(1) > s(2) > \ldots > s(k),$$

having permuted opportunely the h indices.

It is well known from some linear algebra theorems that when $w = 0$ this OE coincides with the OE defined by the price-distribution system on the basis of the maximum rates of profit of the k techniques.

11. Comparison among orders of efficiency

The physical OE [3.21] can be different from the price-distribution OE [3.16] or [3.19]. This means that the activation of processes with NPMP follows a different sequence, according to which OE is used. This has relevant implications on the levels of activity, on the technology, and on the economic system's dynamics.

In the extreme case we can have $\pi(1) > \pi(2) \ldots > \pi(k)$ and $s(1) < s(2) < \ldots < s(k)$, the index of techniques being obviously the same. Needless to say that we are facing the problem of the choice of orders.

Adopting the price-distribution order of efficiency means ordering k general systems of price-distribution, each one containing one additional process with NPMP compared to the previous one. The smallest system contains a single process with NPMP producing PCC1, plus the other m processes for the remaining other m commodities. The greatest system includes k processes with NPMP, plus the usual other m processes.

Each of these systems may be defined as a potential system, in the sense that a choice among them has to be made. Which one will be the effective system depends on the level of activity of the economy, and hence depends on the number of processes with NPMP in activity. This creates sequential relations between the price-distribution system and the physical system. These relations can be represented in the following way. Given π (or w), one may define k potential price-distribution systems and determine the order of efficiency among the k available NPMP; the quantity system allows to determine the number of active processes with NPMP; finally, one may find out the effective price-distribution system.

If, alternatively, the physical order of efficiency is adopted the steps are the following. First one should determine the number of active processes with NPMP, which depends on the quantity system; hence, given π (or w) the actual price-distribution system is established. However, in this case problems of compatibility can emerge. Better, there exist a clear constraint in setting the level of the exogenous variable π (or w) since we need that the processes activated on the basis of both the physical OE and the level of activity show economic feasible cost of production.

On the other hand, the choice of the price-distribution order does not guarantee that the techniques **A**(h) are activated in a sequence of maximum potential growth. Instead, this will happen for each technique if the physical order of efficiency is chosen.

Chapter IV - Production with global technologies in static settings

1. Introduction

Following the economic framework already described (Chapter II, § 11), we can now deal with the problems of production, level of activity, and technology.

The previous analysis identified the OE among processes with NPMP —the order to observe in activating the k processes that produce the primary commodity. Thus, we have k different "technologies" with 1, 2, ..., k active processes employing NPMP. Obviously all the k technologies and the related general system of price-distribution are "potential". The choice of technology and the adoption of an "effective" technology will depend on the actual level of economic activity. The determination and the analysis of the level of economic activity can be carried out by means of two different methods: that of "global technologies or joint techniques"; that of "compound technologies or disjoint techniques" (see Chapter II, § 9).

With these two approaches we are able to analyze the level of activity. The use of both approaches that we shall make is explained by the fact that each of them points out different features of the economic system with NPMP.

First, we consider global technologies (or joint techniques) since they are able to represent synthetically the physical system. The essence of this method, which suites especially static and comparative static analysis, is the inclusion into the same technological matrix of all processes with NPMP sequentially activated, together with the processes producing commodities without NPMP.

Hence, the theoretical framework for global technologies is somewhat original. It takes into account linear production processes, but allows us to introduce new variables linked to the presence of NPMP —namely the "splitting coefficients" which differentiates this framework from the Leontievian analysis.

2. The physical system with one technique

Let us consider the smallest economic system, in which operates only one technique, that is, the technique that includes the most efficient of the k processes with NPMP, according to any one of the efficiency orders described before. The production system that gives a uniform rate of net product is:

$$[(1 + s(1))\, \mathbf{A} - \mathbf{I}]\, \mathbf{q}(1) = \mathbf{o}, \qquad [4.1]$$

[4.2] $$[\mathbf{A} - \lambda(1)\mathbf{I}]\ \mathbf{q}(1) = \mathbf{o},$$

with

[4.3] $$0 < \lambda(1) = 1/(1 + s(1)) < 1,$$

[4.4] $$q_1(1) \leq \bar{q}_1(1) = T(1)/\tau_1(1),$$

[4.5] $$\mathbf{l}(1)'\ \mathbf{q}(1) = 1 \leq \bar{1}.$$

As previously s(1) denotes the uniform rate of net product; λ(1) is the maximum eigenvalue of **A**(1); **q**(1) is the eigenvector of the production associated to λ(1); $\bar{1}$ the existing labor-force. Being **A**(1) non-negative, non-decomposable and viable, the eigenvalue λ(1) is real, positive, non-repeated and less than one; the eigenvector **q**(1) is strictly positive and definite in structure while its scale is determined on the basis of either [4.4] (i.e. the equality of [4.4]) or [4.5].

When only the first technique is active, the system [4.2] represents the whole economic system. When more than one system [4.2] is activated, each one of them becomes a sub-system —the system [4.2] will then become the production sub-system of type 1.

Being h = 1,..., k and substituting the vector $\mathbf{a}_1(1)'$ with vector $\mathbf{a}_1(h)'$ into **A**(1), it thus becomes possible to construct other k–1 sub-systems or techniques [4.2], [4.3], [4.4]. Apart from [4.5], each of these sub-systems is autonomous with maximum production given by [4.4].

Let us consider the relations [4.2], [4.3], [4.5], with [4.5] taken as an equality. If the resulting production vector —that is the vector of full labor employment— does not satisfy [4.4], then the NPMP of type 1 is not sufficient to implement a level of production at full employment. When this is the case, the latter target requires the activation also of process 2 that utilizes NPMP of type 2.

Following the efficiency order —for the moment whatever it is— this process is expressed by

$$\mathbf{a}_1(2)' = [a_{11}(2);\ a_{21}(2);\ \ldots;\ a_{m+1,1}(2)].$$

The technology of the economic system should now be represented either by the method of compound technologies, or by the method of global technologies. As already anticipated, we shall first focus our analysis on the method of global technologies.

3. Global technologies and splitting coefficients

When in the economic system two processes with NPMP are used, in addition to the other m processes, the global technology representing this situation is given by the matrix

$$[4.6] \qquad \mathbf{A}_\alpha(1,2) = \begin{bmatrix} a_{11}(1) & 0 & \alpha_{12}(1) & . & \alpha_{1,m+1}(1) \\ 0 & a_{11}(2) & \alpha_{12}(2) & . & \alpha_{1,m+1}(2) \\ a_{21}(1) & a_{21}(2) & a_{22} & . & a_{2,m+1} \\ . & . & . & . & . \\ . & . & . & . & . \\ a_{m+1,1}(1) & a_{m+1,1}(2) & a_{m+1,2} & . & a_{m+1,m+1} \end{bmatrix}$$

The two processes $\mathbf{a}_1(1)$ and $\mathbf{a}_1(2)$ are now joined in the production of the Pcc1 which is required by the whole economic system. The "splitting coefficients", α, identify the extent to which processes 1 and 2, respectively, supply Pcc1 to the other processes of the economic system. By construction, we thus have

$$\alpha_{ij}(1) + \alpha_{ij}(2) = a_{1j}$$

Therefore, the increase of $\alpha_{1j}(2)$ compared to $\alpha_{1j}(1)$ indicates that process $\mathbf{a}_1(2)$ assumes a greater relative weight in the economic system, as it increasingly replaces process $\mathbf{a}_1(1)$ in the supply of Pcc1 to all other processes of the economic system. In turn, the relative weight of $\mathbf{a}_1(1)$ is reduced in the economic system, even if in absolute terms it remains activated at its maximum level correspondent to the full utilization of T(1) (see [4.4]).

It should be noted that $\mathbf{A}_\alpha(1,2)$ does not include the coefficients that could be defined "reciprocal splitting coefficients", that is, those regarding the flow supplied by process 1 to process 2, and vice versa. The reason is evident: if the level of activity of the economic system were so high such that all $\alpha_{1j}(1)$ were reduced to almost zero, process 1 would still produce a quantity of $q_1(1)$ sufficient for its own utilization, given that $a_{11}(1) < 1$. Supplying process 1 with Pcc1 coming from process 2, that is, introducing a $\alpha_{11}(2) > 0$, would mean that an amount of Pcc1 produced and already utilized by process 1 is released and allocated for utilization in one or more of the j processes. A compensation effect (and not a genuine substitution) would therefore occur which would not have any influence on the activity level. The same reasoning can be carried out for the reciprocal splitting coefficients of process 1 with respect to process 2.

Global technology $\mathbf{A}_\alpha(1,2)$, which is affected by changes in the α, is quite different from the Leontievian matrices, and represents, in our opinion, an innovation in modeling the production system. It includes more processes that produce the same commodity altogether with the traditional processes that produce in a one-to-one relation the other commodities. In addition to the properties already pointed out, matrices of type $\mathbf{A}_\alpha(1,2)$ show also the following features:

a) they are non-negative;
b) they are non-decomposable (except in the extreme potential cases of the limit values assumed by the splitting coefficients);
c) they are viable, that is, they admit some positive uniform rate of net product. This property derives from relation [4.3];

d) they are non-singular. In fact, we exclude the case of productive processes linearly dependent;
e) they are characterized by a particular sequence of coefficients. Without loosing generality, it is assumed that

$$a_{11}(1) \leq a_{11}(2) \leq \ldots \leq a_{11}(k),$$

which is a sufficient condition for the existence of solutions when the analysis moves from aggregate to disaggregate matrices (see later § 6 and § 7).

This is not an excessively restrictive hypothesis —it typically raises if the order followed is that of physical efficiency, though it is not a necessary condition. Moreover, it does not require that the price-distribution order of efficiency coincides to the physical one.

4. The physical system with two techniques

The unknown variables of the economic system, α, s, $\mathbf{q}$, and l, are determined by the following system

$$[4.7] \qquad [(1 + s_\alpha(1,2))\, \mathbf{A}_\alpha(1,2) - \mathbf{I}]\mathbf{q}_\alpha(1,2) = \mathbf{o},$$

with the fulfillment of the following conditions

$$[4.8] \qquad \alpha_{1j}(1) + \alpha_{1j}(2) = a_{1j}; \qquad \alpha_{1j}(1) > 0, \alpha_{1j}(2) > 0, \qquad j = 2, \ldots, m+1$$

$$[4.9] \qquad \bar{q}_1(1) = T(1)/\tau_1(1),$$

$$[4.10] \qquad q_1(1) = \bar{q}_1(1),$$

$$[4.11] \qquad q_1(2) \leq \bar{q}_1(2) = T(2)/\tau_1(2),$$

$$[4.12] \qquad \mathbf{l}(1,2)'\ \mathbf{q}_\alpha(1,2) = 1 \leq \bar{1},$$

with

$$[4.13] \qquad \mathbf{l}(1,2)' = [l_1(1), l_1(2), l_2, \ldots, l_{m+1}],$$

$$\mathbf{q}_\alpha(1,2) = [q_1(1), q_1(2), q_2, \ldots, q_{m+1}].$$

The solution can be found by increasing the $\alpha_{1j}(2)$ in such a way that the constraints given by the full utilization of the NPMP of type 1, that is, by [4.10], does not prevent production processes $\mathbf{q}_\alpha(1,2)$ from growing to that level at which [4.11] becomes an equality, that is, up to the full utilization of the NPMP of type 2.

At that level of $\mathbf{q}_\alpha(1,2)$, there are three alternative scenarios for the labor-force:

a) it is fully employed, and [4.12] is therefore satisfied as an equality;

b) it is insufficient for the full utilization of the NPMP of type 2, and [4.12] is thus violated. In this case, by reducing $\alpha_{1j}(2)$, there will be a fall of $\mathbf{q}_\alpha(1,2)$ up to the point of restoring the equality of [4.12];
c) it is only partially utilized, and [4.12] is thus satisfied as an inequality. In this case, the economic system must expand by introducing a further NPMP, that of type 3.

We imposed the condition that the production processes of the economy based on joint technology were structured in such a way as to generate a uniform rate of net product. However, in this situation the meaning of $s_\alpha(1,2)$ does not coincide with that of s(h). Though both $s_\alpha(1,2)$ and s(h) are proxies of the static efficiency of the economic system, s(h) represents also the maximum uniform growth rate of technique h while $s_\alpha(1,2)$ is only connected to the growth rate of technology $\mathbf{A}_\alpha(1,2)$, and moreover, is not constant.

The comparison between the latter two cases is interesting because it helps to clarify the differences between the dynamics with the use of NPMP compared to the dynamics that does not make use of NPMP.

5. The physical economic system with k techniques

The foregoing analysis showed that the number of active processes with NPMP will depend on the constraints in the quantity of NPMP and labor. The most widely available global technology is that in which the whole k processes with NPMP are active. This technology is given by the previous matrix of order (k + m), which has all the properties defined in § 3, and in which the processes from 1 to k produce PCC1, and the processes from 2 to m + 1 produce the other m commodities (see matrix [4.14]). Such a technology is employed when the first k – 1 processes with NPMP are utilized at their maximum level as established by the available quantity of NPMP.

The economic system as a whole is described by the following relations

[4.14] $$\mathbf{A}_\alpha(1,\dots,k) =$$

$$= \left[\begin{array}{ccccc|cccc}
a_{11}(1) & 0 & 0 & 0 & 0 & \alpha_{12}(1) & \alpha_{13}(1) & \cdot & \alpha_{1,m+1}(1) \\
0 & a_{11}(2) & 0 & 0 & 0 & \alpha_{12}(2) & \alpha_{13}(2) & \cdot & \alpha_{1,m+1}(2) \\
\cdot & \cdot & \cdot & \cdot & \cdot & \cdot & \cdot & \cdot & \cdot \\
\cdot & \cdot & \cdot & \cdot & \cdot & \cdot & \cdot & \cdot & \cdot \\
0 & 0 & 0 & a_{11}(k-1) & 0 & \alpha_{12}(k-1) & \alpha_{13}(k-1) & \cdot & \alpha_{1,m+1}(k-1) \\
0 & 0 & 0 & 0 & a_{11}(k) & \alpha_{12}(k) & \alpha_{13}(k) & \cdot & \alpha_{1,m+1}(k) \\
\hline
a_{21}(1) & a_{21}(2) & & a_{21}(k-1) & a_{21}(k) & a_{22} & a_{23} & \cdot & a_{2,m+1} \\
\cdot & \cdot & & \cdot & \cdot & \cdot & \cdot & \cdot & \cdot \\
\cdot & \cdot & & \cdot & \cdot & \cdot & \cdot & \cdot & \cdot \\
a_{m+1,1}(1) & a_{m+1,1}(2) & & a_{m+1,1}(k-1) & a_{m+1,1}(k) & a_{m+1,2} & a_{m+1.3} & \cdot & a_{m+1,m+1}
\end{array}\right]$$

[4.15] $$[(1 + s_\alpha(1, \dots, k))\, \mathbf{A}_\alpha(1, \dots, k) - \mathbf{I}]\, \mathbf{q}_\alpha(1, \dots, k) = \mathbf{o},$$

[4.16] $$\sum_{h=1}^{k} \alpha_{ij}(h) = a_{ij}, \qquad \alpha_{ij}(h) > 0, \qquad j = 2,\ldots,m+1; h = 1,\ldots,k;$$

[4.17] $$\bar{q}_1(h) = T(h)/\tau_1(h),$$

[4.18] $$q_1(h) = \bar{q}_1(h), \qquad h = 1, \ldots, k-1;$$

[4.19] $$q_1(k) \leq \bar{q}_1(k),$$

[4.20] $$\mathbf{l}(1, \ldots, k)' \, \mathbf{q}_\alpha(1, \ldots, k) = \bar{l},$$

with

$$\mathbf{l}(1, \ldots, k)' = [l_1(1), \ldots, l_1(k), l_2, \ldots, l_{m+1}],$$

$$\mathbf{q}_\alpha(1, \ldots, k)' = [q_1(1), \ldots, q_1(k), q_2, \ldots, q_{m+1}].$$

Alternatively, instead of [4.19] and [4.20], the following relations can be considered

[4.21] $$q_1(k) = \bar{q}_1(k),$$

[4.22] $$\mathbf{l}(1, \ldots, k)' \, \mathbf{q}_\alpha(1, \ldots, k) < \bar{l}.$$

There are three kinds of possible solution to this system.

a) The solution of system [4.15]-[4.20] identifies the uniform rate of net product and the total productions corresponding to the full employment of labor. The NPMP are totally used, apart from the k*th* that cannot be completely employed because of the labor constraint.
b) The solution of system [4.15]-[4.18], [4.21] and [4.22] identifies instead the case in which the NPMP are completely utilized, whereas labor is not completely so, due to the constraints imposed by the availability of NPMP.
c) The solution of system [4.15]-[4.18], [4.20] and [4.21] identifies the case of full employment of both NPMP and labor.

This approach therefore clarifies the changes of technology when are employed two categories of scarce means of production: "labor" and "land". In turn, changes of technology but without technical progress (i.e. without any improvement of single techniques) can be of two kinds.

The first kind is associated with an increase in the weight of the last active process with NPMP, which is required to absorb an increasing labor force. In this case the rate of net product and the level of productions will change, while the processes will not be affected.

The other kind of changes involves an increase in the number of activated processes with NPMP. In this situation changes in the dimensions of the global technology should be added to changes of the above type.

6. Technology and the aggregate economic system

The solution of system [4.15]-[4.20], or system [4.15]-[4.18], [4.21], [4.22] or system [4.15] [4.18], [4.20], [4.21], is not always easy with the usual procedures for calculating eigenvalues and eigenvectors. In fact, the constraints on the vector are at least k–1, as appears from [4.17] and [4.18], while in the standard cases the eigenvector of the quantity can be determined with only one constraint.

However, by taking into account the economic meaning of the problem, the first k–1 processes —activated at their maximum level— can be aggregated into a single process. This approach consists precisely in introducing first the splitting coefficients and the disaggregate global technologies, and then moving to aggregate technologies, as can be immediately seen by defining

[4.23] $$\overline{q}^*_1(k-1) = \sum_{v=1}^{k-1} \overline{q}_1(v),$$

[4.24] $$\gamma(v) = \overline{q}_1(v)/\overline{q}^*_1(k-1), \qquad \sum_{v=1}^{k-1} \gamma(v) = 1,$$

[4.25] $$a^*_{i1}(k-1) = \sum_{v=1}^{k-1} a_{ij}(v)\gamma(v), \qquad i = 1,\ldots,m+1,$$

[4.26] $$l^*_1(k-1) = \sum_{v=1}^{k-1} l_1(v)\gamma(v).$$

The problem of the scale of production of the economy depends, thus, on the relative weight of the k–1 aggregate processes compared to the weight of process k.

The determination of the splitting coefficients can be referred, on the one hand, to the processes obtained by aggregating the first k–1 processes and, on the other hand, to the k*th* process. The splitting coefficients of the same column can be added together, since they represent the same commodity and are multiplied by the same quantity. Therefore we can denote

[4.27] $$\alpha^*_{ij}(k-1) = \sum_{v=1}^{k-1} \alpha_{ij}(v). \qquad j = 2,\ldots,m+1$$

By means of these aggregations the global technology can once again be described by a matrix of order m + 2, as in the case of the economic system with only two techniques. The aggregate global technology is therefore given by

[4.28] $$\mathbf{A}^*_\alpha(k-1, k) =$$

$$
= \left[\begin{array}{c|c|cccc}
a^{*}_{11}(k-1) & 0 & \alpha^{*}_{12}(k-1) & \alpha^{*}_{13}(k-1) & \ldots & \alpha^{*}_{1,m+1}(k-1) \\ \hline
0 & a_{11}(k) & a_{12}(k) & a_{13}(k) & \ldots & \alpha^{*}_{1,m+1}(k) \\ \hline
a^{*}_{21}(k-1) & a_{21}(k) & a_{22} & a_{23} & \ldots & a_{2,m+1} \\
a^{*}_{31}(k-1) & a_{31}(k) & a_{32} & a_{33} & \ldots & a_{3,m+1} \\
. & . & . & . & \ldots & . \\
. & . & . & . & \ldots & . \\
a^{*}_{m+1,1}(k-1) & a_{m+1,1}(k) & a_{m+1,2} & a_{m+1,3} & \ldots & a_{m+1,m+1}
\end{array}\right]
$$

The aggregate economic system is thus given by

[4.29] $$[(1 + s_{\alpha})\, \mathbf{A}^{*}_{\alpha}(k-1, k) - \mathbf{I}]\, \mathbf{q}^{*}_{\alpha}(k-1, k) = \mathbf{o},$$

$$[\mathbf{A}^{*}_{\alpha}(k-1, k) - \lambda_{\alpha}\mathbf{I}]\, \mathbf{q}^{*}_{\alpha}(k-1, k) = \mathbf{o},$$

with

[4.30] $$s_{\alpha} = (1/\lambda_{\alpha}) - 1, \qquad 0 < \lambda_{\alpha} < 1;$$

$$\mathbf{q}^{*}_{\alpha}(k-1, k) = [\ \bar{q}^{*}_{1}(k-1), q_{1}(k), q_{2}, \ldots, q_{m+1}],$$

$$\mathbf{l}^{*}_{\alpha}(k-1, k) = [l^{*}_{1}(k-1), l_{1}(k), l_{2}, \ldots, l_{m+1}],$$

subject to the constraints [4.18], [4.19], and to the constraint

[4.31] $$\mathbf{l}^{*}_{\alpha}(k-1, k)\, \mathbf{q}^{*}_{\alpha}(k-1, k) \le \bar{1}.$$

Also in this formulation there are three alternative kinds of solution:

a) The first solution allows to identify a vector $\alpha_{1j}(k-1)' = [\alpha^{*}_{12}(k-1), \alpha^{*}_{13}(k-1), \ldots, \alpha^{*}_{1,m+1}(k-1)]$, a vector $\alpha_{1j}(k)' = [\alpha_{12}(k), \alpha_{13}(k), \ldots, \alpha_{1,m+1}(k)]$, a quantity vector $\mathbf{q}^{*}_{\alpha}(k-1, k)$, and a rate of net product s_{α}, which give the full employment of labor, whereas the NPMP of type k can remain partially unemployed.
b) The second solution will give the NPMP of type k fully employed with labor unemployed.
c) Finally, the third solution will give full utilization of the NPMP and labor.

In economic terms, the solution follows these steps: the key point are the splitting coefficients. They are related to $\mathbf{q}^{*}_{\alpha}(k-1, k)$ and s_{α} in a way as to satisfy the constraints of full utilization of the first k–1 NPMP. If, however, they do not offer an overall full labor employment, then some action must be taken to reduced $\alpha^{*}_{1j}(k-1)$ and increase $\alpha_{1j}(k)$. In this way, the increase of weight of process k relaxes the constraint of the first k–1 NPMP. This in turn would allow the quantitative increase of all the commodities produced with the use of NPMP as means of production. The reduction of $\alpha^{*}_{1j}(k-1)$ and the corresponding increase of $\alpha_{1j}(k)$ should stop as soon as the constraint [4.21] or [4.22] becomes operative.

7. Technology and the disaggregate economic system

The disaggregation problem consists in splitting the vector $\alpha^*_{1j}(k-1)$ among the k–1 processes in order to switch from the matrix [4.28], $\mathbf{A}^*_\alpha(k-1, \ldots, k)$, to the matrix $\mathbf{A}_\alpha(1, \ldots, k)$, without modifying the solutions obtained.

The mathematical solution determines the splitting coefficients with the distribution of the $\alpha^*_{1j}(k-1)$ among the k–1 processes with NPMP as follows

[4.32] $$\alpha_{1j}(v) = \alpha^*_{1j}(k-1)\,\gamma(v), \qquad v = 1, \ldots, k-1; j = 2, \ldots, m+1.$$

Matrix [4.14], $\mathbf{A}^*_\alpha(1, \ldots, k)$, will thus have k–1 row vectors in the top-right sub-matrix reagion

[4.33] $$[\alpha^*_{12}(k-1)\,\gamma(v), \alpha^*_{13}(k-1)\,\gamma(v), \ldots, \alpha^*_{1,m+1}(k-1)\,\gamma(v)], \quad v = 1, \ldots, k-1.$$

It is worth noting that a distribution of the $\alpha^*_{1j}(k-1)$ with non-uniform weights $\gamma(v)$ in every row, is useless since it would imply only compensations.

Referring to a simple case with three commodities and two processes with NPMP, it can be shown that, if the process with NPMP 1 increases the share of "corn" supplied to the "iron" sector — that is, if $\gamma_{12}(1)$ is increased above $\gamma(1)$ — then the weight of "corn" supplied to the "services" sector must correspondingly diminish — that is, $\gamma_{13}(1)$ falls short $\gamma(1)$.

At the same time, the share of "corn" supplied to the "iron" sector by the process with NPMP of type 2 will have to diminish —that is $\gamma_{12}(2)$ will fall short $\gamma(2)$ — and, correspondingly, the share of "corn" supplied to the "services" sector will have to increase —that is $\gamma_{13}(2)$ will rise above $\gamma(2)$.

The previous analysis allows us to determine the relations between the sequential activation of processes with NPMP and labor employment. If the quantity of NPMP of the different types is sufficiently high, then full employment can be reached. Otherwise, the quantity of NPMP may hinder the target of full employment.

We shall now move to analyze the implications of the growth of production for the efficiency of the economic system.

8. Changes in efficiency, in activity and efficiency proxies: some premises

Let us now suppose that the economic system is in a condition of full employment of labor, with k NPMP activated, but with the k*th* not completely utilized. If the labor force increases, it is necessary for the maintenance of the desired full employment, to further increase the utilization of NPMP of type k. Such a re-adjustment gives rise to the following results:

a) a structural change in the global technology whose dimension, however, do not change, consisting of k processes with NPMP (plus the other m processes);
b) continuous change in the efficiency of the global technology since the k process increases its weight within the technology;

c) growth in production and employment. Within a framework of global technology at constant dimension, this is a first case where we have changes of physical efficiency, namely continuous changes. A second case of changes in physical efficiency occurs with the growing dimension of the global technology, but here changes are discontinuous. This second case rises when the increase of the labor force requires the utilization of a further NPMP process in addition to the last k*th* one. Supposing that this further process, called k + 1, does now exist, we will have:
d) a change of structure and dimensions of the global technology;
e) a discontinuous change in the efficiency of the global technology;
f) an increase in production and employment.

Let us consider the two cases in a comparative static framework without carrying out a proper dynamic analysis, that is, without taking into account the accumulation of the net product.

At first, it is necessary to qualify further the efficiency proxy utilized. A typical measure of "physical efficiency" is given by the uniform rate of net product. This is one among the several possible choices: indeed one of the more synthetic measures (see Chapter III, § 10).

It is well known that in the linear models of production and growth, such as those proposed by von Neumann, the uniform rate of net product and the rate of growth of the economic system coincide. For this reason a more significant measure of dynamic efficiency does not exist.

The previous representation, however, differs in many respects from models *á la* von Neumann. Firstly, it is framed in a static and comparative static analysis. Secondly, the growth of the activity levels, obtained by increasing the weight of the last activated process with NPMP, always affects the uniform rate of net product. The same occurs when any additional process with NPMP is activated. Since the uniform rate of net product, the accumulation rate, and the growth rate are interrelated, any change in the uniform rate of net product ends up to modify the other variables too.

These remarks though confirm the relevance of the uniform rate of net product as proxy for the efficiency of the technology and the physical system show also that its use cannot be always generalized.

9. Changes in efficiency and price efficiency

Now let us analyze the changes in the uniform rate of net product as the activity level increases with both the use of type k NPMP, and the growth of production and employment. From [4.29] we have

$$\lambda_\alpha \mathbf{q}^*_\alpha(k-1,k) = \mathbf{A}^*_\alpha(k-1,k)\,\mathbf{q}^*_\alpha(k-1,k);$$

multiplying both terms of the previous relation by the left eigenvector $\mathbf{p}^*_\alpha(k-1, k)$ of the matrix $\mathbf{A}^*_\alpha(k-1, k)$ and since $\mathbf{p}^*_\alpha(k-1, k)' = [p^*_1(k-1), p_1(k), p_2, \dots, p_{m+1}]$, after re-ordering, we get

$$\lambda_\alpha = \frac{\mathbf{p}^*{}_\alpha(k-1,k)'\mathbf{A}^*{}_\alpha(k-1,k)\mathbf{q}^*{}_\alpha(k-1,k)}{\mathbf{p}^*{}_\alpha(k-1,k)'\mathbf{q}^*{}_\alpha(k-1,k)}$$

and thus

[4.34] $$\frac{\partial\lambda_\alpha}{\partial\alpha_{ij}(k)} = \frac{\partial}{\partial\alpha_{ij}(k)}\{[\mathbf{p}^*{}_\alpha(k-1,k)'\mathbf{A}^*{}_\alpha(k-1,k)\mathbf{q}^*{}_\alpha(k-1,k)]$$

$$[\mathbf{p}^*{}_\alpha(k-1,k)'\,\mathbf{q}^*{}_\alpha(k-1,k)]^{-1}\}$$

from which, simplifying and recalling [4.16], it is possible to obtain

[4.35] $$\frac{\partial\lambda_\alpha}{\partial\alpha_{ij}(k)} = \frac{[p_1(k) - p^*{}_1(k-1)]q_{j+1}}{\mathbf{p}^*{}_\alpha(k-1,k)'\mathbf{q}^*{}_\alpha(k-1,k)};\quad j = 2,\ldots,m+1.$$

Equation [4.35] shows the effect on the maximum eigenvalue of $\mathbf{A}^*{}_\alpha(k-1, k)$ (that is the effect on the rate of net product) produced by an increase in the splitting coefficients of the process with NPMP of type k, and thus the increased weight of this process in the economic system.

From [4.35] we can derive three alternative cases.

a) The case of increasing efficiency

[4.36] $$p_1(k) < p^*{}_1(k-1),$$

which gives:

[4.37] $$\frac{\partial\lambda_\alpha}{\partial\alpha_{1j}(k)} < 0 \quad\text{or}\quad \frac{\partial s_\alpha}{\partial\alpha_{1j}(k)} > 0.$$

b) The case of constant efficiency:

[4.38] $$p_1(k) = p^*{}_1(k-1),$$

which gives:

[4.39] $$\frac{\partial\lambda_\alpha}{\partial\alpha_{1j}(k)} = 0 \quad\text{or}\quad \frac{\partial s_\alpha}{\partial\alpha_{1j}(k)} = 0.$$

c) The case of decreasing efficiency:

[4.40] $$p_1(k) > p^*{}_1(k-1),$$

which gives

[4.41] $$\frac{\partial\lambda_\alpha}{\partial\alpha_{1j}(k)} > 0 \quad\text{or}\quad \frac{\partial s_\alpha}{\partial\alpha_{1j}(k)} < 0.$$

Therefore, the relation between $p^*{}_1(k-1)$ and $p_1(k)$, i.e. the prices of the PCC1 (of "corn") produced respectively by the aggregate process k–1 and by process k, represents the distinctive key that characterizes these three cases.

On the other hand, the vector $\mathbf{p}^*{}_\alpha(k-1, k)$, being the left-hand side eigenvector of the matrix $\mathbf{A}^*{}_\alpha(k-1, k)$, represents the eigenvector of the prices associated with a hypothetical maximum rate of profit for the aggregate global technology.

The prices taken into account here and the hypothetical rate of profit are not those of the general price-distribution system associated with the global technology $\mathbf{A}^*{}_\alpha(k-1, k)$. In fact, in that case, the price of the PCC1 is unique for the whole economy and it is given by the least efficient technique, that is, the technique which includes the least efficient process with NPMP. This is also the technique that determines the rate of profit. As a result, the other processes that produce PCC1 more efficiently within the given technology, will show some levels of rent.

In the current case instead we analyze the processes generating PCC1 as if they would produce two different commodities with two different prices. Therefore, the hypothetical rate of profit is different from that of the usual price-distribution system, because in that framework, purely instrumental to the quantity system, rent does not exist.

These prices are therefore: $p^*_1(k-1)$, the price based on the production cost, given by the circulating capital utilized by the aggregate process k–1; and $p_1(k)$ the price of the process with NPMP of type k. They can be considered proxies for the efficiency of the commodities-means of production utilized by the two processes with NPMP, the aggregate and disaggregate one.

We therefore have increasing efficiency when $p^*_1(k-1) > p_1(k)$, that is, when we increase the weight of the process which utilizes less circulating capital per unit of output. Correspondingly, we have constant efficiency when $p^*_1(k-1) = p_1(k)$, and decreasing efficiency when $p^*_1(k-1) < p_1(k)$.

These three cases are all possible, depending on the order of efficiency. If the level of w does not constitute a constraint, the use of the physical order of efficiency (Chapter III, §10) would result in a shift towards decreasing efficiency in both cases of constant and increasing dimension of the global technology. In the latter case, the introduction of a further process with NPMP causes a discontinuous fall in the uniform rate of profit. One may notice that this is an updated version of the Ricardian analysis —the growth of the economy stops when all the NPMP with viable processes have been utilized. In this situation if another NPMP is introduced, the technique **A**, constructed with the additional process (see [4.1]), would be such that

$$[4.42] \qquad \mathbf{A}(k + x)\, \mathbf{q}(k + x) \geq \mathbf{q}(k + x), \qquad x \geq 1,$$

and thus with either zero or negative rate of net product.

The price-distribution order of efficiency can, however, also give rise to the opposite case, so that the techniques **A**(h) are arranged in such a way that the uniform rates of net product are increasing.

Whenever we would like to inquiry the historical phases of economic development, this situation could be the basis for analyzing a type of technical progress that saves circulating capital. That is, a technical progress that only affects the "new" (i.e. not yet activated) processes with NPMP, and does not temporarily cause the displacement of "old" processes. In this case, obviously, also the historical order of price-distribution efficiency should show an increasing efficiency of the processes.

Though is outside the scope of this volume, the latter remark allows us to stress that a wider analysis of the problems of the orders of efficiency is needed. In particular one should distinguish between orders of efficiency in historical context —which can or cannot include technical progress— and logical orders of efficiency.

Finally, the price-distribution order of efficiency can determine uneven trends in the uniform rate of net product of the global technology, as other processes with NPMP are introduced. This occurs because there is no one-to-one relationship between price-distribution order of efficiency and uniform rate of net product —a given stable ranking of the first is associated with multiple possible rates of the second.

10. Growth of the production activity

The growth of the level of production is the other issue that should be considered, both in the continuous and discontinuous case.

Let us consider the vector $\mathbf{q}^{*}_{\alpha}(k-1, k)'$, obtained by dividing all its elements by $\bar{q}^{*}_{1}(k-1)$. This vector is thus normalized with the first element set equal to 1. We denote with

$$[4.43] \qquad \tilde{\mathbf{q}}^{*}_{a}{}' = [\tilde{q}_1(k), \tilde{q}_2, \ldots, \tilde{q}_{m+1}]$$

the sub-vector consisting of the last m + 1 elements of this normalized vector.

It is possible to demonstrate that

$$[4.44] \qquad \frac{\partial \tilde{\mathbf{q}}_{\alpha}}{\partial \alpha_{ij}(k)} > 0$$

whenever

$$[4.45] \qquad \frac{\partial \lambda_{\alpha}}{\partial \alpha_{ij}(k)} \leq 0, \text{that is} \frac{\partial s_{\alpha}}{\partial \alpha_{ij}(k)} \geq 0 \text{ and } p^{*}_{1}(k-1) \geq p_1(k).$$

Therefore, when the efficiency of the economic system grows (or remains constant) as a consequence of the activation of the process with NPMP of type k, then the produced quantities also increase.

If the efficiency of the economic system decreases, that is,

$$[4.46] \qquad \frac{\partial \lambda_{\alpha}}{\partial \alpha_{ij}(k)} > 0; \ \frac{\partial s_{\alpha}}{\partial \alpha_{ij}(k)} < 0; \ p^{*}_{1}(k-1) < p_1(k).$$

it is possible that either an increase or a decrease in production takes place according to the sign of the elements of vector $\partial \tilde{\mathbf{q}}^{*}_{\alpha} / \partial \alpha_{ij}(k)$. Obviously this sign depends also on the difference between $p_1(k)$ and $p^{*}_{1}(k-1)$.

The economic interpretation of such a condition is not immediately evident on the basis of the mathematical formulation, and requires an analysis in terms of vertically integrated sectors.

However, there is a particular case which supports the conclusion of an increase of the production processes also in the situation considered by [4.46]. The change in vector $\tilde{\mathbf{q}}^{*}_{\alpha}$ of the normalized quantities may be linked to the change of the eigenvector λ_{α} by the simple relation

[4.47] $$\frac{\partial\lambda_\alpha}{\partial\alpha_{1j}(k)} = \frac{\partial\beta_\alpha}{\partial\alpha_{1j}(k)}\tilde{\mathbf{q}}_\alpha + \beta'_\alpha \frac{\partial\tilde{\mathbf{q}}^*{}_\alpha}{\partial\alpha_{1j}(k)}.$$

with

$$\beta'_\alpha = [0,\ \alpha^*{}_{12}(k-1), \alpha^*{}_{13}(k-1), \ldots, \alpha^*{}_{1,m+1}(k-1)].$$

It is possible to verify that [4.47] can be expressed as

[4.48] $$\frac{\partial\lambda_\alpha}{\partial\alpha_{1j}(k)} = [0, -\mathbf{e}_j{}']\tilde{\mathbf{q}}^*{}_\alpha + \beta'_\alpha \frac{\partial\tilde{\mathbf{q}}^*{}_\alpha}{\partial\alpha_{1j}(k)}.$$

By inspecting [4.48] and assuming [4.46] holds, we can obtain the following inequality

[4.49] $$\beta'_\alpha \frac{\partial\tilde{\mathbf{q}}^*{}_\alpha}{\partial\alpha_{1j}(k)} > 0.$$

The increase in a splitting coefficient implies an increase in the utilization of PCC1 as a means of production. This increase is generated by the process k–1, altogether with the reduction of its net product, since it produces a fixed "non-augmenting" quantity of corn. It should be clear that the assumption for increasing the utilization of PCC1 as a means of production, implies that the production of at least one of the other m "industrial" sectors (as distinct from the two "agricultural" processes, k–1 and k), increases so that the demand of "corn" will rise. Having a non-decomposable economic system, it is plausible that the increase of production in both one industrial sector and the agricultural sector k generates an overall increase of production in all other sectors, except for the fixed production of the aggregate "agricultural" sector k – 1. This is because all sectors —included the agricultural one that has not a fixed production— are required to supply additional means of production and these obviously must be produced. Finally, potential compensation effects with falling levels of production induced by sector k – 1 should not occur, since its output is fixed.

11. Conclusions and further lines of analysis

We have started this Chapter clarifying that production problems can be handled within two different theoretical frameworks —that of global technologies, and that of compound technologies.

Then we have sketched an analysis with global technologies that maintains its theoretical originality for the use of splitting coefficients and, consequently, the opportunity of determining the continuous changes in the uniform rate of net product as the weight of the last activated process with NPMP changes.

Based on this analysis of global technologies we shall take into consideration in the following pages the problems of rent, distribution and prices in a static and comparative static setting. This means to focus on the problems listed in Chapter II, §15, §16 and §17, that is, the order of rentability, induced and autonomous changes of income distribution, and the implications for the order of efficiency, and the level of activity.

Indeed, it is clear that the price-distribution system and the physical (or quantity) system show in our theoretical framework a degree of interrelation that lacks in the usual linear models. In the following pages therefore the reader will have to be used in moving easily from one system to the other.

Chapter V - Rent, distribution, prices

1. Introduction

The analysis carried out until now started with the choice of an exogenous distributive variable and determined the order of efficiency (Chapter III), and the level of activity of the economy (Chapter IV).

Building on these premises, we can now determine:

- prices;
- unit rents and unit wage or alternatively profit rate, as well as the total aggregate levels of these distributive variables;
- value added or value of net product.

Moreover we can solve the problems set out in Chapter II (§ 15, 16, 17) by determining:

a) the order of rentability (OR) that is derived from the rent per unit of NPMP. It allows the ordering of the NPMP and the techniques using them, as well as their changes within a given OE;

b) the induced changes in OR, distribution, and prices generated by the growth of the economy's activity level;

c) the autonomous changes in OR, distribution, and prices generated by the exogenous distributive variable. From these changes, it is possible to distinguish two cases: the first, in which the OE is not modified, and the second, in which it is. In the latter case also the technology of the economy as well as the quantity system may change.

This analysis therefore gives form to the particular interdependence between price-distribution system and the physical-quantity system, we already mentioned (Chapter II, § 11).

2. The solving sub-system pwπ and the general system price-distribution

Let us assume that π is exogenously fixed at a level that does not exclude any technique. This means (see Chapter III, § 7 and 9) that we assume $\pi = \bar{\pi} < \max \pi(k)$.

By determining the OE on the basis of the previous distributive variable, it is possible to identify the global technology and the level of activity.

Therefore it is possible to determine the solving sub-system pwπ, that is, that with zero rent (Chapter III, § 3), and hence the unit wage and prices. Finally, on the basis of the sub-system of rents, the latter are calculated (Chapter III, § 4), and we eventually have all the variables of the general system price-distribution determined.

Let us assume that the activity level is such as to involve the use of h* processes with NPMP and that h* < k. An increase in the level of activity can therefore take place, firstly, throughout an extension of scale of the process h*, and, secondly, trough the introduction of further processes with NPMP.

3. Total distributive variables and value of the net product

Once π, w and the level of activity are known, it is possible to determine the total distributive variables.

Total wages are given by

[5.1] $$W(1,\dots,h^*) = \mathbf{l}(1,\dots,h^*)'\,\mathbf{q}_\alpha(1,\dots,h^*)\,w(h^*).$$

The vectors $\mathbf{l}$ and $\mathbf{q}_\alpha$ have h* + m components; w(h*) is the unit wage and W(1,..., h*) is total wage.

Total profits are given by

[5.2] $$\Pi(1,\dots,h^*) = \mathbf{p}(1,\dots,h^*)'\,\mathbf{A}_\alpha(1,\dots,h^*)\,\mathbf{q}_\alpha(1,\dots,h^*)\,\pi(h^*),$$

where

$$\mathbf{p}(1,\dots,h^*)' = [p_1, \dots, p_1, p_2, \dots, p_{m+1}].$$

The price p_1 is repeated h* times, because this is the number of processes with NPMP producing PCC1. As already said all prices depend on process h*.

Total rents are given by

[5.3] $$R(1,\dots,h^*) = \sum_{h=1}^{h^*} \rho(h)\,T(h).$$

This expression, simpler than [3.8], is the sum of h* elements, since rent involves only those processes with NPMP.

The value added of the economic system is therefore given by

[5.4] $$Y(1,\dots,h^*) = W(1,\dots,h^*) + \Pi(1,\dots,h^*) + R(1,\dots,h^*).$$

It is equal to the value of net product of the economic system according to

[5.5] $$Y(1,\dots,h^*) = [\mathbf{p}(1,\dots,h^*)'\,\mathbf{n}_\alpha(1,\dots,h^*)],$$

where

[5.6] $$\mathbf{n}_\alpha(1,\dots,h^*)' = [n_1(1), \dots, n_1(h^*), n_2, \dots, n_{m+1}]$$

or alternatively

[5.7] $$\mathbf{n}_\alpha(1,\dots,h^*)' = s_\alpha(1,\dots,h^*)\,\mathbf{A}_\alpha(1,\dots,h^*)\,\mathbf{q}_\alpha(1,\dots,h^*).$$

We have already said that changes in distributive variables can be either induced or autonomous.

The induced changes have to be studied under two cases: the case with technology of constant dimension, where only the activity of the process employing the NPMP of type h* increases; the case with technology of increasing dimension, when a further process h* + 1 is introduced (see Chapter IV, § 8).

We begin to analyze the induced changes in OR. Then we will investigate those in the aggregate distributive variables Π, W, R.

4. The order of rentability and its induced changes

The OR has been defined (Chapter II, § 15 and Chapter V, § 1) as the sequence of the rents per unit of NPMP.

Now we must analyze this OR and show that:

a) it may not coincide with the OE (in our opinion Sraffa overlooks this property);

b) it may undergo induced changes, that is, it could change when the number of active processes with NPMP grows. Obviously, this second property implies the first one.

On the other hand, if the growth of the activity level does not widen global technology, the OR is not subject to any induced changes.

The relation [3.8] suggests that each rent grows when w and p_j decrease. However the growth of rents can take place at different rates, and hence this uneven patterns can modify their order.

Setting $\mathbf{a}_{j1}' = [a_{21}, \ldots, a_{m+1,1}]$ and $\mathbf{p}_j(h^*) = [p_2(h^*), \ldots, p_{m+1}(h^*)]$, we can write [3.8] as follow

$$[5.8]\quad \rho(h;h^*) = \frac{l_1(h)}{\tau_1(h)}\left\{\left[\frac{[1-a_{11}(h)(1+\bar{\pi})]p_1(h^*)}{l_1(h)} - \frac{1+\bar{\pi}}{l_1(h)}\mathbf{a}_{j1}(h)'\mathbf{p}_j(h^*)\right] - w(h^*)\right\},$$

namely,

$$\rho(h;h^*) = \frac{l_1(h)}{\tau_1(h)}[w(h;h^*) - w(h^*)];$$

where w(h; h*) denotes an hypothetical wage as it will be clear in the next section. From the previous relations emerges that while the sign of ρ depends on circulating capital and labor coefficients, the order of the various ρ with the same sign depends also on the coefficients $\tau_1(h)$. Moreover, the variations in p_j and w affect in a different way the production costs of the processes with NPMP.

For these reasons the OR can change. Since equations [5.8] are linear, it is possible only to experience one change in OR between any couple of processes with NPMP. The maximum number of changes, when the number of processes grows, is therefore given by the combinations $\binom{k}{2}$, where k denotes, as usual, the maximum number of processes with NPMP.

5. A simple case with one primary commodity and one final commodity

The complexity of this analysis requires, at first, some simplifications. Let us consider therefore the general system of price-distribution with only two commodities and a maximum of four active processes with NPMP. In this case, from [5.8] and [3.7] it follows respectively

$$[5.9]\quad \rho(h;h^*) = \frac{l_1(h)}{\tau_1(h)}\left\{\left[\frac{1-a_{11}(h)(1+\bar{\pi})}{l_1(h)} - \frac{a_{21}(h)(1+\bar{\pi})}{l_1(h)}p_2(h^*)\right] - w(h^*)\right\},$$

with h=1, 2, 3, 4;

$$[5.10]\qquad p_2(h^*) = \frac{a_{12}(1+\bar{\pi})}{1-a_{22}(1+\bar{\pi})} + \frac{l_2}{1-a_{22}(1+\bar{\pi})}w(h^*).$$

For h = h*, from [5.9] it follows

$$[5.11]\qquad w(h^*) = \frac{1-a_{11}(h^*)(1+\bar{\pi})}{l_1(h^*)} - \frac{a_{21}(h^*)(1+\bar{\pi})}{l_1(h^*)}p_2(h^*).$$

For each h = h*, we thus have a sub-system pwπ given by [5.10] and [5.11].

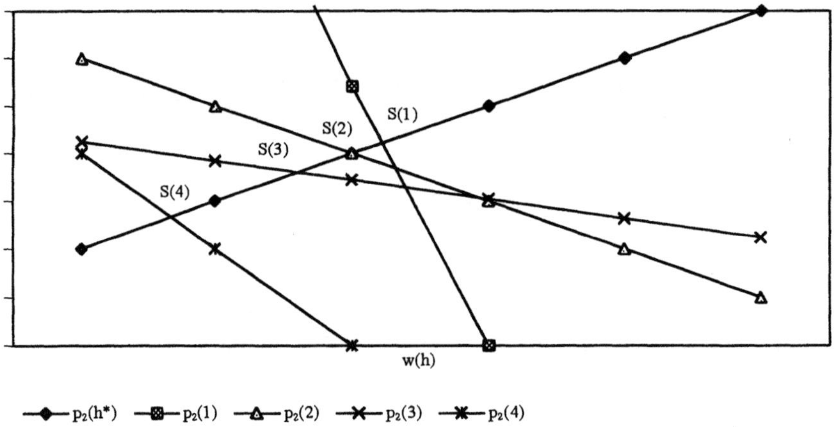

Fig. 5.1. Graphic solution of system [5.10]-[5.11] in the case of two commodities and four processes with NPMP in activity

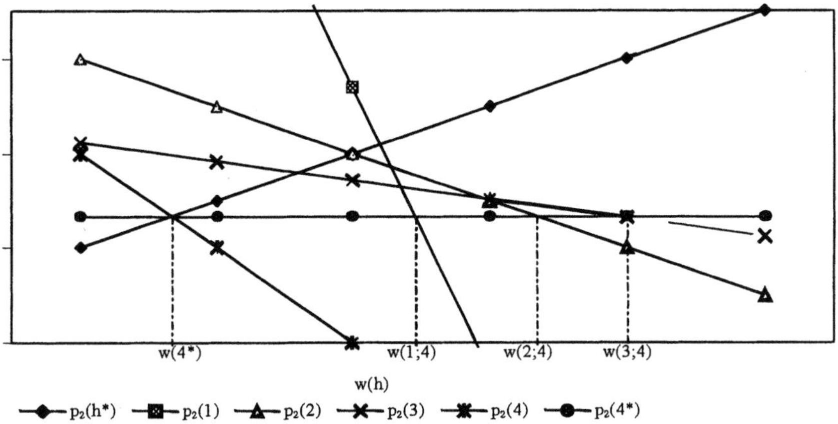

Fig. 5.2. Graphic determination of w(h; h*)

The solutions $p_2(h^*)$ and $w(h^*)$ of system [5.10]-[5.11], inserted into [5.9] give $\rho(h;h^*)$ for $h \neq h^*$. In this way, we obtain four potential price-distribution general systems. Each of these systems becomes effective according to the level of activity, that is, according to the number of processes with NPMP in activity.

In Figure 5.1 we show a graphical representation of the solutions of the four price-distribution general systems.

Equation [5.10] is an upward sloping line; [5.11] are downward sloping lines that we have written down in the following form $p_2(h^*)=f(h^*)w(h^*)$. The particular position of the lines depends on the hypothesis concerning the coefficients.

The co-ordinates of points S(1), S(2), S(3), S(4) show the solutions of the sub-systems pwπ of type 1, 2, 3, 4. In the example, the OE is therefore 1, 2, 3, 4, since $w(1) > w(2) > w(3) > w(4)$.

Let us now take into consideration the sign of the rents. At first, we analyze the term in brackets of [5.9], previously denoted with $w(h;h^*)$. If it is compared to [5.11], we can see that it represents a "hypothetical" unit wage, i.e. the wage that process h would give at price $p_2(h^*)$. This remark allows us to graphically show $w(h;h^*)$ in Figure 5.2. Indeed, the wage that process h would obtain at price $p_2(h^*)$ is determined in the x-axis by the intersection between the straight horizontal line $p_2(h^*)$,which crosses point $S(h^*)$, and one of the lines of [5.11].

If $h^* = 4$, the solutions of system [5.10]-[5.11] are $p_2(4)$ and $w(4)$, which are co-ordinates of point S(4). By tracing the line $p_2(h^*)=p_2(4)$ in Figure 5.2, the determination of $w(1;4)$, $w(2;4)$ and $w(3;4)$ —and more generally of $w(h;h^*)$ for any possible h^*— is straightforward. Since the sign of $\rho(h;h^*)$ is given by $w(h;h^*) - w(h^*)$, for $h^* = 1$ we have $\rho(1) = 0$ and $\rho(h;1) < 0$; for $h^* = 2$ we have $\rho(1;2) > 0$, $\rho(2) = 0$, $\rho(3;2) < 0$, $\rho(4;2) < 0$; for $h^* = 3$ we have $\rho(1;3) > 0$, $\rho(2;3) > 0$, $\rho(3;3) = 0$; $\rho(4;3) < 0$; and finally for $h^* = 4$ $\rho(h;4) > 0$ and $\rho(4) = 0$.

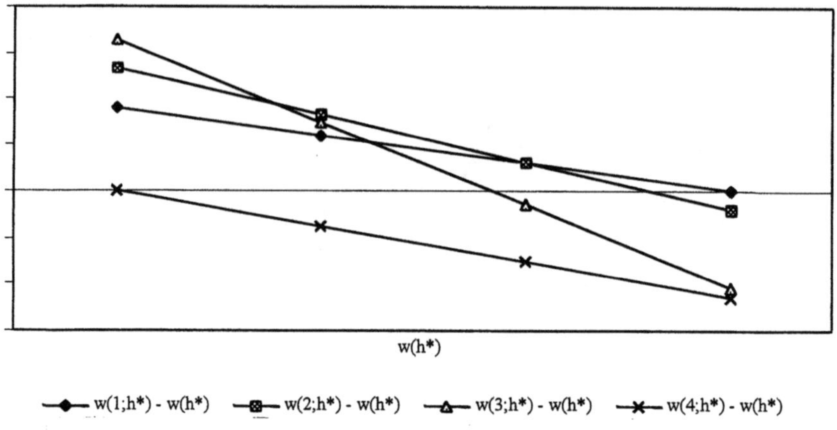

Fig. 5.3. w(h; h*) – w(h*)

Let us now take into consideration the OR. It changes several times —namely at every intersection between two downward sloping lines. The maximum number of changes is $\binom{4}{2}$, that is, 6; but the changes with economic significance are only those falling within the range of values that are meaningful from an economic point of view. This range comprises those solutions placed in the region below the increasing straight line and bounded by the two straight parallel lines which cross S(1) and S(4), that is to say, $\rho(h;h^*) \geq 0$ and $p_2(4) \leq p_2(h) \leq p_2(1)$. Therefore, the significant changes are at points I, L, M. In order to point out these changes it is useful to represent $w(h;h^*) - w(h^*)$ —from which the sign of $\rho(h;h^*)$ depends— for any possible h^*.

One should note that the scale of Figures 5.2 and 5.3 is different and that the lines connecting the points do not represent a continuos change of ρ.

What emerges from the previous figures is that for $h^* = 1$ we have $\rho(1;1) = 0$, whereas all other processes have negative rents. For $h^* = 2$ we have $\rho(1;2) > 0$ and therefore $\rho(1;2) > \rho(2;2)$. For $h^* = 3$ we have $\rho(1;3) > 0$ and $\rho(2;3) > 0$. However, since $[w(2;3)-w(3)] > [w(1;3)-w(3)]$, and assuming that the coefficients $l_1(h)/\tau_1(h)$ do not change the order given by the previous inequality, we have $\rho(2;3) > \rho(1;3)$. Finally, according to the same hypothesis for $h^* = 4$ we have $\rho(3;4) > \rho(2;4) > \rho(1;4)$. This OR is exactly the inverse of the OE.

6. Induced changes of wages and profits

We now investigate other effects on distribution caused by changes in the level of activity. The implications of these effects can be quite relevant, with new situations of "antagonism" in the distribution of income between employed and unemployed workers. The role of NPMP and rents, which will emerge, goes well beyond that of being a residual and a secondary variable compared to wages and profits in the distribution process, though also in our model the latter are determined in advance according to the sub-system pwπ.

Let us begin from the case with technology of constant dimension. Without the introduction of new processes, if the activity level increases —so that the weight of the last active process with NPMP is increased— the effects on distribution are quite straightforward.

Rents remain unchanged, since the increased use of NPMP occurs only in that process with zero rent. Instead, total wages and profits grow because of the raise in employment and means of production, even though prices, unit wage, and profit rate do not change.

The case of technology of increasing dimension, that is to say, the case in which, along with the growth of the activity level, there is also an increase of the number of processes with NPMP, has more complex implications. The consequences on rent have already been analyzed in the two previous sections — total rents increase both if profit rate is given, as well as if unit wage is given.

Concerning the effects on the other distributive variables we distinguish the following cases. Let us begin, in contrast with § 2, by assuming that w —and not π— is exogenously given.

For w = 0, surplus total wages do not change. Total profits can either increase, remain unchanged, or diminish according to whether and to what extent the reduction of π is offset by the increase in the means of production. However, when π reaches zero, total profit also equals zero, and the entire net product goes to rents. But before taking into account this extreme position, we consider the following three cases.

For $w = \bar{w} > 0$, surplus total wages increase with employment. The purchasing power of the surplus unit (and therefore total) wage also grows if w is set up in terms of PCC1 ("corn"). In particular its purchasing power increases compared to the other m commodities because their relative prices diminishes in terms of PCC1 price. The effect is that both employed and job-seeking workers benefit from the growth of production.

This conclusion can change if the numeraire changes. In fact we know that PCC1 is the only production process whose efficiency worsens with the activation of another NPMP. Therefore the changes of prices of the other commodities are dependent on the input of commodity 1.

By an appropriate permutation of the commodity indexes, we define commodity 2 as the numeraire for which p_1 increases, whereas all other prices diminish. Conversely commodity m+1 will be defined as the numeraire for which all the other prices increase. Commodity m+1 is therefore the commodity less dependent on the first production process at the given level of w.

If commodity m+1 were chosen as the numeraire, the result would be the following. The employed workers would suffer a fall of purchasing power, whereas those who find the job from an unemployed position would gain a benefit. In this situation therefore there is an antagonism of interests between these two categories of workers. On the other hand, new employees and the rent earners show converging interests. Finally, if the chosen numeraire is any commodity j with $1 < j < m+1$, it would be necessary to take into account, at the given wage, the composition of the effective expenditure in order to draw conclusions on the changes of purchasing power, and the existence of antagonism among workers.

Concerning the behavior of profits with this new numeraire, what has previously been said for w = 0 remains still true.

Let us now take into consideration the case with π exogenously given. The outcome is that the unit wage always diminishes, even in real terms, compared to any of the m+1 commodities chosen as numeraire. This is because the increasing activation of less efficient processes with NPMP rises the production cost of all commodities and, hence, it rises also prices.

In this case, the real wages of employed workers diminish and an antagonism emerges between them and those workers who already unemployed have found a job and now receive the pay. In contrast with this conflict, a convergence of interest is established between the latter category and rent earners.

As far as profits behavior is concerned, this will depend on both increases of the means of production and changes of prices. The previous remarks still hold whatever is the choice of the numeraire.

Hence, our conclusion is that the presence of NPMP considerably affects prices and income distribution by means of changes of activity level and the number of active NPMP.

7. Autonomous changes in distribution: general propositions

Let us now take into consideration in our model the effects of changes in the exogenous distributive variable, by also analyzing its differences —due to the NPMP— from models of single product.

We focus, in particular, on five stylized cases —we start with a case very similar to models of single product, and we end up with a case that significantly diverge from them. Throughout this analysis, we show how changes in OE affect the activity level, the trade off between π and w, and OR.

Before doing so, it is helpful to summarize some rather well known general propositions.

The use of the "standard commodity" as numeraire in a 'single product system', i.e. in our case the "standard commodity" of each sub-system pwπ, gives the traditional inverse linear relation *à la* Sraffa between π and w, once the value added and the employed labor in the sub-system of the type h* are set equal to one.

[5.12] $$\pi(h^*) = \max\pi(h^*)[1 - w(h^*)]\,.$$

If commodity 1 is used as numeraire, from [3.18] we get

[5.13] $$\mathbf{e}_1'[\mathbf{I} - (1+\pi)\mathbf{A}(h^*)']^{-1}\mathbf{l}(h^*)w(h^*) = 1,$$

where $\mathbf{e}_1'$=[1, 0, …, 0]. Therefore, we can study the relation between π and w as it follows from [5.13]

$$[5.14] \qquad w(h^*) = \frac{\det[\mathbf{I} - (1+\pi)\mathbf{A}(h^*)']}{\mathbf{l}(h^*)\mathbf{c}_{1i}(h^*)}$$

where $\mathbf{c}_{1i}(h^*)$ denotes the vector of the cofactors of the first row of the matrix $[\mathbf{I}-(1+\pi)\mathbf{A}(h^*)]$.

Each of these cofactors is an equation of degree m in the exogenous variable π. Therefore, [5.14] is represented by a polynomial of degree m+1 at the nominator and one of m degree at the denominator. The only certain pattern that emerges from the equation is a monotonic inverse relation between $w(h^*)$ and $\pi(h^*)$.

The great simplification allowed by the standard commodity does not however imply a simplification in studying the relation between π and prices. The changes of π affect prices in a way that depends on both the proportions between the means of production of the single commodities compared to the numeraire, and the interdependence between the economic sectors. Due to the fact that these factors depend on prices too, one cannot resolve one variable without knowing simultaneously the other.

Choosing commodity 1 as numeraire we have

$$[5.15] \qquad p_j(h^*) = \frac{\mathbf{l}(h^*)'\mathbf{c}_{ji}(h^*)}{\mathbf{l}(h^*)'\mathbf{c}_{1i}(h^*)} \qquad j=2, \ldots, m+1.$$

Prices are therefore given by the ratio between the two polynomials of degree m, being $\mathbf{c}_{ji}(h^*)$ the vector of cofactors of the j-th row of the matrix $[\mathbf{I}-(1+\pi)\mathbf{A}(h^*)]$. From this, it follows that also the relative efficiency of the processes can change with π.

What may occur is the case known as "reswitching of techniques" outlined by Sraffa and developed by Pasinetti and others, which involves several changes in the efficiency order of two techniques. Let us compare the wage-profit frontiers of the sub-systems pwπ of type 1 and 2 in Figure 5.4.

The changes of π and the consequent changes of prices have similar implications on rents. Differentiating [5.8] we get

$$[5.16] \qquad \frac{\partial\rho(h;h^*)}{\partial\pi} = \frac{l_1(h)}{\tau_1(h)}\left[\frac{\partial w(h;h^*)}{\partial\pi} - \frac{\partial w(h^*)}{\partial\pi}\right] =$$

$$= \frac{l_1(h)}{\tau_1(h)}\left\{\left[\frac{a_{11}(h^*) + \mathbf{a}_{j1}(h^*)'\mathbf{p}_j(h^*)}{l_1(h^*)} - \frac{a_{11}(h) + \mathbf{a}_{j1}(h)'\mathbf{p}_j(h^*)}{l_1(h)}\right] + \right.$$

$$\left. + (1+\pi)\left[\frac{1}{l_1(h^*)}\mathbf{a}_{j1}(h^*)'\frac{\partial\mathbf{p}_j(h^*)}{\partial\pi} - \frac{1}{l_1(h)}\mathbf{a}_{j1}(h)'\frac{\partial\mathbf{p}_j(h^*)}{\partial\pi}\right]\right\}.$$

The sign of this relation cannot, in general, be determined. The first term, which expresses the effect due to the capital-labor composition, may be either positive or negative and it changes according to π. Some possible remarks on the signs that can come about in the case of $l_1(h) > l_1(h^*)$ are of little use in finding the result. Moreover, nothing can be said on the sign of the second term.

Therefore, as π grows, $\rho(h;h^*)$ can either increase or diminish without a clear well-defined pattern.

8. Autonomous changes with a stable solving sub-system and the effects on rents

Let us now consider a first case by assuming that the movements of π, which is the exogenous variable, occur within the range $0 \leq \pi \leq \max \pi(h^*)$ and neither change the processes in activity nor the least efficient process, h*. In this case the solving sub-system pwπ remains unchanged. Though changes in the OE of the first h*–1 processes in operation are not excluded, it is assumed that these variations do not interfere with process h* and the remaining k–h* inactive processes with NPMP.

The relations between π and w can be studied within a unique sub-system: the solving sub-system h*. Also the standard commodity does not change with π.

What may change is only the sub-system of rents —let us see in which way.

A first aspect that should be noted is that in the first h*–1 processes with NPMP, OE and hence OR may change at different levels of π. Let us consider the previous Figure 5.4 based on a very simple case: three processes with NPMP that produce PCC1 and one process that generate commodity 2. We shall refer to this two-commodity example also in the following Figures.

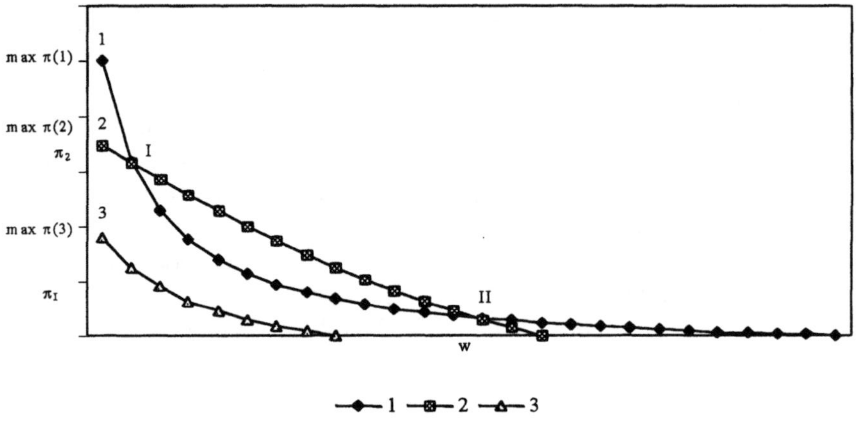

Fig. 5.4. Wage-profit frontier of sub-systems 1, 2, and 3

Changes in OE, which occur at points I and II of Figure 5.4, do not necessarily involve changes in OR. Let us consider [5.9] and assume that $[l_1(1)/\tau_1(1)] = [l_1(2)/\tau_1(2)]$. In this case, $\rho(1;3)$ would be equal to $\rho(2;3)$ only if $w(1;3) = w(2;3)$. This condition would be satisfied only if $p_2 = p_2(1) = p_2(2)$. Due to the fact that in the economic system the actual p_2 is $p_2(3)$, it is very unlikely that the equality between w(1;3) and w(2;3) takes place. Therefore, the changes in OR would not coincide with the points of change of the techniques.

A second aspect that must be taken into account concerns the number of changes in OR. This number cannot exceed the changes in OE. To see why, let us take [3.8] and substitute $\mathbf{p}(h^*)$ and $w(h^*)$ with [5.14] and [5.15]. Thus, we get

$$[5.17]\quad \rho(h;h^*) = \left\{1 - a_{11}(h)[1+\pi(h^*)] - \sum_{j=2}^{m+1} a_{j1}(h)'\frac{\mathbf{l}(h^*)\mathbf{c}_{ji}(h^*)}{\mathbf{l}(h^*)\mathbf{c}_{li}(h^*)}[1+\pi(h^*)] + \right.$$

$$\left. -l_1(h)\frac{\det[\mathbf{I}-(1+\pi(h^*))\mathbf{A}(h^*)']}{\mathbf{l}(h^*)'\mathbf{c}_{li}(h^*)}\right\}[\tau_1(h)]^{-1}$$

which at the numerator is a polynomial of degree m+1 in the variable π, and at the denominator is a polynomial of degree m, that is, the same degree of [5.14].

Changes in OR take place for values of π that equalize two rents. By placing

$$[5.18]\qquad \rho(h;h^*) = \rho(h^+;h^*)$$

we obtain the polynomial of degree m+1 in the variable π

$$[5.19]\qquad \mathbf{l}(h^*)'\mathbf{c}_{li}(h^*)\{\tau_1(h^+)[1-a_{11}(h)(1+\pi(h^*))]+$$

$$-\tau_1(h)[1-a_{11}(h^+)(1+\pi(h^*)]\} - \tau_1(h^+)\sum_{j=2}^{m+1} a_{j1}(h)\mathbf{l}(h^*)'\,\mathbf{c}_{ji}(h^*)[1+\pi(h^*)]+$$

$$+\tau_1(h)\sum_{j=2}^{m+1} a_{j1}(h^+)\mathbf{l}(h^*)'\,\mathbf{c}_{ji}(h^*)[1+\pi(h^*)] + \det\{\mathbf{I}-[1+\pi(h^*)]\mathbf{A}(h^*)'\}$$

$$[\tau_1(h)l_1(h^+) - \tau_1(h^+)l_1(h)] = 0,$$

whose maximum number of real roots in the unknown quantity π, is m+1.

9. Autonomous changes with a stable solving sub-system and discontinuous rent

A second case concerns the changes in the active processes with NPMP, but leaving unchanged the solving process h* and hence the standard commodity. This case should be regarded as a change in technology without change in the relation between π and w. Among the many different scenarios, Figure 5.5 shows a simplified one.

The following analysis sets aside process 2b, and focuses the attention on processes 1 and 2a. Let us assume that in the range $\pi_I > \pi \geq 0$ only process 1 is active because the available quantity of NPMP of type 1 is sufficient to satisfy the production objectives of the economy. Thus rent equals zero.

In the range $\pi_{II} > \pi > \pi_I$ process 2a becomes more efficient than process 1. If the production objectives of the economy are not reached because of [3.9] constraint of NPMP of type 2a, both process 1 and process 2a will be activated. The solving process remains 1, and process 2a will have a rent that follows a pattern outlined in Figure 5.6 by line 2.

In the range max $\pi(2) > \pi > \pi_{II}$ the situation returns back to the range $\pi_I > \pi \geq 0$ —only the NPMP of type 1 is active and the rent on NPMP of type 2a disappears. Finally, for $\pi = \pi_I$ or $\pi = \pi_{II}$, either process 1 or processes 1 and 2a can be jointly in activity. However, in this case there is no rent.

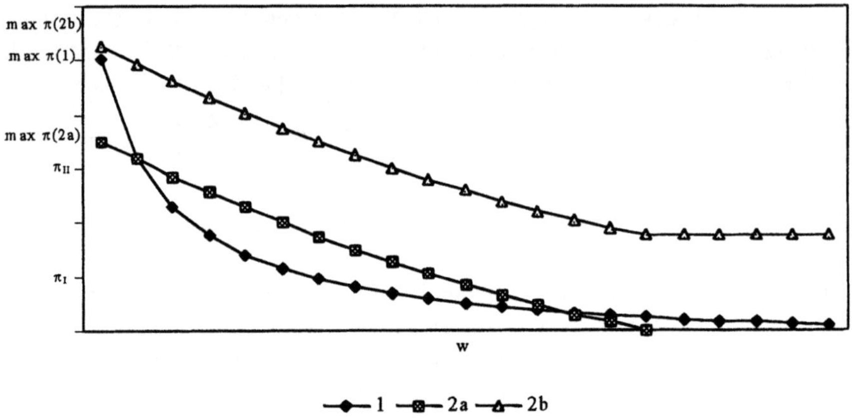

Fig. 5.5. Wage-profit frontier of sub-systems 1, 2a, and 2b

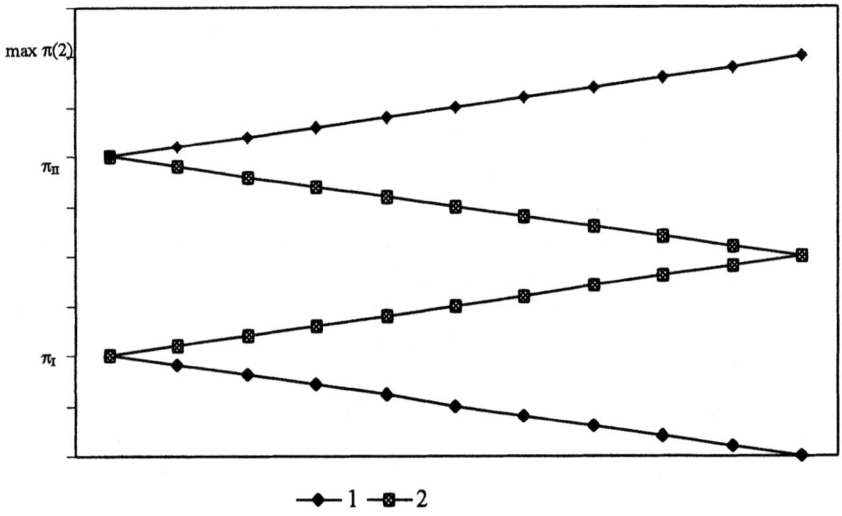

Fig. 5.6. Relationship between rent and profit rate

To sum up, in the range max $\pi(1) \geq \pi \geq 0$ the relation between π and w depends only on the solving sub-system pwπ of type 1, and the standard commodity does not change. Concerning rent, its presence emerges only for some values of π —at first it raises and then it falls. This differs from the relation between w and π, which is always an inverse relation.

From a qualitative point of view, the same conclusions are reached in the opposite case —namely when process 1 cannot be in operation without 2a, while the reverse is possible. In this case the relation between w and π is given by the solving sub-system pwπ of type 2a. As it is shown by line 1 in Figure 5.6, only process 1 will have rent.

10. Autonomous changes with variable rents

A third case shows variations in OE that do not affect the processes in activity, but do affect the solving process h*. Therefore, those processes which compose the production technology do not change, whereas the relation between w and π changes —a situation that does never occur in a single product model. Let us take into account the changes in OE of the processes 1 and 2a as represented in Figure 5.5, with the assumption that the latter are always jointly in activity to satisfy the production objectives of the economy. The rent will always be positive, except for the case $\pi = \pi_{I} = \pi_{II}$. In the range $0 \leq \pi \leq$ max $\pi(2a)$, —as the example in Figure 5.6 shows— the rent will shift from process 1 to process 2a and then back to process 1 again.

The solving sub-system pwπ will change twice in order to determine the relation between w and π. Therefore, the standard commodity will be modified, whereas the processes in activity will be not.

11. Autonomous changes in the solving sub-system with permanent rent

The fourth case regards changes in OE which modify both the activated processes and the process involved in the solving sub-system pwπ, without removing the rent.

Let us refer to the case shown in Figure 5.5, by assuming that to reach the target of production, process 2b is always active either with process 1 or with process 2a.

For π growing in the interval from 0 to max $\pi(1)$, the solving process will move from 1 to 2a, and from 2a back again to 1. The standard commodity will change twice. Processes 1 and 2a will never have rent, whereas process 2b will always have rent whose behavior could be represented, following the changes of π, by a continuos curve at the right of the existing curves 1 and 2 in Figure 5.6.

12. Reduction in the technology dimension and effects on the distributive variables

Finally we shall examine the case of π greater than max $\pi(h^*)$. In this case, process h* is disactivated and both the activity level of the economy and employment level fall.

Therefore, frontier $f(w,\pi)$ shows a discontinuity and w, which is equal to zero at max $\pi(h^*)$, becomes positive (see example of Figure 5.5). This movement of w and π in the same direction is due to the transfer of rent of process 1 to wages. At this point, it is interesting to compare the increase of the surplus wages with the decrease of the subsistence wages due to the reduction of employment. If the rise of the former is greater or equal than the fall of the latter, then in some economic and institutional contexts the surplus wages could be used, totally or partially, to subsidize the unemployed. In other social situations, a coalition between profit earners and subsistence wage earners could be formed in order to contrast the rent earners. In all these cases, some relations among π, the exogenous variable, and activity-employment level of the economy are always established.

13. Conclusions

Rent complicates —or better enriches— the economic picture and, at the same time, it makes the relation between wages and profits more realistic. The order of efficiency, the rentability order, the non-produced means of production and the influence of the latter over the former generate new situations never discussed in the traditional models of pure production. The previous analysis has provided interesting insights which go well beyond the demonstration of the cryptic nature of some Sraffa's propositions such as "the order of fertility [...] is not defined independently of the rents; that order, as well as the magnitude of the rents themselves, may vary with the variation of π and w. " (Sraffa, 1960, p. 75). In fact, from these sentences one cannot make any distinction between the order of efficiency and that of rentability —a distinction that we believe is quite important.

In particular, we showed that the autonomous variations in the distribution of income face the heavy interference of rent that reshapes the traditional relationship between wages and profits. Moreover, the distribution may face also induced variations from changes in the activity level. To sum up, our investigation points out that univocal relations among wages, profits, and rents do not exist, just as they do not exist between the interests of employed workers and unemployed workers.

Chapter VI - Non-equiproportional dynamics with compound technologies: productions

1. Introduction

In Chapters III, IV and V, we have developed a general theoretical framework which has been applied to economic issues on the bases of two assumptions:

a) there were no dynamics and accumulation, i.e. the study was limited to static one-period analysis and comparative statics;
b) there was no technical progress.

Both hypotheses greatly narrow the scope of the analysis. As a matter of fact, dynamics with accumulation is the phenomenon that generates scarcity. Technical progress, in turn, plays an important role in determining the magnitude of relative scarcity that we have also called technological scarcity. Ruling out the presence of technical progress implies that the relative scarcity shortly becomes absolute scarcity, whereas, the existence of high rates of technical progress could completely eliminate the scarcity altogether.

However, the present and similar theories allow for the removal of the two assumptions, so that the range of analysis is significantly widen.

In this Chapter we begin by taking into account dynamics, but without technical progress.

2. Towards dynamic systems: accumulation and residuals

This Chapter focuses primarily on the physical system, and on the accumulation of net product.

Let us assume that the OE adopted is the physical one (see Chapter III, § 10). One may also adopt alternatively the static price-distribution OE, but in this case the order should show the same sequence of techniques **A**(h) of the physical OE.

The rise of activity in the last process with NPMP or the introduction of a new process with NPMP increase all the quantities produced, and also change the physical efficiency of the quantity system. The analysis already developed in a comparative static setting (Chapter IV, § 8 and § 9) shows that the reduction of the uniform rate of net product jeopardizes the physical efficiency of the economic system. This means also the decrease in the potential rate of accumulation of the system itself.

This statement, however, is incomplete and requires some further qualifications. In fact, one possible effect in activating a new process is the change of structure of the technology. There is then the problem of the accumulation of net product with a technology whose structure differs from that in which the net product itself has been created.

In short, changes of technology —even in the absence of technical progress— may rise the problem of residual net products which cannot be (immediately) accumulated.

The dynamics of the economic system thus depends on both the size of the net products of the already active techniques, the structure of the new active techniques, the dimension of the residuals, and the levels of net products of these new techniques.

3. Introduction to compound technologies

The outlined analysis can be carried out in a simplified framework that represents the economic system by utilizing the concept of compound technologies rather than global technologies (see Chapter II, § 9).

Also the compound technologies are based on techniques [**A**(h); **l**(h); τ_1(h)] (see [2.5]) which —as opposed to global technologies— are kept disconnected one from the other, though they remain linked over time since the activation of any new technique occurs with those means of production generated by the already active techniques. These disconnected, but linked over time, techniques form a compound technology, which, as far as NPMP are concerned, constitutes a good approximation to reality.

In order to clarify the meaning of compound technologies, let us consider an economic system in which only **A**(1) is the active technique; assuming that the production structure is such as to have a uniform rate of net product, the activation of technique **A**(1) allows the whole economic system to grow at its internal growth rate s(1) until the constraint given by the endowment T(1) becomes effective, that is, until the constraint $\bar{q}_1(1)$ (see [4.4]). Once this level is eventually approached, the production of sub-system 1 enters in its steady state.

At that point alongside **A**(1) is required technique [**A**(2); **l**(2); τ_1(2)]. Given the previous hypotheses concerning the structure of production and accumulation, the production sub-system of type 2 grows at its internal growth rate s(2) until the productive constraint $\bar{q}_1(2)$ is reached (see [4.11]).

Therefore, the technology of the economic system becomes

[6.1] $$[\mathbf{A}(1), \mathbf{A}(2); \mathbf{l}(1), \mathbf{l}(2); \tau_1(1), \tau_1(2)]$$

[6.2] $$q_1(1) = \bar{q}_1(1); \qquad q_1(2) \le \bar{q}_1(2).$$

As the process of expansion proceeds the other NPMP constraints bound the system and the technology grows in dimension with the activation of techniques **A**(3), **A**(4), …, **A**(k).

The problem, however, becomes more complex when one decides to analyze the temporal relationship between the various techniques by studying the accumulation of net products generated by one technique, and invested with the use of the subsequent technique. As already pointed out, it is at this point that the problem of residuals emerges. With this rather complex problem we shall engage in shortly.

There is a contradiction that however is convenient to highlight immediately. One of the cornerstones of the von Neumann, Leontief, and Sraffa's production frameworks is that, in the case of accumulation of entire net product, the rates of growth of production and of surplus are equal and constant. On the contrary, one of the cornerstones of the dynamics of the economy with non-reproduced means of production, as we shall see in the following analysis, is the absence of the previous identities and the variability over time of the rates of growth.

Because of the presence of different types of non-reproduced means of production sequentially activated, the economy may pass from situations in which the entire net product can be accumulated to situations in which residuals are created, and back again to situations of total accumulation. We have already notice that these residuals may be used for consumption or exported in the international markets when the internal conditions do not allow their accumulation.

The intertwining of the above phenomena may give rise to various types of dynamics. The growth rates of production and net product may either increase or decrease and frequently change behavior over time. For example, the activation of a less efficient process with NPMP, characterized however by a bundle of means of production much closer in quantity and quality with the available residuals, may bring about an increase in the growth rates rather than a dynamic slow down.

To sum up, though framed in very abstract terms, we think our theory is able to give account and explain with good approximation the real dynamic processes, where lack of uniformity appears to be the rule. This lack of uniformity is here explained by phenomena of structural nature.

4. Equiproportional maximum growth with only one sub-system

Without inquiry further, let us say that we have already chosen OE. Then, at the beginning of a dynamic process the economic system depends only on the activation of technique **A**(1) and the production system is that described by [4.1], with the difference that the variables are now also depending on time t as follows

[6.3] $$[(1 + s(1))\,\mathbf{A}(1) - \mathbf{I}]\,\mathbf{q}(1;t) = \mathbf{o} \qquad t_0 \leq t \leq \bar{t}_1 .$$

The notation t_0 indicates the beginning of the period of the productive activity; $\bar{t}_1$ indicates the temporal limit when the system represented by [6.3] stops growing for the full utilization of NPMP of type 1.

Let us assume that the initial supply of means of production is anticipated once for all. The scale of the production system at time t_0 is therefore given by the quantity of the anticipated means of production. $\mathbf{A}(1)\ \mathbf{q}(1;t_0)$. Let us assume, moreover, that labor does not constrain growth, which in the current conditions of the economies is a quite realistic assumption.

Since the standard consumption is already included in the matrix coefficients, the economic system which coincides with sub-system $\mathbf{A}(1)$ can accumulate the entire net product in each period, and grow at rate s(1). Productions $\mathbf{q}(1;t)$ and all other variables, therefore, grow dynamically at the same rate until the constraint of the endowment T(1), becomes binding, that is, until the constraint $\bar{q}_1(1)$ is reached.

This constraint may rise in two possible ways:

a) the total accumulation of the available net product at $(\bar{t}_1 - 1)$ leads to the full employment of T(1) and thus exactly to the production of max $\bar{q}_1(t)$ at time $\bar{t}_1$;

b) a share of available net product at $(\bar{t}_1 - 1)$ cannot be accumulated with $\mathbf{A}(1)$, because this would imply the violation of the constraint given by the availability of T(1).

In the first case, at $\bar{t}_1$, the economic system shown in [6.3] can no longer grow, thus entering into the steady state. From that period onwards, the system generates net products that cannot be internally accumulated. This means that the net products obtained with technique $\mathbf{A}(1)$ at $\bar{t}_1$, namely

$$[6.4] \qquad \mathbf{n}(1;\bar{t}_1) = \mathbf{q}(1;\bar{t}_1) - \mathbf{A}(1)\ \mathbf{q}(1;\bar{t}_1) = s(1)\ \mathbf{A}(1)\ q(1;\ \bar{t}_1),$$

may be utilized as means of production for activating another technique $\mathbf{A}(2)$.

Instead, in the second case the technique $\mathbf{A}(2)$ must be activated before reaching the constraint imposed by NPMP of type 1. In other words we face a situation where the new NPMP is utilized before the fully exploitation of the previous more efficient NPMP.

There is, however, in both cases the same problem: how the net product of sub-system 1 that cannot be internally accumulated should be accumulated in sub-system 2.

At aggregate level, therefore, the production system is based on two techniques, each one representing a production sub-system. The two techniques are disconnected and the technology they give rise to is compound.

The dynamics developed with these two techniques becomes rather complex, being the dynamic process neither equiproportional among the various sectors, nor constant in its rate of growth.

5. Non-equiproportional growth with two techniques: compound technology and residuals

Let us assume for the sake of simplicity that at time $\bar{t}_1$ the production is precisely $\bar{q}_1(t)$. At that time system [6.3] enters into a steady state and thus the activation of technique **A**(2) begins. Production sub-system 2 is given by:

$$[(1 + s(2))\, \mathbf{A}(2) - \mathbf{I}]\, \mathbf{q}(2;t) = \mathbf{o} \qquad \bar{t}_1 < t \leq \bar{t}_2 . \tag{6.5}$$

The production system is now composed of two sub-systems: one based on technique **A**(1) in steady state; the other based on technique **A**(2) which is growing.

In studying the dynamics of this economic system several problems must be solved — the main one concerns the residuals. In this context, two cases should be considered:

a) the case where structural differences between techniques **A**(1) and **A**(2) makes impossible to transfer completely the internally non-accumulated net products from sub-system 1 to sub-system 2, thus implying the formation of residuals;
b) the case where techniques **A**(1) and **A**(2) have the same structure and the net products generated by technique 1 may be fully accumulated in the production system 2.

As implied by case a), if the structures of techniques **A**(1) and **A**(2) are different, the entire accumulation of $\mathbf{n}(1;\bar{t}_1)$ in **A**(2) cannot occur, and the residuals that emerge are given by

$$\mathbf{r}(1,2;\bar{t}_1 +1) = \mathbf{n}(1;\bar{t}_1) - \mathbf{A}(2)\, \mathbf{q}(2;\bar{t}_1 +1) \geq \mathbf{o}. \tag{6.6}$$

To achieve maximum accumulation requires to squeeze the residuals at minimum and, therefore, the means of production $\mathbf{A}(2)\, \mathbf{q}(2;\bar{t}_1 +1)$ should be set at their highest level. In particular one may identify m+1 vectors of the means of production $\mathbf{A}(2)\, \mathbf{q}(2;\bar{t}_1 +1)$, each of which implying the full employment of one of the net product of vector $\mathbf{n}(1;\bar{t}_1)$.

In other words, the eigenvector $\mathbf{q}(2;\bar{t}_1 +1)$ associated to the maximum eigenvalue of [6.5] can be normalized in m+1 different ways, as follows

$$\mathbf{e}_i'\, \mathbf{n}(1;\bar{t}_1) = \mathbf{e}_i'\, \mathbf{A}(2)\, \mathbf{q}(2;\bar{t}_1 +1) \tag{6.7}$$

or

$$\mathbf{e}_i'\, \mathbf{n}(1;\bar{t}_1)/\lambda(2) = \mathbf{e}_i'\, \mathbf{q}(2;\bar{t}_1 +1),$$

where $\mathbf{e}_i'$ = [0,0, ... ,1(i), ... , 0] for i = 1, ... , m+1, is a vector with null components, except the i-th component which is equal to unity.

Among the m+1 vectors $\mathbf{q}(2;\bar{t}_1 +1)$ so obtained only one of them satisfies the non-negativity condition [6.6] — namely that vector $\mathbf{q}(2;\bar{t}_1 +1)$ which gives the smallest residuals. In this case for at least one of the m+1 commodities of the production vector, the residual of net product will be null; this commodity is marked by the index i*.

The allocation of the residuals that are formed in each period that follows $\bar{t}_1$, may differ: they may be stocked, exported, or consumed. For the sake of simplicity, let us assume that residuals are consumed and, therefore, do not affect growth. The consumption of residuals is added to the level of consumption already included in matrix **A**, as expressed by the coefficients of necessary consumption (see Chapter II, § 5).

To grasp immediately the dynamics involved by the use of compound technologies, Figure 6.1 offers a first impressionistic overview.

The economic system grows at the maximum internal growth rate of technique **A**(1) until $\bar{t}_1$. At that point the technique reaches its maximum level, $\bar{q}_1(1)$. Therefore from $\bar{t}_1$ onwards the production sub-system 1 approaches its steady state — the same quantities $\mathbf{q}(1;\bar{t}_1)$ and the same net products $\mathbf{n}(1;\bar{t}_1)$ are produced in each period.

The vector of net products generated by this technique that cannot be accumulated in the production sub-system 1 can be utilized in activating the technique which follows **A**(1) in OE, that is, **A**(2).

Production sub-system 2 may grow at the maximum and constant rate s(2) which represents its internal growth rate, and differs from that of the whole economic system.

Starting from $\bar{t}_1$+2, the rate of growth of sub-system 2 becomes autonomous and independent from $\mathbf{n}(1;\bar{t}_1)$. In fact, at time $\bar{t}_1$+2 the vector of net products $\mathbf{n}(1;\bar{t}_1+1)$, which continues to be generated by the sub-system 1, is utilized as means of production in order to activate a second sub-system of type **A**(2).

Therefore, at $\bar{t}_1$+2 the production system will be composed by three active sub-systems: one based on **A**(1) in steady state and described in [6.3], and two, based on **A**(2) which are growing at rate s(2).

Hence, in each period after $\bar{t}_1$ a new production sub-system 2 is activated which utilizes, as initial means of production, the net products of production sub-system 1. Each production sub-system 2 continues to grow at rate s(2) by accumulating completely its internal net product.

Figure 6.1 shows that in period $\bar{t}_1$+1 production sub-system 1 and a production sub-system 2 are active; at $\bar{t}_1$+2 production sub-system 1 and two production sub-systems 2 become active; in period $\bar{t}_1$+3 this occurs for production sub-system 1 and three production sub-systems 2.

With reference to the productions of those sub-systems based on **A**(2), we can therefore note

$$\text{[6.8]} \qquad \mathbf{A}(2)\,\mathbf{q}(2;\bar{t}_1+1)\,[1+s(2)] = \mathbf{q}(2;\bar{t}_1+1),$$

$$\text{[6.9]} \qquad \mathbf{q}(2;\bar{t}_1+1)\,[1+s(2)] = \mathbf{A}(2)\,\mathbf{q}(2;\bar{t}_1+1)\,[1+s(2)]^2 = \mathbf{q}\,(2;\bar{t}_1+2).$$

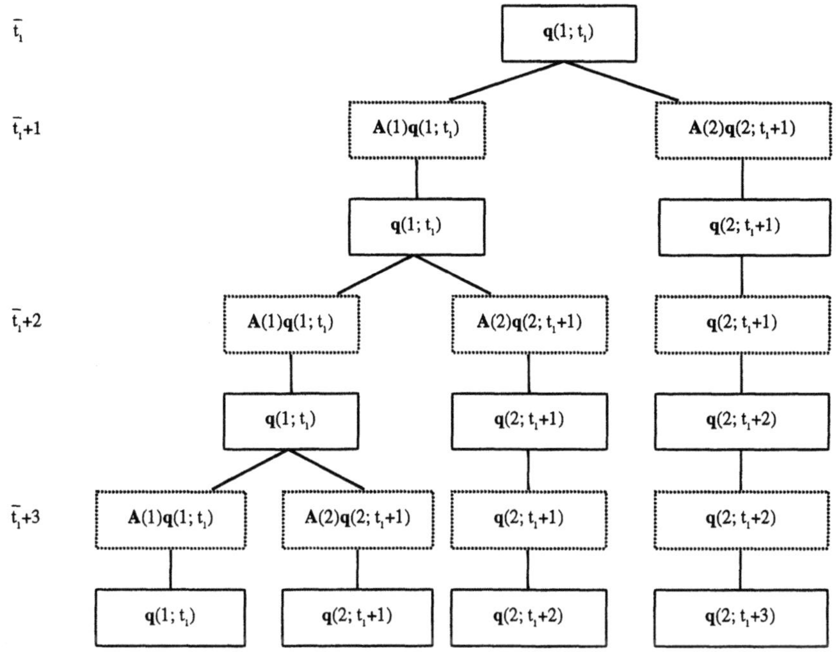

Figure 6.1 Dynamics with compound technologies

Let us assume that at $\bar{t}_2 = \bar{t}_1 + n$, the constraint of NPMP of type 2 halts the expansion of further sub-systems based on **A**(2). The situation at that point will be that of having n active sub-systems based on **A**(2); the last sub-system to enter in activity is represented in purely quantitative terms by [6.8], while the first sub-system of type 2 by the following relationship

[6.10] $$\mathbf{A}(2)\,\mathbf{q}(2;t_1+1)\,[1 + s(2)]^n = \mathbf{q}(2;t_1+n).$$

Figure 6.1 summarizes this situation. It must be noted that the quantities contained in the continuous rectangles refer to "the end" of a period, while those in the dashed rectangles refer to "the beginning" of a period. Taking each commodity separately and excluding the commodity without residuals, we notice that the sum of the quantities contained in a continuous row is greater than those contained in the following dashed row, because of the presence of residuals.

When the progressive expansion of techniques **A**(2) reaches the constraint $\bar{q}_1(2)$, those net products generated in production systems of type 1 and 2 that cannot be internally accumulated will feed the activation of techniques of type 3.

6. The residuals and their possible utilization

We have seen how residuals are formed. Let us now consider their utilization. There are three possible and not mutually excludable allocations:

a) consumption. This is possible for some, but not for all, commodities. Previously we assumed that all residuals were consumed, and we maintain this hypothesis in our analysis;
b) total or partial storage of residuals that cannot be immediately accumulated for future utilization when new proper techniques are activated;
c) international trade; i.e. export of the non-accumulated residuals or import of the missing commodities.

In the latter case, the economic system imports commodities which are partially lacking to fully accumulate the net product, and accordingly it readjusts the vectors of means of production with the use of international trade.

In all these cases, we assume that residuals have their own demand and their price coincides with the cost of production. This hypothesis may change with reference to the international trade of residuals, given that international prices and domestic prices are not usually the same.

7. The total variables of the compound technology

Before proceeding further, it is useful to single out clearly the aggregate variables of the economic system; namely, the means of production, the productions, the net products, and the residuals. For the sake of simplicity, we consider the case in which technology is composed of only two techniques.

The *total means of production* employed by the active sub-systems 1 and 2 in period t_2, with $\bar{t}_1 < t_2 < \bar{t}_2$, are as follow

$$[6.11] \qquad \mathbf{m}(1,2;t_2) = \mathbf{A}(1)\mathbf{q}(1;\bar{t}_1) + \mathbf{A}(2)\mathbf{q}(2;\bar{t}_1+1)\sum_{t=0}^{t_2-\bar{t}_1-1}[1+s(2)]^t =$$

$$= \mathbf{A}(1)\mathbf{q}(1;\bar{t}_1) + \mathbf{A}(2)\mathbf{q}(2;\bar{t}_1+1)\frac{\{[1+s(2)]^{t_2-\bar{t}_1}-1\}}{s(2)}.$$

For the commodity without residuals, its total use as means of production is given by

$$[6.12] \quad m_{i*}(1,2;t_2) = \mathbf{e}'_{i*}\mathbf{A}(1)\mathbf{q}(1;\bar{t}_1) + \mathbf{e}'_{i*}\mathbf{A}(2)\mathbf{q}(2;\bar{t}_1+1)\sum_{t=0}^{t_2-\bar{t}_1-1}[1+s(2)]^t =$$

$$\mathbf{e}'_{i*}\mathbf{A}(1)\mathbf{q}(1;\bar{t}_1)\left\{1+s(1)\frac{[1+s(2)]^{t_2-\bar{t}_1}-1}{s(2)}\right\}.$$

Among the previous means of production, $\mathbf{A}(1)\mathbf{q}(1;\bar{t}_1)$ and $\mathbf{A}(2)\mathbf{q}(2;\bar{t}_1+1)$, for $(t_2 - \bar{t}_1)$ times are produced by the sub-system based on technique $\mathbf{A}(1)$; all other means of production are produced by the sub-system based on technique

$\mathbf{A}(2)$. At time t_2, the techniques or sub-systems of type $\mathbf{A}(2)$ in activity are $(t_2 - \bar{t}_1)$.

The *total productions* obtained in period t_2 by the active sub-systems 1 and 2 are given by

$$[6.13] \qquad \mathbf{q}(1,2;t_2) = \mathbf{q}(1;\bar{t}_1) + \mathbf{A}(2)\mathbf{q}(2;\bar{t}_1+1)\sum_{t=1}^{t_2-\bar{t}_1}[1+s(2)]^t =$$

$$= \mathbf{q}(1;\bar{t}_1) + \mathbf{A}(2)\mathbf{q}(2;\bar{t}_1+1)[1+s(2)]\frac{[1+s(2)]^{t_2-\bar{t}_1}-1}{s(2)}.$$

Concerning the commodity that does not have residuals, we obtain

$$[6.14] \quad q_{1*}(1,2;t_2) = \mathbf{e}'_{i*}\mathbf{q}(1;\bar{t}_1) + \mathbf{e}'_{i*}\mathbf{A}(2)\mathbf{q}(2;\bar{t}_1+1)[1+s(2)]\frac{[1+s(2)]^{t_2-\bar{t}_1}-1}{s(2)} =$$

$$= \mathbf{e}'_{i*}\mathbf{A}(1)\mathbf{q}(1;\bar{t}_1)\left\{1+s(1)+s(1)[1+s(2)]\frac{[1+s(2)]^{t_2-\bar{t}_1}-1}{s(2)}\right\}.$$

The *total net products* obtained in period t_2 by the active sub-systems 1 and 2 are the result of

$$[6.15] \quad \mathbf{n}(1,2;t_2) = s(1)\mathbf{A}(1)\mathbf{q}(1;\bar{t}_1) + s(2)\mathbf{A}(2)\mathbf{q}(2;\bar{t}_1+1)\sum_{t=0}^{t_2-\bar{t}_1-1}[1+s(2)]^t =$$

$$= s(1)\mathbf{A}(1)\mathbf{q}(1;\bar{t}_1) + \mathbf{A}(2)\mathbf{q}(2;\bar{t}_1+1)\left\{[1+s(2)]^{t_2-\bar{t}_1}-1\right\}.$$

With regards to the commodity without residuals, we obtain

$$[6.16] \quad n_{i*}(1,2;t_2) = \mathbf{e}'_{i*}s(1)\mathbf{A}(1)\mathbf{q}(1;\bar{t}_1) + \mathbf{e}'_{i*}\mathbf{A}(2)\mathbf{q}(2;\bar{t}_1+1)\left\{[1+s(2)]^{t_2-\bar{t}_1}-1\right\} =$$

$$= \mathbf{e}'_{i*}s(1)\mathbf{A}(1)\mathbf{q}(1;\bar{t}_1)[1+s(2)]^{t_2-\bar{t}_1}.$$

8. The rates of growth of productions

In the traditional linear dynamic models, such as that proposed by von Neumann, the growth rates of production of all commodities and the growth rates of net products are equal. Furthermore, the growth rates of productions and net products are equal to the uniform rate of net product. In our theory, with compound technologies, many of these equalities are not satisfied, and our economic system shows clearly non-uniform dynamics for the various commodities and sectors. We shall analyze these dynamics by starting to the growth rates of productions.

We indicate the growth rate of production of commodity i in period t with the notation $\beta_i(1,2;t)$. This rate is a weighted average that depends on the internal growth rate of techniques $\mathbf{A}(1)$ and $\mathbf{A}(2)$, the net products of technique $\mathbf{A}(1)$ that can be accumulated in technique $\mathbf{A}(2)$, and the non-accumulated residuals. On the basis of the productions obtained in two subsequent periods, say t_2 and t_2-1, and considering [6.13], we obtain

$$[6.17] \qquad 1+\beta_1(1,2;t_2)=\frac{\mathbf{e}_i'\mathbf{q}(1,2;t_2)}{\mathbf{e}_i'\mathbf{q}(1,2;t_2-1)}=$$

$$=\{\mathbf{e}_i'\mathbf{q}(1;\bar{t}_1)s(2)+\mathbf{e}_i'\mathbf{A}(2)\mathbf{q}(2;\bar{t}_1+1)[1+s(2)][(1+s(2))^{t_2-\bar{t}_1}-1]\}$$

$$\{\mathbf{e}_i'\mathbf{q}(1;\bar{t}_1)s(2)+\mathbf{e}_i'\mathbf{A}(2)\mathbf{q}(2;\bar{t}_1+1)[1+s(2)][(1+s(2)^{t_2-\bar{t}_1-1}-1]\}^{-1}=\frac{N_i}{D_i}.$$

In order to highlight the role of residuals, we re-write [6.17] by recalling that the initial means of production of techniques **A**(2) are given by the difference between the net products of technique **A**(1) that cannot be internally accumulated, and the residuals given by in [6.6]. Equation [6.17] therefore becomes

$$\{\mathbf{e}_i'\mathbf{A}(1)\mathbf{q}(1;\bar{t}_1)[(1+s(1))s(2)+s(1)(1+s(2))((1+s(2))^{t_2-\bar{t}_1}-1)]+$$
$$-\mathbf{e}_i'\mathbf{r}(1,2;\bar{t}_1+1)[1+s(2)][(1+s(2))^{t_2-\bar{t}_1}-1]\}\{\mathbf{e}_i'\mathbf{A}(1)\mathbf{q}(1;\bar{t}_1)$$
$$[(1+s(1))s(2)+s(1)(1+s(2))((1+s(2))^{t_2-\bar{t}_1-1}-1]+$$
$$-\mathbf{e}_i'\mathbf{r}(1,2;\bar{t}_1+1)[1+s(2)][(1+s(2))^{t_2-\bar{t}_1-1}-1]\}^{-1}.$$

For commodity i*, whose residual is null, we obtain with the use of [6.14]

$$[6.18]\, 1+\beta_{i*}(1,2;t_2)=\frac{\mathbf{e}_{i*}'\mathbf{q}(1,2;t_2)}{\mathbf{e}_{i*}'\mathbf{q}(1,2;t_2-1)}=\frac{s(2)+s(1)[1+s(2)]^{t_2-\bar{t}_1+1}-s(1)}{s(2)+s(1)[1+s(2)]^{t_2-\bar{t}_1}-s(1)}=\frac{N_{i*}}{D_{i*}}.$$

In order to illustrate the evolution of these rates, we refer to the numerical simulations with different techniques given in Appendix A. Here, we focus our analysis on some general properties.

The first property, which derives from the behavior of these growth rates, is the exclusion of any equiproportional dynamics. In fact, we always find

$$[6.19] \qquad \beta_{i*}(1,2;t)>\beta_i(1,2;t) \qquad t>\bar{t}_1,\ i(\neq i^*)=1,\ldots,m+1.$$

Commodity i* is the commodity without residuals, and the inequality is due to other commodities' residuals. The growth rates of production are all likely to be different, even though equal rates cannot be excluded in principle.

The second property is embodied in the inequality

$$[6.20] \qquad s(1)>\beta_{i*}(1,2;t) \qquad t>\bar{t}_1,$$

due to the lower efficiency of sub-system 2 compared to sub-system 1. The introduction of technique **A**(2) thus determines a change in the production growth rates; this change is related to the quantity of residuals— if the latter are small the former will be irrelevant, if the gap between s(2) and s(1) is high, the change will be consistent.

The third property is more complex and concerns the relationships between β_i, β_{i*} and s(2). Sub-system 1 is more efficient than sub-system 2, but the presence of residuals may nullify the effect of this greater efficiency and compromise the potential higher rates of growth of the economy than those assured by sub-system 2.

Therefore, while commodity i*, which does not have residuals, maintains

[6.21] $\beta_{i*}(1,2;\,t) > s(2) \qquad t > \bar{t}_1,$

the other commodities show

[6.22] $\beta_i(1,2;t) \gtreqless s(2) \qquad t > \bar{t}_1,$

that is, recalling [6.17],

$$N_i - [1+s(2)]D_i \gtreqless 0,$$

according to the scale of the residuals. In fact, with some transformations, [6.22] may be re-written as follows

[6.23] $$s(1) - s(2) \gtreqless [1+s(2)]\frac{\mathbf{e}_i'\mathbf{r}(1,2;\bar{t}_1+1)}{\mathbf{e}_i'\mathbf{A}(1)\mathbf{q}(1;\bar{t}_1)}.$$

Inequality [6.23] suggests that the smaller the share of residuals and the greater the gap between s(1) and s(2), the more likely is to find $\beta_i(1,2;\,t)$ greater than s(2), and vice versa.

The fourth property concerns the convergence over time of the growth rates β_i to rate s(2) —a value that usually can only be approximated given the scarce and therefore temporally limited nature of NPMP of type 2. The convergence may occur from a starting point either higher or lower than s(2). This depends on the sign shown by [6.22]. The fact that the growth rates of production tend asymptotically to s(2) finds its rationale on the decreasing relative weights of both sub-system 1 and the residuals while production of sub-system 2 experiences positive growth.

Formally, from [6.17] it follows

[6.24] $$\frac{\partial[1+\beta_i(1,2;t_2)]}{\partial t_2} = \frac{\frac{\partial N_i}{\partial t_2}D_i - N_i\frac{\partial D_i}{\partial t_2}}{D_i^2} =$$

$$= \{\mathbf{e}_i'\mathbf{A}(2)\mathbf{q}(2;\bar{t}_1+1)[1+s(2)][(1+s(2)^{t_2-\bar{t}_1}\log[1+s(2)]D_i +$$

$$- N_i\mathbf{e}_i'\mathbf{A}(2)\mathbf{q}(2;\bar{t}_1+1)[1+s(2)][1+s(2)]^{t_2-\bar{t}_1-1}\log[1+s(2)]\}D_i^{-2} =$$

$$= \{\mathbf{e}_i'\mathbf{A}(2)\mathbf{q}(2;\bar{t}_1+1)[1+s(2)]\log[1+s(2)][1+s(2)]^{t_2-\bar{t}_1-1}\}D_i^{-2}$$

$$\{D_i[1+s(2)] - N_i\}.$$

And so

$$\frac{\partial[1+\beta_i(1,2;t_2)]}{\partial t_2} \gtreqless 0$$

according to whether

[6.25] $$D_i[1+s(2)] - N_i \gtreqless 0.$$

The signs of [6.25] are opposite to those of [6.22]. Therefore, if $\beta_1(1,2;t_2) > s(2)$ we have $\dfrac{\partial[1+\beta_i(1,2;t_2)]}{\partial t_2} < 0$ and vice versa.

Furthermore, from [6.17] and [6.18] we have that

$$[6.26] \qquad \lim_{t_2\to\infty}[1+\beta_i(1,2;t_2)] = \lim_{t_2\to\infty}[1+\beta_{i*}(1,2;t_2)] = 1+s(2).$$

9. The rates of growth of net products

Let us now consider the growth rates of net products, indicated by $\mu_i(1,2;t)$.

On the basis of the net products obtained in two subsequent periods, say t_2 and t_2 - 1, by taking [6.15] and [6.6] into account we obtain

$$[6.27] \qquad 1+\mu_1(1,2;t_2) = \frac{\mathbf{e}_i'\mathbf{n}(1,2;t_2)}{\mathbf{e}'\mathbf{n}(1,2;t_2-1)} =$$

$$= \{\mathbf{e}_i's(1)\mathbf{A}(1)\mathbf{q}(1;\bar{t}_1)+\mathbf{e}_i'\mathbf{A}(2)\mathbf{q}(2;\bar{t}_1+1)[(1+s(2))^{t_2-\bar{t}_1}-1]\}$$
$$\{\mathbf{e}_i's(1)\mathbf{A}(1)\mathbf{q}(1;\bar{t}_1)+\mathbf{e}_i'\mathbf{A}(2)\mathbf{q}(2;\bar{t}_1+1)[(1+s(2))^{t_2-\bar{t}_1-1}-1]^{-1}\} =$$
$$= \{\mathbf{e}_i's(1)\mathbf{A}(1)\mathbf{q}(1;\bar{t}_1)+\mathbf{e}_i'[\mathbf{n}(1;\bar{t}_1)-\mathbf{r}(1,2;\bar{t}_1+1)][1+s(2)]^{t_2-\bar{t}_1}-1\}$$
$$\{\mathbf{e}_i's(1)\mathbf{A}(1)\mathbf{q}(1;\bar{t}_1)+\mathbf{e}_i'[\mathbf{n}(1;\bar{t}_1)-\mathbf{r}(1,2;\bar{t}_1+1)][(1+s(2))^{t_2-\bar{t}_1-1}-1]\}^{-1} = \frac{N_i'}{D_i'}.$$

Concerning commodity i^*, by taking [6.16] into account we get that

$$[6.28] \qquad 1+\mu_{i*}(1;2;t_2) = \frac{\mathbf{e}_{i*}\mathbf{n}(1,2;t_2)}{\mathbf{e}_{i*}\mathbf{n}(1,2;t_2-1)} = 1+s(2).$$

The growth rate of net product of the commodity without residuals turns out to be equal to the rate of net product of technique **A**(2).

A second property of the growth rates of net products is

$$[6.29] \qquad \mu_{i*}(1,2;\, t_2) > \mu_i(1,2;\, t), \qquad t > \bar{t}_1,$$

and thus the growth rate of net product of the commodity without residuals is maximum; furthermore, [6.29] shows that also net products do not grow with an equiproportional pattern.

The previous properties imply that the net product of the economic system grows less rapidly than that of sub-system 2 due to the residuals that cannot be accumulated.

A third property involves those growth rates lower than s(2); they will converge asymptotically over time to this level.

In particular from [6.27] and with $i \neq i^*$ we have that

$$[6.30] \qquad \frac{\partial[1+\mu_i(1,2;t_2)]}{\partial t_2} =$$

$$= \frac{\partial N_i'}{\partial t_2}\{\mathbf{e}_i's(1)\mathbf{A}(1)\mathbf{q}(1;\bar{t}_1)+\mathbf{e}_i'\mathbf{A}(2)\mathbf{q}(2;\bar{t}_1+1)[(1+s(2))^{t_2-\bar{t}_1-1}-1]\}D_i'^{-2} +$$
$$-\{\mathbf{e}_i's(1)\mathbf{A}(1)\mathbf{q}(1;\bar{t}_1)+\mathbf{e}_i'\mathbf{A}(2)\mathbf{q}(2;\bar{t}_1+1)[(1+s(2))^{t_2-\bar{t}_1}-1]\}\frac{\partial D_i'}{\partial t_2}D_i'^{-2} =$$

$$= \frac{\mathbf{e}_i^{'} s(1)\mathbf{A}(1)\mathbf{q}(1;\overline{t_1})\left(\frac{\partial N_i^{'}}{\partial t_2} - \frac{\partial D_i^{'}}{\partial t_2}\right)}{D_i^{'2}} + \frac{\mathbf{e}_i^{'}\mathbf{A}(2)\mathbf{q}(2;\overline{t_1}+1)\left(\frac{\partial D_i^{'}}{\partial t_2} - \frac{\partial N_i^{'}}{\partial t_2}\right)}{D_i^{'2}} =$$

$$= \left(\frac{\partial N_i^{'}}{\partial t_2} - \frac{\partial D_i^{'}}{\partial t_2}\right)[\mathbf{e}_i^{'} s(1)\mathbf{A}(1)\mathbf{q}(1;\overline{t_1}) - \mathbf{e}_i^{'}\mathbf{A}(2)\mathbf{q}(2;\overline{t_1}+1)]D_i^{'-2} > 0.$$

Again, from [6.27] we finally obtain

$$[6.31] \qquad \lim_{t_2 \to \infty} [1 + \mu_{i*}(1,2;t_2)] = 1 + s(2).$$

10. Comparisons between growth rates of productions and net products

With reference to the comparison between growth rates of productions and net products it is easily shown that

$$[6.32] \qquad \beta_i(1,2;t) > \mu_i(1,2;t), \;\; \beta_{i^*}(1,2;t) > \mu_{i^*}(1,2;t), \qquad t > \overline{t_1}.$$

Given that the growth rates of net products and productions do not coincide, it is useful to point out that the latter determine the quantity of utilized NPMP (and therefore the level of labor employment), whereas the growth rates of net products determine the pace of accumulation.

11. The rates of net product

Let us now take into consideration the rates of net product of different commodities, indicated by $\delta_i(1,2;t)$.

From [6.13] and [6.11] we obtain

$$[6.33] \qquad 1 + \delta_i(1,2;t_2) = \frac{\mathbf{e}_i^{'}\mathbf{q}(1,2;t_2)}{\mathbf{e}_i^{'}\mathbf{m}(1,2;t_2)} =$$

$$= \{\mathbf{e}_i^{'}\mathbf{q}(1;\overline{t_1})s(2) + \mathbf{e}_i^{'}\mathbf{A}(2)\mathbf{q}(2;\overline{t_1}+1)[1+s(2)][1+s(2))^{t_2-\overline{t_1}} - 1]\}$$

$$\{\mathbf{e}_i^{'}\mathbf{A}(1)\mathbf{q}(1;\overline{t_1})s(2) + \mathbf{e}_i^{'}\mathbf{A}(2)\mathbf{q}(2;\overline{t_1}+1)[(1+s(2))^{t_2-\overline{t_1}} - 1]\}^{-1}.$$

Concerning the commodity without residuals, from [6.14] and [6.12] we have

$$[6.34] \qquad 1 + \delta_{i*}(1,2;t_2) = \frac{\mathbf{e}_{i*}^{'}\mathbf{q}(1,2;t_2)}{\mathbf{e}_{i*}^{'}\mathbf{m}(1,2;t_2)} =$$

$$= \frac{s(2) + s(1)\{[1+s(2)]^{t_2-\overline{t_1}+1} - 1\}}{s(2) + s(1)\{[1+s(2)]^{t_2-\overline{t_1}} - 1\}}.$$

The properties of the rates of net product are the following

$$[6.35] \qquad \delta_i(1,2;\, t) > \beta_i(1,2;\, t) \qquad t > \bar{t}_1,$$

as it is easy to demonstrate, and furthermore

$$[6.36] \qquad \delta_{i*}(1,2;\, t) = \beta_{i*}(1,2;\, t) \qquad t > \bar{t}_1,$$

as result of [6.18] and [6.34].

12. Equiproportional growth with two techniques

The previous analysis has been undertaken by assuming a structural diversity between **A**(1) and **A**(2), that is, the net products that cannot be internally accumulated by sub-system 1 are only partially transferred to sub-system 2. However, as we have already noted, when the net products generated by technique 1 are entirely accumulated by sub-system 2, the economy may continue to grow along an equiproportional path. This possibility holds if the values of the technical coefficients of sub-system 2 are such as to eliminate residuals, or, in other words, if the following system can be solved

$$[6.37] \qquad [\mathbf{A}(2) - \lambda(2)\mathbf{I}]\mathbf{q}(2;\bar{t}_1 + 1) = \mathbf{o},$$

$$[6.38] \qquad 1 > \lambda(2) > \lambda(1) > 0,$$

$$[6.39] \qquad \mathbf{r}(1,2;\bar{t}_1 + 1) = \mathbf{n}(1;\bar{t}_1) - \mathbf{A}(2)\,\mathbf{q}(2;\bar{t}_1 + 1) = \mathbf{o}.$$

This is a system with 2 + m equations and unknowns, namely $\lambda(2)$, $\mathbf{e}_i'\,\mathbf{A}(2)\,\mathbf{q}(2;\bar{t}_1 + 1)$. It can be shown that this system has positive solutions, and developing [6.3], [6.7], and [6.9] we obtain

$$[6.40] \qquad \mathbf{q}(2;\bar{t}_1 + 1) = \mathbf{q}(1;\bar{t}_1)\left(\frac{1}{\lambda(1)} - 1\right)\frac{\lambda(1)}{\lambda(2)} = \mathbf{q}(1;\bar{t}_1)s(1)\frac{1+s(2)}{1+s(1)}.$$

The productions, and therefore net products and the means of production of sub-system 1 and 2, maintain in this case their proportions. We shall call these "critical proportions".

The dynamics of the economy is now expressed for all commodities by equation [6.12] for the means of production, by [6.14] for productions, by [6.16] for net products, by [6.18] for the growth rates of productions, and by [6.28] for the growth rates of net products.

More generally this case keeps valid all the properties identified in the previous sections for commodity i*. The expression [6.23] is thus confirmed and, therefore, even with equiproportional growth, the equality between the growth rates of productions and net products is not satisfied for finite values of t.

The changes of growth rates when moving from a single sub-system to two sub-systems are much more relevant, the greater the gap between s(1) and s(2). In fact, we have

[6.41] $$\frac{\partial[1+\beta_{i^*}(1,2;t_2)]}{\partial s(2)} > 0,$$

as it can be shown with some elaborations.

If s(2) decreases, the capability of the economy of generating net product is obviously reduced. Changes in s(2) determine also changes in the difference between β_{i^*} and μ_{i^*}.

After a certain period therefore we have

[6.42] $$\frac{\partial[(1+\beta_{i^*}(1,2;t_2)) - (1+\mu_{i^*}(1,2;t_2))]}{\partial s(2)} < 0.$$

In the extreme case of s(2) null, μ_{i^*} is null, while β_{i^*} is positive. In such hypothetical scenario with the use of [6.13], we obtain

[6.43] $$1+\beta_{i^*}(1,2;t_2) = \frac{1+s(1)(t_2+1-\bar{t}_1)}{1+s(1)(t_2-\bar{t}_1)}.$$

The positive rate of growth of productions, with null growth rate of the net product, can be explained by observing that production increases in each period by the net product of sub-system 1 which is wholly accumulated and reproduced in one of the sub-systems 2. Of course, as t tends to infinite, the growth rate of productions will tend to zero. Indeed, from [6.3] it follows

[6.44] $$\lim_{t_1 \to \infty} [1+\beta_{i^*}(1,2;t_2)] = 1.$$

13. Summary of the essential features

The production system that we have described differs in many respects from the standard prototype of dynamic multisectoral model, such as von Neumann's one. In that model there is equiproportional growth and the net product rate, the production growth rate, and the net product growth rate are all equal.

On the contrary, in our theoretical framework:

a) the rates of net product, the production growth rates, and the net product growth rates do not coincide;
b) the rates of net product, and the growth rates of production and net product can be as numerous as the commodities of the economic system;
c) these rates are not uniform over time even when techniques do not change;
d) the internal growth rate of a single technique, which in the case of maximum accumulation coincides with s, loses its central economic role for the dynamics of the system.

At this point, it should be clear that the growth of the economic system that uses NPMP, depends on a great variety of factors that are neglected in models such as that proposed by von Neumann.

In particular, the following additional elements emerge as important in our framework

a) the time $\bar{t}_1$ when sub-system 1 stops growing, which is affected by the available quantity of T(1);

b) the size of the net product generated by sub-system 1 and available for accumulation by technique **A**(2); this dimension, moreover, depends on $\bar{t}_1$;
c) the level of s(1) and s(2);
d) the size of the residuals of net products generated by **A**(1) and that cannot be accumulated by **A**(2);
e) the time when sub-system 2 stops growing which also depends on the quantity of T(2),.

14. The relation between technological change and technological dimension

An important feature emerged from our analysis is that the dynamic process shows continuous technological change, even in the absence of technical progress.

In fact, technological change comes about when a new NPMP and a new technique is introduced. In such a case, the dimension of the technology grows (cf. the difference with Chapter II, § 10) both in qualitative terms (depending on the type of techniques and processes) and in quantitative terms (depending on the number of techniques and processes).

But technological change comes about also when the dimension of the technology grows only in quantitative terms by increasing the number of active techniques of type 2.

Moreover, technological change does not only depend on the efficiency level of each technique, but also on the degree of compatibility between the various techniques that are activated over time. In this context, residuals play a crucial role.

In the following Chapters we shall deal with other issues that further illustrate the range of features of a dynamic analysis based on compound technologies.

Chapter VII – Choice of technologies and dynamic-physical order of efficiency

1. Introduction

From the analysis of the foregoing Chapter, we came up with some key variables in studying the dynamic process; namely, the techniques **A**(h), the derived compound technologies, the internal growth rate of each technique, and the residuals that could emerge from the increasing technological dimension.

Undoubtedly, the presence of NPMP complicates the relations between economic efficiency and choice of techniques. Whereas the degree of physical efficiency of a single technique **A**(h) is given by its internal growth rate s(h), this is not the case for those technologies that, by including various techniques, become compound structures with problems of compatibility.

We have already seen that the behavior of the growth rates of compound technologies cannot be defined in general terms, even if the adopted order of efficiency coincides with the physical one in which the single techniques are arranged according to the decreasing order of their own internal growth rates.

In Chapter VI we based our investigation on the order of physical efficiency among techniques and we analyzed the dynamics of a compound technology.

It is now necessary to analyze deeply the role of residuals, which are a new and important element of our dynamics. More precisely, they affect:
- the choice of techniques and technologies;
- the definition of efficiency;
- the definition of technical and technological progress.

2. Choice of techniques: previous hypotheses and their re-examination

The issue concerning the choice of techniques must be built upon the determination of the efficiency order that has been already discussed (cf. Chapter II, § 12; Chapter III, in particular § 6, § 10, § 11).

The analysis in those previous Chapters was elaborated on the basis of the following criteria:

1) We assumed that for each NPMP there was only one production process. More generally, we assumed that for each NPMP there was one process with the wage-profit frontier dominant over all the other processes utilizing the same

NPMP. This restriction may be partially relaxed by assuming that numerous processes have the same maximum rate of growth and hence the same uniform rate of net product. However, we shall postulate that one of these processes has higher growth rate for the range of all possible values of the exogenous distributive variable, so that it becomes dominant. This superiority occurs despite the fact that in terms of the physical efficiency order —as previously defined— there are more processes equally efficient.

2) Each problem about efficiency order was concerned with techniques utilizing different NPMP.

The presence of residuals requires the re-examination of these two hypotheses. In fact, in some cases this could advantage techniques, that appear inferior in terms of both the static order of price-distribution efficiency, and the physical efficiency. Residuals, therefore, rule out hypothesis 1), and in its place, we should take into account a plurality of techniques related to the same NPMP —there is then the problem of their choice. Moreover, residuals may modify also the efficiency —as established by the criteria of price-distribution and physical efficiency— among processes with different NPMP. In other words, we must identify a new order of efficiency with which the techniques are activated, that explicitly includes the role of residuals.

3. New efficiency orders, choice of techniques and of technologies

The foregoing discussion pointed out the analytical need for different OE with the introduction of new criteria side by side with those considered in the past Chapters. We shall immediately consider two types of OE:

- that among techniques, which can be ordered on the basis of both physical efficiency and the values assumed by the distributive variables. We have already dealt with this order;
- that among technologies, containing different techniques using both equal and different NPMP. Also in this case, we should determine one order based on the physical efficiency of the technologies, and one derived from the price-distribution system.

As we shall see shortly, the choice of the physical order of efficiency among techniques may turn out to be non-optimal in a dynamic context. In this case the techniques would be activated following their decreasing sequence of uniform rates of net product, but the effects caused by residuals would be completely dismissed. Instead, the physical efficiency order among technologies, which we shall also name for short dynamic order of efficiency, turns out to be optimal because it brings about maximum growth, evaluated with criteria that we shall specify. This order in some cases is established simply with the comparison of the physical variables, whereas in others cases it is necessary to refer to values.

The distinction we made requires probably some further qualifications concerning the difference between the choice of techniques and the choice of technologies. In dealing with the choice of techniques we shall not consider the possible effects that it could have on technologies —in this sense we should speak of 'pure choice of techniques'. In dealing with the choice of technologies, we shall still refer to the choice of techniques, but with the explicit target of considering technology. Therefore, the term 'choice of techniques', without the qualification of "pure", refers also to the choice of technology.

Finally, it must be noted that the previous problems concern choices of already existing techniques and technologies. They can be either realized instantly and once and for all, or dynamically and only for a limited time, so that they can be modified as soon as new clearly predictable conditions arise.

In order to determine the dynamic OE we must compare technologies composed of techniques that refer to both the same and to different NPMP. As we shall see later, the problem of the order is analogous in these two cases; we shall, however, start with techniques that are using the same NPMP.

4. Dynamic-physical OE among technologies relative to the same NPMP and the same time horizon

The determination of the dynamic OE, that is to say of that order which guarantees the maximum growth, cannot be based on the degree of physical efficiency of each single technique as expressed by its uniform rate of net product, but also on the structural compatibility among the various techniques activated through time. The dynamic OE is heavily affected by the presence of residuals, the availability of each NPMP, the degree of its utilization, and the length of time in which each technique allows for growth.

For the moment in the attempt of maintaining the analysis as simple as possible, let us assume only two types of NPMP and the same given time horizon in which techniques will grow. Based on this hypothesis, in the following sections, we shall compare technologies that utilize these two types of NPMP. We shall in particular analyze those cases in which the dynamic efficiency order can be established by comparing physical magnitudes.

5. Techniques with equal NPMP and s, and orderable residuals

The first case that we consider deals with the comparison of two technologies which make use of NPMP of type 1 and 2, that allow for growth during the same period of time. The first technology is composed of techniques **A**(1) and **A**(2a), and the second one of **A**(1) and **A**(2b).

Whereas techniques **A**(1), relative to NPMP of type 1, are equal in the two technologies, techniques **A**(2a) and **A**(2b), relative to NPMP of type 2, show the same uniform rate of net product, but different structures. The fact that s(2a)=s(2b) means that the two techniques have the same physical efficiency according to the earlier classification.

Techniques **A**(1), **A**(2a), and **A**(2b) differ only by the process producing PCC1. Introducing this hypothesis and focusing on the change of the process of PCC1 seems rather plausible since it is only because of this process and its NPMP that the economy moves from technique **A**(1) to a compound technology.

Let us begin with the simplest case and assume that the structural diversity among technologies [**A**(1); **A**(2a)] and [**A**(1); **A**(2b)] brings about the production of different residuals, but that these residuals can be compared and in particular that $\mathbf{r}(1,2a;t) \geq \mathbf{r}(1,2b;t)$.

Let us now analyze how it is possible to determine the dynamic-physical OE.

The two technologies are composed of techniques with the same physical efficiency. Because of different residuals, however, the second technology shows a higher dynamic efficiency, being characterized by both greater productions, net products, and growth rates for each commodity, with the only exception of the commodity without residuals that has in the two technologies the same values.

By indicating with $\bar{t}_{2a}$ and $\bar{t}_{2b}$ the time when NPMP of type 2 is fully utilized by respectively the technologies that include **A**(2a) and **A**(2b), and comparing their sectoral productions, net products, and growth rates at time t_2 with

$$t_1 < t_2 \leq \bar{t}_{2a} = \bar{t}_{2b},$$

from [6.13] and [6.14], it follows that

$$[7.1] \qquad \mathbf{e}_i'\mathbf{q}(1,2a;t_2) < \mathbf{e}_i'\mathbf{q}(1,2b;t_2), \qquad \text{for } i \neq i^*;$$

and

$$[7.2] \qquad \mathbf{e}_{i*}'\mathbf{q}(1,2a;t_2) = \mathbf{e}_{i*}'\mathbf{q}(1,2b;t_2).$$

From [6.15] and [6.16], the net products are

$$[7.3] \qquad \mathbf{e}_i'\mathbf{n}(1,2a;t_2) < \mathbf{e}_i'\mathbf{n}(1,2b;t_2), \qquad \text{for } i \neq i^*;$$

and

$$[7.4] \qquad \mathbf{e}_{i*}'\mathbf{n}(1,2a;t_2) = \mathbf{e}_{i*}'\mathbf{n}(1,2b;t_2).$$

Concerning the rates of growth of productions and net products for each commodity, it is possible to show that

$$[7.5] \qquad \beta_i\,(1, 2a; t_2) < \beta_i\,(1, 2b; t_2), \qquad \text{for } i \neq i^*;$$

$$[7.6] \qquad \beta_{i^*}\,(1, 2a; t_2) = \beta_{i^*}\,(1, 2b; t_2)$$

$$[7.7] \qquad \mu_i(1, 2a; t_2) < \mu_i(1, 2b; t_2), \qquad \text{for } i \neq i^*;$$

$$[7.8] \qquad \mu_{i^*}\,(1, 2a; t_2) = \mu_{i^*}\,(1, 2b; t_2).$$

It should, therefore, be quite evident that the second technology is preferred to the first. This also appears from some numerical simulations drawn from the data in Appendix A. In these examples we assume that the highest production obtainable with the available NPMP of type 1 is reached at time t = 3. Therefore, at time t = 4, the net product that no longer can be accumulated within the technique that employs NPMP of type 1 is utilized to activate a second technique. The following Figures illustrate the dynamics of the system with technologies [**A**(1); **A**(2a)] and [**A**(1); **A**(2b)], from the period in which the availability of NPMP of type 1 becomes a binding constraint, that is to say from t = 3.

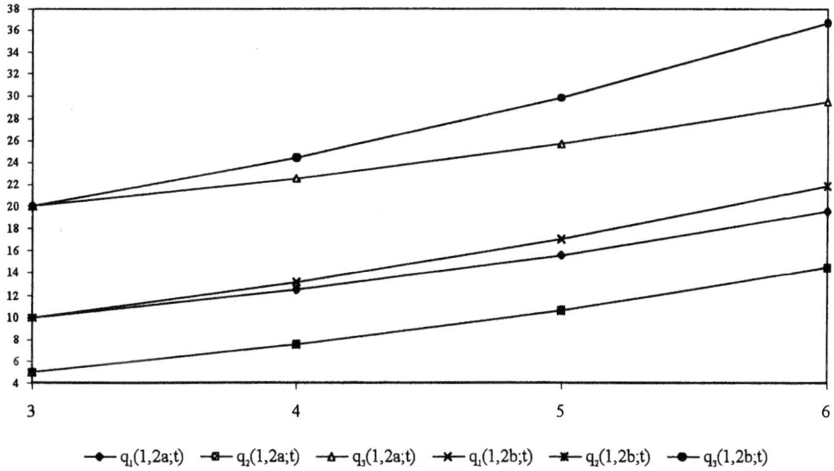

Fig. 7.1 Total productions with [**A**(1); **A**(2a)] and [**A**(1); **A**(2b)]

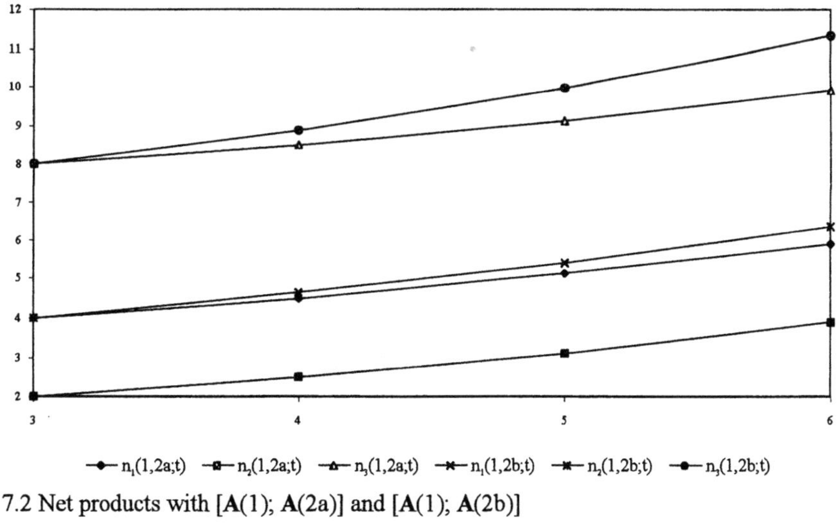

Fig. 7.2 Net products with [**A**(1); **A**(2a)] and [**A**(1); **A**(2b)]

The Figures show that technology [**A**(1); **A**(2b)] has a greater dynamic efficiency allowing to obtain for each commodity greater production, net product, and higher growth rates, except the case of the commodity without residuals, for which production, net product, and growth rates are the same for the two technologies.

More precisely, Figures 7.1 and 7.2 shows that productions and total net products of commodities 1 and 3 are greater and grow more rapidly with [**A**(1); **A**(2b)], that is, the technology with lower residuals of these commodities. Concerning the commodity without residuals for both technologies, i.e. commodity 2, the situation is the same.

Figure 7.3 gives evidence of the growth rates of production of each commodity. At the beginning these rates are either higher, equal, or smaller than the uniform rate of net product of the less efficient technique. This is dependent on the relative weights of the residuals, and the difference between the uniform rate of net products of the techniques activated through time, as is shown by [6.23]. In particular, the rate of growth of production of the commodity without residuals is always higher than the uniform rate of net product of the less efficient technique, though the gap decreases over time as the weight of the latter technique increases. Figure 7.3 shows for both technologies the unique rate of growth of production of commodity 2, and how it is higher than the other commodities' rate of growth and decreases over time (0.5 for $t = 4$; 0.42 for $t = 5$; 0.37 for $t = 6$). This is the obvious result from the fact that the production of commodity 2 does not form residuals.

The growth rate of production of commodity 1 with the use of technology [**A**(1); **A**(2b)] is higher than the uniform rate of net product of technique **A**(2b) and it decreases over time. However the same commodity experiences a constant rate of growth when produced with technology [**A**(1); **A**(2a)]. The analysis of the productive trend of commodity 3 shows that its growth rate is smaller than the uniform rate of net product of the less efficient technique of both technologies, but it increases over time.

Figure 7.4 shows the growth rates of net products. They are always smaller than the uniform rate of net product of the less efficient technique —always with the exception of the commodity without residuals, for which they coincide. Moreover these rates increase over time due to the fall of the relative weight of residuals, and tend to the uniform rate of net product of the second technique. In the example that has been just illustrated, the rates of growth of net products are higher with technology [**A**(1); **A**(2b)] —with the obvious exception of commodity 2 whose rate is the same with both technologies, constant and higher than the growth rates of net products of the other commodities.

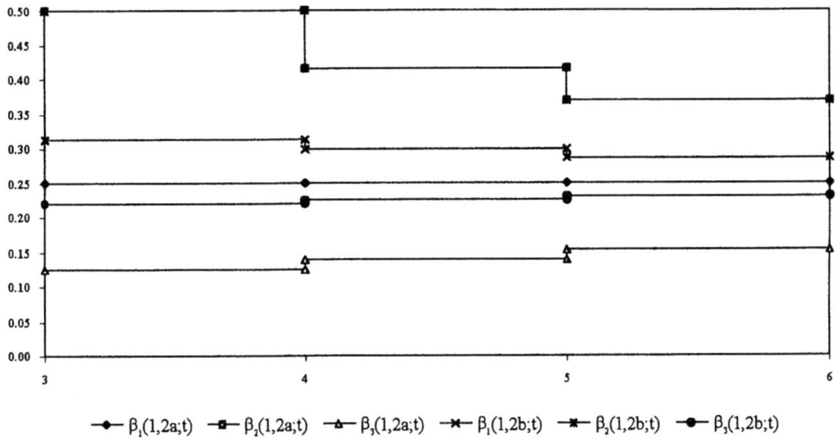

Fig. 7.3 Rates of growth of productions with [**A**(1); **A**(2a)] and [**A**(1); **A**(2b)]

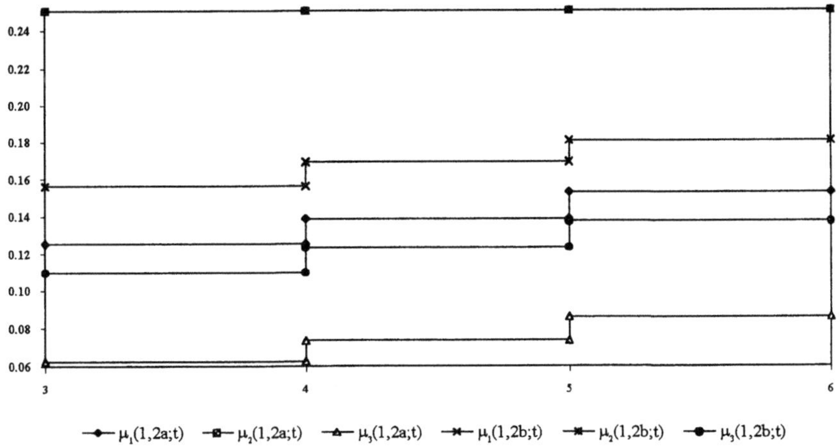

Fig. 7.4 Rates of growth of net products with [**A**(1); **A**(2a)] and [**A**(1); **A**(2b)]

6. Techniques with equal NPMP and s, one of which without residuals

The second case that we consider is a particular case of the previous one, because we assume that the new technique **A**(2c) employing the NPMP of type 2, when it is activated in the right proportions for achieving steady growth, shows exactly the same productive structure of the already active technique, that is to say, without comporting the formation of residuals.

In fact, let us take into account technologies [**A**(1); **A**(2a)] and [**A**(1); **A**(2c)]. The first includes two techniques that we have already analyzed. Technique **A**(1) is equal in both technologies, while techniques **A**(2a) and **A**(2c) have the same uniform rate of net product, but different structure because only technology [**A**(1); **A**(2a)] shows residuals. Hence, the vectors of residuals necessarily turn out to be orderable.

The characteristics of technique **A**(2c) have already been analyzed in Chapter VI, where we studied what conditions the technical coefficients of the process producing Pcc1 must satisfy in order to avoid the formation of residuals.

Also in this case, although the technologies are composed of techniques with the same physical efficiency, the second technology shows a superior dynamic efficiency, due to its absence of residuals.

In particular, when compared to [**A**(1); **A**(2a)], the utilization of technology [**A**(1); **A**(2c)] brings about higher productions, net products, and growth rates for all commodity, with the exception of the commodity that do not have residuals in either cases.

From [6.13] and [6.14] we have the following relationships in the levels of production

$$[7.9] \qquad \mathbf{e}_i'\mathbf{q}(1,2a;t_2) < \mathbf{e}_{i*}'\mathbf{q}(1,2c;t_2),$$

$$[7.10] \qquad \mathbf{e}_{i*}'\mathbf{q}(1,2a;t_2) = \mathbf{e}_{i*}'\mathbf{q}(1,2c;t_2).$$

From [6.15] and [6.16] we note for the net products that

$$[7.11] \qquad \mathbf{e}_i'\mathbf{n}(1,2a;t_2) < \mathbf{e}_{i*}'\mathbf{n}(1,2c;t_2),$$

$$[7.12] \qquad \mathbf{e}_{i*}'\mathbf{n}(1,2a;t_2) = \mathbf{e}_{i*}'\mathbf{n}(1,2c;t_2).$$

Finally, the growth rates of production and net product show that

$$[7.13] \qquad \beta_i(1,2a;t_2) < \beta_{i*}(1,2c;t_2),$$

$$[7.14] \qquad \beta_{i*}(1,2a;t_2) = \beta_{i*}(1,2c;t_2);$$

and

$$[7.15] \qquad \mu_i(1,2a;t_2) < \mu_{i*}(1,2c;t_2),$$

$$[7.16] \qquad \mu_{i*}(1,2a;t_2) = \mu_{i*}(1,2c;t_2).$$

The absence of residuals, now possible thanks to the use of technology [**A**(1); **A**(2c)], implies that the growth rates of productions and of net products with this technology are the same for each commodity. However, while the growth rates of net products are constant and equal to s(2c) (which in the example is equal to 0.25), growth rates of productions change over time. Indeed, they turn out to be higher than s(2c), but with a decreasing trend as the weight of technique **A**(2c) increases.

Therefore, even if there are no residuals, the analysis of the system with the method of compound technologies involves different results from those obtained in models *á la* von Neumann. Indeed, in our analysis there is no correspondence between the rates of growth of productions and net products.

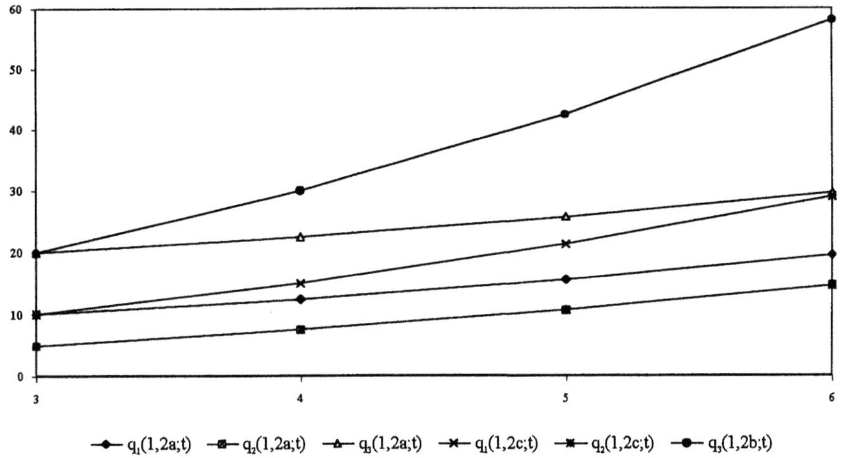

Fig. 7.5 Total production with [**A**(1); **A**(2a)] and [**A**(1); **A**(2c)]

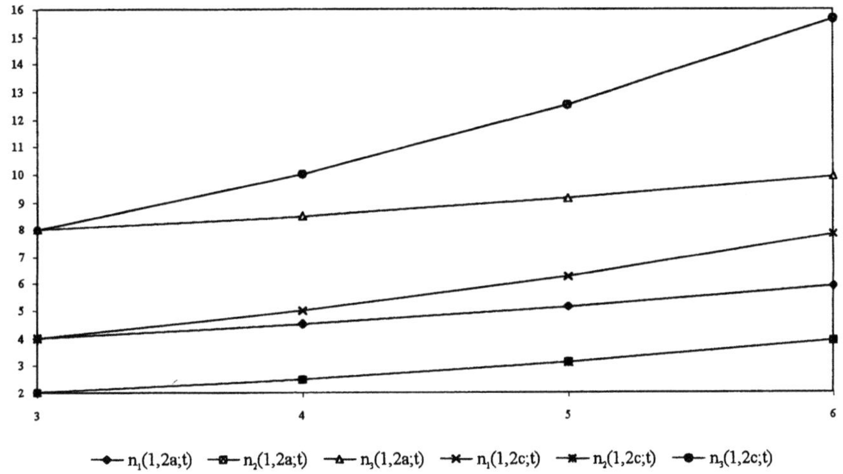

Fig. 7.6 Net product with [**A**(1); **A**(2a)] and [**A**(1); **A**(2c)]

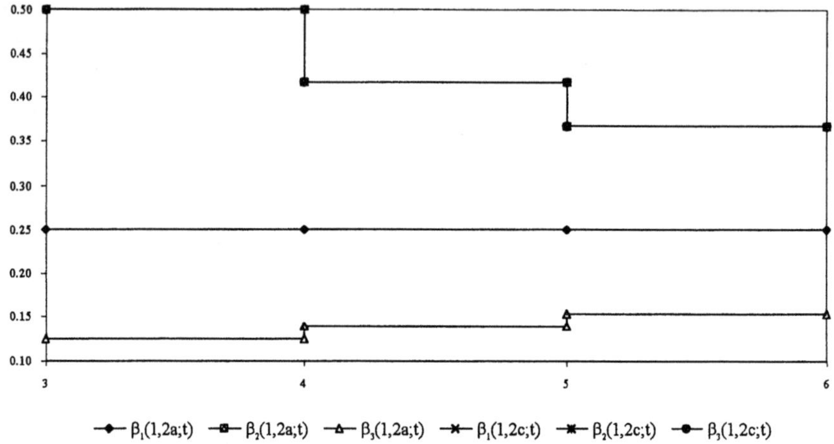

Fig. 7.7 Rates of growth of productions with [**A**(1); **A**(2a)] and [**A**(1); **A**(2c)]

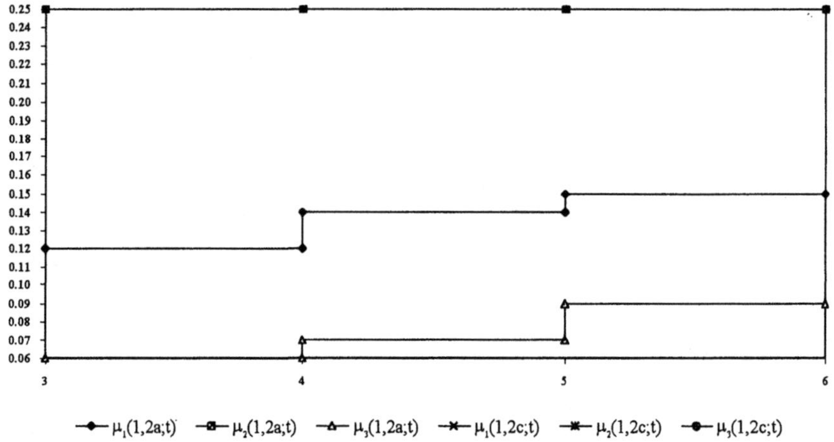

Fig. 7.8 Rates of growth of net products with [**A**(1); **A**(2a)] and [**A**(1); **A**(2c)]

The Figures 7.5-7.8, based on some simulations made by the authors, show for finite values of t, the superiority of technology [**A**(1); **A**(2c)] compared to [**A**(1); **A**(2a)]. However, it should be quite clear that when t tends to infinity, the growth rates of the two technologies eventually coincide.

7. Techniques with equal NPMP and s, and with non orderable residuals

The third case that we consider comes about when at given equal internal rates of growth of the techniques, the residuals are not orderable. In other words, we consider two technologies [**A**(1); **A**(2a)] and [**A**(1); **A**(2d)] composed of techniques with the same uniform rates of net product, but with residuals unevenly distributed —for some commodities they are higher with the first technology, whereas for other commodities they are higher with the second technology.

If technologies show non-orderable vectors of residuals, it is no longer possible, if we limit our analysis to the information provided by the physical system, to determine a dynamic OE. For those commodities that show smaller residuals with one of the two technologies, they will have within their respective technology also higher production, net product and growth rates.

Indeed, from [6.13], [6.15], [6.17], and [6.27] it follows

[7.17] $$\mathbf{e}_i'\mathbf{q}(1,2a;t_2) \gtrless \mathbf{e}_i'\mathbf{q}(1,2d;t_2),$$

[7.18] $$\mathbf{e}_i'\mathbf{n}(1,2a;t_2) \gtrless \mathbf{e}_i'\mathbf{n}(1,2d;t_2),$$

[7.19] $$\beta_i(1,2a;t_2) \gtrless \beta_i(1,2d;t_2),$$

[7.20] $$\mu_i(1,2a;t_2) \gtrless \mu_i(1,2d;t_2),$$

depending on

$$\mathbf{e}_i'\mathbf{r}_i(1,2a;\bar{t}_1+1) \lesseqgtr \mathbf{e}_i'\mathbf{r}_i(1,2d;\bar{t}_1+1).$$

The dynamics of the system with technology [**A**(1); **A**(2a)] and [**A**(1); **A**(2d)] is represented in Figures 7.9-7.12. From these Figures it emerges that the adoption of technology [**A**(1); **A**(2a)] compared to [**A**(1); **A**(2d)], brings about the following patterns. For the commodity with smaller residuals, that is, commodity 1, production, net product, and their relative rates of growth are higher. On the contrary, for the commodity with greater residuals, that is, commodity 3, we have that these variables are lower. Finally they precisely coincide for the commodity with the same residuals, that is commodity 2.

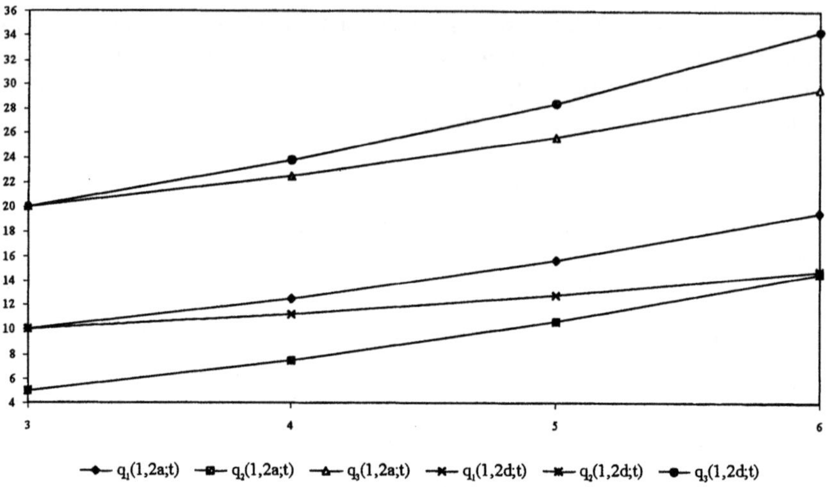

Fig. 7.9 Total production with [**A**(1); **A**(2a)] and [**A**(1); **A**(2d)]

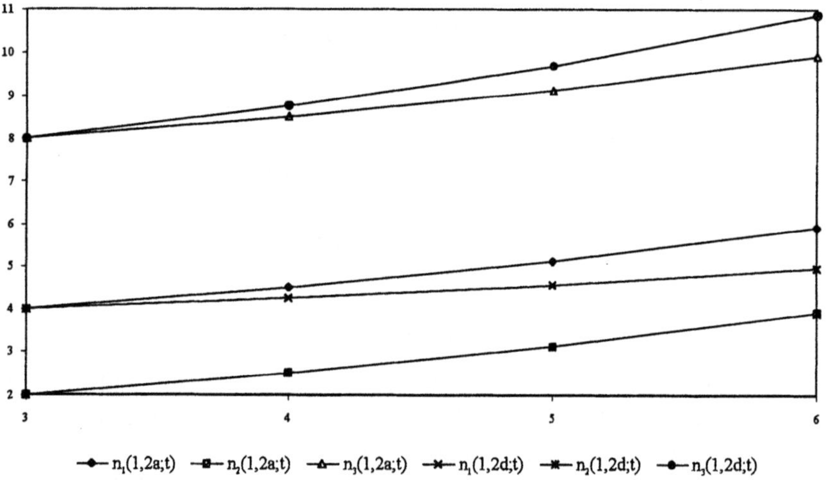

Fig. 7.10 Net product with [**A**(1); **A**(2a)] and [**A**(1); **A**(2d)]

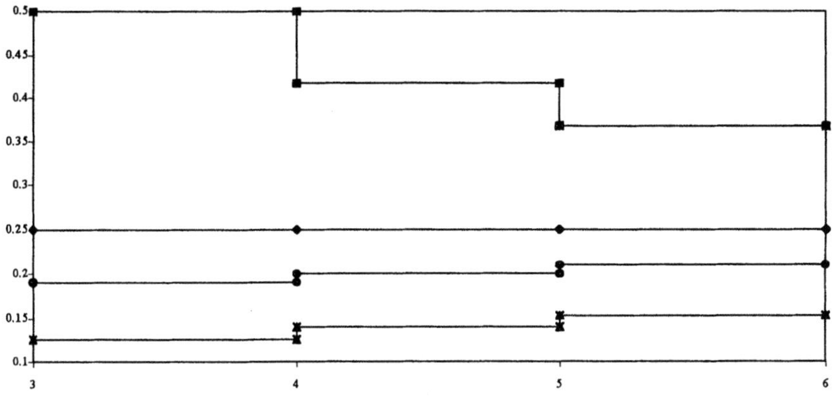

$\beta_1(1,2a;t)$ $\beta_2(1,2a;t)$ $\beta_3(1,2a;t)$ $\beta_1(1,2d;t)$ $\beta_2(1,2d;t)$ $\beta_3(1,2d;t)$

Fig. 7.11 Rates of growth of productions with [**A**(1); **A**(2a)] and [**A**(1); **A**(2d)]

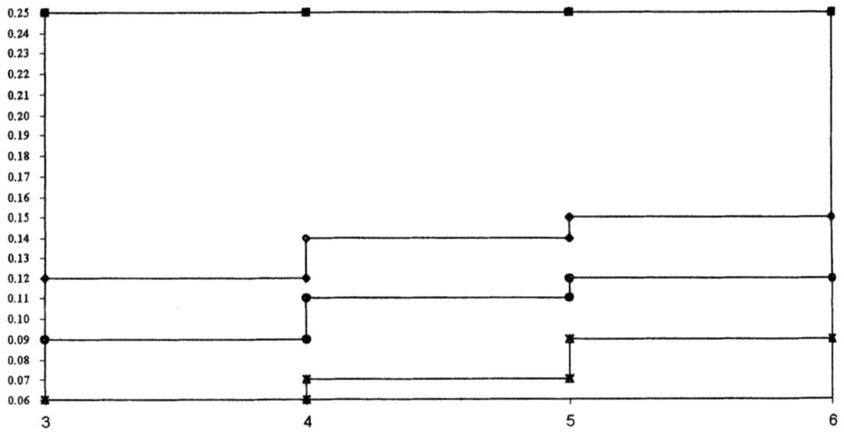

$\mu_1(1,2a;t)$ $\mu_2(1,2a;t)$ $\mu_3(1,2a;t)$ $\mu_1(1,2d;t)$ $\mu_2(1,2d;t)$ $\mu_3(1,2d;t)$

Fig. 7.12 Rates of growth of net products with [**A**(1); **A**(2a)] and [**A**(1); **A**(2d)]

It is, therefore, impossible to order, in terms of efficiency, the two technologies on the basis of the physical system. This result seems to be of great importance because it proves that the efficiency criterion, which is based on the growth rates of net products and largely employed in dynamic models, is correct in only some cases.

In the present context, to establish an efficiency order, it is necessary to shift the comparison between the values of productions and net products obtainable with the two technologies.

8. Techniques with equal NPMP and s, but with several commodities without residuals

The fourth case that we consider is a particular case of the previous one. We assume that the commodity without residuals is different for the two technologies. Therefore, the residual vectors are not orderable. In fact, let us take into consideration technologies [**A**(1); **A**(2a)] and [**A**(1); **A**(2e)] which are still composed of techniques with the same internal growth rates, but with not the same commodity without residuals.

In this case, it is impossible to order technologies on the basis of the information obtained from the physical system, because production, net product and, rates of growth of the commodity for which residuals are formed with technology [**A**(1); **A**(2a)] —but not with technology [**A**(1); **A**(2e)]— are higher if the second technology is used. Conversely, the opposite occurs for the commodity that forms residuals with [**A**(1); **A**(2e)], but not with [**A**(1); **A**(2a)].

More precisely, from [6.13], [6.15], [6.17] and [6.27], productions, net products, and their growth rates follow these inequalities

[7.21] $$\mathbf{e}_i'\mathbf{q}(1,2a;t_2) < \mathbf{e}_{i*}'\mathbf{q}(1,2e;t_2);$$

[7.22] $$\mathbf{e}_{i*}'\mathbf{q}(1,2a;t_2) > \mathbf{e}_i'\mathbf{q}(1,2e;t_2);$$

[7.23] $$\mathbf{e}_i'\mathbf{n}(1,2a;t_2) < \mathbf{e}_{i*}'\mathbf{n}(1,2e;t_2);$$

[7.24] $$\mathbf{e}_{i*}'\mathbf{n}(1,2a;t_2) > \mathbf{e}_i'\mathbf{n}(1,2e;t_2).$$

Moreover

[7.25] $$\beta_i(1,2a;t_2) < \beta_{i*}(1,2e;t_2);$$

[7.26] $$\beta_{i*}(1,2a;t_2) > \beta_i(1,2e;t_2);$$

and

[7.27] $$\mu_i(1,2a;t_2) < \mu_{i*}(1,2e;t_2);$$

[7.28] $$\mu_{i*}(1,2a;t_2) > \mu_i(1,2e;t_2).$$

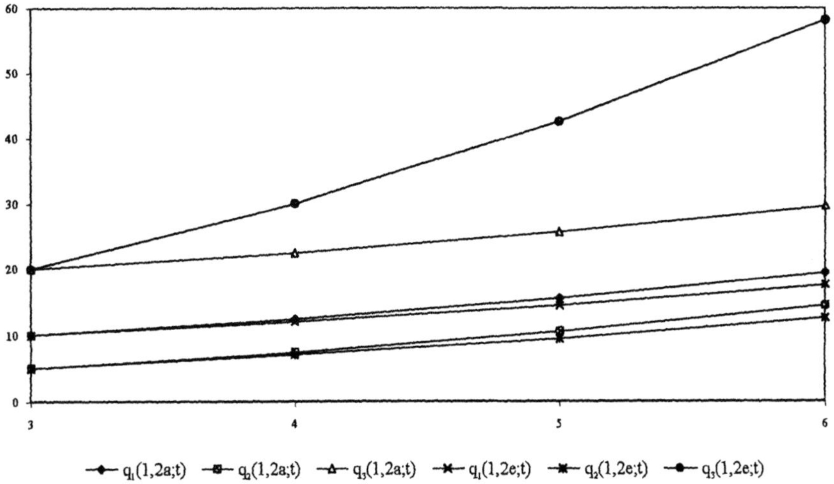

Fig. 7.13 Total production with [**A**(1); **A**(2a)] and [**A**(1); **A**(2e)]

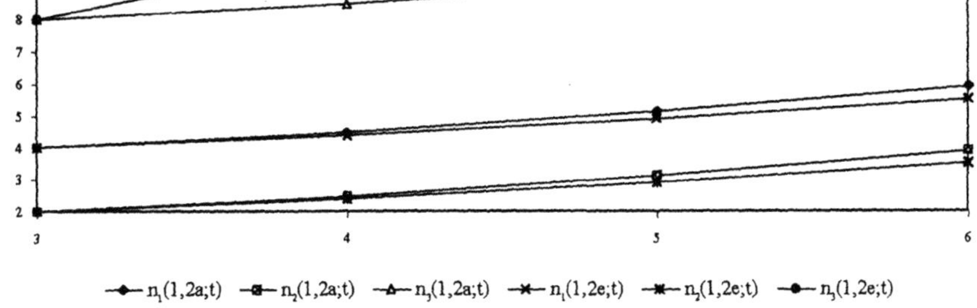

Fig. 7.14 Net product with [**A**(1); **A**(2a)] and [**A**(1); **A**(2e)]

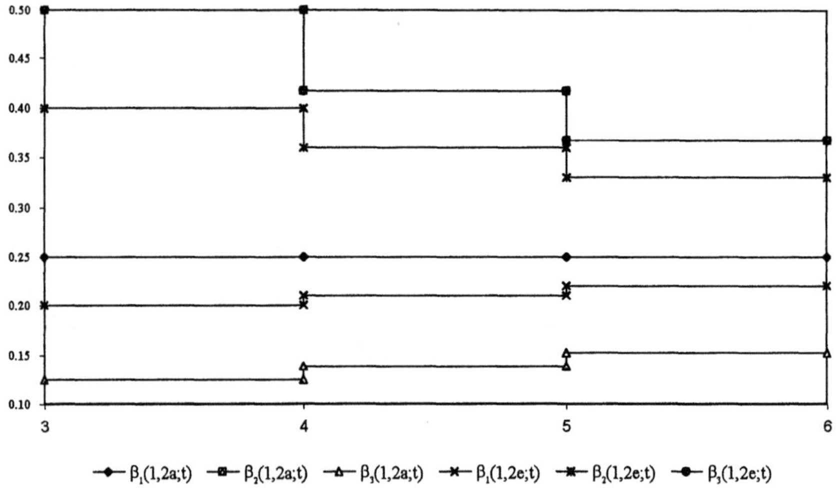

Fig. 7.15 Rates of growth of productions with [**A**(1); **A**(2a)] and [**A**(1); **A**(2e)]

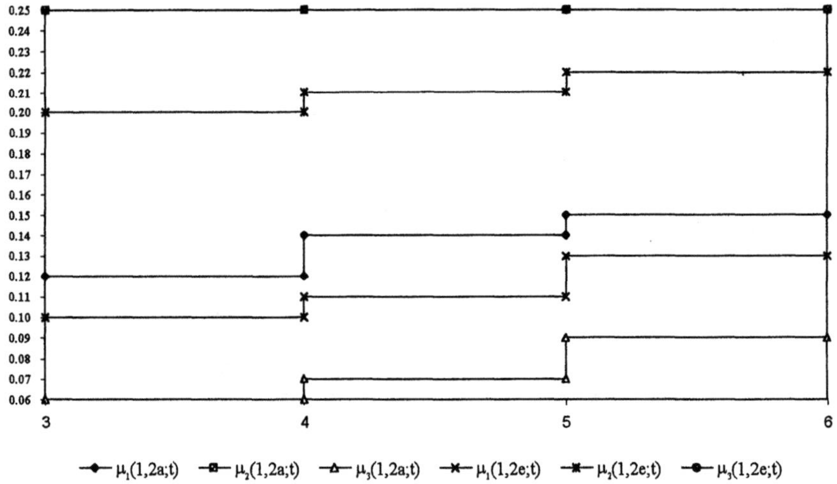

Fig. 7.16 Rates of growth of net products with [**A**(1); **A**(2a)] and [**A**(1); **A**(2e)]

The dynamics of that system with [**A**(1); **A**(2a)] and [**A**(1); **A**(2e)] is shown in Figures 7.13-7.16. From them it turns out that productions, net products, and growth rates with technology [**A**(1);**A**(2a)] are lower for commodity 3 and higher for commodities 1 and 2. In fact this technology embodies smaller residuals of these two latter commodities and greater residuals for commodity 3 and greater residuals for commodity 3.

9. Techniques with equal NPMP and different s

The last case we consider is that of technologies containing techniques characterized by different uniform rates of net product.

If we were to take into consideration only the efficiency of techniques, we would choose that technology with the most efficient techniques. But the efficiency of technology does not depend only on this: it is also necessary to assess the impact of residuals.

Let us take into consideration two generic technologies [**A**(1); **A**(2n)] and [**A**(1); **A**(2p)] composed of techniques with s(2n) > s(2p). From [6.13] it follows

$$[7.29] \qquad \mathbf{e}_i'\mathbf{q}(1,2n;t_2) \gtreqless \mathbf{e}_i'\mathbf{q}(1,2p;t_2)$$

according to whether

$$\sum_{t=1}^{t_2-\bar{t}_1}[1+s(2n)]^t \gtreqless \sum_{t=1}^{t_2-\bar{t}_1}[1+s(2p)]^t \frac{[\mathbf{e}_i'\mathbf{n}(1;\bar{t}_1)-\mathbf{e}_i'\mathbf{r}(1,2p;\bar{t}_1+1)]}{[\mathbf{e}_i'\mathbf{n}(1;\bar{t}_1)-\mathbf{e}_i'\mathbf{r}(1,2n;\bar{t}_1+1)]}.$$

From [6.15] it follows that

$$[7.30] \qquad \mathbf{e}_i'\mathbf{n}(1,2n;t_2) \gtreqless \mathbf{e}_i'\mathbf{n}(1,2p;t_2)$$

according to whether

$$\{[1+s(2n)]^{t_2-\bar{t}_1}-1\} \gtreqless \{[1+s(2p)]^{t_2-\bar{t}_1}-1\} \frac{[\mathbf{e}_i'\mathbf{n}(1;\bar{t}_1)-\mathbf{e}_i'\mathbf{r}(1,2p;\bar{t}_1+1]}{[\mathbf{e}_i'\mathbf{n}(1;\bar{t}_1)-\mathbf{e}_i'\mathbf{r}(1,2n;\bar{t}_1+1)]}.$$

Moreover, it is

$$[7.31] \qquad \beta_i(1,2n;t_2) \gtreqless \beta_i(1,2p;t_2)$$

according to whether

$$\mathbf{e}_i'\mathbf{q}(1;\bar{t}_1)[1+s(2n)]^{t_2-\bar{t}_1}[\mathbf{e}_i'\mathbf{n}(1;\bar{t}_1)-\mathbf{e}_i'\mathbf{r}(1,2n;\bar{t}_1+1)] \gtreqless$$

$$\mathbf{e}_i'\mathbf{q}(1;\bar{t}_1)[1+s(2p)]^{t_2-\bar{t}_1}[\mathbf{e}_i'\mathbf{n}(1;\bar{t}_1)-\mathbf{e}_i'\mathbf{r}(1,2p;\bar{t}_1+1)]+$$
$$+[\mathbf{e}_i'\mathbf{n}(1;\bar{t}_1)-\mathbf{e}_i'\mathbf{r}(1,2n;\bar{t}_1+1)][\mathbf{e}_i'\mathbf{n}(1;\bar{t}_1)-\mathbf{e}_i'\mathbf{r}(1,2p;\bar{t}_1+1)]$$

$$\{[1+s(2p)]^{t_2-\bar{t}_1}\sum_{t=1}^{t_2-\bar{t}_1-1}[1+s(2n)]^t-[1+s(2n)]^{t_2-\bar{t}_1}\sum_{t=1}^{t_2-\bar{t}_1-1}[1+s(2p)]^t\};$$

and also

$$[7.32] \qquad \mu_i(1,2n;t_2) \gtreqless \mu_i(1,2p;t_2)$$

according to whether

$$\mathbf{e}_i^{'}s(1)\mathbf{A}(1)\mathbf{q}(1;\bar{t}_1)[\mathbf{e}_i^{'}\mathbf{n}(1;\bar{t}_1)-\mathbf{e}_i^{'}\mathbf{r}(1,2n;\bar{t}_1+1)]s(2n)[1+s(2n)]^{t_2-\bar{t}_1-1} \gtreqless$$

$$\mathbf{e}_i^{'}s(1)\mathbf{A}(1)\mathbf{q}(1;\bar{t}_1)[\mathbf{e}_i^{'}\mathbf{n}(1;\bar{t}_1)-\mathbf{e}_i^{'}\mathbf{r}(1,2p;\bar{t}_1+1)]$$

$$s(2p)[1+s(2p)]^{t_2-\bar{t}_1-1}+[\mathbf{e}_i^{'}\mathbf{n}(1;\bar{t}_1)-\mathbf{e}_i^{'}\mathbf{r}(1,2n;\bar{t}_1+1)][\mathbf{e}_i^{'}\mathbf{n}(1;\bar{t}_1)-\mathbf{e}_i^{'}\mathbf{r}(1,2p;\bar{t}_1+1)]$$

$$\{[1+s(2p)]^{t_2-\bar{t}_1-1}\sum_{t=0}^{t_2-\bar{t}_1-2}[1+s(2n)]^t-[1+s(2n)]^{t_2-\bar{t}_1-1}\sum_{t=0}^{t_2-\bar{t}_1-2}[1+s(2p)]^t\}s(2n)s(2p).$$

To determine the dynamic Oe between technologies [**A**(1); **A**(2n)] and [**A**(1); **A**(2p)] the order —which is established on the basis of the productions of each commodity with the two technologies— should be the same for all the commodities and should coincide with the order established on the basis of net products and of the respective growth rates.

Such an order depends on the sign of the relations [7.29]-[7.32], and this is determined by three elements:

- the gap between the uniform rates of net product of the single techniques;
- the weight of the residual of each commodity within each technology;
- the time t_2 at which the comparison takes place.

However, these elements affect each inequality in a different way. Therefore, the order established on the basis of the production of one commodity may not coincide with the order established on the basis of the net product of the same commodity or on the basis of the rates of growth. Moreover, because the weight of residuals may be different from commodity to commodity, each relation [7.29]-[7.32] may show a different sign according to which commodity is considered.

Finally, given that residuals are constant, their impact on production and total net product decreases as the dynamic process continues, while the impact of physical efficiency of the technique with a higher uniform rate of net product increases over time, since the divergence between rates is constant The implications of this phenomenon are the potential change of sign of each inequality [7.29]-[7.32] over time.

From the previous remarks emerges that it is not always possible to determine the dynamic Oe by comparing the physical magnitudes of technologies which have different internal growth rates.

What we may affirm is that technology [**A**(1); **A**(2p)] with $s(2p) < s(2n)$, can never be preferred to [**A**(1); **A**(2n)] on the basis of the information contained in the physical system. The explanation follows from relations [7.29]-[7.32], where technology [**A**(1); **A**(2n)] is surely preferred at least for the commodity which does not generate residuals within it. This, however, does not imply that [**A**(1); **A**(2n)] is preferred in any sense to [**A**(1); **A**(2p)], but it means that in some cases the efficiency order among technologies may be established only by comparing the values of productions and net products obtainable from them.

10. Dynamic efficiency: orderable and non-orderable cases

In general, when comparing two technologies with different internal rates of growth, the following situations may be observed:

a) technology [**A**(1); **A**(2n)] has a higher dynamic efficiency than technology [**A**(1); **A**(2p)], if s(2n) > s(2p) and **r**(1,2n;t) ≤ **r**(1,2p;t);
b) technology [**A**(1); **A**(2n)] has a higher dynamic efficiency than technology [**A**(1); **A**(2p)] though may generate residuals not comparable or even higher than those of the other technology, given that the difference between s(2n) and s(2p) is sufficiently wide.
c) technology [**A**(1); **A**(2n)] is not comparable to technology [**A**(1); **A**(2p)], on the basis of the information contained in the physical system, because in the interval that goes from the beginning up to the full utilization of NPMP of type 2, for some commodities the adoption of the first technology is preferable and for some other commodities the adoption of the second one is preferable;
d) technology [**A**(1); **A**(2n)] is not comparable to technology [**A**(1); **A**(2p)] on the basis of the information contained in the physical system only for a given number of periods, after which it becomes comparable and preferable.

The above cases deserve some detailed remarks: technology [**A**(1); **A**(2n)], for which s(2n) > s(2p), would allow for a given commodity higher production and net product than that allowed by technology [**A**(1); **A**(2p)] only if the greater physical efficiency, highlighted by the difference between s(2n) and s(2p), is not counterbalanced by internal higher residuals. Thus it may occur, such as in case a), that technology [**A**(1); **A**(2n)] is preferable on both grounds —because of higher efficiency and because of its smaller residuals, comporting surely a higher dynamic efficiency.

It may also occur, such as in case b), that the difference between s(2n) and s(2p) is so advantageous as to compensate the eventual higher weight of the residuals.

It may, however, also occur that, at least for some commodities, the burden of the residual is so high as to preclude the use of the information of the physical system to make the choice between the two technologies. Yet, because the residual weight compared to the total means of production shrinks over the time, after a certain period of time the technology [**A**(1); **A**(2n)] gains higher productions, net products, and growth rates than the technology [**A**(1); **A**(2p)]. In fact, beyond a certain period, which may not be the same for the various inequalities, [7.29]-[7.32] are surely satisfied for the 'greater than' case.

Given the limited availability of NPMP of type 2 we cannot exclude in principle that the period of time for which the earlier condition is satisfied will be never reached. This is precisely the case considered in point c). Even if the period would be eventually reached, such as in the case indicated in point d), the ordinability problem between the two technologies would not be immediately solved for the difficulties raised from the inter-temporal comparisons.

11. Orderable and non-orderable cases: a numerical example

To clarify further the cases in which the efficiency order can be established by comparing productions, net products, and growth rates, it is useful to refer to some numerical examples.

We take into consideration the following technologies [**A**(1); **A**(2c)], [**A**(1); **A**(2f)], [**A**(1); **A**(2g)], [**A**(1); **A**(2l)], [**A**(1); **A**(2m)] which have only one technique in common, **A**(1), while the other —either **A**(2c), **A**(2f), **A**(2g), **A**(2l), **A**(2m)— is different. These techniques are characterized by different internal growth rates and by different residuals.

In particular, let us assume that s(2g) > s(2m) > s(2l) > s(2c) > s(2f), and moreover that $\mathbf{r}(1,2c;t_2) = \mathbf{o}$, $\mathbf{r}(1,2g;t_2) \leq \mathbf{r}(1,2f;t_2)$ and $\mathbf{r}(1,2l;t_2) \leq \mathbf{r}(1,2m;t_2)$, but that $\mathbf{r}(1,2g;t_2)$ and $\mathbf{r}(1,2f;t_2)$ are not comparable to $\mathbf{r}(1,2l;t_2)$ and $\mathbf{r}(1,2m;t_2)$.

The dynamics of the system with the previous technologies is indicated in Table 7.1 and in the subsequent Figures 7.17-7.28, where it is possible to find the levels of production, net product, and growth rates of each commodity by using the different technologies. The starting point is period 4, that is, the period when a new technique starts to become active. Let us begin by comparing [**A**(1); **A**(2c)] and [**A**(1); **A**(2f)]. Because the adoption of technology [**A**(1); **A**(2c)] allows for the re-investment of all the available net products and, moreover, because technique **A**(2c) has a higher uniform rate of net product than **A**(2f), the technology in question —namely [**A**(1); **A**(2c)]— turns out to be more efficient, having for each commodity higher productions, net products, and growth rates. Let us now compare technology [**A**(1); **A**(2c)] and [**A**(1); **A**(2g)]. Technique **A**(2g) has a uniform rate of net product which is higher than **A**(2c). Its production structure is, however, different from that of **A**(1), and thus technology [**A**(1); **A**(2g)] generates some residuals. The gap between the internal growth rates of the two technologies, respectively [**A**(1); **A**(2g)] and [**A**(1); **A**(2c)], is still so high, that the first technology is able to overcome the deadweight loss of residuals and gain, for each commodity, greater productions, net products, and rates of growth.

Therefore, on the basis of the physical system, one is able to determine the dynamic efficiency order of the previous technologies, that is, [**A**(1); **A**(2g)], [**A**(1); **A**(2c)], [**A**(1); **A**(2f)].

We now broaden the comparison by considering also technologies [**A**(1); **A**(2l)] and [**A**(1); **A**(2m)]. The latter technology includes the technique with NPMP of type 2, which is more efficient if it is taken alone, but have the drawback of forming higher residuals than both commodity 1 and commodity 3. These residuals counterbalance the effect of higher uniform rate of net product, and make impossible the direct comparison of productions, net products, and growth rates in establishing the order of efficiency.

To see much more clearly the point, let us once again refer to Table 7.1 and to Figures 7.17-7.28. It emerges that there are several orders of efficiency among these technologies, depending on which variable is taken into account

Table 7.1 Dynamics with different technologies

t	Technology	s(2)	Total production commodity 1	Total production commodity 2	Total production commodity 3	Net product commodity 1	Net product commodity 2	Net product commodity 3	$\beta_1(1;2)$	$\beta_2(1;2)$	$\beta_3(1;2)$	$\mu_1(1;2)$	$\mu_2(1;2)$	$\mu_3(1;2)$
3	[A(1);A(2c)]	0.25	10	5	20	4	2	8	0.6667	0.6667	0.6667	0.6667	0.6667	0.6667
4	[A(1);A(2c)]	0.25	15	7.5	30	5	2.5	10	0.5	0.5	0.5	0.25	0.25	0.25
5	[A(1);A(2c)]	0.25	21.25	10.63	42.50	6.25	3.13	12.50	0.4167	0.4167	0.4167	0.25	0.25	0.25
6	[A(1);A(2c)]	0.25	29.06	14.53	58.13	7.81	3.91	15.63	0.3676	0.3676	0.3676	0.25	0.25	0.25
3	[A(1);A(2f)]	0.18	10	5	20	4	2	8	0.6667	0.6667	0.6667	0.6667	0.6667	0.6667
4	[A(1);A(2f)]	0.18	14.71	7.05	28.43	4.71	2.31	9.26	0.4706	0.4099	0.4213	0.1765	0.1537	0.1580
5	[A(1);A(2f)]	0.18	20.24	9.46	38.34	5.54	2.67	10.75	0.3765	0.3420	0.3487	0.1765	0.1567	0.1605
6	[A(1);A(2f)]	0.18	26.76	12.30	50.00	6.51	3.09	12.50	0.3218	0.2998	0.3042	0.1765	0.1594	0.1627
3	[A(1);A(2g)]	0.54	10	5	20	4	2	8	0.6667	0.6667	0.6667	0.6667	0.6667	0.6667
4	[A(1);A(2g)]	0.54	16.15	7.77	31.69	6.15	2.97	12.09	0.6154	0.5538	0.5846	0.5385	0.4846	0.5115
5	[A(1);A(2g)]	0.54	25.62	12.03	49.68	9.47	4.46	18.39	0.5861	0.5484	0.5676	0.5385	0.5022	0.5206
6	[A(1);A(2g)]	0.54	40.19	18.58	77.35	14.57	6.75	28.07	0.5685	0.5449	0.5570	0.5385	0.5143	0.5267
3	[A(1);A(2l)]	0.33	10	5	20	4	2	8	0.6667	0.6667	0.6667	0.6667	0.6667	0.6667
4	[A(1);A(2l)]	0.33	14.56	7.67	30.33	5.14	2.67	10.58	0.4556	0.5333	0.5167	0.2847	0.3333	0.3229
5	[A(1);A(2l)]	0.33	20.63	11.22	44.11	6.66	3.56	14.03	0.4173	0.4638	0.4542	0.2955	0.3333	0.3255
6	[A(1);A(2l)]	0.33	28.73	15.96	62.48	8.68	4.74	18.62	0.3926	0.4224	0.4165	0.3041	0.3333	0.3274
3	[A(1);A(2m)]	0.43	10	5	20	4	2	8	0.6667	0.6667	0.6667	0.6667	0.6667	0.6667
4	[A(1);A(2m)]	0.43	14.06	7.86	30.67	5.22	2.86	11.20	0.4063	0.5714	0.5333	0.3048	0.4286	0.4000
5	[A(1);A(2m)]	0.43	19.87	11.94	45.90	6.96	4.08	15.77	0.4128	0.5195	0.4969	0.3337	0.4286	0.4082
6	[A(1);A(2m)]	0.43	28.16	17.77	67.67	9.45	5.83	22.30	0.4174	0.4884	0.4742	0.3574	0.4286	0.4141

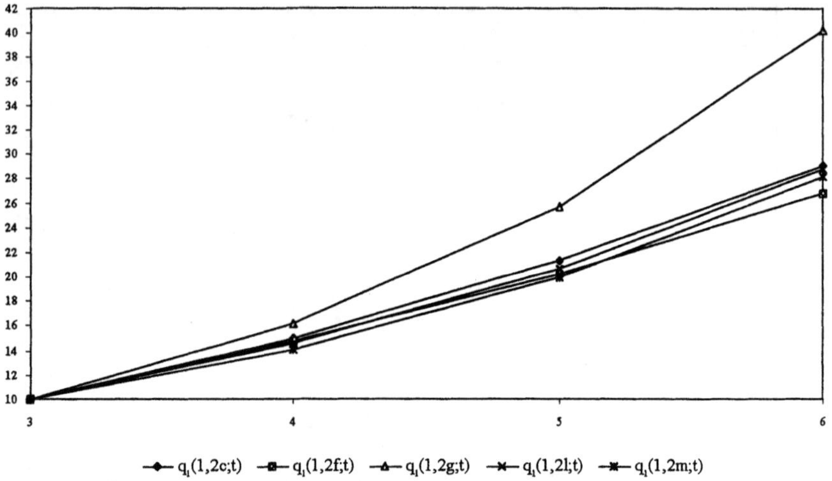

Fig. 7.17 Total production of commodity 1 with different technologies

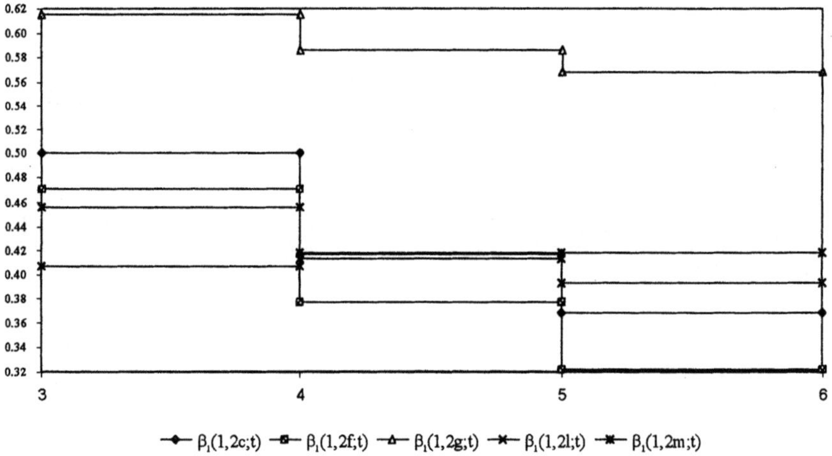

Fig. 7.18 Rates of growth of total production of commodity 1 with different technologies

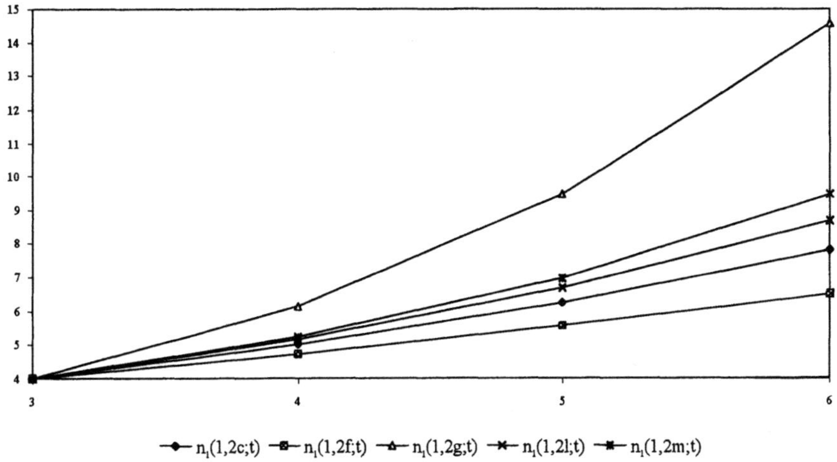

Fig. 7.19 Total net product of commodity 1 with different technologies

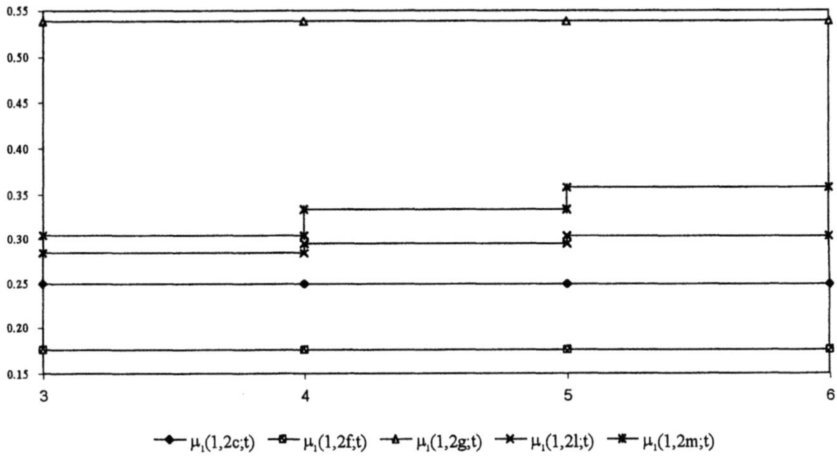

Fig. 7.20 Rates of growth of total net product of commodity 1 with different technologies

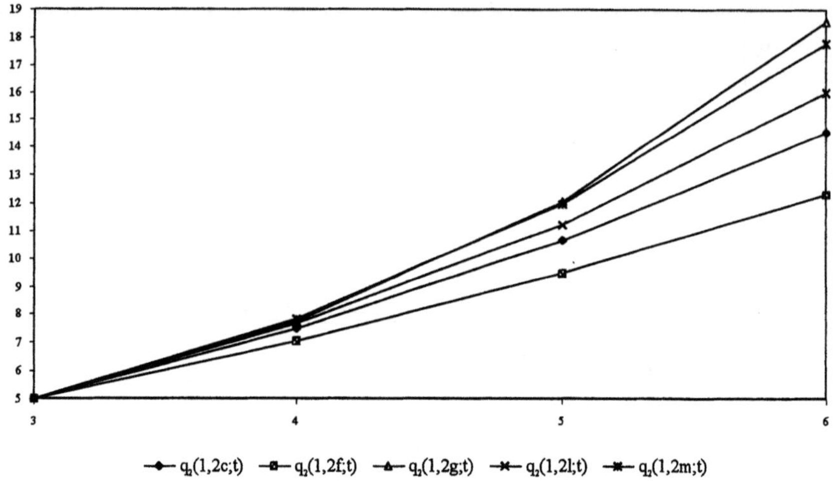

Fig. 7.21 Total production of commodity 2 with different technologies

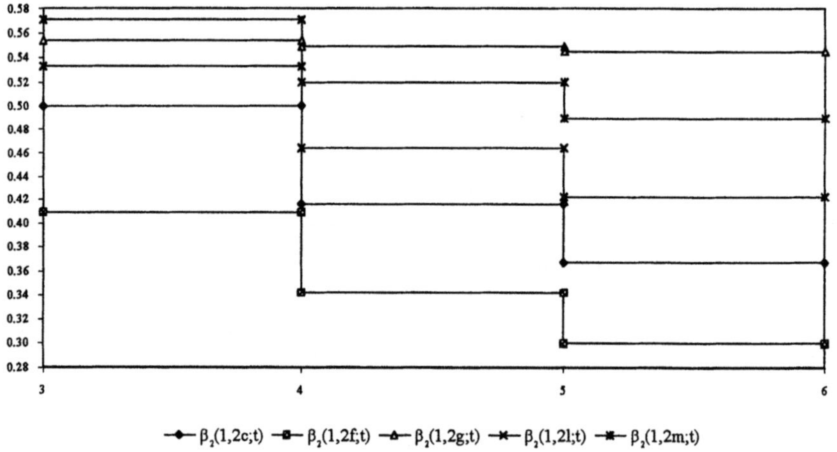

Fig. 7.22 Rates of growth of total production of commodity 2 with different technologies

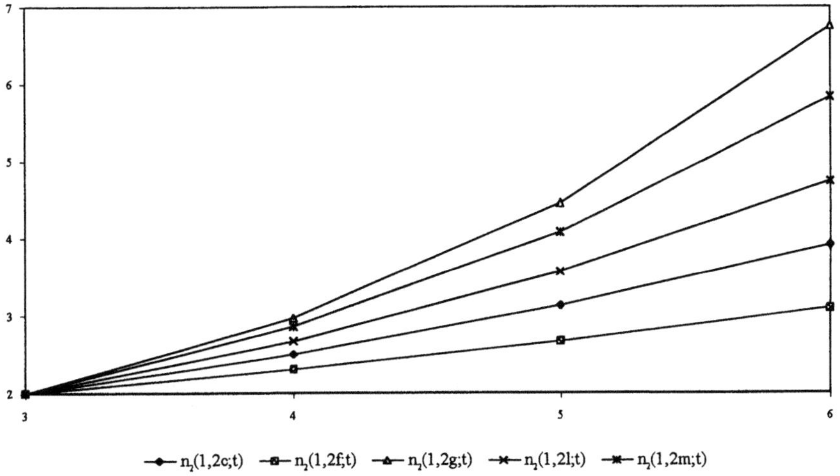

Fig. 7.23 Total net product of commodity 2 with different technologies

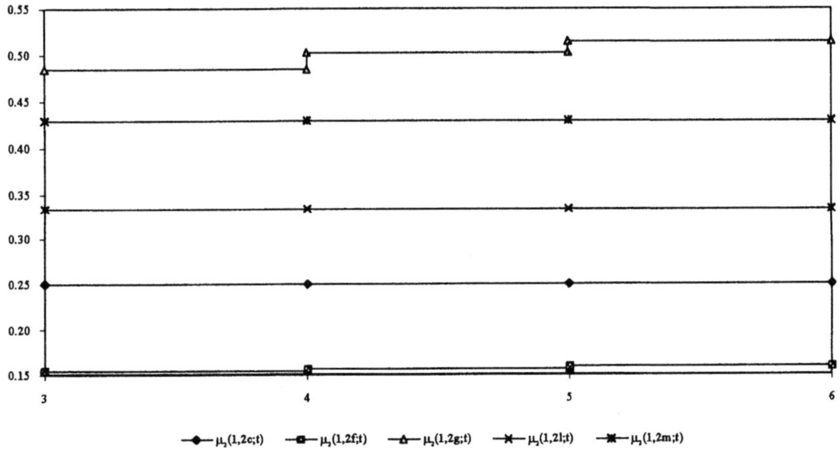

Fig. 7.24 Rates of growth of total net product of commodity 2 with different technologies

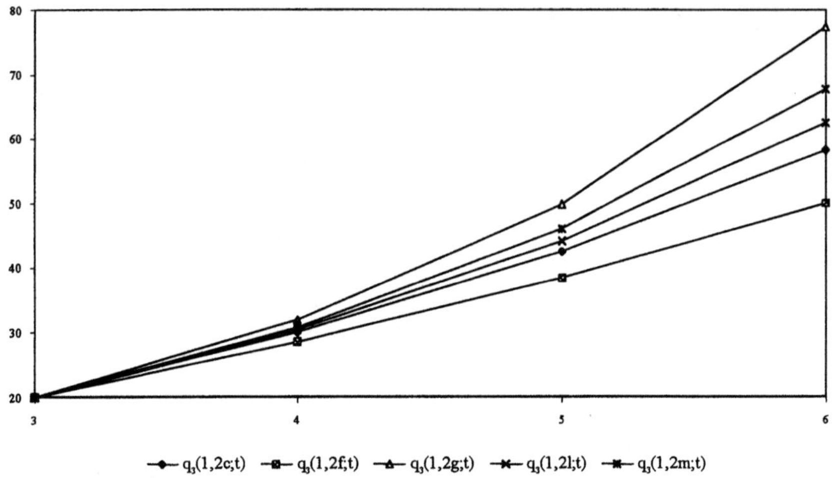

Fig. 7.25 Total production of commodity 3 with different technologies

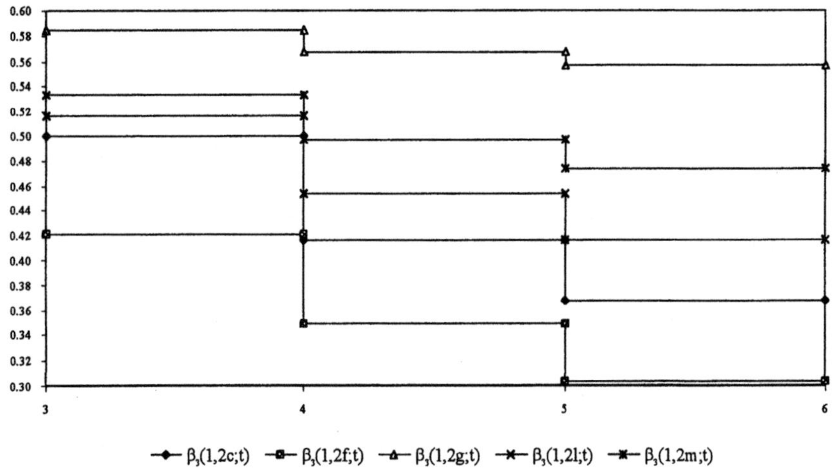

Fig. 7.26 Rates of growth of total production of commodity 3 with different technologies

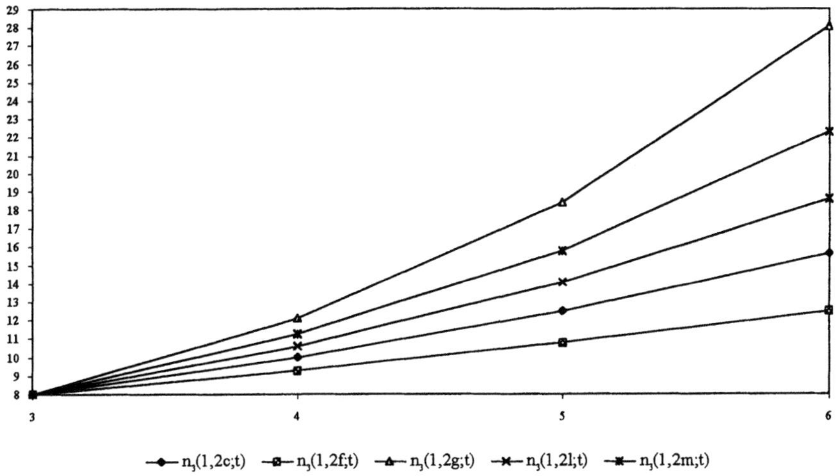

Fig. 7.27 Total net product of commodity 3 with different technologies

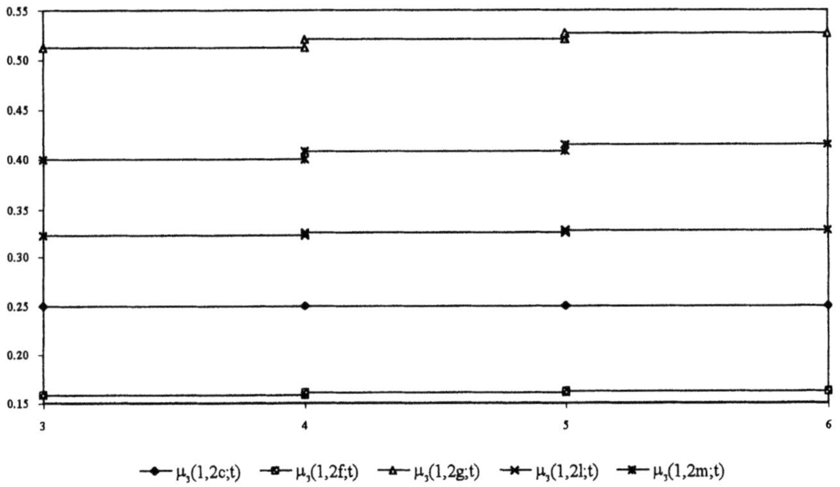

Fig. 7.28 Rates of growth of total net product of commodity 3 with different technologies

(production, net product, growth rates), the commodity considered, and the period of time in which the comparison is carried out.

Let us consider the first period in which a second technique is employed, that is t = 4. If we consider the production variable for the various commodities we get

$$q_1(1,2g;4) > q_1(1,2c;4) > q_1(1,2f;4) > q_1(1,2l;4) > q_1(1,2m;4),$$

$$q_2(1,2m;4) > q_2(1,2g;4) > q_2(1,2l;4) > q_2(1,2c;4) > q_2(1,2f;4),$$

$$q_3(1,2g;4) > q_3(1,2m;4) > q_3(1,2l;4) > q_3(1,2c;4) > q_3(1,2f;4),$$

Instead, in the next period we obtain

$$q_1(1,2g;5) > q_1(1,2c;5) > q_1(1,2l;5) > q_1(1,2f;5) > q_1(1,2m;5),$$

$$q_2(1,2g;4) > q_2(1,2m;4) > q_2(1,2l;4) > q_2(1,2c;4) > q_2(1,2f;4),$$

while, with regards to commodity 3, the order is the same as in the preceding period.

Furthermore, whereas in period 4 the order established by comparing the production of each commodity coincides with the order determined by comparing the growth rates of production for the same commodity, in period 5 this correspondence is lost for commodity 1. We have in particular

$$\beta_1(1,2g;5) > \beta_1(1,2l;5) > \beta_1(1,2c;5) > \beta_1(1,2m;5) > \beta_1(1,2f;5).$$

Similar remarks can be made when considering the net products of the different commodities and their growth rates.

Beyond a certain period of time, however, the order determined on the basis of the internal rates of growth, productions, net products, and of their growth rates become the same. These orders already coincide in period 4 for commodity 3, and in period 5 for commodity 2. Instead, for commodity 1 the coincidence between the order given by the growth rates of productions and that given by the internal rates of growth is reached in period 6; and only in period 7 the order determined on the basis of the productions coincides with that determined on the basis of the internal growth rates.

12. Conclusions

The previous analysis has allowed for the determination of the dynamic OE based on the information contained in the physical system. Firstly, we assumed that the technologies in question were composed of only two techniques with a process of growth in the same time horizon, and, secondly, we concentrated only on specific cases, as follow:

1) the case of two technologies [**A**(1); **A**(2i)] and [**A**(1); **A**(2j)] composed of techniques for which s(2i) = s(2j) and **r**(1,2i;t) ≥ **r**(1,2j;t) analyzed in § 5;

2) the case of two technologies [**A**(1); **A**(2i)] and [**A**(1); **A**(2j)] composed of techniques for which s(2i) = s(2j) and **r**(1,2i;t) ≥ **r**(1,2j;t).] = **o**, analogous to the former case, analyzed in §6;
3) the case of two technologies [**A**(1); **A**(2i)] and [**A**(1); **A**(2j)] composed of techniques for which s(2i) < s(2j) and **r**(1,2i;t) ≥ **r**(1,2j;t), analyzed in § 9;
4) the case of two technologies [**A**(1); **A**(2i)] and [**A**(1); **A**(2j)] composed of techniques for which s(2i) < s(2j) and despite the relation **r**(1,2i;t) ≥ **r**(1,2j;t) is not true (and thus it is true either **r**(1,2i;t) < **r**(1,2j;t) or the vectors of residual associated to the two technologies are not orderable), the inequalities [7.29]-[7.32] all turn out to be satisfied in terms of the upper sign in each period due to the gap between s(2j) and s(2i). This was shown in § 9.

In conclusion, it was possible to determine the order of dynamic efficiency on the basis of the physical system by making particular hypotheses concerning the time horizon and the techniques included in the technology. In particular, we have assumed that these techniques could be compared and ordered according to some criteria. Given the fact that the dynamic efficiency of one specific technology depends on the physical efficiency of its single techniques and on the structural compatibility among them, the problem of the order has to be resolved by jointly considering these two dimensions.

Whether the order of dynamic efficiency in the case of technologies with equal physical efficiency of their techniques can or cannot be determined is a question of structure compatibility among the techniques activated through time. Namely, it is a question if the residuals that dynamically emerge from these techniques can or cannot be ordered. In the case of techniques with different physical efficiency, the order of dynamic-physical efficiency can be determined if the structural compatibility can be compared and if the order established on its basis do not contrast with that of the physical efficiency. However, there exists the chance that the order of dynamic-physical efficiency can be determined also when there is no structural compatibility order or even when the latter order does exist but it is at odds with that obtained on the basis of the physical efficiency. This occurs when the difference of physical efficiency is so great as to downplay the weight of the residuals.

There are other cases, however, that make impossible to order the technologies by only considering the physical system. It is then necessary to generalize our analysis by resolving the problem of the determination of the dynamic efficiency order when these and other complications arise. For example, the uneven availability of NPMP, that is, the case in which the different technologies allow for growth in different periods; the case in which the techniques cannot be ordered on the basis of the previous criteria, i.e., technologies which must be compared do not satisfy the requirements indicated in points 1)-4); and even the case in which more than two NPMP exist.

Chapter VIII – Choice of technologies and dynamic values efficiency order

1. Introduction

In the previous Chapter we established both the potential and the limits of the dynamic physical efficiency order. Even in the simpler case, in which the determination of the order is achieved with the comparison of techniques employing the same NPMP, this OE cannot be resolved when:

a) the technologies have the same uniform rates of net product, but non-orderable residuals (Chapter VII, § 7);
b) the technologies have the same uniform rates of net product, but the commodity that can be entirely accumulated by the two technologies' is different (Chapter VIII, § 8);
c) the technologies have different uniform rates of net product (except for some particular cases discussed in Chapter VII, § 9)

Furthermore, in the previous Chapter the physical dynamic OE among technologies [**A**(1); **A**(2j)] and [**A**(1); **A**(2i)] was determined by assuming $\bar{t}_{2i} = \bar{t}_{2j}$, that is, the NPMP of type 2 gains full employment at the same time for both the two technologies which include **A**(2i) and **A**(2j) respectively.

If we assume the case

$$[8.1] \qquad \bar{t}_1(2j) > \bar{t}_1(2i),$$

it is possible to show that technology [**A**(1); **A**(2j)] (of course, when conditions 1)-4) of Chapter VII, § 12, still hold) has a higher dynamic efficiency, since it allows for a longer period of growth than that allowed by technology with technique **A**(2i).

If we assume the opposite case

$$[8.2] \qquad \bar{t}_1(2j) < \bar{t}_1(2i)$$

the problem of determining the dynamic OE becomes more complex, because technique **A**(2j) allows for faster growth but for a shorter time horizon.

To sum up, if technologies satisfy the requirements of points 1)-4) in Chapter VII, § 12, but the technology which allows for a faster growth can be used for a shorter time horizon than the other available; or conversely if technologies do not satisfy the above requirements, the conclusion we draw is the same. The information derived from the physical system does not allow us to establish an order among the technologies.

The dynamic OE can be determined in these cases only by means of inter-temporal comparisons and by taking into account the price-distribution system. In order to search this new OE, that we shall name "dynamic values OE", it is useful to stress since the beginning the difficulties brought about by the inter-temporal analysis and the price-distribution system.

2. Discount rate and prices

In order to make inter-temporal comparisons among vectors of productions and of net products, thereby identifying the order of technologies, we need to know the level of prices and the inter-temporal rate of discount. Only in this way, we are able to sum heterogeneous physical variables and referred them to a given period of time.

The discount rate may be interpreted either as an interest rate or as an inter-temporal preference rate. Admittedly, this issue could be further developed.

Another problem is the choice of the price vector utilized to compare heterogeneous commodities. To this respect, it is useful to remind (see Chapters III and V) that, within the theoretical framework of compound technologies, we can determine the relative prices for each technique as function of an exogenously given distributive variable —wage or profit— and assuming that this technique is the least efficient among those in activity according to the price-distribution order, that is, assuming null rent for the NPMP employed in it.

For the whole economic system, only one production-price system exists: that associated to the least efficient active technique in the price-distribution order or, in other words, that system which allows all the active NPMP for non-negative rents. These relative prices, among other things, depend also on the value of the exogenously given distributive variable.

When it is impossible to compare technologies in physical terms to define an order, one must pay attention to the values of individual productions and net products, and for each technology assess productions and net products in terms of their prices. We should, however, point out that the results of this comparison of values are highly dependent on the choice of the *numeraire*.

The problem to be faced in determining the dynamic values OE, therefore, is that of finding a proper efficiency proxy for the different technologies, which is independent from the chosen numeraire.

The dynamic values OE can nonetheless change as distribution changes. Indeed, given the interdependence between prices and income distribution, any change in distribution involves some changes in the order established among technologies by comparing the individual values of productions and net products obtained from each technology.

3. The dynamic values OE and the inter-temporal average rate of value added: a simplified case

Determining the dynamic values OE may be a very complex task: therefore we first take into account the problem of the order only in the simplified case of comparisons among techniques that use the same NPMP. Hence, we assume, as we already did in the previous Chapter, that

- only two NPMP exist, and thus the technologies to compare include only two techniques;
- only one technique employing NPMP of type 1 exists;
- it is possible to compare different technologies by taking into account a finite time horizon, denoted by $\bar{t}_2$. This means that any consideration after $\bar{t}_2$ is irrelevant to the determination of the dynamic OE.

If technologies cannot be compared on the basis of the physical variables, we need to follow different strategies to find the order of dynamic efficiency. For example, one may consider for each technology [**A**(1); **A**(2)] the ratio between the present value of that technology's net products and the present value of the means of production employed for obtaining those net products, as follows

$$[8.3] \qquad \frac{\displaystyle\sum_{t=1}^{\bar{t}_2-\bar{t}_1} \frac{\mathbf{p}(2)'\mathbf{n}(1,2;\bar{t}_1+t)}{(1+i)^t}}{\displaystyle\sum_{t=1}^{\bar{t}_2-\bar{t}_1} \frac{\mathbf{p}(2)'\mathbf{m}(1,2;\bar{t}_1+t)}{(1+i)^{t-1}}}.$$

Thanks to the previous hypothesis, the determination of the order among technologies is restricted only to the interval between period $\bar{t}_1$ and $\bar{t}_2$.

In [8.3] **n**(1,2;t) represents the vector of net products of technology [**A**(1); **A**(2)], **m**(1,2;t) the vector of means of production, **p**(2) the vector of existing prices when technology [**A**(1);**A**(2)] is active, and i the inter-temporal discount rate which is assumed to be exogenously given.

Alternatively, if we decide to emphasize the role of residuals, the order of dynamic efficiency should be determined by taking into consideration for each technology [**A**(1); **A**(2)] the ratio between the present value of that technology's net products and the present value of the available means of production that are used to obtain such net products —means of production that, however, may only be partially employed due to the structural incompatibilities among present and future techniques. To put it more precisely

$$[8.4] \qquad \frac{\displaystyle\sum_{t-1}^{\bar{t}_2-\bar{t}_1} \frac{\mathbf{p}(2)'\mathbf{n}(1,2;\bar{t}_1+t)}{(1+i)^t}}{\displaystyle\sum_{t=1}^{\bar{t}_2-\bar{t}_1} \frac{\mathbf{p}(2)'[\mathbf{m}(1,2;\bar{t}_1+t)+\mathbf{r}(1,2;\bar{t}_1+t)]}{(1+i)^{t-1}}} = \frac{\displaystyle\sum_{t=1}^{\bar{t}_2-\bar{t}_1} \frac{\mathbf{p}(2)'\mathbf{n}(1,2;\bar{t}_1+t)}{(1+i)^t}}{\displaystyle\sum_{t=1}^{\bar{t}_2-\bar{t}_1} \frac{\mathbf{p}(2)'\mathbf{q}(1,2;\bar{t}_1+t-1)'}{(1+i)^{t-1}}},$$

where **m**(1,2;t) + **r**(1,2;t) represents the vector of means of production available for technology [**A**(1); **A**(2)] which is so split up: **m**(1,2;t) is the vector of the means actually employed and **r**(1,2;t) is that of residuals. Therefore we have that **m**(1,2;t) + **r**(1,2;t) = **q**(1,2;t-1).

By adopting one of the previous criteria, it is possible to show that [**A**(1); **A**(2i)] has a higher dynamic efficiency than [**A**(1); **A**(2j)] if the value of [8.3] and [8.4] is greater when using the first technology than the second one.

Yet, with these ordering criteria, there is the crucial choice of the inter-temporal discount rate —it is so fundamentally important because different discount rates may change the dynamic OE altogether.

Another possible method for determining the dynamic OE, which has the advantage of eliminating the arbitrary choice of the discount rate, takes into account the average inter-temporal rate of value added (I). This is the rate that, for each technology, equalizes the present value of the available means of production with the present value of the levels of production, by assuming maximum accumulation and growth.

In the simplified case already considered, the inter-temporal average rate of value added in the time interval between $\bar{t}_1$ and $\bar{t}_2$ is defined as follows

$$[8.5] \qquad \sum_{t=1}^{\bar{t}_2-\bar{t}_1} \frac{\mathbf{p}(2)'[\mathbf{m}(1,2;\bar{t}_1+t)+\mathbf{r}(1,2;\bar{t}_1+t)]}{(1+I)^{t-1}} = \sum_{t=1}^{\bar{t}_2-\bar{t}_1} \frac{\mathbf{p}(2)'\mathbf{q}(1,2;\bar{t}_1+t)}{(1+I)^{t}},$$

where **m**(1,2;t) + **r**(1,2;t) = **q**(1,2;t-1) represents the available means of production vector of technology [**A**(1); **A**(2)], **q**(1,2;t) the vector of the productions obtainable with that technology, and **p**(2) the production prices vector of the same technology.

It is possible to show that [**A**(1); **A**(2i)] has a greater dynamic efficiency than [**A**(1); **A**(2j)] if the inter-temporal average rate of value added is greater with the first technology than with the second one.

We define the dynamic values OE that order established among technologies on the basis of the inter-temporal average rate of value added.

4. The determination of the inter-temporal average rate of value added: an example

In order to exemplify the determination of the inter-temporal average rate of value added we refer to technologies [**A**(1); **A**(2a)], [**A**(1); **A**(2b)], [**A**(1); **A**(2c)], [**A**(1); **A**(2d)], [**A**(1); **A**(2e)] previously discussed in Chapter VII.

The first three technologies can be compared on the basis of physical magnitudes. From Chapter VII, § 5 and § 6, it follows that [**A**(1); **A**(2c)] is more efficient than [**A**(1); **A**(2b)] which in turn is more efficient than [**A**(1); **A**(2a)]. However, technologies [**A**(1); **A**(2d)] and [**A**(1); **A**(2e)] cannot be ordered on the basis of their physical variables. Let us therefore take into consideration the inter-temporal average rate of value added for each technology. As we have already seen, the determination of this rate requires that the vector of prices is known and, therefore, requires assuming one distributive variable —wage or the rate of profit— exogenously given. We shall later determine the inter-temporal average rate of value added in the case in which the wage is zero and thus the rate of profit is maximum.

Moreover, we continue to assume that the initial endowment of the means of production is such as to activate technique **A**(1) without any residual. Under this assumption, since s(1) is higher than the correspondent rates of net product of techniques which employ NPMP of type 2 and once we put the wages equal to zero we gain the following result. The general price vector that exists when one technique employing the type 2 NPMP is activated, is precisely that one associated to the newcomer technique.

The techniques **A**(2a), **A**(2b), **A**(2c), **A**(2d) and **A**(2e) differ one from each other for the production process of commodity 1. However, due to the fact that they have the same uniform rate of net product, the vector of production prices of these techniques, at maximum growth rate, is always the following

[8.6] $$\mathbf{p} = \left[1, \frac{10}{17}, \frac{4}{17}\right].$$

By taking this vector into account we can determine the inter-temporal average rate of value added for each of the previous technologies.

We continue to refer only to the time interval between $\bar{t}_1$ and $\bar{t}_2$, where $\bar{t}_1$ denotes the period during which the full utilization of NPMP of type 1 is reached, and $\bar{t}_2$ —which in the given example is equal to $\bar{t}_1 + 3$— denotes the period during which the full utilization of NPMP of type 2 occurs. In order to keep the analysis manageable, we have assumed that this period is the same for each technique employing NPMP of type 2.

Table 8.1 makes use of relation [8.5] and the price vector [8.6] and determines the inter-temporal average rates of value added of technologies [**A**(1); **A**(2a)], [**A**(1); **A**(2b)], [**A**(1); **A**(2c)], [**A**(1); **A**(2d)], [**A**(1); **A**(2e)].

Among the technologies taken into account for the case of maximum growth rate, we can establish the following order:

[**A**(1); **A**(2c)], [**A**(1); **A**(2b)], [**A**(1); **A**(2e)], [**A**(1); **A**(2a)], [**A**(1); **A**(2d)].

The example suggests that the order established on the basis of the inter-temporal average rate of value added —that we called dynamic values efficiency order— is compatible with the physical dynamic efficiency order, in all the cases the latter can be determined. Technology [**A**(1); **A**(2c)] precedes the other technologies because its techniques are characterized by the same uniform rates of the other technologies, but it can entirely accumulate the available net products.

Technology [**A**(1); **A**(2b)] precedes [**A**(1); **A**(2a)], because it includes techniques with the same net product rates, but it generates less residuals.

The determination of the inter-temporal average rate of value added allows us also to order technologies [**A**(1); **A**(2d)] and [**A**(1); **A**(2e)], which cannot be compared one to each other, and cannot be compared neither with [**A**(1); **A**(2a)] and [**A**(1); **A**(2b)] on the basis of physical magnitudes.

Table 8.1 Determination of the inter-temporal average rate of value added (I)

Technology	t	**m**(1,2h)+**r**(1,2h)	**q**(1,2h)	**p**(2h)	**p** (2h)'[**m**(1,2h)+**r**(1,2h)]	**p** (2h)'**q**(1,2h)	I
[**A**(1);**A**(2a)]	4	10	12.5	1	10.00	12.50	
		5	7.5	0.59	2.94	4.41	
		20	22.5	0.24	4.71	5.29	
					17.65	22.21	
	5	12.5	15.63	1	12.50	15.63	
		7.5	10.63	0.59	4.41	6.25	
		22.5	25.63	0.24	5.29	6.03	
					22.21	27.90	
	6	15.63	19.53	1	15.63	19.53	
		10.63	14.53	0.59	6.25	8.55	
		25.63	29.53	0.24	6.03	6.95	
					27.90	35.03	0.2567

[**A**(1);**A**(2b)]	4	10	13.13	1	10	13.13	
		5	7.50	0.59	2.94	4.41	
		20	24.38	0.24	4.71	5.74	
					17.65	23.27	
	5	13.13	17.03	1	13.13	17.03	
		7.50	10.63	0.59	4.41	6.25	
		24.38	29.84	0.24	5.74	7.02	
					23.27	30.30	
	6	17.03	21.91	1	17.03	21.91	
		10.63	14.53	0.59	6.25	8.55	
		29.84	36.68	0.24	7.02	8.63	
					30.30	39.09	0.3036

Table 8.1 (continued)

Technology	t	**m**(1,2h)+**r**(1,2h)	**q**(1,2h)	**p**(2h)	**p** (2h) [**m**(1,2h)+**r**(1,2h)]	**p** (2h) **q**(1,2h)	**I**
[**A**(1);**A**(2c)]	4	10	15	1	10	15	
		5	7.5	0.59	2.94	4.41	
		20	30	0.24	4.71	7.06	
					17.65	26.47	
	5	15	21.25	1	15	21.25	
		7.5	10.63	0.59	4.41	6.25	
		30	42.50	0.24	7.06	10	
					26.47	37.50	
	6	21.25	29.06	1	21.25	29.06	
		10.63	14.53	0.59	6.25	8.55	
		42.50	58.13	0.24	10	13.68	
					37.50	51.29	0.4271

[**A**(1);**A**(2d)]	4	10	11.25	1	10	11.25	
		5	7.50	0.59	2.94	4.41	
		20	23.75	0.24	4.71	5.59	
					17.65	21.25	
	5	11.25	12.81	1	11.25	12.81	
		7.50	10.63	0.59	4.41	6.25	
		23.75	28.44	0.24	5.59	6.69	
					21.25	25.75	
	6	12.81	14.77	1	12.81	14.77	
		10.63	14.53	0.59	6.25	8.55	
		28.44	34.30	0.24	6.69	8.07	
					25.75	31.38	0.2116

Table 8.1 (continued)

Technology	t	**m**(1,2h)+**r**(1,2h)	**q**(1,2h)	**p**(2h)	**p** (2h)'[**m**(1,2h)+**r**(1,2h)]	**p**(2h)'**q**(1,2h)	I
[**A**(1);**A**(2e)]	4	10	12	1	10	12	
		5	7	0.59	2.94	4.12	
		20	30	0.24	4.71	7.06	
					17.65	23.18	
	5	12	14.5	1	12	14.5	
		7	9.5	0.59	4.12	5.59	
		30	42.5	0.24	7.06	10	
					23.18	30.09	
	6	14.5	17.63	1	14.50	17.63	
		9.5	12.63	0.59	5.59	7.43	
		42.5	58.13	0.24	10	13.68	
					30.09	38.73	0.2995

In concluding this example, it is useful to emphasize the complexity of the dynamic values efficiency order. Indeed, the determination of the inter-temporal average rate of value added has been carried out by taking into account particular cases. In the previous example, we assumed that only two NPMP and only one technique employing NPMP of type 1 existed. Hence, the technologies differ only in terms of those techniques employing NPMP of type 2.

In the following section, we remove the limit of carrying out comparisons only among technologies employing the same NPMP. However, the simplification of an equal time horizon, during which the steady state is reached among all technologies, is much more difficult to remove. This simplification has allowed us to determine the order by taking into consideration productions of different technologies in a finite interval. However, given that technologies can utilize different NPMP, which in turn can have different coefficients of utilization, the technologies may reach the steady state at different times.

Yet, a common time horizon is necessary if we want to make the comparison among the growth paths meaningful. Following this consideration, it should be also maintained that the periods outside the time horizon are irrelevant for the determination of the dynamic efficiency order.

5. The impossibility of having a technology of type [A(1); A(2j); A(2i)]

According to the previous analysis, if technologies are activated following the dynamic OE, we can never find a technology of type [**A**(1); **A**(2j); **A**(2i)]. In fact, technique **A**(2j) would be preferred to **A**(2i), only if that preference is maintained throughout the period in which **A**(2j) is activated, that is, up to time $\bar{t}_{2j}$.However, at time $\bar{t}_{2j}$ the production of $\bar{q}_1(2j)$ involves the full utilization of NPMP of type 2, and therefore such a NPMP is no longer available and cannot be utilized to activate **A**(2i).

Moreover, we indirectly exclude the possibility of having **A**(2i) and **A**(2j) simultaneously active in a single technology by splitting between them NPMP of type 2. If from an analytical point of view, a combination of **A**(2i) and **A**(2j) (or even of more **A**(2) techniques) is conceivable and could reduce the residuals with an increase of growth, from a substantial point of view, this assumption implies the flexibility of the technical coefficients. In other words, this would force the second technique's coefficients to change up to the point at which residuals are eliminated. In our opinion, reality suggests that technical coefficients should be kept quite rigid rather than allow them to be completely flexible.

6. The dynamic OE among technologies composed of techniques with the same and different NPMP

In the first Chapters of this volume we assumed that there was only one technique for each NPMP and we dealt with the problem of OE as if it were equivalent to that of ordering the activation of the various NPMP. In Chapter VII we also studied the choice among techniques that used the same NPMP —an analysis complicated, as we have seen, by the presence of residuals. We now generalize our analysis by considering the problem of the choice among technologies that include techniques of both types, that is, techniques with either equal or different NPMP.

Determining the dynamic OE is quite complex in this general framework. In particular we notice that

1) among techniques **A**(3) (and in general among techniques **A**(h), for h = 4,...,k) the ordering problems could be the same of those depicted for **A**(2);
2) the techniques that use NPMP of type 2 do not only need to be compared with those using NPMP of type 3, but also with all the techniques employing NPMP of type h, for h = 4,...,h. Similar argument holds for those techniques that use NPMP of type 3 and in general for techniques **A**(h).

We must, therefore, identify an OE of technologies for the general case, that is, referred to all non-produced means of production and all the available techniques.

If we assume to have k types of NPMP, by means of permutations of the k techniques it is possible to identify k! technologies which include all the k techniques in their different orders. If we then assume that for each NPMP there are n techniques alternatively utilizable, it follows that the available technologies become $n^k k!$ which brings quickly to very high numbers.

To give an idea, if k = 10 and n = 2 that is to say if the available NPMP were 10 and for each one of them two techniques were available, there would be 3,715,891,200 technologies.

If we assume, as we have done until now, that for each NPMP there is only one technique, the technologies that can be built-up would nonetheless be 3,628,800. And among them an OE should be established.

In ordering techniques with different NPMP, there is the chance of finding similar situations of those considered in ordering the techniques **A**(2i) and **A**(2j). The criteria previously analyzed are therefore useful even though they necessitate further extensions.

In some particular cases (similar to those considered in Chapter VII) the efficiency order among techniques concerning different NPMP can be established on the basis of the physical system. In the majority of cases, however, the efficiency order can only be determined by comparing the values of productions and net products from each technology. To avoid that the choice of the *numeraire* affects the final order, we shall again order technologies according to the inter-temporal average rate of value added which, however, is very complex to derive.

In the previous Chapters, the assumptions we made limited the comparison among technologies and the analysis of prices within the interval between $\bar{t}_1$

and $\bar{t}_2$. The assumptions that there exists only one technique which uses NPMP of type 1 and that the initial means of production are such as to activate this technique in those proportions that guarantee uniform rate of growth and no residuals bring us to the conclusion that what happens before $\bar{t}_1$ is irrelevant for the determination the dynamic OE. The available technologies do not differ in that period because they have in activity the same technique.

Moreover, the assumption that the techniques employing NPMP of type 2 reach their full utilization at the same time, and that only two NPMP exist brings us to the conclusion that in the period after $\bar{t}_2$ no further technique can be activated.

Admittedly, in a more general analysis all these hypotheses should be removed. Yet, this elimination would render the determination of the dynamic OE so complex that in this section we are only able to tackle some possible extensions.

If different techniques exist that can use NPMP of type 1, then the period before $\bar{t}_1$ becomes important. In particular, it is necessary to determine the existing price system to correctly assess net products and productions. In this case the proportions among the initial endowments of means of production also matter.

If more then two NPMP exist, it is no longer possible to limit the comparison to the period in which the full employment of NPMP of type 2 is reached, even by means of the technology with the smaller coefficients $\tau_1(h)$. In this case, it is necessary to determine a meaningful horizon for comparing the different technologies, and furthermore we should also know the changes that affect the price systems of each technology when further NPMP of different qualities are employed.

7. Conclusions

We conclude that the efficiency order among technologies is conceptually different from that among techniques. This is because only by following the order of technologies we can deal with the problems of the interconnection among techniques and residuals. The analysis has allowed us to establish two dynamic OE: the dynamic physical OE and the dynamic values OE. The first can only be established on the basis of the information contained in the physical system, and thus it is much more meaningful, because it does not depend on prices and income distribution. However, the physical dynamic OE can only be determined with particular technologies —those that include techniques that are comparable and orderable on the basis of their physical efficiency and structural compatibility.

If the physical dynamic OE cannot be determined, technologies can still be ordered by taking into consideration the dynamic values OE.

Two problems arise, however, from the previous discussion. The first concerns the complexity of the dynamic OE, in particular for the high number of technologies that should be compared —a direct result of the presence of many NPMP alternatively employable by many techniques.

The problem can be handled with the introduction of further additional hypotheses that scale down the number of technologies to be compared in determining the efficiency order.

The second problem concerns the kind of relation between dynamic physical and dynamic values OE on the one hand and dynamic price-distribution OE on the other. The first gives the maximum growth of the economic system and the second is the ordered followed by the profit-maker operator. So far the analysis has been carried out by assuming maximum accumulation of the available net product, that is we made the choice that offered maximum growth. It is thus useful at this point to analyze also the behavior of the profit earners who choose the technologies and determines the accumulation dynamics with the narrower aim of maximizing profits.

Before studying this relation, however, it is necessary to define the dynamic price-distribution OE. This is the aim of the next Chapter.

Chapter IX - Choice of technologies and dynamic price-distribution order of efficiency

1. Introduction

In this Chapter we will analyze the criteria according to which technologies are chosen by the profit earners, that is, by that economic operator who selects technologies and drives accumulation. We shall refer to this category therefore indifferently as profit-maker, technology-maker, or accumulation-maker operator. It is commonly assumed that this operator aims at profit maximization, which, in turn, is a matter also dependent on the dynamics of accumulation.

The first problem we deal with is the determination of the dynamic price-distribution order of efficiency, that is, the order that should be followed in activating techniques in such a way as to maximize profits.

In Chapter III we determined the static price-distribution order of efficiency. In other words, we have ordered the techniques on the basis of the decreasing values of the rate of profit, once we fixed an exogenous unit wage (or vice versa). Now we should assess if this criterion, which allows us to order techniques, is also useful for ordering technologies. In particular we should inquiry if this order ranks techniques in such a sequence as to allow the profit-makers to maximize profits.

The analysis of the two previous Chapters tells us that the order of techniques according to their physical efficiency is not sufficient to resolve the problem of the order of technologies formed by these techniques. In fact, there is the problem of residuals and that of dynamic compatibility.

Therefore we proceed cautiously. Firstly, we want to verify if the static price-distribution order coincides with the dynamic price-distribution order of efficiency, that is, if this type of ordering also shows problems of mismatch between the order of efficiency established among techniques, and the order established among technologies composed by the above techniques.

The conclusion we reach is that the dynamic price-distribution order of efficiency that should be considered for the choice of technology may not coincide with the static order of efficiency.

The second problem we want to deal with in this Chapter concerns the dynamic accumulation. So far we have developed a dynamic model with the assumption of maximum growth, and therefore we indirectly assumed that such a growth was supported by the process of accumulation. However, there are at least three "market" problems that the profit-maker operator must resolve before starting the accumulation.

First, the operators who drive accumulation —i.e. the profit-maker operators— base their decisions also on the dynamic expectation of profits. One of their characteristics is that of reacting to each profit reduction by searching different solutions in the attempt to regain back the same or higher level of profits.

Second, the financial resources required for the accumulation process may be supplied by other categories of income. In some cases this becomes a necessary condition if the maximum growth is the final target. The result is that other operators will assess the accumulation process from the standpoint of their expectations of income distribution.

Hence, the wage earners, or the labor operator, are interested in the unit wage and employment, variables that may well come into conflict with each other.

Finally, there is the particular problem of rent earners, which we call also resource operators. They make decisions concerning scarce resources, and it is equally plausible that their behavior is dependent from the income these resources are able to generate.

Such remarks do not intend to reformulate our framework in terms of maximizing behavior of these social operators. Our aim is only that of analyzing the consequences of their choices (this Chapter), as well the effects that different accumulation paths generate on their income (next Chapter).

It is clear that in reality the principle of maximization affects the behavior of all operators. Without investigating this principle further —a topic outside the aims of this book— we focus our attention on its consequences for the price-distribution ordering. This attention rises from the fact that there exists a connection between the objective of profit maximization and the dynamics of accumulation. More precisely, we shall deal with the dynamic price-distribution order by referring to only two cases:

i) the case of maximum growth, as considered up till now, that is, the case in which profits, wages and rents are accumulated as much as possible;
ii) the case in which only part of profits is accumulated.

Obviously these are particular cases, but as we have already asserted, the main aim of this analysis is that of determining the dynamic price-distribution order of efficiency and not that of investigating the specific behavior held by operators during the accumulation process.

2. The dynamic price-distribution OE

In Chapter III we saw that the static price-distribution order of efficiency depends on the sequence levels followed by one distributive variable when the other is exogenously chosen. Within this ordering, the techniques are activated according to the decreasing sequence of the rates of profit given the exogenous level of the unit wage (or vice versa). We must now inquiry whether this criterion can also be used for ordering technologies.

To set the stage, let us refer back to some features of the price-distribution system. We have already seen in the previous Chapters that it is possible to determine a price-distribution system for any single technique. The economic system as a whole is associated to the price-distribution system of the least efficient technique in activity, as determined by the price-distribution order. If this was not so, several techniques would have negative rents.

Each time an additional technique is activated, the dimension of technology changes and the price-distribution system associated with the technology can change as well, since the one taken into consideration is always connected to the least efficient technique in activity.

Changes in the price-distribution system take place if the newly activated technique happens to be the least efficient in the price-distribution order. Following this order also the endogenous distributive variable decreases for the whole economic system.

Let us turn the attention now to the profit-maker operator that has to choose the more advantageous sequence in activating the techniques and selecting the technologies.

In a static setting the choice among techniques ends up with that technique which offers the greater rate of profit at the given unit wage. However, the analysis carried out in Chapter VII and VIII has already shown that choosing among techniques and choosing among technologies could be two different matters. This is because of the problems concerning the dynamic compatibility. Activating in sequence techniques during the process of accumulation makes possible the formation of residuals which affect the system's potential of growth, and hence its capacity to produce value added and profits —the higher the residuals, the lower the value added and profits gained over time. Moreover, there are other problems linked to the time horizon of growth of each technology.

To sum up, the choice of a technique which, for a given unit wage, maximizes the rate of profit, does not necessarily guarantee the maximization of total profits from the technology that includes this technique.

3. The dynamic price-distribution OE among techniques with the same NPMP

To clarify what was previously said, and given the impossibility of having a formal solution, we shall propose some cases with the use of numerical simulations.

We assume that, given a certain unit wage, at the beginning a technique, called **A**(1), is activated which guarantees the higher rate of profit and the right proportions for having maximum growth. Since there is scarce availability of NPMP of type 1, after a certain production level it becomes necessary to activate another technique.

Let us assume that there are two techniques, **A**(2c) and **A**(2n), which use the same NPMP of type 2. The available technologies are therefore either [**A**(1); **A**(2c)] or [**A**(1); **A**(2n)]. The matrices of the technical coefficients of these technologies are shown in Appendix A.

Therefore, we should decide whether to activate technique **A**(2c) or technique **A**(2n), and the decision is made on the following ground. First, a comparison between the two technique shows that s(2n) = 21/79 = 0.2658 > s(2c) = 0.25. From the viewpoint of the internal growth rate, **A**(2n) is therefore preferable to **A**(2c). By choosing commodity 1 as *numeraire*, we shall now compare the profit-wage frontier of technique **A**(2n) and **A**(2c) which are respectively

$$[9.1] \qquad w[\mathbf{A}(2n)] = -0.4\{869[\pi(\mathbf{A}(2n))]^3 - 5998[\pi(\mathbf{A}(2n))]^2 + $$
$$+ 34397[\pi(\mathbf{A}(2n))] - 8736\}$$
$$\{2761[\pi(\mathbf{A}(2n))]^2 + 6662[\pi(\mathbf{A}(2n))] + 2391\}^{-1};$$

$$[9.2] \qquad w[\mathbf{A}(2c)] = 0.8\{\pi(\mathbf{A}(2n)) - 4\}\{4[\pi(\mathbf{A}(2n))]^2 +$$
$$- 77[\pi(\mathbf{A}(2n))] + 9\} \{59[\pi(\mathbf{A}(2n))]^2 - 82[\pi(\mathbf{A}(2n))] - 541\}^{-1}.$$

The representation of [9.1] and [9.2] in Figure 9.1 shows that the profit-wage frontier of technique **A**(2n) dominates that of technique **A**(2c) for all the possible values of the distributive variables.

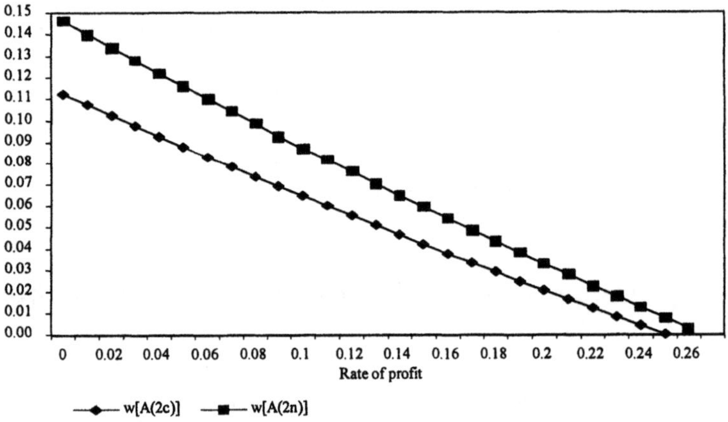

Fig. 9.1 Comparison between profit-wage frontiers

Hence, in the ranking list technique **A**(2n) precedes technique **A**(2c), both for its internal growth rate and the price-distribution order. Having to choose between the two techniques, obviously, **A**(2n) is preferred.

However, we have already said that within a dynamic context, given that the choice is not among techniques but rather among technologies, the profit-makers address their attention to the total profits and not to the rate of profit available from activating a single technique. Indeed, total profits are connected to the choice of technology and are strictly dependent also on the structural compatibility between techniques that are activated through time.

Table 9.1 Comparison among the physical magnitudes of technologies [**A**(1);**A**(2c)] and [**A**(1);**A**(2n)]

t	**q**(1)	**n**(1)	**m**(1)	**q**(1,2h)	**n**(1,2h)	**m**(1,2h)	**r**(1,2h)
1	3.6	1.44	2.16				
[**A**(1)]	1.8	0.72	1.08				
	7.2	2.88	4.32				
2							
[**A**(1)]	6	2.4	3.6				
	3	1.2	1.8				
	12	4.8	7.2				
3							
[**A**(1)]	10	4	6				
	5	2	3				
	20	8	12				
4							
[**A**(1);**A**(2c)]	10	4	6	15	5	10	0
	5	2	3	7.5	2.5	5	0
	20	8	12	30	10	20	0
4	10	4	6	11.95	4.41	7.54	2.46
[**A**(1);**A**(2n)]	5	2	3	7.53	2.53	5	0
	20	8	12	21.95	8.41	13.54	6.46
5	10	4	6	21.25	6.25	15	0
[**A**(1);**A**(2c)]	5	2	3	10.63	3.13	7.5	0
	20	8	12	42.50	12.50	30	0
5	10	4	6	14.41	4.93	9.49	2.46
[**A**(1);**A**(2n)]	5	2	3	10.74	3.20	7.53	0
	20	8	12	24.41	8.93	15.49	6.46
6	10	4	6	29.06	7.81	21.25	0
[**A**(1);**A**(2c)]	5	2	3	14.53	3.91	10.63	0
	20	8	12	58.13	15.63	42.5	0
6	10	4	6	17.53	5.58	11.95	2.46
[**A**(1);**A**(2n)]	5	2	3	14.79	4.06	10.74	0
	20	8	12	27.53	9.58	17.95	6.46

Table 9.2 Prices, value added and total profits of technologies [**A**(1);**A**(2c)] and [**A**(1);**A**(2n)] at t_4

	w	π(1,2h)	**p**(1,2h)	**n**(1,2h)	[**p**(1,2h)'**n**(1,2h)]	**m**(1,2h)	[**p**(1,2h)'**m**(1,2h)]	[π**p**(1,2)'**m**(1,2h)]	π**p**(1,2h)'**m**(1,2h) / **p**(1,2h)'**n**(1,2h)
4	0	0.25	1	5	5	10	10	2.50	
[**A**(1);**A**(2c)]			0.588	2.5	1.47	5	2.94	0.74	
			0.235	10	2.35	20	4.71	1.18	
					8.82			4.41	0.5
4	0	0.27	1	4.41	4.41	7.54	7.54	2.00	
[**A**(1);**A**(2n)]			0.605	2.53	1.53	5	3.03	0.80	
			0.241	8.41	2.03	13.54	3.27	0.87	
					7.97			3.68	0.461
4	0	0.25	1.7	5	8.5	10	17	4.25	
[**A**(1);**A**(2c)]			1	2.5	2.50	5	5	1.25	
			0.4	10	4.00	20	8	2.00	
					15.00			7.50	0.5
4	0	0.27	1.653	4.41	7.29	7.54	12.46	3.31	
[**A**(1);**A**(2n)]			1	2.53	2.53	5	5.00	1.33	
			0.399	8.41	3.35	13.54	5.40	1.43	
					13.17			6.08	0.461

Table 9.2 (continued)

4	0	0.25	4.25	5	21.25	10	42.5	10.63	
[**A**(1);**A**(2c)]			2.5	2.5	6.25	5	12.5	3.13	
			1	10	10.00	20	20	5.00	
					37.50			18.75	0.5
4	0	0.27	4.146	4.41	18.28	7.54	31.25	8.31	
[**A**(1);**A**(2n)]			2.508	2.53	6.35	5	12.54	3.33	
			1	8.41	8.41	13.54	13.54	3.60	
					33.04			15.24	0.461
4	0.02	0.2014	1	5	5	10	10	2.01	
[**A**(1);**A**(2c)]			0.596	2.5	1.49	5	2.98	0.60	
			0.251	10	2.51	20	5.03	1.01	
					9.00			3.63	0.402
4	0.02	0.2254	1	4.41	4.41	7.54	7.54	1.70	
[**A**(1);**A**(2n)]			0.621	2.53	1.57	5	3.10	0.70	
			0.260	8.41	2.19	13.54	3.52	0.79	
					8.17			3.19	0.391

Table 9.2 (continued)

	w	$\pi(1,2h)$	$\mathbf{p}(1,2h)$	$\mathbf{n}(1,2h)$	$[\mathbf{p}(1,2h)'\mathbf{n}(1,2h)]$	$\mathbf{m}(1,2h)$	$[\mathbf{p}(1,2h)'\mathbf{m}(1,2h)]$	$[\pi\mathbf{p}(1,2)'\mathbf{m}(1,2h)]$	$\frac{\pi\mathbf{p}(1,2h)'\mathbf{m}(1,2h)}{\mathbf{p}(1,2h)'\mathbf{n}(1,2h)}$
4	0.02	0.2014	1.678	5	8.39	10	16.78	3.38	
[**A**(1);**A**(2c)]			1	2.5	2.50	5	5	1.01	
			0.422	10	4.22	20	8.44	1.70	
					15.11			6.09	0.402
4	0.02	0.2254	1.610	4.41	7.10	7.54	12.14	2.74	
[**A**(1);**A**(2n)]			1	2.53	2.53	5	5	1.13	
			0.419	8.41	3.53	13.54	5.68	1.28	
					13.16			5.14	0.391
4	0.02	0.2014	3.977	5	19.88	10	39.77	8.01	
[**A**(1);**A**(2c)]			2.370	2.5	5.92	5	11.85	2.39	
			1	10	10.00	20	20	4.03	
					35.81			14.42	0.402
4	0.02	0.2254	3.841	4.41	16.93	7.54	28.96	6.53	
[**A**(1);**A**(2n)]			2.385	2.53	6.04	5	11.93	2.69	
			1	8.41	8.41	13.54	13.54	3.05	
					31.38			12.27	0.391

To prove this statement we assume that the technique employing NPMP of the type 2 is active in those proportions which guarantee maximum growth. Moreover, we also assume that technology [**A**(1); **A**(2c)] allows for the total accumulation of the net product of **A**(1) which can no longer be internally accumulated by this technique. This is perfectly plausible in our example because the means of production required by technique **A**(2c) to achieve the maximum growth are in the same proportions of the net products obtained with technique **A**(1). On the contrary, the activation of technique **A**(2n) implies the formation of large residuals due to the fact that the proportions of the means of production required by technique **A**(2n) for its maximum growth are quite different from the proportions of net products of technique **A**(1) that can no longer be internally accumulated by it. The situation is shown in Table 9.1, where under the assumption of maximum accumulation and growth one can follow the dynamics of both productions and net products respectively with technologies [**A**(1); **A**(2c)] and [**A**(1); **A**(2n)].

If the choice between [**A**(1); **A**(2c)] and [**A**(1); **A**(2n)] were to be based upon the "unit" levels of the distributive variables, the choice should advantage [**A**(1); **A**(2n)], whose profit-wage frontier dominates that of [**A**(1); **A**(2c)].

Instead, when taking into account the compatibility among techniques, that is the dynamic technological problems with their implications on total profits, the choice of technology [**A**(1); **A**(2n)] might not be optimal.

To clarify this statement, let us consider the dynamic price-distribution order of efficiency when the profit-maker operators view only period t_4, or, in other words, only the first period in which it is necessary to activate a new technique. The hypothesis of taking into account only one period, apart from its explanatory power in our example, may be explained by the high uncertainty that would surround the outcome if the choices of the operators were made in a multi-period context.

Table 9.2 shows the prices of technologies [**A**(1); **A**(2c)] and [**A**(1); **A**(2n)] by making different hypotheses concerning the value of the distributive exogenous variable, and by considering, alternatively, one of the three commodities as numeraire. Firstly, we assume $w = 0$ and therefore the maximum profit rate, then $w = 0.02$ and therefore respectively π[**A**(1); **A**(2c)] = 20.14% and π [**A**(1); **A**(2n)] = 22.54%.

In Table 9.2 we have determined the value added and the total profits that can be obtained by the activation of one of the two technologies using the relative prices implied by its adoption. This table shows that the value added of technology [**A**(1); **A**(2c)] is higher than that of technology [**A**(1); **A**(2n)] no matter which commodity is chosen as numeraire. The same may be argued for total profit, and the profit share on value added. All prior remarks bring us to the conclusion that it is more convenient for the profit-maker operators to choose technology [**A**(1); **A**(2c)] in spite of the fact that, for each possible wage level, the rate of profit results higher with the other technology [**A**(1); **A**(2n)].

In the last example, technology [**A**(1); **A**(2c)] is preferred to [**A**(1); **A**(2n)] no matter which numeraire is chosen. In other cases, the ordering might depend on the adopted numeraire, and change with it. Therefore, to determine the dynamic price-distribution order of efficiency, we need to make several hypotheses concerning the profit-makers' behavior. In particular, one should establish which good or bundle of goods is utilized by these operators to determine the purchasing power of their profits, and the time horizon they are considering.

4. The static and dynamic price-distribution OE

In the last Section we presented a particular case and concluded that the profit-maker operators follow an efficiency order among techniques that may not be uniquely determined by the rate of profit, given the unit wage. This analysis, therefore, shows the limited scope of the static price-distribution order in casting light on dynamic phenomena with compound technologies. In fact, the dynamic OE concerns technologies, whereas the static price-distribution OE concerns techniques. It is true that, by choosing techniques indirectly we form preferences upon technologies, but at the level of technology there is an element that is not present at the level of technique: the residuals.

Despite the fact that the static price-distribution OE does not necessarily coincide with the dynamic price-distribution OE, the static price-distribution relation continues to be important in order to assess the trade-off between rate of profit, unit wage, and rent. Moreover such a relation is still essential for the determination of both the dynamic values OE and the dynamic price-distribution OE.

5. Endowment of NPMP, growth time-horizon and consequences on the price-distribution OE

As we return to the previous numerical analysis it should be clear that it refers to an extreme case, given that the difference in terms of physical efficiency between techniques **A**(2c) and **A**(2n) is almost irrelevant. On the contrary, their structural diversity strongly affects the potential accumulation of the net product. Moreover, the analysis of the previous Chapters shows that the longer is the period for which a certain type of NPMP is available for accumulation, the higher is the weight of the physical efficiency, and the lesser is that of the residuals. Having assumed that the operators take into account only the first period in which it is necessary to activate a new technique, we have further reduced the impact that could exercise the higher physical efficiency and widened the role of residuals. We may ask now what will be the behavior of the profit-makers, if we relax the assumption that the choice is limited only to period t_4.

Table 9.3 shows the evolution of value added obtainable by activating technologies [**A**(1); **A**(2c)] and [**A**(1); **A**(2n)], the evolution of profits and their rate of growth. In particular, the values are determined by assuming null wages, and maximum accumulation of net products. Technology [**A**(1); **A**(2c)] allows for total accumulation, while technology [**A**(1); **A**(2n)] produces some residuals

Table 9.3 Prices associated to technologies [**A**(1);**A**(2c)] and [**A**(1);**A**(2n)], value added and growth rate of profits

t	π(1,2h)	**p**(1,2h)	**n**(1,2h)	**p**(1,2h)'**n**(1,2h)	**m**(1,2h)	**p**(1,2h)'**m**(1,2h)	π**p**(1,2h)'**m**(1,2h)	ΔΠ/Π
4	0.25	1	5	5	10	10	2.5	
[**A**(1);**A**(2c)]		0.588	2.5	1.47	5	2.94	0.74	
		0.235	10	2.35	20	4.71	1.18	
				8.82		17.65	4.41	
5	0.25	1	6.25	6.25	15	15	3.75	
[**A**(1);**A**(2c)]		5.888	3.13	1.84	7.5	4.41	1.10	
		0.235	12.50	2.94	30	7.06	1.76	
				11.03		26.47	6.62	0.5
6	0.25	1	7.81	7.81	21.25	21.25	5.31	
[**A**(1);**A**(2c)]		0.588	3.91	2.30	10.63	6.25	1.56	
		0.235	15.63	3.68	42.5	10.00	2.50	
				13.79		37.50	9.38	0.4167
7	0.25	1	9.77	9.77	29.06	29.06	7.27	
[**A**(1);**A**(2c)]		0.588	4.88	2.87	14.53	8.55	2.14	
		0.235	19.53	4.60	58.13	13.68	3.42	
				17.23		51.29	12.82	0.3676

Table 9.3 (continued)

...								
66	0.25	1	5,097,894	5,097,894	20,391,566	20,391,566	5,097,892	
[**A**(1);**A**(2c)]		0.588	2,548,947	1,499,381	10,195,783	5,997,520	1,499,380	
		0.235	10,195,788	2,399,009	40,783,133	9,596,031	2,399,008	
				8,996,284		35,985,117	8,996,279	0.2500
67	0.25	1	6,372,368	6,372,368	25,489,461	25,489,461	6,372,365	
[**A**(1);**A**(2c)]		0.588	3,186,184	1,874,226	12,744,730	7,496,900	1,874,225	
		0.235	12,744,735	2,998,761	50,978,921	11,995,040	2,998,760	
				11,245,355		44,981,401	11,245,350	0.2500
68	0.25	1	7,965,460	7,965,460	31,861,828	31,861,828	7,965,457	
[**A**(1);**A**(2c)]		0.588	3,982,730	2,342,782	15,930,914	9,371,126	2,342,781	
		0.235	15,930,919	3,748,452	63,723,656	14,993,802	3,748,450	
				14,056,693		56,226,756	14,056,689	0.2500
69	0.25	1	9,956,824	9,956,824	39,827,288	39,827,288	9,956,822	
[**A**(1);**A**(2c)]		0.588	4,978,412	2,928,478	19,913,644	11,713,908	2,928,477	
		0.235	19,913,649	4,685,564	79,654,576	18,742,253	4,685,563	
				17,570,867		70,283,449	17,570,862	0.2500

Table 9.3 (continued)

t	π(1,2h)	**p**(1,2h)	**n**(1,2h)	**p**(1,2h)'**n**(1,2h)	**m**(1,2h)	**p**(1,2h)'**m**(1,2h)	π**p**(1,2h)'**m**(1,2h)	ΔΠ/Π
4	0.2658	1	4.41	4.41	7.54	7.54	2.00	
[**A**(1);**A**(2n)]		0.605	2.53	1.53	5.00	3.03	0.80	
		0.241	8.41	2.03	13.54	3.27	0.87	
				7.97		13.83	3.68	
5	0.2658	1	4.93	4.93	9.49	9.49	2.52	
[**A**(1);**A**(2n)]		0.605	3.20	1.94	7.53	4.56	1.21	
		0.241	8.93	2.15	15.49	3.74	0.99	
				9.02		17.78	4.73	0.2855
6	0.2658	1	5.58	5.58	11.95	11.95	3.18	
[**A**(1);**A**(2n)]		0.605	4.06	2.45	10.74	6.50	1.73	
		0.241	9.58	2.31	17.95	4.33	1.15	
				10.35		22.78	6.05	0.2812
7	0.2658	1	6.41	6.41	15.07	15.07	4.01	
[**A**(1);**A**(2n)]		0.605	5.13	3.11	14.79	8.95	2.38	
		0.241	10.41	2.51	21.07	5.08	1.35	
				12.03		29.10	7.74	0.2778

Table 9.3 (continued)

...								
66	0.2658	1	4,330,920	4,330,920	16,292,499	16,292,499	4,330,917	
[**A**(1);**A**(2n)]		0.605	5,630,193	3,406,658	21,180,243	12,815,519	3,406,657	
		0.241	4,330.924	1,044,663	16,292,505	3,929,917	1,044,662	
				8,782,240		33,037,935	8,782,236	0.2658
67	0.2658	1	5,482,176	5,482,176	20,623,416	20,623,416	5,482,174	
[**A**(1);**A**(2n)]		0.605	7,126,826	4,312,225	26,810,436	16,222,177	4,312,224	
		0.241	5,482,180	1,322,357	20,623,422	4,974,578	1,322,356	
				11,116,759		41,820,172	11,116,754	0.2658
68	0.2658	1	6,939,463	6,939,463	26,105,590	26,105,590	6,939,461	
[**A**(1);**A**(2n)]		0.605	9,021,299	5,458,513	33,937,262	20,534,402	5,458,512	
		0.241	6,939,467	1,673,870	26,105,596	6,296,934	1,673,869	
				14,071,845		52,936,926	14,071,841	0.2658
69	0.2658	1	8,784,130	8,784,130	33,045,050	33,045,050	8,784,127	
[**A**(1);**A**(2n)]		0.605	11,419,365	6,909,510	42,958,561	25,992,915	6,909,509	
		0.241	8,784,134	2,118,822	33,045,056	7,970,803	2,118,821	
				17,812,462		67,008,768	17,812,457	0.2658

because the proportions of techniques **A**(1) and **A**(2n) related to maximum growth are different.

From the above Table, we notice that until period t_{67}, technology [**A**(1); **A**(2c)] gains higher profits than [**A**(1); **A**(2n)], not only in terms of commodity 1, but, as results from simple calculations, in terms of any numeraire. In periods t_{68} and t_{69}, the profits obtained by [**A**(1); **A**(2c)] are lower than those of [**A**(1); **A**(2n)] in terms of commodity 1, but in terms of commodity 2 and 3 they are still greater. In period t_{70}, the profits of [**A**(1); **A**(2c)] fall short of those of [**A**(1); **A**(2n)] in terms of commodity 1 and 3, but they still exceed in terms of commodity 2. Beginning from period t_{71} the profits of [**A**(1); **A**(2n)] become higher than those of [**A**(1); **A**(2c)], no matter which commodity is chosen as numeraire.

These remarks remind us how difficult is the choice of the numeraire when at stake there is the comparison between technologies with different price-distribution systems.

The fact that, after a certain period, [**A**(1); **A**(2n)] obtains higher profits than [**A**(1); **A**(2c)] must not be surprising. The hypotheses made on accumulation force the profits of [**A**(1); **A**(2c)] to grow at the rate of 25%, whereas those of [**A**(1); **A**(2n)] growth at the rate of 26.58%. This confirms the idea that the longer the period for which a certain type of NPMP can feed accumulation, the greater will be the weight of the physical efficiency, and the lesser that of residuals. Hence, beyond a certain period, [**A**(1); **A**(2n)] —i.e. the technology that includes techniques with higher physical efficiency— comes to be preferred even if it involves greater residuals. If the endowment of NPMP of type 2 is sufficiently abundant so to allow the system to reach this period, the profit-maker operators shall face, among others, the problem of inter-temporal choice.

6. Partial accumulation and its consequences on the dynamic price-distribution OE

In Chapter VIII we suggested the utilization the inter-temporal average rate of value added as proxy of the dynamic efficiency. In order to determine the price-distribution OE among technologies we need a similar index, which should not depend on the chosen numeraire and which should make comparable the dynamic efficiency of economic system with different relative prices. Yet, compared to Chapter VIII, we have here an additional problem. To determine the dynamic price-distribution order of efficiency is not sufficient to introduce an assumption on one of distributive variables —as always we have done. It is also necessary to make assumptions on the dynamics of accumulation. In fact, the example shown in Section 3 proves that this order depends not only on the rate of profit, given the wage level, but also on the structural compatibility among techniques activated through time. This is because total profits are also dependent on value of the anticipated means of production. In such an example the concern was that of maximizing the accumulation. Without this objective, the influence of residuals is greatly reduced or it is even nullified.

Table 9.4 Comparison between technologies [**A**(1);**A**(2c)] and [**A**(1);**A**(2n)] in the case of partial accumulation of profits

t	**q**(1)	**n**(1)	**m**(1)	**p**(1)	**p**(1)'**n**(1)	**m**(2c)	**p**(1)'**m**(2c)	**m**(2n)	**p**(1)'**m**(2n)
3	10	4	6	1	4	1.55	1.55	1.27	1.27
A(1)	5	2	3	1.29	2.59	0.77	1	1.65	2.13
	20	8	12	0.47	3.76	3.09	1.45	1.27	0.60
					10.35		4		4

t	**q**(1)	**n**(1)	**m**(1)	**m**(1,2h)	**q**(1,2h)	**n**(1,2h)
4	10	4	6	7.55	11.93	4.39
[**A**(1);**A**(2c)]	5	2	3	3.77	5.97	2.19
	20	8	12	15.09	23.86	8.77
4	10	4	6	7.27	11.61	4.34
[**A**(1);**A**(2n)]	5	2	3	4.65	7.09	2.44
	20	8	12	13.27	21.61	8.34

Table 9.5 Prices associated to technologies [**A**(1);**A**(2c)] and [**A**(1);**A**(2n)], value added and income distribution

	w	π(1,2h)	**p**(1,2h)	**n**(1,2h)	**p**(1,2h)'**n**(1,2h)	**m**(1,2h)	**p**(1,2h)'**m**(1,2h)	π**p**(1,2h)'**m**(1,2h)	π**p**(1,2h)'**m**(1,2h) / **p**(1,2h)'**n**(1,2h)
4	0	0.25	1	4.39	4.39	7.55	7.55	1.89	
[**A**(1);**A**(2c)]			0.588	2.19	1.29	3.77	2.22	0.55	
			0.235	8.77	2.06	15.09	3.55	0.89	
					7.74			3.33	0.43
4	0	0.27	1	4.34	4.34	7.27	7.27	1.93	
[**A**(1);**A**(2n)]			0.605	2.44	1.48	4.65	2.81	0.75	
			0.241	8.34	2.01	13.27	3.20	0.85	
					7.82			3.53	0.45

To simplify the previous statement, let us consider technologies [**A**(1); **A**(2c)] and [**A**(1); **A**(2n)]. We still assume null wage; additionally we assume that only a part of the available profit at the end of period t_3 is invested in the means of production of the following period. In particular, let us suppose that only a profit equal to 4 (in terms of commodity 1) is accumulated in period t_4. Table 9.4 shows the dynamics of the system with technologies [**A**(1); **A**(2c)] and [**A**(1); **A**(2n)] and Table 9.5 indicates the evolution of value added, profits, and the profit share on value added. From these tables, one can note that the purchasing power of the profits obtained with the activation of technology [**A**(1); **A**(2n)] is higher then those associated with technology [**A**(1); **A**(2c)]. In this case technology [**A**(1); **A**(2n)] precedes [**A**(1); **A**(2c)] in the price-distribution order of efficiency.

These examples lead to the following conclusion: if we have maximum accumulation, then it is initially more important, for the price-distribution dynamic efficiency, a superior structural compatibility among techniques, which makes possible the accumulation of all means of production. However, if there is no maximum accumulation, then the role of residuals is strongly reduced, up to the point of becoming irrelevant. In this case, instead, what becomes fundamental is the level of the rate of profit, once fixed exogenously the unit wage.

7. The relation between the dynamic values OE and the dynamic price-distribution OE

From Chapter III, we know that there exists always a static price-distribution OE that determines also their physical OE. Now we must inquiry whether a dynamic price-distribution OE exists —that is, an OE which is followed in order to maximize profits— that guarantees also the determination of an OE between technologies compatible with the maximum growth as expressed in terms of value added.

Since the dynamic price-distribution OE cannot be determined only on the basis of the rate of profit, it is necessary to take into account the system's capacity to produce value added. For having a dynamic price-distribution OE compatible with an OE of technologies at their maximum growth we should opportunely manipulate the level of wage chosen as the exogenous distributive variable. There is no doubt that under the hypothesis of null wage and maximum accumulation the two orders perfectly coincide.

8. Some final remarks

The investigation of the dynamic price-distribution OE has been carried out with some numerical analysis, and limited to the case of ordering techniques, **A**(2c) and **A**(2n), which employ the same NPMP. However, despite the simplifications, we may eventually draw some general propositions that maintain their validity also for ordering techniques with different NPMP.

The static price-distribution OE is not always compatible with the dynamic price-distribution order. No synthetic proxy can be singled out for the dynamic price-distribution OE similar to the inter-temporal average rate of value added found in the last Chapter. The techniques are activated according to the dynamic price-distribution OE if the chosen sequence maximizes the present value of the profits obtainable in a certain interval —a magnitude that depends on both the rate of profit and the value of the accumulated means of production. Finally, to determine the price-distribution dynamic order among technologies, one must know in advance:
- the value of the exogenous distributive variable;
- the time horizon taken into account;
- the inter-temporal discount rate;
- the accumulation dynamics.

Chapter X – The dynamics of income distribution: total wages and their shares

1. Introduction

In our dynamic framework we shall now introduce the behavior of the distributive variables. The analysis undertaken in Chapter V on unit wage, profit rate and rent will now be further developed in a dynamic context. The following sections will study how distribution changes during the process of growth in the case of maximum accumulation.

2. Total distributive variables and net product value

We shall refer to technology [**A**(1); **A**(2); **A**(3); ...; **A**(k)] which has been chosen as the most efficient on the basis of a certain OE that we assume to be compatible with both the price-distribution and the physical efficiency order of efficiency. We shall examine the growth process from the very beginning.

When only technique **A**(1) is activated, the distributive variables are as follows.

Total wages are

$$W(1;t_1) = \mathbf{l}(1)'\,\mathbf{q}(1;t_1)\,w(1), \tag{10.1}$$

and total profits are

$$\Pi(1;t_1) = \mathbf{p}(1)'\,\mathbf{m}(1;t_1)\,\pi(1) = \mathbf{p}(1)'\,[\mathbf{A}(1)\,\mathbf{q}(1;t_1)]\,\pi(1). \tag{10.2}$$

The rent is obviously zero whereas w(1) and π(1) depend on which of the two variables is exogenously chosen.

The value of the economic system's net product is

$$Y(1;t_1) = \mathbf{p}(1)'\,\mathbf{n}(1;t_1). \tag{10.3}$$

It is obviously equal to the value added of the economic system

$$Y(1;t_1) = W(1;t_1) + \Pi(1;t_1). \tag{10.4}$$

From a dynamic point of view, when technology [**A**(1); **A**(2)] is activated, the total distributive variables, calculated for any $t_2 \geq t_1 + 1$, become the following.

Total wages are

[10.5] $$W(1,2,t_2)=[\mathbf{l}(1)'\mathbf{q}(1,\overline{t_1})+\mathbf{l}(2)'\sum_{i=1}^{t_2-\overline{t_1}}\mathbf{q}(2;\overline{t_1}+i)]\,w(2)$$

where $\sum_{i=1}^{t_2-\overline{t_1}}\mathbf{q}(2;\overline{t_1}+i)$ represents the quantitative vector of productions of all techniques $\mathbf{A}(2)$ in activity in period t_2.

Total profits are

[10.6] $$\Pi(1,2;t_2) = \mathbf{p}(2)'\,\mathbf{m}(1,2;t_2)\,\pi(2),$$

where $\mathbf{m}(1,2;t_2)$ denotes the vector of the means of production employed by techniques $\mathbf{A}(1)$ and $\mathbf{A}(2)$ active in period t_2.

Total rents are

[10.7] $$R(1,2;t_2) = \rho(1)\,T(1).$$

The determination of w(2), and $\pi(2)$ is established, as already seen in Chapters III and V, on the basis of the sub-system associated to $\mathbf{A}(2)$ and the rent based on the comparison with the system associated to $\mathbf{A}(1)$.

The value of net product is

[10.8] $$Y(1,2;t_2) = \mathbf{p}(2)'\,\mathbf{n}(1,2;t_2).$$

It is obviously equal to the value added of the economic system

[10.9] $$Y(1,2;t_2) = W(1,2;t_2) + \Pi(1,2;t_2) + R(1,2;t_2).$$

When all technologies are active we have the following distributive variables.

Total wages are

[10.10] $$W(1,2,\ldots,k;t_k)=[\mathbf{l}(1)'\mathbf{q}(1;\overline{t_1})+\mathbf{l}(2)'\sum_{i=1}^{\overline{t_2}-\overline{t_1}}\mathbf{q}(2;\overline{t_1}+i)+$$
$$+\mathbf{l}(3)'\sum_{i=1}^{\overline{t_3}-\overline{t_2}}\mathbf{q}(3;\overline{t_2}+i)+\ldots+\mathbf{l}(k)'\sum_{i=1}^{t_k-\overline{t_{k-1}}}\mathbf{q}(k;\overline{t_{k-1}}+i)]\,w(k),$$

where $\sum_{i=1}^{t_h-\overline{t_{h-1}}}\mathbf{q}(h;\overline{t_{h-1}}+i)$ represents in its quantitative dimensions, the vector of productions of all the techniques $\mathbf{A}(h)$ (for h = 2, 3, ..., k) active in period t_h.

Total profits and rents are respectively:

[10.11] $$\Pi(1,2,\ldots,k;t_k) = \mathbf{p}(k)'\,\mathbf{m}(1,2,\ldots,k;t_k)\,\pi(k),$$

[10.12] $$R(1,2,\ldots,k;t_k)=\sum_{h=1}^{k-1}\rho(h)T(h).$$

The value of net product or the value added of the economic system can be expressed as follows

[10.13] $$Y(1,2,\ldots,k;t_k) = \mathbf{p}(k)'\,\mathbf{n}(1,2,\ldots,k;t_k);$$

[10.14] $$Y(1,2,\ldots,k;t_k) = W(1,2,\ldots,k;t_k) + \Pi(1,2,\ldots,k;t_k) + R(1,2,\ldots,k;t_k).$$

The variables w (k), $\pi(k)$, $\rho(h)$ and $\mathbf{p}(k)$ are determined on the basis of the sub-system associated to $\mathbf{A}(k)$, and by comparing the latter to those sub-systems associated to the other k–1 techniques $\mathbf{A}(h)$ in order to resolve the level of rents.

3. An overview on distribution and prices

We now analyze wages, profits, and rents, in their aggregate values and relative shares on the value added. The dynamics of unit wage, the rate of profit, and unit rent has already been dealt with in chapter V and it will be recalled here only when required. The problem of distributive shares is of great importance and its ancient roots stem back to the Classics and reach the present days [Quadrio Curzio 1994]. As exemplification it can be mention the long-lasting theoretical and empirical debate on the stability of the share of income devoted to the labor factor. Generally speaking, the evolution of the distributive shares is important because they measure the "weight" of the different factors on the national income and therefore the "weight" of the corresponding productive operators with their bargaining power.

It should be quite obvious that an economic system in which 80% of income is represented by wages is dominated by the labor factor: as it would be true for the other two factors if similar shares occurred to capital or scarce resource owners.

In our analysis we assume a unit wage given exogenously: therefore total wages always grow except the case in which the unit wage becomes semi-exogenous. The wage share may instead have various behaviors disclosing changes of labor "weight" in the distribution of the value added.

The dynamics of total profits is more complex because it is subject to different forces: changes in the rate of profit as well as changes of capital. These complex changes affect also the profit shares.

Then there is the dynamics of rent. Our assumption that the order utilized for activating the techniques is compatible with the static price-distribution efficiency order has the following implication: the rates of rent and total rent increase every time there are changes in the dimension of the technology. More complex it appears the dynamics followed by the rent shares instead.

The previous propositions must be further qualified with reference to prices and the choice of the numeraire. As we have already analyzed (Chapters III and V) the behavior of prices is crucial in our framework. We must recall that the adoption of the static price-distribution efficiency order implies the reduction of prices because the process that produces commodity 1, which has been chosen as *numeraire,* diminishes its efficiency. It is the increase of its production cost that reduces the prices of all other commodities and makes room for the rise of rents. The change of prices and purchasing power requires some further remarks. Firstly, if we were to choose the commodity with the lowest direct and indirect content of commodity 1 as numeraire, then the prices of the other commodities would grow with the following effects on the distributive variables. The purchasing power will be reduced for given wages and nominal profits, while the rent earners, that precisely on the increased prices found their source of income, will take advantage.

The choice of commodity 1 as numeraire was preferred because it allows us to determine without ambiguities the price-distribution efficiency order although it makes less intuitive the previous conclusion on income distribution. It is useful, however, to underline the fact that, no matter which numeraire is chosen, the broadening of the dimension of technology by means of new and less efficient techniques, generates a whole set of rents. We shall examine these cases with the use of some numerical simulations.

Having exogenously set-up the unit wage in terms of the numeraire-commodity 1, the decrease of all prices in terms of this numeraire determines an increase in the unit wage in real terms, an hypothesis that we shall briefly analyze in the following section.

The analysis of the profit is more complex. The changing of technology brings about decreasing rates of profit, and prices, whereas the employed means of production are increasing. These different movements have conflicting effects on real profits. Usually —as a closer look at the various cases could reveal— we notice that the efficiency lost in the production of the numeraire-commodity with its negative consequences on the rate of profit and prices will be able to transfer purchasing power to the rent.

In the following analysis we will use some simulations that aim not only to clarify the conclusions and making them more intuitive, but also to single out various cases that analytically are difficult to disentangle. Therefore, it is worth starting with some remarks on the features of the general numerical model.

In the case of a technique **A**(1), as Table 10.1 shows, profits and total wages grow over time, whereas rent is null. Profit and wage shares remain constant, respectively at 93.3% and 6.7%.

Therefore, as the economic system grows, the technology-maker operator takes advantage of the growing profit, whereas the labor operator takes advantage of the growing employment.

These results are obvious since that distribution depends exclusively on the initial level of w.

The case of transition to technology [**A**(1); **A**(2)], which occurs at time t_4, brings about a much more complex situation and each distributive variable must be examined individually. We shall do this with our simulation by examining the following cases:

a) changes of technology without residuals and without changes in the labor coefficients; in this case the efficiency of the economy is reduced because the process which produces the commodity 1 becomes less efficient;
b) changes of technology without residuals but with the increase of labor coefficients: in this case the efficiency of the economy is reduced because of the pressure of both circulating capital and labor;
c) changes of technology with the formation of residuals but without changes in labor coefficients;
d) changes of technology with the formation of residuals and with the increase of labor coefficients;

e) expansion of activity without changes of technology.

It is worth noting that the case of reductions in labor coefficients is not taken into account here —we shall dealt explicitly with it when we focus on the analysis of technical progress and technological change in Chapter XII.

4. Wage dynamics

The dynamic analysis on wage must deal with three variable's categories: unit wage, total wages, and share of wages on the value added or the value of net product. The analysis is developed, as we have already said, by taking into account the case of constant dimension of the technology —where growth is only possible by intensifying the use of the last active technique— and the case of changes in the technological dimension with the activation of new techniques.

Because we assume that wages are set-up in terms of commodity 1, it follows that their purchasing power increases as the technology efficiency falls, implying for this distributive variable a high degree of determinacy. More precisely, in our model the wage variable grows according to the reduction of efficiency, and not on the basis of movements in demand and supply of labor. In so doing, we have a complete wage indexation which keeps its real level constant in terms of commodity 1, i.e. that commodity that experiences higher increases of both production costs and price than any other commodity.

Though with some lack of realism, this hypothesis is useful for a model that aims to investigate in detail the dynamic changes of the total distributive variables as well as their shares. The problem of scarce realism, however, appears relevant in dealing with the cause of the rise of wages rather than the effects of such a rise. A well recognized stylized fact in economic history is, in fact, the persistence of this phenomenon and any theoretical effort should not entirely overlook it.

The hypothesis we made appears more realistic and attracting if we consider that the dynamic economic process with its decreasing efficiency tends to benefit in terms of unitary rewards the two non-produced factors, "land" and "labor". This surely represents an incentive for the technology-maker operator in charge of the produced factors —"capital" and "technology"— to introduce innovations that modify such a trend to his or her own advantage.

Still, if the hypothesis concerning unit wage appears unsuitable, it could be easily reformulated in other ways. One way would be that of establishing a bundle of goods and imposing a constant ratio over time between nominal wage and the value of this fixed bundle. Given that, on the basis of the identified dynamics, prices diminish over time, in order to maintain the real wage constant it would be necessary to reduce the nominal wage. In other words, the nominal wage should be determined by the following equation

$$w = w_r \, \mathbf{p}' \, \mathbf{q}_b,$$

where w_r is the real wage assumed to be constant, and $\mathbf{q}_b$ is the vector representing the chosen bundle of goods.

All other intermediate hypotheses between the two that we have mentioned are possible once the function of the nominal wage is specified.

A completely alternative strategy is that of leaving the rate of profit as the exogenous variable. Yet, the hypothesis of fixing the wage level with a downward rigidity still appears to be the most realistic assumption we can make.

4.1 General propositions

Accordingly with the latter remark, we assume that the exogenous distributive variable is the unit wage, and that this does not change when either the last active technique increases its level of production or new techniques are introduced. In this case if the chosen technology were [**A**(1); **A**(2); **A**(3); …; **A**(k)], we should note

$$\max w(k) \geq w = \bar{w} \geq 0. \qquad [10.15]$$

If on the contrary we were to note

$$\max w(h^*) \geq w = \bar{w} \geq \max w(h^* + x), \qquad x = 1, \ldots, k-h^*, \qquad [10.16]$$

namely, if the exogenous wage level were greater than the maximum wage of technique **A**(h*+1), then, with the activation of this technique, the unit wage should diminish thus becoming a semi-exogenous or semi-endogenous variable, as we have already seen in Chapter V.

Total wages turns out to be

$$W(1,2,\ldots,k;t_k) = [\mathbf{l}(1)'\mathbf{q}(1;\bar{t}_1) + \mathbf{l}(2)'\sum_{i=1}^{\bar{t}_2-\bar{t}_1}\mathbf{q}(2;\bar{t}_1+i) + \mathbf{l}(3)'\sum_{i=1}^{\bar{t}_3-\bar{t}_2}\mathbf{q}(3;\bar{t}_2+i) + \ldots + \mathbf{l}(k)'\sum_{i=1}^{t_k-\bar{t}_{k-1}}\mathbf{q}(k;\bar{t}_{k-1}+i)]\bar{w}(k), \qquad [10.17]$$

where $\bar{w}(k)$ is the exogenous unit wage within the conditions given by [10.15].

Nominal wages grow both for the growth of production of the single techniques and for the adding of new techniques. Therefore they always grow during the dynamic process. If the order utilized for activating the techniques is compatible with the price-distribution OE we have $\mathbf{p}(1) \geq \mathbf{p}(2) \geq \ldots \geq \mathbf{p}(k)$; having chosen commodity 1 as numeraire, the purchasing power of wages grows even more rapidly.

The share of wages on the value added or on the value of net product is given by

$$\omega_w(t_k) = \frac{W(1,2,\ldots,k;t_k)}{Y(1,2,\ldots,k;t_k)}. \qquad [10.18]$$

To analyze the dynamics of this share we shall continue to refer to the case of maximum accumulation.

4.2. The dynamics of the share of wages with one technique

When only technique **A**(1) is activated, with the use of [10.1] and [10.3], we obtain

[10.19] $$\omega_w(t_1) = \frac{\overline{w}(1)\mathbf{l}(1)'\mathbf{q}(1;t_1)}{\mathbf{p}(1)'\mathbf{n}(1;t_1)}, \quad t_0 \leq t_1 \leq \overline{t_1}.$$

Assuming, as usual, that we know the initial endowment of means of production $\mathbf{m}(1;t_0)$, and that this endowment is in such proportions as to allow technology **A**(1) to grow at the uniform rate without generating residuals, we can re-write [10.19] as follows

[10.20] $$\omega_w(t_1) = \frac{\overline{w}(1)\mathbf{l}(1)'\mathbf{m}(1;t_0)[1+s(1)]^{t_1+1-t_0}}{\mathbf{p}(1)'\mathbf{m}(1;t_0)\,s(1)[1+s(1)]^{t_1-t_0}} =$$
$$= \frac{\overline{w}(1)\mathbf{l}(1)'\mathbf{m}(1;t_0)[1+s(1)]}{\mathbf{p}(1)'\mathbf{m}(1;t_0)s(1)} = c, \qquad t_0 \leq t_1 \leq \overline{t_1},$$

where c denotes a constant. By increasing the level activity of the first technique, the share of wages on the value added remains constant, as one should expect at first sight.

Let us consider, for example, that part of Table 10.1 in which only technique **A**(1) is active, that is, up to period t_3. Given exogenously the unit wage, total wages grow according to the productive expansion of technique **A**(1), but the share of wages on value added remains constant at 6.7%. Hence, growth does not modify the distribution shares, as this case shows clearly.

4.3. The dynamics of the share of wages when technology changes dimension

At $\overline{t_1}$ the constraint of NPMP of type 1 becomes effective, and, to allow further growth, technique **A**(2) —i.e. the next technique in OE after **A**(1)— has to be activated. From now onwards, the analysis of changes in ratio between wages and value added, are limited for the sake of simplicity to the case in which s(2) < s(1), and π(2) < π(1). That is, we shall focus on the case where the chosen OE is compatible with both the physical OE and the price-distribution OE.

When technology [**A**(1); **A**(2)] is activated, with the use of [10.5] and [10.8], we obtain

[10.21] $$\omega_w(t_2) = \frac{[\mathbf{l}(1)'\mathbf{q}(1;\overline{t}_1) + \mathbf{l}(2)'\sum_{i=1}^{t_2-\overline{t_1}}\mathbf{q}(2;t_1+i)]\overline{w}(2)}{\mathbf{p}(2)'\mathbf{n}(1,2;t_2)}, \quad \overline{t_1}+1 \leq t_2 \leq \overline{t_2}.$$

The first element to inquiry is whether the employment of NPMP of type 2, given $\overline{w} = \overline{w}(1) = \overline{w}(2)$, involves a change in the share of wages on value added. Therefore, we intend to study the following inequality

[10.22] $$\omega_w(\overline{t}_1) \gtrless \omega_w(\overline{t_1}+1),$$

Table 10.1 Prices and distribution with technology [**A**(1);**A**(2*c*)] at unchanged labor coefficients and total accumulation

t	w	π(1)	**p**(1)	**q**(1)	**n**(1)	Y(1)	**m**(1)	**l**	Π(1)	W(1)	R(1)	Π/Y	W/Y	R/Y
1	0.02	0.62	1	3.6	1.44	1.44	2.16	1	1.34	0.07				
A(1)			1.278	1.8	0.72	0.92	1.08	1	0.86	0.04				
			0.481	7.2	2.88	1.38	4.32	1	1.29	0.14				
						3.74			3.49	0.25	0	0.933	0.067	0
2			1	6	2.4	2.4	3.6	1	2.24	0.12				
A(1)			1.278	3	1.2	1.53	1.8	1	1.43	0.06				
			0.481	12	4.8	2.31	7.2	1	2.15	0.24				
						6.24			5.82	0.42	0	0.933	0.067	0
3			1	10	4	4	6	1	3.73	0.20				
A(1)			1.278	5	2	2.56	3	1	2.38	0.10				
			0.481	20	8	3.85	12	1	3.59	0.40				
						10.40			9.70	0.70	0	0.933	0.067	0

Table 10.1 (continued)

t	w	π(2c)	**p**(2c)	**q**(1,2c)	**n**(1,2c)	Y(1,2c)	**m**(1,2c)	**l**	Π	W	R	Π/Y	W/Y	R/Y
4	0.02	0.201	1	15	5	5	10	1	2.01	0.30				
[**A**(1);**A**(2c)]			0.596	7.5	2.5	1.49	5	1	0.60	0.15				
			0.251	30	10	2.51	20	1	1.01	0.60				
						9.00			3.63	1.05	4.33	0.403	0.117	0.481
5	0.02	0.201	1	21.25	6.25	6.25	15	1	3.02	0.43				
[**A**(1);**A**(2c)]			0.596	10.63	3.13	1.86	7.5	1	0.90	0.21				
			0.251	42.50	12.50	3.14	30	1	1.52	0.85				
						11.26			5.44	1.49	4.33	0.483	0.132	0.384
6	0.02	0.201	1	29.06	7.81	7.81	21.25	1	4.28	0.58				
[**A**(1);**A**(2c)]			0.596	14.53	3.91	2.33	10.63	1	1.28	0.29				
			0.251	58.13	15.63	3.93	42.5	1	2.15	1.16				
						14.07			7.71	2.03	4.33	0.548	0.145	0.308
7	0.02	0.201	1	38.83	9.77	9.77	29.06	1	5.85	0.78				
[**A**(1);**A**(2c)]			0.596	19.41	4.88	2.91	14.53	1	1.74	0.39				
			0.251	77.66	19.33	4.91	58.13	1	2.94	1.55				
						17.59			10.54	2.72	4.33	0.599	0.155	0.246

Table 10.1 (continued)

t	w	π(2c)	**p**(2c)	**q**(1,2c)	**n**(1,2c)	Y(1,2c)	**m**(1,2c)	**l**	Π	W	R	Π/Y	W/Y	R/Y
8	0.02	0.201	1	51.04	12.21	12.21	38.83	1	7.82	1.02				
[**A**(1);**A**(2c)]			0.596	25.52	6.10	3.64	19.41	1	2.33	0.51				
			0.251	102.07	24.41	6.14	77.66	1	3.93	2.04	4.33	0.641	0.163	0.197
						21.98			14.08	3.57				
9	0.02	0.201	1	66.29	15.26	15.26	51.04	1	10.28	1.33				
[**A**(1);**A**(2c)]			0.596	33.15	7.63	4.55	25.52	1	3.06	0.66				
			0.251	132.59	30.52	7.67	102.07	1	5.17	2.65				
						27.48			18.51	4.64	4.33	0.674	0.169	0.157
...														
40	0.02	0.201	1	77,027.20	15,407.44	15,407.44	61,619.76	1	12,411.01	1,540.54				
[**A**(1);**A**(2c)]			0.596	38,513.60	7,703.72	4,590.71	30,809.88	1	3,697.91	770.27				
			0.251	154,054.40	30,814.88	7,748.92	123,239.52	1	6,241.91	3,081.08				
						27,747.07			22,350.83	5,391.90	4.33	0.806	0.194	0.000
41	0.02	0.201	1	96,286.50	19,259.30	19,259.30	77,027.20	1	15,514.27	1,925.73				
[**A**(1);**A**(2c)]			0.596	48,143.25	9,629.65	5,738.39	38,513.60	1	4,622.54	962.86				
			0.251	192,572.99	38,518.60	9,686.15	154,054.40	1	7,802.64	3,851.46				
						34,683.83			27,939.45	6,740.05	4.33	0.806	0.194	0.000

that is

$$[10.23] \qquad \frac{\overline{w}\mathbf{l}(1)'\mathbf{q}(1;\overline{t_1})}{\mathbf{p}(1)'\mathbf{n}(1;\overline{t_1})} \gtrless \frac{\overline{w}[\mathbf{l}(1)'\mathbf{q}(1;\overline{t_1})+\mathbf{l}(2)'\mathbf{q}(2;\overline{t_1}+1)]}{\mathbf{p}(2)'\mathbf{n}(1,2;\overline{t_1}+1)}.$$

To study the dynamics of this share we should make a distinction between different cases, depending on the degree of compatibility between techniques activated through time, and the labor requirements of the different techniques.

4.3.1 The case of absence of residuals and equal labor coefficients

First, we shall consider the case in which $\mathbf{l}(1) = \mathbf{l}(2)$ and the net product not internally accumulable by the first technique can be entirely employed by the second technique.

We should verify whether the activation of technique $\mathbf{A}(2c)$, that we assume follows $\mathbf{A}(1)$ in OE, implies some sort of change in the share of wages on value added. The matrices of the technical coefficients are given in Appendix A, and the labor coefficients are assumed to be $\mathbf{l}(1) = \mathbf{l}(2c) = [1, 1, 1]$. Before determining the solutions of [10.23] we observe that if $\pi(1) > \pi(2)$ then $\mathbf{p}(1) \geq \mathbf{p}(2)$, hence

$$[10.24] \qquad \frac{\overline{w}\mathbf{l}(1)'\mathbf{q}(1;\overline{t_1})}{\mathbf{p}(2)'\mathbf{n}(1;\overline{t_1})} > \frac{\overline{w}\mathbf{l}(1)'\mathbf{q}(1;\overline{t_1})}{\mathbf{p}(1)'\mathbf{n}(1;\overline{t_1})}.$$

Therefore let us now consider the following inequality

$$[10.25] \qquad \frac{\overline{w}\mathbf{l}(1)'\mathbf{q}(1;\overline{t_1})}{\mathbf{p}(2)'\mathbf{n}(1;\overline{t_1})} \gtrless \frac{\overline{w}\mathbf{l}(1)'[\mathbf{q}(1;\overline{t_1})+\mathbf{l}(2)'\mathbf{q}(2;\overline{t_1}+1)]}{\mathbf{p}(2)'\mathbf{n}(1,2;\overline{t_1}+1)}.$$

Remembering that in the case taken into account residuals are not formed, from [10.25] it follows

$$[10.26] \qquad \frac{\overline{w}\mathbf{l}(1)'\mathbf{q}(1;\overline{t_1})}{\mathbf{p}(2)'\mathbf{n}(1;\overline{t_1})} \gtrless \frac{\overline{w}\mathbf{l}(1)'\mathbf{q}(1;\overline{t_1})+\overline{w}\mathbf{l}(1)'\mathbf{n}(1;\overline{t_1})[1+s(2)]}{\mathbf{p}(2)'\mathbf{n}(1;\overline{t_1})+\mathbf{p}(2)'\mathbf{n}(1;\overline{t_1})s(2)},$$

depending on

$$[10.27] \qquad \frac{\overline{w}\mathbf{l}(1)'\mathbf{q}(1;\overline{t_1})}{\mathbf{p}(2)'\mathbf{n}(1;\overline{t_1})} \gtrless \frac{\overline{w}\mathbf{l}(1)'\mathbf{n}(1;\overline{t_1})[1+s(2)]}{\mathbf{p}(2)'\mathbf{n}(1;\overline{t_1})s(2)}.$$

From [10.27] we have

$$[10.28] \qquad \overline{w}\mathbf{l}(1)'\mathbf{n}(1,\overline{t_1})[1+s(1)]\,\mathbf{p}(2)'\mathbf{n}(1,\overline{t_1})s(2) \gtrless \overline{w}\mathbf{l}(1)'\mathbf{n}(1,\overline{t_1})[1+s(2)]\,\mathbf{p}(2)'\mathbf{n}(1,\overline{t_1})s(1),$$

that is

$$[10.29] \qquad s(2) \gtrless s(1).$$

Because $s(2) < s(1)$, the inequality [10.26] holds for the 'less than' case, hence, taking into consideration [10.24], we have

$$[10.30] \qquad \frac{\overline{w}\mathbf{l}(1)'\mathbf{q}(1;\overline{t_1})}{\mathbf{p}(1)'\mathbf{n}(1;\overline{t_1})} < \frac{\overline{w}\mathbf{l}(1)'[\mathbf{q}(1;\overline{t_1})+\mathbf{q}(2;\overline{t_1}+1)]}{\mathbf{p}(2)'\mathbf{n}(1,2;\overline{t_1}+1)}.$$

When the activation of technique **A**(2c) does not modify the labor coefficients and does not form residuals, the share of wages on value added, given exogenously the unit wage, grows with such a technique.

Let us refer back to Table 10.1 that shows the dynamics of distribution with technology [**A**(1); **A**(2c)]. To gain maximum growth, technique **A**(2c) requires the same productive proportions of technique **A**(1), thus allowing the employment of the entire net product available at t_3. When **A**(2c) becomes active, total wages increase as well as the share of wages on value added.

More precisely, it turns out from the simulation that the share of wages moves from 6.7% to 11.7% during the change of technology from **A**(1) to [**A**(1); **A**(2c)]. Subsequently, this share continues to grow, reaching asymptotically the level of 19.4%, as we shall show shortly in §4.4.

The decrease of efficiency as a consequence of the change of technology, therefore, hits the profit share, which from t_3 to t_4 drops from 93.3% to 40.3%. Over time, both the share of wages and the share of profits increase at the expenses of the share of rents, whereas employment and circulating capital also increase, and the scarce NPMP remains constant.

Given both the unit wage and labor coefficients, the dynamics shows how the labor factor acquires a greater weight in terms of income distribution,. Hence, there are no reasons why this operator should resist to the change of technology.

Negative effects are primary faced by the profit-maker or technology-maker operators so that an antagonism arises between them and the resource owners and the labor factor.

4.3.2 The case without residuals and increasing labor coefficients

Let us now consider the case in which $\mathbf{l}(1) \leq \mathbf{l}(2)$ and the net product of the first technique is still entirely accumulated, and we analyze the evolution of the share of wages on the value added when **A**(2) is activated. The change of labor coefficients is a feature of the increasing labor-intensity of the production process, which can be interpreted as the compensation effect for the reduced efficiency of the system.

Now we analyze the following inequality

$$[10.31] \qquad \frac{\overline{w}\mathbf{l}(1)'\mathbf{q}(1;\overline{t_1})}{\mathbf{p}(1)'\mathbf{n}(1;\overline{t_1})} \gtrless \frac{\overline{w}[\mathbf{l}(1)'\mathbf{q}(1;\overline{t_1})+\mathbf{l}(2)'\mathbf{q}(2;\overline{t_1}+1)]}{\mathbf{p}(2)'\mathbf{n}(1{,}2;\overline{t_1}+1)}$$

In this case also we first consider the relation

$$[10.32] \qquad \frac{\overline{w}\mathbf{l}(1)'\mathbf{q}(1;\overline{t_1})}{\mathbf{p}(2)'\mathbf{n}(1;\overline{t_1})} \gtrless \frac{\overline{w}\mathbf{l}(1)'\mathbf{q}(1;\overline{t_1})+\overline{w}\mathbf{l}(2)'\mathbf{n}(1;\overline{t_1})[1+s(2)]}{\mathbf{p}(2)'\mathbf{n}(1;\overline{t_1})+\mathbf{p}(2)'\mathbf{n}(1;\overline{t_1})s(2)};$$

which can be rewritten as

$$[10.33] \qquad \frac{\overline{w}\mathbf{l}(1)'\mathbf{q}(1;\overline{t_1})}{\mathbf{p}(2)'\mathbf{n}(1;\overline{t_1})} \gtrless \frac{\overline{w}\mathbf{l}(2)'\mathbf{n}(1;\overline{t_1})[1+s(2)]}{\mathbf{p}(2)'\mathbf{n}(1;\overline{t_1})s(2)}$$

and hence

$$[10.34] \qquad \overline{w}\mathbf{l}(1)'\mathbf{n}(1;\overline{t_1})[1+s(1)]\mathbf{p}(2)'\mathbf{n}(1;\overline{t_1})\,s(2) \gtrless$$

$$\overline{w}\mathbf{l}(2)'\mathbf{n}(1;\overline{t_1})[1+s(2)]\mathbf{p}(2)'\mathbf{n}(1;\overline{t_1})\,s(1).$$

If $\mathbf{l}(2) - \mathbf{l}(1) = \mathbf{d} \geq \mathbf{o}$, namely by assuming that the technique which follows $\mathbf{A}(1)$ in the OE shows a lower internal rate of growth and not a lower quantity of labor per unit product, then [10.34] becomes

$$[10.35] \qquad \overline{w}\mathbf{l}(1)'\mathbf{n}(1;\overline{t_1})[1+s(1)]\mathbf{p}(2)'\mathbf{n}(1;\overline{t_1})\,s(2) \gtrless$$

$$\overline{w}\mathbf{l}(1)'\mathbf{n}(1;\overline{t_1})[1+s(2)]\mathbf{p}(2)'\mathbf{n}(1;\overline{t_1})\,s(1) +$$

$$+\,\overline{w}\mathbf{d}'\mathbf{n}(1;\overline{t_1})[1+s(2)]\mathbf{p}(2)'\mathbf{n}(1;\overline{t_1})\,s(1).$$

As we have already seen, the term on the left hand-side is lesser than the first term on the right hand side, and thus, to the whole term on the right hand side. Hence, assuming given the unit wage and null residuals, also in the case in which the labor coefficients increase with the activation of $\mathbf{A}(2)$ the share of wages on value added grows with the introduction of this technique.

This result is not surprising. Total wages grow more rapidly with the activation of a technique that requires higher inputs of labor per unit of output, while the value added is affected by the reduction of efficiency.

If compared to the case considered in the previous Section, given the same unit wage, the profit rate decreases further, whereas the share of wages marks an additional increase. Let us refer to Table 10.2 that shows the dynamics of distribution with technology [$\mathbf{A}(1)$; $\mathbf{A}(2c')$]. The second technique has the same matrix of technical coefficients of that shown in Table 10.1, but the vector of labor coefficients is higher. Indeed, we have assumed $\mathbf{l}(2c') = [2,1,1]$. From Table 10.2 we notice that when $\mathbf{A}(2c')$ is activated, total wages increase as well as the share of wages on value added. Moreover by comparing Tables 10.1 and 10.2, we find that this increase is higher than that associated with $\mathbf{A}(2c)$. This is obvious because, with the same unit wage, the labor employed has increased, while the value added has lowered (8.92 versus 9 at period t_4). In the period in which the technology changes from $\mathbf{A}(1)$ to [$\mathbf{A}(1)$; $\mathbf{A}(2c')$], the share of wages grows from 6.7% to 12.9%, whereas in the transition from $\mathbf{A}(1)$ to [$\mathbf{A}(1)$; $\mathbf{A}(2c)$] it shifts from 6.7% to 11.7%. Finally, the increase in labor coefficients shrinks profit and implies a lower level of efficiency for $\mathbf{A}(2c')$, thus causing the rent of technique $\mathbf{A}(1)$ to further increase, namely from 4.33 (Table 10.1) to 4.43 (Table 10.2).

The rise of labor coefficients is thus detrimental for profits and not for rents. This contrasting effect strengths the antagonism between labor and technology-maker operators, who, in turn, continue to maintain their antagonism towards the resource operators, as it was in the previous case.

4.3.3. The case with residuals

We now take into consideration the case in which the net product of the first technique not internally accumulable cannot be entirely used by the second

Table 10.2 Prices and distribution with technology [**A**(1);**A**(2c')] with increasing labor coefficients and total accumulation

t	w	π(1)	**p**(1)	**q**(1)	**n**(1)	Y(1)	**m**(1)	**l**	Π(1)	W(1)	R(1)	Π/Y	W/Y	R/Y
1	0.02	0.62	1	3.6	1.44	1.44	2.16	1	1.34	0.07				
A(1)			1.278	1.8	0.72	0.92	1.08	1	0.86	0.04				
			0.481	7.2	2.88	1.38	4.32	1	1.29	0.14				
						3.74			3.49	0.25	0	0.933	0.067	0
2			1	6	2.4	2.4	3.6	1	2.24	0.12				
A(1)			1.278	3	1.2	1.53	1.8	1	1.43	0.06				
			0.481	12	4.8	2.31	7.2	1	2.15	0.24				
						6.24			5.82	0.42	0	0.933	0.067	0
3			1	10	4	4	6	1	3.73	0.20				
A(1)			1.278	5	2	2.56	3	1	2.38	0.10				
			0.481	20	8	3.85	12	1	3.59	0.40				
						10.40			9.70	0.70	0	0.933	0.067	0

Table 10.2 (continued)

	w	π(2c')	**p**(2c')	**q**(1, 2c')	**n**(1, 2c')	Y(1, 2c')	**m**(1, 2c')	**l**	Π	W	R	Π/Y	W/Y	R/Y
4	0.02	0.187	1	15	5	5	10	2	1.87	0.40				
[**A**(1);**A**(2c')]			0.581	7.5	2.5	1.45	5	1	0.54	0.15				
			0.246	30	10	2.46	20	1	0.92	0.60				
						8.92			3.33	1.15	4.43	0.374	0.129	0.497
5	0.02	0.187	1	21.25	6.25	6.25	15	2	2.80	0.65				
[**A**(1);**A**(2c')]			0.581	10.63	3.13	1.82	7.5	1	0.81	0.21				
			0.246	42.50	12.50	3.08	30	1	1.38	0.85				
						11.14			5.00	1.71	4.43	0.449	0.154	0.398
6	0.02	0.187	1	29.06	7.81	7.81	21.25	2	3.97	0.96				
[**A**(1);**A**(2c')]			0.581	14.53	3.91	2.27	10.63	1	1.15	0.29				
			0.246	58.13	15.63	3.85	42.5	1	1.96	1.16				
						13.93			7.08	2.42	4.43	0.508	0.173	0.318
7	0.02	0.187	1	38.83	9.77	9.77	29.06	2	5.43	1.35				
[**A**(1);**A**(2c')]			0.581	19.41	4.88	2.84	14.53	1	1.58	0.39				
			0.246	77.66	19.53	4.81	58.13	1	2.68	1.55				
						17.41			9.69	3.29	4.43	0.556	0.189	0.255

technique, thus giving rise to residuals. The effects of residuals on distribution are quite interesting, because a strictly technological element, which causes an incomplete accumulation of physical net products, affects the distribution system. Once again we show that the physical-technological system, which is shaped so heavily by features dependent on scarcity, has fundamental implications for the distribution of income.

Let us analyze the following inequality

$$[10.36] \qquad \frac{\overline{w}\mathbf{l}(1)'\mathbf{q}(1;\overline{t_1})}{\mathbf{p}(1)'\mathbf{n}(1;\overline{t_1})} \gtrless \frac{\overline{w}[\mathbf{l}(1)'\mathbf{q}(1;\overline{t_1})+\mathbf{l}(2)'\mathbf{q}(2;\overline{t_1}+1)]}{\mathbf{p}(2)'\mathbf{n}(1,2;\overline{t_1}+1)}.$$

We start, as always we have done, from the relation

$$[10.37] \qquad \frac{\overline{w}\mathbf{l}(1)'\mathbf{q}(1;\overline{t_1})}{\mathbf{p}(2)'\mathbf{n}(1;\overline{t_1})} \gtrless \frac{\overline{w}[\mathbf{l}(1)'\mathbf{q}(1;\overline{t_1})+\mathbf{l}(2)'\mathbf{q}(2;\overline{t_1}+1)]}{\mathbf{p}(2)'\mathbf{n}(1,2;\overline{t_1}+1)},$$

from which, recalling that in this case there is a rise of residuals, we obtain

$$\frac{\overline{w}\mathbf{l}(1)'\mathbf{q}(1;\overline{t_1})}{\mathbf{p}(2)'\mathbf{n}(1;\overline{t_1})} \gtrless$$

$$\frac{\overline{w}\mathbf{l}(1)'\mathbf{q}(1;\overline{t_1})+\overline{w}\mathbf{l}(2)'[\mathbf{n}(1;\overline{t_1})-\mathbf{r}(1,2;\overline{t_1}+1)][1+s(2)]}{\mathbf{p}(2)'\mathbf{n}(1;\overline{t_1})+\mathbf{p}(2)'[\mathbf{n}(1;\overline{t_1})-\mathbf{r}(1,2;\overline{t_1}+1)]s(2)}$$

depending on

$$[10.38] \qquad \frac{\overline{w}\mathbf{l}(1)'\mathbf{q}(1;\overline{t_1})}{\mathbf{p}(2)'\mathbf{n}(1;\overline{t_1})} \gtrless \frac{\overline{w}\mathbf{l}(2)'[\mathbf{n}(1;\overline{t_1})-\mathbf{r}(1,2;\overline{t_1}+1)][1+s(2)]}{\mathbf{p}(2)'[\mathbf{n}(1;\overline{t_1})-\mathbf{r}(1,2;\overline{t_1}+1)]s(2)}$$

from which follows

$$\overline{w}\mathbf{l}(1)'\mathbf{n}(1;\overline{t_1})[1+s(1)]\mathbf{p}(2)'[\mathbf{n}(1;\overline{t_1})-\mathbf{r}(1,2;\overline{t_1}+1)]s(2) \gtrless$$

$$\overline{w}\mathbf{l}(2)'[\mathbf{n}(1;\overline{t_1})-\mathbf{r}(1,2;\overline{t_1}+1)][1+s(2)]\mathbf{p}(2)'\mathbf{n}(1;\overline{t_1})s(1),$$

and thus

$$[10.39] \qquad \overline{w}\mathbf{l}(1)'\mathbf{n}(1;\overline{t_1})\mathbf{p}(2)'\mathbf{n}(1;\overline{t_1})[1+s(1)]s(2)+$$

$$+\overline{w}\mathbf{l}(2)'\mathbf{r}(1,2;\overline{t_1}+1)\mathbf{p}(2)'\mathbf{n}(1;\overline{t_1})[1+s(2)]s(1) \gtrless$$

$$\overline{w}\mathbf{l}(2)'\mathbf{n}(1;\overline{t_1})\mathbf{p}(2)'\mathbf{n}(1;\overline{t_1})[1+s(2)]s(1)+$$

$$+\overline{w}\mathbf{l}(1)'\mathbf{n}(1;\overline{t_1})\mathbf{p}(2)'\mathbf{r}(1,2;\overline{t_1}+1)][1+s(1)]s(2).$$

Let us first take into consideration the case in which $\mathbf{l}(1) = \mathbf{l}(2)$. From [10.39] it follows

$$\mathbf{p}(2)'\mathbf{n}(1;\overline{t_1})\{\overline{w}\mathbf{l}(1)'\mathbf{n}(1;\overline{t_1})s(2)+\overline{w}\mathbf{l}(1)'\mathbf{r}(1,2;\overline{t_1}+1)[1+s(2)]s(1)\} \gtrless$$

$$\overline{w}\mathbf{l}(1)'\mathbf{n}(1;\overline{t_1})\{\mathbf{p}(2)'\mathbf{n}(1;\overline{t_1})s(1)+\mathbf{p}(2)'\mathbf{r}(1,2;\overline{t_1}+1)[1+s(1)]s(2)\}$$

and thus

$$[10.40] \qquad \frac{\mathbf{l}(1)'\mathbf{r}(1,2;\overline{t_1}+1)}{\mathbf{l}(1)'\mathbf{n}(1;\overline{t_1})}[1+s(2)]s(1)+$$

$$-\frac{\mathbf{p}(2)'\mathbf{r}(1,2;\overline{t_1}+1)}{\mathbf{p}(2)'\mathbf{n}(1,2;\overline{t_1}+1)}[1+s(1)]\,s(2)\gtrless s(1)-s(2).$$

The sign of the last relation depends on the gap between the physical efficiency of the two techniques, and the relationship between two ratios: a) the ratio of the labor quantities required for producing the residuals to the labor quantities required for producing the maximum net product of the first technique; b) the ratio of the value of the residuals to the value of the maximum net product of the first technique. Moreover, since we are interested in the solutions of [10.36], we can argue that the sign of this relation depends also on the price differentials between the first and the second technique.

When the structure of techniques activated through time is such as to produce residuals, the activation of the second technique may change the share of wage on value added in both directions. The chance to find a reduction of this share therefore cannot be ruled out. The explanation of this result is given by considering [10.38], where the presence of residuals reduces total wages compared with the previous case of perfect compatibility among techniques of an amount equal to

$$\overline{w}\mathbf{l}(2)'\mathbf{r}(1,2;\overline{t_1}+1)[1+s(2)];$$

while it reduces the value added, again compared to the case of perfect compatibility, of an amount equal to

$$\mathbf{p}(2)'\mathbf{r}(1,2;\overline{t_1}+1)\,s(2)$$

and hence, in general, with different proportions.

The overall result is that, whereas in the case of absence of residuals the wage share grows, here it may diminish because of the different dynamics between the slowing down of employment growth and accumulation.

Table 10.3 engages in a simulation where the wage share diminishes as the second technique is activated.

We assume that the matrix of coefficients of the first active technique is **A**(1) and that of the second is **A**(2o) (the matrices are detailed in Appendix A). The labor coefficients are taken as **l**(1) = **l**(2o) = [15, 1, 15]; commodities 1 and 3, for which residuals are formed, need, therefore, greater labor inputs per unit of output than the commodity for which the net product can be entirely accumulated.

Table 10.3 shows that when **A**(2o) is activated, total wages increase but the share of wages on value added diminishes. This is due to the fact that the residuals of commodities that require high labor coefficients hit harder total wage growth than the value added growth.

Let us now consider the case in which **l**(2) – **l**(1) = **d** ≥ **o**. From [10.39] it follows

$$\mathbf{p}(2)'\mathbf{n}(1;\overline{t_1})\{\overline{w}\mathbf{l}(1)'\mathbf{n}(1;\overline{t_1})\,s(2)+\overline{w}\mathbf{l}(2)'\mathbf{r}(1,2;\overline{t_1}+1)[1+s(2)]\,s(1)+$$
$$-\overline{w}\mathbf{d}'\mathbf{n}(1;\overline{t_1})[1+s(2)]\,s(1)\}\gtrless\overline{w}\mathbf{l}(1)'\mathbf{n}(1;\overline{t_1})\{\mathbf{p}(2)'\mathbf{n}(1;\overline{t_1})\,s(1)+$$
$$+\mathbf{p}(2)'\mathbf{r}(1,2;\overline{t_1}+1)[1+s(1)]\,s(2)\},$$

Table 10.3 Prices and distribution with technology [**A**(1);**A**(2o)] assuming constant labor coefficients and accumulation with residuals

t	w	π(1)	**p**(1)	**q**(1)	**n**(1)	Y(1)	**m**(1)	**l**	Π(1)	W(1)	R	Π/Y	W/Y	R/Y
1	0.02	0.085	1	3.6	1.44	1.44	2.16	15	0.18	1.08				
A(1)			0.747	1.8	0.72	0.54	1.08	1	0.07	0.04				
			0.616	7.2	2.88	1.77	4.32	15	0.23	2.16				
						3.75			0.48	3.28	0	0.127	0.873	0
2		0.085	1	6	2.4	2.4	3.6	15	0.30	1.80				
A(1)			0.747	3	1.2	0.90	1.8	1	0.11	0.06				
			0.616	12	4.8	2.96	7.2	15	0.38	3.60				
						6.25			0.79	5.46	0	0.127	0.873	0
3		0.085	1	10	4	4	6	15	0.51	3.00				
A(1)			0.747	5	2	1.49	3	1	0.19	0.10				
			0.616	20	8	4.93	12	15	0.63	6.00				
						10.42			1.32	9.10	0	0.127	0.873	0

Table 10.3 (continued)

	w	π(2o)	**p**(2o)	**q**(1,2o)	**n**(1,2o)	Y(1,2o)	**m**(1,2o)	**l**	Π	W	R	Π/Y	W/Y	R/Y
4	0.02	0.083	1	11.45	4.45	4.45	7	15	0.58	3.43				
[**A**(1);**A**(2o)]			0.746	7.90	2.90	2.16	5	1	0.31	0.16				
			0.615	22.90	8.90	5.48	14	15	0.72	6.87				
						12.09			1.61	10.46	0.01	0.133	0.866	0.001
5	0.02	0.083	1	13.55	5.10	5.10	8.45	15	0.70	4.06				
[**A**(1);**A**(2o)]			0.746	12.10	4.20	3.13	7.90	1	0.49	0.24				
			0.615	27.10	10.20	6.28	16.90	15	0.87	8.13				
						14.51			2.06	12.44	0.01	0.142	0.857	0.001
...														
17	0.02	0.083	1	588.54	183.35	183.35	405.20	15	33.73	176.56				
[**A**(1);**A**(2o)]			0.746	1,162.09	360.70	268.92	801.39	1	49.73	23.24				
			0.615	1,177.09	366.70	225.65	810.39	15	41.51	353.13				
						677.92			124.97	552.93	0.01	0.184	0.816	0.000
18	0.02	0.083	1	849.92	264.37	264.37	585.54	15	48.74	254.98				
[**A**(1);**A**(2o)]			0.746	1,684.84	522.75	389.74	1.162.09	1	72.12	33.70				
			0.615	1,699.84	528.75	325.36	1.171.09	15	59.98	509.95				
						979.48			180.84	798.62	0.01	0.185	0.815	0.000

that is

$$[10.41]\qquad \frac{[\mathbf{l}(2)'\mathbf{r}(1,2;\bar{t_1}+1)-\mathbf{d}'\mathbf{n}(1;\bar{t_1})][1+s(2)]\,s(1)}{\mathbf{l}(1)'\mathbf{n}(1;\bar{t_1})}+$$
$$-\frac{\mathbf{p}(2)'\mathbf{r}(1,2;\bar{t_1}+1)[1+s(1)]\,s(2)}{\mathbf{p}(2)'\mathbf{n}(1;\bar{t_1})}\gtrless s(1)-s(2).$$

The sign of this inequality, apart from those variables taken into account when analyzing the sign of [10.40], depends on the difference between the labor coefficients associated to the first and the second technique.

To sum up, in the case of residuals the share of wages on value added can increase, remain constant, or diminish according to the order of magnitude of the variables previously taken into account.

4.4. The dynamics of the share of wages when the activity level of the last technique increases

In the last Sections we focused on the dynamics of the share of wages on income. In particular, we saw that, given the unit wage, this share remains constant if **A**(1) is the only active technique. When technique **A**(2) is activated, the share increases if the structural compatibility between the two techniques avoids the production of residuals. If it happens, the evolution of the wage share will depend on the relations between the different variables previously considered. Now we aim to study the evolution of the share with the extension of activity of technique **A**(2).

Therefore we shall consider a period $t_2 > \bar{t_1} + 1$. The share of wages on value added is

$$[10.42]\qquad \omega_w(t_2)=\frac{W(1,2;t_2)}{Y(1,2;t_2)}=$$
$$=\bar{w}\left\{\mathbf{l}(1)'\mathbf{q}(1;\bar{t_1})+\mathbf{l}(2)'\mathbf{A}(2)\mathbf{q}(2;\bar{t_1}+1)[1+s(2)]\frac{\left\{[1+s(2)]^{t_2-\bar{t_1}}-1\right\}}{s(2)}\right\}$$
$$\left\{\mathbf{p}(2)'\left\{s(1)\mathbf{A}(2)\mathbf{q}(1;\bar{t_1})+\mathbf{A}(2)\mathbf{q}(2;\bar{t_1}+1)[1+s(2)]^{t_2-\bar{t_1}}-1\right\}\right\}^{-1}$$

In order to determine how this share changes over time, we shall study the sign of the first derivative of [10.42] with respect to t_2 as follows

$$[10.43]\qquad \frac{\partial\omega_w(t_2)}{\partial t_2}=\left\{\bar{w}\mathbf{l}(2)'\mathbf{A}(2)\mathbf{q}(2;\bar{t_1}+1)\frac{[1+s(2)]^{t_2+1-\bar{t_1}}}{s(2)}\right.$$
$$\log[1+s(2)]Y(1,2;t_2)-W(1,2;t_2)\mathbf{p}(2)'\mathbf{A}(2)\mathbf{q}(2;\bar{t_1}+1)$$
$$\left.[1+s(2)]^{t_2-\bar{t_1}}\log[1+s(2)]\right\}/[Y(1,2;t_2)]^2\gtrless 0.$$

The solutions to the inequality are therefore obtained by solving

$$[10.44] \qquad \overline{w}\mathbf{l}(2)'\mathbf{A}(2)\mathbf{q}(2;\overline{t_1}+1)\frac{[1+s(2)]^{t_2+1-\overline{t_1}}}{s(2)}\log[1+s(2)]$$

$$\mathbf{p}(2)'s(1)\mathbf{A}(1)\mathbf{q}(1;\overline{t_1}) - \overline{w}\mathbf{l}(1)'\mathbf{q}(1;\overline{t_1})\mathbf{p}(2)'\mathbf{A}(2)\mathbf{q}(2;\overline{t_1}+1)$$

$$[1+s(2)]^{t_2-\overline{t_1}}\log[1+s(2)] =$$

$$= \overline{w}[\mathbf{l}(2)'\mathbf{A}(2)\mathbf{q}(2;\overline{t_1}+1)\frac{1+s(2)}{s(2)}\mathbf{p}(2)'s(1)\mathbf{A}(1)\mathbf{q}(1;\overline{t_1}) +$$

$$-\mathbf{l}(1)'\mathbf{q}(1;\overline{t_1})\mathbf{p}(2)'\mathbf{A}(2)\mathbf{q}(2;\overline{t_1}+1)][1+s(2)]^{t_2-\overline{t_1}}$$

$$\log[1+s(2)] \gtreqless 0.$$

To discuss the solutions of the previous inequality, we consider, as we have done in the past, different cases.

Let us first assume that $\mathbf{l}(1) = \mathbf{l}(2)$ and that the activation of technique employing NPMP of type 2 does not generate residuals. In such a case, [10.44] is satisfied for the signs 'greater than', 'equal' or 'less than', according to

$$[10.45] \qquad \mathbf{l}(1)'\mathbf{n}(1;\overline{t_1})\mathbf{p}(2)'\mathbf{n}(1;\overline{t_1})\left[\frac{1+s(2)}{s(2)} - \frac{1+s(1)}{s(1)}\right] \gtreqless 0,$$

that is $s(1) \gtreqless s(2)$.

Because of s(1) > s(2), the first derivative of [10.42] turns out to be positive, and thus with the extension of activity of technique **A**(2) the share of wages on value added increases. An exemplification is given in Table 10.1. We notice that by extending the activity of the technique that employs NPMP of type 2, the share of wages on value added grows.

In the case in which residuals are not formed but $\mathbf{l}(2) - \mathbf{l}(1) = \mathbf{d} \geq \mathbf{o}$, we obtain in place of [10.45] the following relation

$$[10.46] \qquad \mathbf{l}(1)'\mathbf{n}(1;\overline{t_1})\mathbf{p}(2)'\mathbf{n}(1;\overline{t_1})\left[\frac{1+s(2)}{s(2)} - \frac{1+s(1)}{s(1)}\right] +$$

$$+\mathbf{d}(1)'\mathbf{n}(1;\overline{t_1})\mathbf{p}(2)'\mathbf{n}(1;\overline{t_1})\frac{1+s(2)}{s(2)} \gtreqless 0.$$

Given that [10.46] is surely positive, also in this case, the extension of activity of technique **A**(2) brings an increase of the share of wages on value added.

Let us now consider the case in which $\mathbf{l}(1) = \mathbf{l}(2)$, but the structure of the techniques is such as to give rise to residuals.

In this case [10.44] is satisfied with the signs 'greater than', 'equal' or 'less than' according to

$$[10.47] \qquad s(1) - s(2) \gtreqless \frac{\mathbf{l}(1)'\mathbf{r}(1,2;\overline{t_1}+1)][1+s(2)]s(1)}{\mathbf{l}(1)'\mathbf{n}(1;\overline{t_1})} +$$

$$-\frac{\mathbf{p}(2)'\mathbf{r}(1,2;\overline{t_1}+1)][1+s(1)]s(2)}{\mathbf{p}(2)'\mathbf{n}(1;\overline{t_1})},$$

which is obtained with similar manipulations to those developed for [10.40]. In particular, by comparing [10.47] with [10.40] and by taking into consideration [10.37] and [10.43], we arrive at the following inequality

$$[10.48] \qquad \frac{\bar{w}\mathbf{l}(1)'\mathbf{q}(1;\bar{t}_1)}{\mathbf{p}(2)'\mathbf{n}(1;\bar{t}_1)} > \frac{\bar{w}[\mathbf{l}(1)'\mathbf{q}(1;\bar{t}_1)+\mathbf{l}(1)'\mathbf{q}(2;\bar{t}_1+1)]}{\mathbf{p}(2)'\mathbf{n}(1,2;\bar{t}_1+1)},$$

then

$$\frac{\partial\omega_w(t_2)}{\partial t_2} < 0,$$

on the contrary, if it turns out that

$$[10.49] \qquad \frac{\bar{w}\mathbf{l}(1)'\mathbf{q}(1;\bar{t}_1)}{\mathbf{p}(2)'\mathbf{n}(1;\bar{t}_1)} < \frac{\bar{w}[\mathbf{l}(1)'\mathbf{q}(1;\bar{t}_1)+\mathbf{l}(1)'\mathbf{q}(2;\bar{t}_1+1)]}{\mathbf{p}(2)'\mathbf{n}(1,2;\bar{t}_1+1)},$$

then

$$\frac{\partial\omega_w(t_2)}{\partial t_2} > 0.$$

In interpreting [10.48] and [10.49], it is useful to note that the first term of these inequalities does not represent the share of wages on value added in the period in which only NPMP of type 1 is employed, since the value added is assessed with the prices associated to the technique which employs NPMP of type 2.

However, in the case in which

$$\frac{\bar{w}\mathbf{l}(1)'\mathbf{q}(1;\bar{t}_1)}{\mathbf{p}(1)'\mathbf{n}(1;\bar{t}_1)} > \frac{\bar{w}[\mathbf{l}(1)'\mathbf{q}(1;\bar{t}_1)+\mathbf{l}(1)'\mathbf{q}(2;\bar{t}_1+1)]}{\mathbf{p}(2)'\mathbf{n}(1,2;\bar{t}_1+1)}$$

and hence, the case in which, the activation of the technique with NPMP of type 2 brings about a reduction of the share of wages on income, since $\mathbf{p}(1) \geq \mathbf{p}(2)$ the following inequalities are necessarily implied

$$\frac{\bar{w}\mathbf{l}(1)'\mathbf{q}(1;\bar{t}_1)}{\mathbf{p}(2)'\mathbf{n}(1;\bar{t}_1)} > \frac{\bar{w}\mathbf{l}(1)'\mathbf{q}(1;\bar{t}_1)}{\mathbf{p}(1)'\mathbf{n}(1;\bar{t}_1)} > \frac{\bar{w}[\mathbf{l}(1)'\mathbf{q}(1;\bar{t}_1)+\mathbf{l}(1)'\mathbf{q}(2;\bar{t}_1+1)]}{\mathbf{p}(2)'\mathbf{n}(1,2;\bar{t}_1+1)},$$

and therefore, considering [10.48], also

$$\frac{\partial\omega_w(t_2)}{\partial t_2} < 0.$$

Table 10.3 reports the case in which the activation of the technique employing NPMP of type 2 causes a reduction in the share of wages on income: applying the previous analysis, it turns out that a further utilization of this technique yields further decreases in the wage shares.

The case in which $\mathbf{l}(2) - \mathbf{l}(1) = \mathbf{d} \geq \mathbf{o}$, and there is still the formation of residuals, the inequality [10.44] is satisfied with the signs 'greater than', 'equal' or 'less than', according to

$$[10.50] \qquad s(1)-s(2) \gtreqless \frac{[\mathbf{l}(2)'\mathbf{r}(1,2;\bar{t}_1+1)-\mathbf{d}'\mathbf{n}(1;\bar{t}_1)][1+s(2)]s(1)}{\mathbf{l}(1)'\mathbf{n}(1;\bar{t}_1)}+$$

$$-\frac{\mathbf{p}(2)'\mathbf{r}(1,2;\bar{t}_1+1)[1+s(1)]s(2)}{\mathbf{p}(2)'\mathbf{n}(1;\bar{t}_1)}.$$

In this case also, it is useful to take into consideration [10.50] and [10.41], in order to conclude that, if

$$\frac{\bar{w}\mathbf{l}(1)'\mathbf{q}(1;\bar{t}_1)}{\mathbf{p}(2)'\mathbf{n}(1;\bar{t}_1)} > \frac{\bar{w}[\mathbf{l}(1)'\mathbf{q}(1;\bar{t}_1)+\mathbf{l}(1)'\mathbf{q}(2;\bar{t}_1+1)]}{\mathbf{p}(2)'\mathbf{n}(1,2;\bar{t}_1+1)},$$

then the result is

$$\frac{\partial\omega_w(t_2)}{\partial t_2}<0,$$

and vice versa. Thus we can argue, as we have done earlier, that if the activation of the technique employing NPMP of type 2 implies a reduction of the share of wages on income, the further extension of this technique will yield further decreases in the wage share.

In conclusion, when the second technique requires at least the same quantity of labor per unit of output of the first one, and does not generate residuals, the increase of its activity level will have the effect of rising the share of wages on value added, given exogenously the unit wage.

When, instead, the activation of this second technique generates residuals because of its inability of accumulating the entire available net product, the share of wages on value added can change in both directions. However, in the specific case in which the activation of this second technique implies at first a reduction of the share of wages on value added, any further increase of its activity level involves further reductions of the wage share.

Before concluding the analysis of the changes of the share of wages on value added, it is interesting to remark that if the endowment of NPMP of type 2 is not excessively binding, such a share will tend in the long run to stabilize itself.

We can in fact note that

$$\lim_{t_2\to\infty}\omega_w(t_2)=$$

$$=\lim_{t_2\to\infty}\bar{w}\left\{\mathbf{l}(1)'\mathbf{q}(1;\bar{t}_1)+\mathbf{l}(2)'\mathbf{A}(2)\mathbf{q}(2;\bar{t}_1+1)[1+s(2)]\frac{[1+s(2)]^{t_2-\bar{t}_1}-1}{s(2)}\right\}$$

$$\left\{\mathbf{p}(2)'\{s(1)\mathbf{A}(1)\mathbf{q}(1;\bar{t}_1)+\mathbf{A}(2)\mathbf{q}(2;\bar{t}_1+1)[1+s(2)]^{t_2-\bar{t}_1}-1\}\right\}^{-1},$$

from which, by applying the theorem of de L'Hospital, we obtain

[10.51]
$$\lim_{t_2\to\infty}\omega_w(t_2)=$$

$$=\lim_{t_2\to\infty}\frac{\bar{w}\mathbf{l}(2)'\mathbf{A}(2)\,\mathbf{q}(2;\bar{t}_1+1)\dfrac{[1+s(2)]^{t_2+1-\bar{t}_1}}{s(2)}\log[1+s(2)]}{\mathbf{p}(2)'\mathbf{A}(2)\,\mathbf{q}(2;\bar{t}_1+1)[1+s(2)]^{t_2-\bar{t}_1}\log[1+s(2)]}=$$

$$=\frac{\bar{w}\mathbf{l}(2)'\mathbf{A}(2)\,\mathbf{q}(2;\bar{t}_1+1)[1+s(2)]}{\mathbf{p}(2)'\mathbf{A}(2)\,\mathbf{q}(2;\bar{t}_1+1)s(2)}.$$

The limit [10.51] suggests that the share of wages on value added with technology [**A**(1); **A**(2)] tends to the value given by the ratio between the wages paid only in those production processes belonging to the technique that employs NPMP of type 2 and the net product value of this technique. Such a result is not surprising: we know that the higher the contribution of the second technique to total production, the closer the share of wages of the whole economic system to the share that would be obtained if **A**(2) was the only active technique.

For technology [**A**(1); **A**(2c)], the value of this share is 0.194; in Table 10.1 we observe that with the use of NPNP of type 2 the ratio between wages and value added grows from the initial value of 0.117 to the value 0.194.

For technology [**A**(1); **A**(2o)], the ratio shown by [10.51] is equal to 0.815; in Table 10.3 we can observe that the share of wages on value added, when type 2 NPMP is utilized, from the initial value of 0.866 diminishes tending to the value 0.815.

5. Conclusions

In the foregoing Sections we have reached several conclusions. Here we sum up them by giving particular attention to the effects that growth and technological change produce on income distribution and the behavior of economic operators. It is once again useful to stress that these conclusions have been obtained with the following simplifying assumptions: maximum possible growth for the economic system; techniques activated with a dynamic efficiency order compatible with both the physical OE and the static price-distribution OE; unit wage exogenously given in terms of commodity 1.

In the case of growth with a unique technique, there is an increase of total profits and total wages, without changes in the distributive shares. The technology-maker operator gains more profits and the labor operator obtains more employment. The process of growth yields an advantage for everyone.

In the case of growth with widening technology, the analysis should distinguish between different scenarios. If there are no residuals and the labor coefficients remain unchanged or increase, then growth determines an increase in the share of wages on income, and therefore the labor operator has no reasons for contrasting the change of technology. However, the dynamics of profits and rents generates conflict between the following operators: labor versus profit-makers an resource-owners on the one hand, but also profit-makers versus resource-owners on the other. In the case in which the structure of the techniques activated through time generates residuals, growth does no longer necessarily imply an increase in the share of wages on income. In fact, the presence of residuals affects both the growth of wages and the value added, and, in some cases, could greatly compromise the growth of total wages, thus implying a reduction of the share of wages on income. In this case the labor operator could still take advantage in terms of higher employment and growth of real wages (given our assumption of unit wage constant in terms of commodity 1), but the other categories of income earners could gain far greater advantages from the growth process.

In the case of two active techniques and growth due to an increase of activity level of the second technique, the share of wages on income grows if two conditions are met: no residuals, and labor inputs per unit of output of the second technique at least equal to those of the first technique. Instead, if the activation of the second technique gives rise to residuals, an increase in the activity level of the second technique does no longer necessarily imply an increase in the share of wages on income, but it may greatly favor the technology-maker operator.

The analysis, therefore, suggests that an increase in the activity level of the second technique can lead to either an increase or a reduction in the share of wages on income. However, if the endowment constraint of NPMP of type 2 is not excessively binding, this share tends to become eventually stable.

Chapter XI - Dynamics of profits, rents and their shares

1. Introduction

Profits and rents are two distributive variables that depend on quite different production factors and economic operators. Profits depend on capital, a producible factor, and entrepreneurship. Rents depend on a scarce factor, either non-producible, non-reproducible or non-reproduced, and ownership. It could therefore appear advisable to deal with rents and profits separately. In particular, considering rent alone would seem the natural corollary of having in our analysis NPMP as scarce factor of production. However, there are also reasons for dealing jointly with these two categories of income because, given the unit wage, we notice that in the long run the real antagonism is between profits and rents. Moreover, because technology and accumulation, which are decided by the technology-maker operator, affect the distributive weights of profit and rent, it is useful to analyze these two variables together. A different choice would have been required if we assumed given the rate of profit instead of the unit wage. An exogenous rate of profit rises conflicting interests between rents and wages, and in this situation the two latter categories should be studied together.

2. Profit dynamics: general propositions

Also in this case our dynamic analysis takes three variables into consideration: profit rate, total profits, and profit shares on value added, and examines both the case of technology of fixed dimension and the case of technology of changing dimension.

The dynamics of profits is crucial because who takes the investment decision and therefore shapes the accumulation is the technology-maker (i.e. the profit-maker) operator. For the sake of analytical convenience in our model we assume maximum growth, implying therefore a particular behavior of the operators. Yet, this does not undermine the necessity to assess the effects of growth on profits and to point out whether and to what extent these effects appear convenient to those operators that ultimately decide the accumulation process.

To study the dynamics of the profit rate, total profits, and profit shares on value added, we need to specify the order in which techniques $\mathbf{A}(h)$ are activated. We need also to assume an exogenous distributive variable: the unit wage still plays this role.

3. The profit rate

As already noticed in Chapters III and V, when the unit wage is given exogenously and the order utilized for activating techniques is compatible with the static price-distribution OE, the result is that the profit rate changes discontinuously every time a different type of technique is introduced.

4. Total profits

Total profits obviously depend on the amount of the means of production employed and the process of accumulation. The technology-maker operator targets this variable very carefully because discontinuous reductions of the profit rate can be reflected in non-univocal changes in total profits. If accumulation and the change of technology were to reduce systematically total profits, the technology-maker operator would certainly not remain indifferent to this outcome. Hence we must examine the various possible cases.

4.1 Total profits with a single technique

As long as only technique **A**(1) is active, the profit rate is $\pi(1)$ and total profits grow over time. As we have already shown

[11.1] $\Pi(1; t_1) = \pi(1)\, \mathbf{p}(1)'\mathbf{A}(1)\mathbf{q}(1; t_1) = \pi(1)\mathbf{p}(1)'\mathbf{m}(1; t_1), \qquad t_0 \le t_1 \le \bar{t}_1 .$

When this technique has utilized all the available NPMP it reaches its steady state with constant and no longer cumulative total profits. In Table 10.1 one notes that from t_3 onwards, without the employment of further NPMP, total profits in each period would be equal to 9.70.

4.2 Total profits with two techniques

When technique **A**(2) becomes active, granted that the sequence of techniques is compatible with the static price-distribution OE, we have

[11.2] $\pi(1) > \pi(2) \;\text{ and }\; \mathbf{p}(1) \ge \mathbf{p}(2).$

Total profits are

[11.3] $\Pi(1, 2 ;t_2) = \pi(2)\, \mathbf{p}(2)\mathbf{m}(1; \bar{t}_1) + \pi(2)\mathbf{p}(2)\mathbf{m}(2; t_2), \qquad \bar{t}_1 + 1 \le t_2 \le \bar{t}_2 .$

The first question we address is how the utilization of **A**(2) affects the amount of total profits. We therefore compare the value of [11.1] for $t_1 = \bar{t}_1$ with $\Pi(1,2; \bar{t}_1 +1)$. From this comparison it results that it can be both cases $\Pi(1;\bar{t}_1) \gtrless \Pi(1,2;\bar{t}_1 +1)$ depending on the difference between $\pi(1)$ and $\pi(2)$, **p**(1) and **p**(2), and on the amount of net product of the first technique that, being no longer internally exploitable, is employed as mean of production to activate the second technique. This amount of net product transferred to the second technique depends obviously on s(1), and the structural compatibility between the two techniques. Accordingly nominal profits can thus grow, remain constant, or diminish.

The evolution of real profits is no less complex because it is connected with the pattern with which prices decrease, the employed capital increases and the rate of profit falls. For example, in the following section we consider a case of both decrease and increase of real profits.

With technology [**A**(1); **A**(2c)], total profits in terms of the *numeraire*-commodity 1 diminish from t_3 to t_4 as Table 10.1 and Figure 11.1 show. In this case the purchasing power of total profits is also reduced in terms of commodity 2 and 3, hence in terms of any commodity. In particular Table 11.1 reports the number of units of the three commodities that can be alternatively bought with total profits at t_3 and t_4.

Table 11.1 - Comparison between purchasing power of profits gained at t_3 and t_4, respectively with **A**(1) and [**A**(1); **A**(2c)]

t	Π(1)	**p**(1)	Π(1)/p_i
3	9.70	1	9.70
A(1)		1.278	7.59
		0.481	20.18
4	3.63	1	3.63
[**A**(1); **A**(2c)]		0.596	6.09
		0.251	14.42

With technology [**A**(1); **A**(2o)] total profits, in terms of commodity 1, grow from t_3 to t_4 as shown in Table 10.3 and Figure 11.2. The purchasing power of total profits during transition from t_3 to t_4 also grows in terms of commodity 2 and 3, and hence in terms of any commodity (see Table 11.2).

Table 11.2 - Comparison between purchasing power of profits gained at t_3 and t_4, respectively with **A**(1) and [**A**(1); **A**(2o)]

t	Π(1)	**p**(1)	Π(1)/p_i
3	1.32	1	1.32
A(1)		0.747	1.77
		0.616	2.15
4	1.61	1	1.61
[**A**(1); **A**(2o)]		0.746	2.16
		0.615	2.62

Therefore in this case, in spite of the reduced efficiency of the economic system, real profits rise.

The previous examples show that with the activation of a less efficient technique the trend of total profits can change in both directions: either with its reduction or increase. This is because a less efficient NPMP, by shrinking the rate of profit, involves in the drop also the profits obtained through the use of more efficient NPMP.

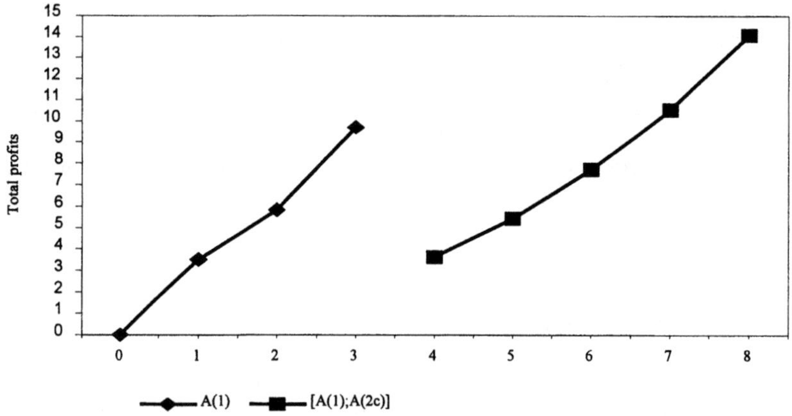

Fig. 11.1. Trend in total profits with technology [**A**(1); **A**(2c)]

However this activation, by allowing the employment of more means of production, generates also further profits which may or may not counter-balance the previous drop.

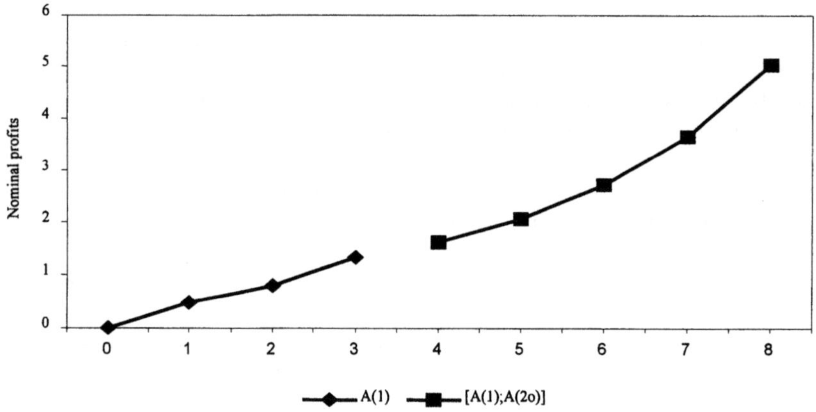

Fig. 11.2. Trend in total profits with technology [**A**(1); **A**(2o)]

Table 11.3 Comparison between the purchasing power of profits obtained by using NPMP of type 1 at t_3 and t_4 respectively with [**A**(1)], [**A**(1);**A**(2c)] and [**A**(1);**A**(2o)]

t	π(1)	**l**	**p**(1)	**m**(1)		Π(1)			Π(1)/p_i
3	0.62	1	1	6		3.73			9.70
A(1)		1	1.278	3		2.38			7.59
		1	0.481	12		3.59			20.18
						9.70			
	π(2c)	**l**	**p**(2c)	**m**(1)	**m**(2c)	Π(1)	Π(2c)	Π(1,2c)	Π(1)/p_i
4	0.201	1	1	6	4	1.21	0.81		2.18
[**A**(1);**a**(2c)]		1	0.596	3	2	0.36	0.24		3.65
		1	0.251	12	8	0.61	0.41		8.65
						2.18	1.45	3.63	
t	π(1)	**l**	**p**(1)	**m**(1)		Π(1)			Π(1)/p_i
3	0.085	15	1	6		0.51			1.32
A(1)		1	0.747	3		0.19			1.77
		15	0.616	12		0.63			2.15
						1.32			
	π(2o)	**l**	**p**(2o)	**m**(1)	**m**(2o)	Π(1)	Π(2o)	Π(1,2o)	Π(1)/p_i
4	0.083	15	1	6	1	0.50	0.08		1.30
[**A**(1);**A**(2o)]		1	0.746	3	2	0.19	0.12		1.74
		15	0.615	12	2	0.61	0.10		2.11
						1.30	0.31	1.61	

Table 11.3 shows the profits obtained with the employment of NPMP of type 1, 2c, and 2o. We notice that profits obtained with NPMP of type 1 shrink when NPMP of type 2 becomes active. This is not only the case of the profits expressed in terms of commodity 1, which change from 9.70 to 2.18 and from 1.32 to 1.30, but in terms of any commodity as the last column makes clear with the list of number of units of the different commodities that Π(1) can alternatively buy at t_3 and t_4.

4.3 Total profits with the increase of the activity level of the second technique

By extending the employment of the technique with NPMP of type 2, Π(1, 2; t_2) grows because the last term of equation [11.3] rises, as Figures 11.1 and 11.2 suggest.

We have previously shown that in the passage from one to two active techniques, total profit may rise, remain equal, or fall. However, if t_2 is sufficiently large, it is possible that the increase in the used means of production compensates for the fall in the rate of profit and prices, thereby allowing the increase of total profits expressed in terms of commodity 1.

Figure 11.1 makes clear that even technology [**A**(1); **A**(2c)], that at the beginning with the employment of NPMP of type 2 brings about a reduction in total profits, after a certain period (period t_7 to be precise) exhibits an increase of this variable.

Table 10.1 specifies the magnitudes of this change. The fall of the rate of profit, from 62% to 20.1% during the transition to technology [**A**(1); **A**(2c)], determines the drop of total profits to 3.63 at t_4. Then the process of accumulation rises total profits again and at t_7 they recover the level of t_3 in nominal terms, and in the following periods they keep growing. In particular, total profits accumulated from t_4 to t_9 are equal to 59.91 and thus, excluding inter-temporal discounts, they are higher than those obtained by maintaining technique **A**(1) at its steady state until t_9 (58.21). Hence, if total profit maximization is the aim of the technology-maker operator, changing technological dimension is advantageous if NPMP of type 2 is available for a sufficiently large number of periods —the number of periods that allow total profits to recover and overtake the previous position.

4.4 Total profits with growth in the dimension of technology

The remarks made in the last sections hold also in the case in which further techniques are introduced and the dimension of technology grows. It is still therefore impossible to determine the behavior of total profit —its evolution depends on the interplay of the rate of profit, prices, and circulating capital.

For example, with technology [**A**(1); **A**(2); **A**(3)], by comparing the maximum achievable total profit when one, two, and three NPMP are respectively employed, there are 3! (i.e. 6) cases of different possible relations among Π(1; $\bar{t}_1$), Π(1, 2; $\bar{t}_2$), Π(1, 2, 3; $\bar{t}_3$).

If, in the proceeding of the dynamics process and the introduction of new techniques, the profit rate tends to zero, then obviously total profit would become also zero —and it would fall short compared to the previous cases. However, if the profit rate remains positive and the time-horizon of growth is sufficiently wide, the economic system can experience the case in which the fall of profit rate is shadowed by effects of the other variables, so that total profits reach higher levels than those possible with fewer techniques.

5. The share of profits on value added

The share of profits on value added, or value of net product, is given by

$$\omega_\pi(t_k)=\frac{\Pi(1,2,...,k;t_k)}{Y(1,2,...,k;t_k)}. \qquad [11.4]$$

In studying the dynamics of this share, the analysis follows the framework already employed for the wage shares —we refer only to the case of maximum accumulation and consider the situation without residuals and that with residuals.

5.1 The dynamics of the share of profits with only one active technique

When the only active technique is **A**(1), from [11.1] and [10.3] we write

$$\omega_\pi(t_1)=\frac{\pi(1)\mathbf{p}(1)'\mathbf{m}(1;t_1)}{\mathbf{p}(1)'\mathbf{n}(1;t_1)}, \quad t_0\le t_1\le \bar{t}_1. \qquad [11.5]$$

We assume that the initial endowment of means of production $\mathbf{m}(1; t_0)$ is in such proportions as to allow technology **A**(1) to grow at a uniform rate without producing residuals. Recalling [10.20], we can rewrite equation [11.5] as follows

$$\omega_\pi(t_1)=\frac{\pi(1)\mathbf{p}(1)'\mathbf{m}(1;t_0)[1+s(1)]^{t_1-t_0}}{\mathbf{p}(1)'\mathbf{m}(1;t_0)s(1)[1+s(1)]^{t_1-t_0}}=\frac{\pi(1)}{s(1)}=1-c, \quad t_0\le t_1\le \bar{t}_1. \qquad [11.6]$$

Even by increasing the activity level of the first technique, the share of profits on value added remains constant and in particular it is equal to the ratio between profit rate and rate of net product. Indeed, given that we are dealing with a system growing at a uniform rate, there is a linear relationship between the rate of profit and rate of net product.

Table 10.1 shows that until t_3 the share of profits is 93.3% and that of wages is 6.7%.

5.2 The dynamics of the share of profits when technology changes dimension

Once the constraint of NPMP of type 1 becomes effective, the technique **A**(2) which follows **A**(1) in the OE, is activated. With technology [**A**(1); **A**(2)] we have

$$\omega_\pi(t_2)=\frac{\pi(2)\mathbf{p}(2)'\mathbf{m}(1,2;t_2)}{\mathbf{p}(2)'\mathbf{n}(1,2;t_2)}, \quad \bar{t}_1+1\le t_2\le \bar{t}_2. \qquad [11.7]$$

To determine what kind of effects in the share of profits on value added the employment of NPMP of type 2 brings about, we must discuss the following inequalities

[11.8] $$\omega_\pi(\bar{t}_1) \gtrless \omega_\pi(\bar{t}_1+1),$$

namely

[11.9] $$\frac{\pi(1)\,\mathbf{p}(1)'\mathbf{m}(1;\bar{t}_1)}{\mathbf{p}(1)'\mathbf{n}(1;\bar{t}_1)} \gtrless \frac{\pi(2)[\mathbf{p}(2)'\mathbf{m}(1;\bar{t}_1)+\mathbf{p}(2)'\mathbf{m}(2;\bar{t}_1+1)]}{\mathbf{p}(2)'\mathbf{n}(1,2;\bar{t}_1+1)}.$$

The dynamic changes of this share depend on the difference between the profit rate and the growth rates associated to the first and the second technique, and the degree of compatibility between the two techniques, that is, on the presence or not of residuals.

5.2.1 The case of accumulation without residuals

When the net product of the first technique is no longer internally exploitable, but it is compatible and then entirely employed by the second technique, the inequality [11.9] can be written as follow

[11.10] $$\frac{\pi(1)\,\mathbf{p}(1)'\mathbf{n}(1;\bar{t}_1)}{s(1)\mathbf{p}(1)'\mathbf{n}(1;\bar{t}_1)} \gtrless \frac{\pi(2)\,\mathbf{p}(2)'\mathbf{n}(1;\bar{t}_1)[1/s(1)+1]}{\mathbf{p}(2)'\mathbf{n}(1;\bar{t}_1)[1+s(2)]}$$

and thus

[11.11] $$\frac{\pi(1)}{1+s(1)} \gtrless \frac{\pi(2)}{1+s(2)}.$$

Let us take into account the relation between the profit rate and the growth factor, that is, the sign of [11.11]. The underlying assumption that we maintain in this analysis is that the activation of technique employing NPMP of type 2 does not reduce the labor coefficients.

During the period in which only technique **A**(1) is active in such proportions as to allow for a uniform rate of growth, we have

$$\mathbf{A}(1)\,\mathbf{q}(1;t_1) = \frac{\mathbf{q}(1;t_1)}{1+s(1)}.$$

The price-distribution system associated to **A**(1) can therefore be written in the following way

$$[1+\pi(1)]\mathbf{p}(1)'\frac{\mathbf{q}(1;t_1)}{1+s(1)} + w(1)\mathbf{l}(1)'\mathbf{q}(1;t_1) = \mathbf{p}(1)'\mathbf{q}(1;t_1), \quad 0 \le t_1 \le \bar{t}_1,$$

from which it follows that, for $t_1 = \bar{t}_1$,

[11.12] $$\frac{s(1)-\pi(1)}{1+s(1)} = \frac{w(1)\mathbf{l}(1)'\mathbf{q}(1;\bar{t}_1)}{\mathbf{p}(1)'\mathbf{q}(1;\bar{t}_1)}.$$

Similarly, from the price-distribution system associated to **A**(2) we obtain for $t_2 = \bar{t}_2 + 1$,

[11.13] $$\frac{s(2)-\pi(2)}{1+s(2)}=\frac{w(2)\mathbf{l}(2)'\mathbf{q}(2;\overline{t_1}+1)}{\mathbf{p}(2)'\mathbf{q}(2;\overline{t_1}+1)}.$$

Granted that every technique grows at the uniform rate, and that there are no residuals, from [11.12] and [11.13] we achieve respectively

$$\frac{\pi(1)}{1+s(1)}=1-\frac{1}{1+s(1)}-\frac{w(1)\mathbf{l}(1)'\mathbf{n}(1;\overline{t_1})}{\mathbf{p}(1)'\mathbf{n}(1;\overline{t_1})},$$

$$\frac{\pi(2)}{1+s(2)}=1-\frac{1}{1+s(2)}-\frac{w(2)\mathbf{l}(2)'\mathbf{n}(1;\overline{t_1})}{\mathbf{p}(2)'\mathbf{n}(1;\overline{t_1})}.$$

Because in this case we have $w(1) = w(2) = \overline{w}$ and $\mathbf{l}(1) \leq \mathbf{l}(2)$, and being $\mathbf{p}(2) \leq \mathbf{p}(1)$, we get the following result

$$\frac{\pi(1)}{1+s(1)}>\frac{\pi(2)}{1+s(1)}.$$

Without residuals and with no reduction of labor coefficients, *ex-hypothesi,* the previous relation suggests that the share of profits decreases when technique utilizing NPMP of type 2 is activated.

Let us consider, for example, Tables 10.1 and 10.2. With the second technique in activity, the share of profits drops from 93.3% to, respectively, 40.3% and 37.4%.

5.2.2 The case with residuals

The case when the net product no internally exploitable by the first technique cannot be entirely transferred to the second technique either is expressed from [11.9] by

[11.14] $$\frac{\pi(1)}{s(1)} \gtrless \frac{\pi(2)\,\mathbf{p}(2)'\mathbf{n}(1;\overline{t_1})[1/s(1)+1]-\pi(2)\,\mathbf{p}(2)'\mathbf{r}(1,2;\overline{t_1}+1)}{\mathbf{p}(2)'\mathbf{n}(1;\overline{t_1})[1+s(2)]-s(2)\,\mathbf{p}(2)'\mathbf{r}(1,2;\overline{t_1}+1)},$$

and it follows that

$$[\pi(1)+\pi(1)s(2)-\pi(2)-\pi(2)s(1)]\mathbf{p}(2)'\mathbf{n}(1;\overline{t_1}) \gtrless$$

$$[\pi(1)s(2)-\pi(2)s(1)]\mathbf{p}(2)'\mathbf{r}(1,2;\overline{t_1}+1).$$

If it were $\mathbf{p}(2)'\mathbf{r}(1, 2;\ \overline{t_1}+1) = 0$, we would obtain [11.11], that is satisfied by the 'grater than' relation, as the previous section shows. In the absence of residuals, therefore, the share of profits decreases. Instead, if residuals are formed, the share of profits may also increase; inequality [11.14] is satisfied by the 'greater than', 'equal', or 'less than' relation according to whether

[11.15] $$\frac{\mathbf{p}(2)'\mathbf{n}(1;\overline{t_1})}{\mathbf{p}(2)'\mathbf{n}(1;\overline{t_1})-\mathbf{p}(2)'\mathbf{r}(1,2;\overline{t_1}+1)} \gtrless \frac{\pi(2)s(1)-\pi(1)s(2)}{\pi(1)-\pi(2)},$$

Therefore, the share of profits increases if the left-hand side of [11.15] is less than the right one.

The data of Table 10.3 implies that [11.15] is satisfied with the 'less than' relation; in this case the activation of the technique employing NPMP of type 2 rises the share of profits.

5.3 The dynamics of the share of profits when the activity level of the last technique increases

We now analyze the evolution of the share of profits in the case of extension of the activity of technique **A**(2).

Therefore, let us take into consideration a period $t_2 > \bar{t}_1 + 1$. The share results to be

[11.16]
$$\omega_\pi(t_2) = \frac{\Pi(1,2;t_2)}{Y(1,2;t_2)} =$$
$$= \pi(2)\left\{ \mathbf{p}(2)'\mathbf{m}(1;\bar{t}_1) + \mathbf{p}(2)'\mathbf{A}(2)\mathbf{q}(2;\bar{t}_1+1)\frac{[1+s(2)]^{t_2-\bar{t}_1}-1}{s(2)} \right\}$$
$$\left\{\mathbf{p}(2)'\{\mathbf{n}(1;\bar{t}_1) + \mathbf{A}(2)\mathbf{q}(2;\bar{t}_1+1)[(1+s(2))^{t_2-\bar{t}_1}-1]\}\right\}^{-1}.$$

Let us study the sign of the first derivative of the [11.16] with respect to t_2, as follows

[11.17]
$$\frac{\partial\omega_\pi(t_2)}{\partial t_2} =$$
$$= \{\pi(2)\mathbf{p}(2)'\mathbf{A}(2)\mathbf{q}(2;\bar{t}_1+1)\frac{[1+s(2)]^{t_2-\bar{t}_1}}{s(2)}\log[1+s(2)]Y(1,2;t_2) +$$
$$-\Pi(1,2;t_2)\mathbf{p}(2)'\mathbf{A}(2)\mathbf{q}(2;\bar{t}_1+1)[1+s(2)]^{t_2-\bar{t}_1}\log[1+s(2)]\}\frac{1}{[Y(1,2;t_2)]^2} \gtrless 0.$$

The solutions of the previous inequality can be obtained by solving

[11.18]
$$\pi(2)\mathbf{p}(2)'\mathbf{A}(2)\mathbf{q}(2;\bar{t}_1+1)\frac{[1+s(2)]^{t_2-\bar{t}_1}}{s(2)}\log[1+s(2)]\mathbf{p}(2)'\mathbf{n}(1;t_1) +$$
$$-\pi(2)\mathbf{p}(2)'\mathbf{m}(1;\bar{t}_1)\mathbf{p}(2)'\mathbf{A}(2)\mathbf{q}(2;\bar{t}_1+1)[1+s(2)]^{t_2-\bar{t}_1}\log[1+s(2)] =$$
$$= \pi(2)\mathbf{p}(2)'\mathbf{A}(2)\mathbf{q}(2;\bar{t}_1+1)[1+s(2)]^{t_2-\bar{t}_1}\log[1+s(2)]\mathbf{p}(2)'\mathbf{m}(1;\bar{t}_1)\left(\frac{s(1)}{s(2)}-1\right) \gtrless 0.$$

Because the sign of [11.18] is positive, the extension of activity of the technique employing NPMP of type 2 always determines an increase of the share of profits on value added.

More precisely also in this case we observe that if the endowment of NPMP of type 2 is not excessively binding, the share of profits tends to stabilize in the long run.

In fact we have

$$\lim_{t_2\to\infty}\omega_\pi(t_2) = \lim_{t_2\to\infty}\{\pi(2)[\mathbf{p}(2)'\mathbf{m}(1;\bar{t}_1) + \mathbf{p}(2)'\mathbf{A}(2)\mathbf{q}(2;\bar{t}_1+1)$$
$$\frac{[1+s(2)]^{t_2-\bar{t}_1}-1}{s(2)}\}\{\mathbf{p}(2)'\{\mathbf{n}(1;\bar{t}_1) + \mathbf{A}(2)\mathbf{q}(2;\bar{t}_1+1)[(1+s(2))^{t_2-\bar{t}_1}-1]\}\}^{-1},$$

by applying the theorem of de l'Hopital, we obtain

[11.19]
$$\lim_{t_2\to\infty}\omega_\pi(t_2) = \lim_{t_2\to\infty}\{\pi(2)\mathbf{p}(2)'\mathbf{A}(2)\mathbf{q}(2;\bar{t}_1+1)\frac{[1+s(2)]^{t_2-\bar{t}_1}}{s(2)}$$

$$\log[1+s(2)]\{\mathbf{p}(2)'\mathbf{A}(2)\mathbf{q}(2;\overline{t_1}+1)[1+s(2)]^{t_2-\bar{t}_1}-\log[1+s(2)]\}^{-1}\}=\frac{\pi(2)}{s(2)}$$

From [11.19] it turns out that the share of profits with technology [**A**(1); **A**(2)] tends to the value given by the ratio between the rate of profit and the uniform rate of net product of the second technique.

With technology [**A**(1); **A**(2c)] the level of such a share is 0.806 as Table 10.1 shows; starting from a value of 0.403, it is reached at period t_{40}.

For technology [**A**(1); **A**(2o)], the ratio indicated by [11.19] is equal to 0.185 and Table 10.3 shows that, starting from 0.133, it is reached at period t_{18}.

6. Rents dynamics

Also in this case we take into consideration three variables: rent per unit of NPMP, total rents, and share of rents on value added.

For the analysis of unit rent and its changes over time with one, two and, k NPMP and active techniques, we already referred in Chapters III and V.

6.1 Unit rent

In the present context we only recall that when technique **A**(1) is the only active technique, ρ(1) is zero. Once the number of active techniques increases and the order followed is compatible with the dynamic price-distribution OE, we have

$$\rho(1) < \rho(1;2) < \rho(1;3) < \ldots < \rho(1;k);$$

and the rent per unit of NPMP of type 1 increases. More generally, the rent per unit of NPMP of type h increases by activating further techniques

$$\rho(h) < \rho(h;h+1) < \rho(h;h+2) < \ldots < \rho(h;k).$$

6.2 Total rents

As long as only technique **A**(1) is active, we have R(1) = 0. With technique **A**(2) also in activity we have

$$R(1,2;t_2) = \rho(1;2)\,T(1),$$

and so on, as further techniques are activated

Table 11.4 Dynamics of prices and of income distribution with technology [A(1);A(2c);A(3)]

t	w	π(1)	p(1)	q(1)	n(1)	Y(1)	m(1)	l	Π(1)	W(1)	R(1)	R	Π/Y	W/Y	R/Y
1	0.02	0.62	1	3.6	1.44	1.44	2.16	1	1.34	0.07					
A(1)			1.278	1.8	0.72	0.92	1.08	1	0.86	0.04					
			0.481	7.2	2.88	1.38	4.32	1	1.29	0.14					
						3.74			3.49	0.25	0	0	0.933	0.067	0
2			1	6	2.4	2.4	3.6	1	2.24	0.12					
A(1)			1.278	3	1.2	1.53	1.8	1	1.43	0.06					
			0.481	12	4.8	2.31	7.2	1	2.15	0.24					
						6.24			5.82	0.42	0	0	0.933	0.067	0
3			1	10	4	4									
A(1)			1.278	5	2	2.56	6	1	3.73	0.20					
			0.481	20	8	3.85	3	1	2.38	0.10					
						10.40	12	1	3.59	0.40					
									9.70	0.70	0	0	0.933	0.067	0

Table 11.4 (continued)

	w	π(2c)	p(2c)	q(1,2c)	n(1,2c)	Y(1,2c)	m(1,2c)	l	Π	W	R(1;2)	R(2)		R	Π/Y	W/Y	R/Y
4	0.02	0.201	1	15	5	5	10	1	2.01	0.30							
[A(1);A(2c)]			0.596	7.5	2.5	1.49	5	1	0.60	0.15							
			0.251	30	10	2.51	20	1	1.01	0.60							
						9.00			3.63	1.05	4.33	0		4.33	0.403	0.117	0.481
5	0.02	0.201	1	21.25	6.25	6.25	15	1	3.02	0.43							
[A(1);A(2c)]			0.596	10.63	3.13	1.86	7.5	1	0.90	0.21							
			0.251	42.50	12.50	3.14	30	1	1.52	0.85							
						11.26			5.44	1.49	4.33	0		4.33	0.483	0.132	0.384
6	0.02	0.201	1	29.06	7.81	7.81	21.25	1	4.28	0.58							
[A(1);A(2c)]			0.596	14.53	3.91	2.33	10.63	1	1.28	0.29							
			0.251	58.13	15.63	3.93	42.5	1	2.15	1.16							
						14.07			7.71	2.03	4.33	0		4.33	0.548	0.145	0.308
	w	π(3)	p(3)	q(1,2c,3)	n(1,2c,3)	Y(1,2c,3)	m(1,2c,3)	l	Π	W	R(1;3)	R(2;3)	R(3)	R	Π/Y	W/Y	R/Y
7	0.02	0.191	1	38.75	9.69	9.69	29.06	1	5.56	0.78							
[A(1);A(2c); A(3)]			0.586	19.38	4.84	2.84	14.53	1	1.63	0.39							
			0.248	77.50	19.38	4.80	58.13	1	2.76	1.55							
						17.33			9.95	2.71	4.40	0.26	0	4.66	0.574	0.157	0.269

$$R(1,2,\ldots,k;t_k) = \sum_{h=1}^{k-1} \rho(h;k)T(h).$$

Rent always grows as the system grows. This is the combined result of the fact that the rent per unit of NPMP grows, and that the number of NPMP paying rent rises. This growth takes place discontinuously, since the rent on T(1) emerges at $\bar{t}_1+1$, that on T(2) at $\bar{t}_2+1$, and so on.

For example, let us examine Table 11.4 which shows the dynamics of income distribution with technology [**A**(1); **A**(2c); **A**(3)], and Figure 11.3 which illustrates the rent of each NPMP and the total rents. From them, we conclude that total rents discontinuously grow every time a further NPMP is activated, and the rent of each employed NPMP grows every time a less efficient NPMP is utilized.

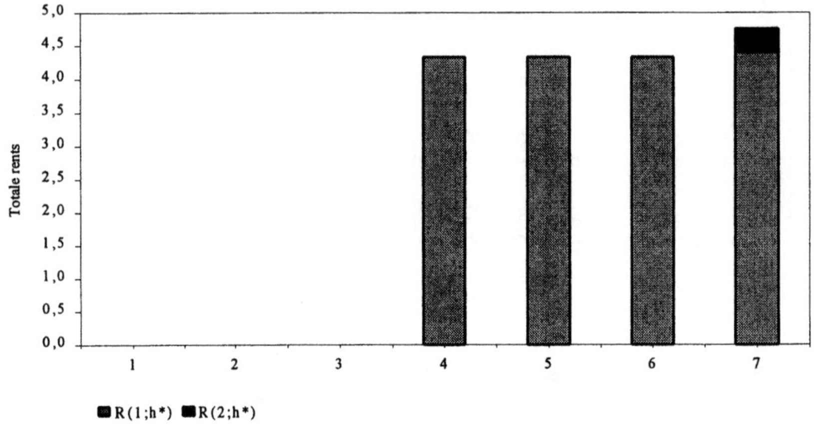

Fig. 11.3. Trends in total rents and rent of each NPMP

7. The share of rents on value added with technology composed by one and two techniques

The share of rents on value added is given by

[11.20] $$\omega_R(t_k) = \frac{R(1,2,\ldots,k;t_k)}{Y(1,2,\ldots,k;t_k)}.$$

Obviously, when the only active technique is **A**(1), we have

[11.21] $$\omega_R(t_1) = 0, \quad t_0 \le t_1 \le \bar{t}_1.$$

When technique **A**(2) is activated, the rent on T(1) emerges and, thus, we have

[11.22] $$\omega_R(t_2) = \frac{\rho(1;2)T(1)}{\mathbf{p}(2)'\mathbf{n}(1,2;t_2)} > \omega_R(t_1) = 0, \ \bar{t}_1 + 1 \le t_2 \le \bar{t}_2.$$

The evolution of the share of rents on value added with the extension of activity of technique **A**(2) is sufficiently clear —the numerator of [11.22] is constant whereas the denominator grows with the increasing use of NPMP of type 2.

Therefore the share decreases and asymptotically it tends to zero as Tables 10.1 and 10.3 show.

8. Antagonism between the different distributive shares

After the analysis of the dynamics of the different distributive shares, when the technique employing NPMP of type 2 is active, we shall make some remarks concerning the antagonism among the different classes of income earners.

The utilization of the less efficient NPMP of type 2 generates rent; therefore a part of the value added is taken away from profits and wages. If the activation of the technique with NPMP of type 2 does not generate residuals, the analysis carried out in this and in the previous Chapter suggests an increase of the share of wages and a fall of the share of profits.

Table 10.1 (and similarly Table 10.2) shows that during the transition from technology **A**(1) to technology [**A**(1); **A**(2c)] the share of rent moves from zero to 48.1%, while the share of profit falls from 93.3% to 40.3%, and the share of wages rises from 6.7% to 11.7%. Hence, the greatest change in the distributive shares is at the expense of profits, and in favor of rents and the antagonism between the categories of capital and NPMP emerges clearly in this case. Yet, with the expansion of the accumulation and growth process, the share of profits regains positions and the share of rents falls back, because total rents remain constant whereas the value added grows.

The analysis of the antagonism between the distributive shares in the case of technique with NPMP of type 2 that produces residuals is more complex. In this case, both the share of wages and the share of profits may either grow, remain constant, or diminish with the activation of **A**(2). However, by extending the use of this technique, the share of profits surely increases, whereas it is not possible to establish in advance the trend followed by the share of wages.

Table 10.3, which shows the dynamics with residuals, presents one among many scenarios. During the transition from technology **A**(1) to technology [**A**(1); **A**(2o)] the share of rents rises from zero to 0.1%, whereas the share of profits moves from 12.7% to 13.3% and keeps growing. On the contrary, the share of wages decreases from 87.3% to 86.6% and continues to reduce. In this case, thus, the share of rents hits primarily the wage category.

9. The dynamics of the share of rents with technology composed by three techniques

The activation of technique **A**(3) makes rent appearing on both T(1) and T(2), and thus we have

[11.23] $$\omega_R(t_3) = \frac{\rho(1;3)T(1) + \rho(2;3)T(2)}{\mathbf{p}(3)'\mathbf{n}(1,2,3;t_3)}, \quad \bar{t}_2 + 1 \le t_3 \le \bar{t}_3.$$

By comparing [11.23] and [11.21] we immediately obtain

$$\omega_R(t_3) > \omega_R(t_1).$$

To verify whether the share of rents grows or does not grow when NPMP of type 3 is activated, we shall analyze the following inequalities

$$\omega_R(\overline{t_2}) \gtrless \omega_R(\overline{t_2}+1)$$

namely

$$[11.24] \qquad \frac{\rho(1;2)T(1)}{\mathbf{p}(2)'\mathbf{n}(1,2;\overline{t_2})} \gtrless \frac{\rho(1;3)T(1)+\rho(2;3)T(2)}{\mathbf{p}(3)'\mathbf{n}(1,2,3;\overline{t_2}+1)}.$$

It is not possible however to establish in advance the sign of [11.24]. It depends on several factors: the internal growth rate of each technique, the structural compatibility among the techniques activated through time, the change in prices which follows the change of technology, and the availability of NPMP.

Let us consider the examples given in Tables 11.4 and 11.5. In both cases the technology employed is [**A**(1); **A**(2c); **A**(3)]. By construction Table 11.4 assumes that the full employment of NPMP of type 2c is reached in period t_6; whereas in Table 11.5 this occurs in period t_{10}. In Table 11.4 we have $\omega_R(6) > \omega_R(7)$; while in Table 11.5 we have $\omega_R(10) < \omega_R(11)$.

To sum up, while an extension of the utilization of the less efficient active technique involves the reduction of the share of rents on value added, the introduction of a further NPMP may change this share in the opposite direction.

Table 11.4 shows that at t_7, the introduction of the less efficient NPMP of type 3 determines an increase in total profits, total wages and total rents; however, whereas the share of profits and the share of wages increase, that of rents tends to decrease.

Table 11.5 shows that at t_{11}, the introduction of NPMP of type 3, even though it still determines an increase of profits, wages, and rents, it also involves an increase of the share of wages and of rents, and a reduction of the share of profits.

10. Conclusions

After our formal theorizing, the investigation on the dynamics of the distribution of income was essentially carried out with the use of some simulations to highlight some characteristic cases. The numerical analysis emphasized the importance, for the problem of distribution, of both NPMP and technological factors which prevent the total accumulation of the available net products.

We have seen how residuals rule out the possibility of determining in advance the evolution of the distributive shares, and how they bring about a great variety of antagonisms between the different categories of income earners. The problem of income distribution derives therefore not only from the conflicting interdependence between operators, but also from important aspects of technological nature linked to the presence of scarce resources.

The previous analysis would become even more complex, if an OE different from the static price-distribution one were to be utilized in the activation of techniques. We analyze this issue, from a different viewpoint, in the following Chapters.

Table 11.5 Dynamics of prices and income distribution with technology [**A**(1);**A**(2c);**A**(3)]

t	w	π(1)	**p**(1)	**q**(1)	**n**(1)	Y(1)	**m**(1)	**l**	Π(1)	W(1)	R(1)	R	Π/Y	W/Y	R/Y
1	0.02	0.62	1	3.6	1.44	1.44	2.16	1	1.34	0.07					
A(1)			1.278	1.8	0.72	0.92	1.08	1	0.86	0.04					
			0.481	7.2	2.88	1.38	4.32	1	1.29	0.14					
						3.74			3.49	0.25	0	0	0.933	0.067	0
2			1	6	2.4	2.4	3.6	1	2.24	0.12					
A(1)			1.278	3	1.2	1.53	1.8	1	1.43	0.06					
			0.481	12	4.8	2.31	7.2	1	2.15	0.24					
						6.24			5.82	0.42	0	0	0.933	0.067	0
3			1	10	4	4	6	1	3.73	0.20					
A(1)			1.278	5	2	2.56	3	1	2.38	0.10					
			0.481	20	8	3.85	12	1	3.59	0.40					
						10.40			9.70	0.70	0	0	0.933	0.067	0

Table 11.5 (continued)

t	w	π(2c)	p(2c)	q(1,2c)	n(1,2c)	Y(1,2c)	m(1,2c)	l	Π	W	R(1;2)	R(2)	R	Π/Y	W/Y	R/Y
4	0.02	0.201	1	15	5	5	10		2.01	0.30						
[A(1);A(2c)]			0.596	7.5	2.5	1.49	5		0.60	0.15						
			0.251	30	10	2.51	20	1	1.01	0.60						
						9.00			3.63	1.05	4.33	0	4.33	0.403	0.117	0.481
5	0.02	0.201	1	21.25	6.25	6.25	15	1	3.02	0.43						
[A(1);A(2c)]			0.596	10.63	3.13	1.86	7.5	1	0.90	0.21						
			0.251	42.50	12.50	3.14	30	1	1.52	0.85						
						11.26			5.44	1.49	4.33	0	4.33	0.483	0.132	0.384
6	0.02	0.201	1	29.06	7.81	7.81	21.25	1	4.28	0.58						
[A(1);A(2c)]			0.596	14.53	3.91	2.33	10.63	1	1.28	0.29						
			0.251	58.13	15.63	3.93	42.5	1	2.15	1.16						
						14.07			7.71	2.03	4.33	0	4.33	0.548	0.145	0.308
7	0.02	0.201	1	38.83	9.77	9.77	29.06	1	5.85	0.78						
[A(1);A(2c)]			0.596	19.41	4.88	2.91	14.53	1	1.74	0.39						
			0.251	77.66	19.53	4.91	58.13	1	2.94	1.55						
						17.59			10.54	2.72	4.33	0	4.33	0.599	0.155	0.246

8	0.02	0.201	1	51.04	12.21	12.21	38.83	1	7.82	1.02							
[**A**(1);**A**(2c)]			0.596	25.52	6.10	3.64	19.41	1	2.33	0.51							
			0.251	102.07	24.41	6.14	77.66	1	3.93	2.04							
						21.98			14.08	3.57	4.33	0		4.33	0.641	0.163	0.197
9	0.02	0.201	1	66.29	15.26	15.26	51.04	1	10.28	1.33							
[**A**(1);**A**(2c)]			0.596	33.15	7.63	4.55	25.52	1	3.06	0.66							
			0.251	132.59	30.52	7.67	102.07	1	5.17	2.65							
						27.48			18.51	4.64	4.33	0		4.33	0.674	0.169	0.157
10	0.02	0.201	1	85.37	19.07	19.07	66.29	1	13.35	1.71							
[**A**(1);**A**(2c)]			0.596	42.68	9.54	5.68	33.15	1	3.98	0.85							
			0.251	170.73	38.15	9.59	132.59	1	6.72	3.41							
						34.35			24.05	5.98	4.33	0		4.33	0.700	0.174	0.126

	w	π(3)	**p**(3)	**q**(1,2c,3)	**n**(1,2c,3)	Y(1,2c,3)	**m**(1,2c,3)	**l**	Π	W	R(1;3)	R(2;3)	R(3)	R	Π/Y	W/Y	R/Y
11	0.02	0.191	1	109.02	23.65	23.65	85.37	1	16.35	2.18							
[**A**(1);**A**(2c);			0.586	54.51	11.83	6.93	42.68	1	4.79	1.09							
A(3)]			0.248	218.04	47.30	11.73	170.73	1	8.10	4.36							
						42.30			29.24	7.63	4.40	1.04	0	5.44	0.691	0.180	0.128

Chapter XII – Technical progress and technological change

1. Introduction

The aim of this Chapter is to clarify some aspects of our theoretical framework of production based on compound technologies; namely, the meaning of technical and technological progress, the differences between these two concepts, and the implications of the choice of technology for the price-distribution system and the growth process. Such a theoretical setting has profound implications for the analysis of technological change. The models put forward in the previous Chapters in which non-produced means of production (NPMP) play a key role, imply an autonomous and partially new taxonomy of technological and technical progress. This novelty may rise some doubts among those used to the traditional technological classifications.

In this Chapter we also clarify the concepts of relative scarcity and technological scarcity which are fundamental for our study.

The following analysis will take into consideration the sequence of techniques ordered according to the dynamic physical and the dynamic values OE, that is that OE which maximizes growth. Moreover, we assume that the two orders of efficiency are compatible one to each other.

2. First distinction between technical and technological progress

In the previous Chapters, we pointed out that the crucial variables for the dynamic analysis are techniques **A**(h), the compound technologies made up from these techniques, the internal rate of growth of each technique, and the residuals generated by increasing the dimension of the technology. We have already seen that the whole dynamics is pervaded by technological change, a general category that includes both the choice of techniques and the problem of residuals. The presence of NPMP makes particularly difficult to work out the relationships that there exist between the degree of efficiency, choice of techniques and technical progress.

The physical efficiency of a single technique **A**(h) is given by its uniform rate of net product s(h), which coincides with its internal rate of growth. However, the efficiency of a compound technology with several techniques **A**(h) does not depend only on the physical efficiency of the single techniques, but also on the structural compatibility between techniques activated through time —a factor which affects the whole assessment of the technical and technological progress experienced by the system.

The interconnection between natural resources, primary commodities, and NPMP discloses a variety of technical progresses that cannot be fully examined in this study.

The variety of cases depends on the fact that, within the framework of compound technology, technical progress can be classified only by referring to many different variables and their combinations. Therefore the analysis cannot be resolved only by knowing the changes in the coefficients of a technical matrix or the changes in labor coefficients as the traditional single production models do. We need, instead, also to consider the changes of the NPMP coefficients, the availability of NPMP, and the changes of the production structure, which in turn affects the amount of residuals and the potential of accumulation.

For the sake of simplicity we focus on two categories of change:

a) changes that bring about an increase in the physical efficiency of a single technique that we define technical progress;
b) changes that bring about an increase in the physical efficiency of a compound technology that we define technological progress.

The distinction between technical progress and technological progress is quite important, because, as it will be clear shortly, the former does not necessarily implies the latter and vice versa. Obviously they may be associated.

Each of these two categories resembles different forms of technological change which is different from those changes due to the dynamics of the compound technologies based, as we have already seen in the previous Chapters, on given techniques.

Let us consider here only the most important cases, and see what are the effects of these changes on both the process of growth and the distribution of income. These effects depend on whether such a change involves an already active technique or a technique not yet activated. In the latter case, the effects also depend on whether the intensity of change makes this technique convenient to be adopted.

In the following Section we propose a taxonomy to take into account the effects of technological change on the choice of techniques.

Generally the analysis ahead will consider that order of efficiency that gives the maximum growth of the economic system, that is, the dynamic physical OE. Only in some cases, we shall mention what would come about once we follow the static price-distribution OE when its sequence of activation differs from the dynamic physical OE.

3. Cases of technical progress

We know that each technique is represented by a matrix **A**(h), by a vector of labor coefficients **l**(h), and by a technical coefficient $\tau_1(h)$ of NPMP of type h. Furthermore, its scale of activity is limited by the availability T(h) of NPMP type h, because the quantity of commodity 1 (NPMP1) that can be produced from process h is subject to the constraint $q_1(h) \leq T(h)/\tau_1(h)$. Therefore, it is possible to distinguish different cases of technical progress according to the effects generated by the "invention-innovation". Namely:

- change in the technological matrix **A**(h);
- reduction of the vector of labor coefficients **l**(h);
- reduction of the technical coefficient $\tau_1(h)$ of NPMP of type h;
- increase of the availability of the employed NPMP.

Combinations of these cases are obviously feasible. At the extreme, we may define as general technical progress the case that occurs when the technical coefficients of a matrix A(h), the labor coefficients, and the coefficient of NPMP are all simultaneously reduced, and the available quantity of NPMP of type h increases.

By speaking of "invention-innovation" we use a quite broad and general definition of technical progress compared to those typically found in the literature. However, the relevance of our definition will emerge more clearly from its applications in the following sections.

3.1. Structural technical progress: changes in the inter-industry coefficients

We know that the most synthetic index of physical efficiency for the single matrix **A**(h) is its uniform rate of net product: an increase in this rate is evidence of technical progress. This increase certainly occurs if the technical coefficients of the technological matrix decrease, but such outcome is also possible even if the changes of coefficients do not all move in this same direction. In general, the increase of s(h) brings about, unless all coefficients are reduced proportionally, a change in the production structure which allows for uniform growth and an improvement in the profit-wage frontier of **A**(h).

If h is the least efficient active technique, we can also note an improvement in the profit-wage frontier of the whole economic system.

We define this progress as structural because it regards the technical matrix. It modifies the uniform rate of net product and usually the proportions between the productions related to the maximum growth.

Obviously it may also occur that s(h) grows without any change in the production structure.

In the previous Chapters we assumed that the differences between techniques A(h) were due only to the process using NPMP. This hypothesis, which emphasizes the role of NPMP, can be removed without altering the previous analysis by assuming another condition. Namely, that the diversity among the technical coefficients of matrices **A**(h) is not such as to prevent the identification of the price-distribution efficiency order, that is, for $\pi(1) > \pi(2) > ... > \pi(k)$ we have $\mathbf{p}(1) > \mathbf{p}(2) > ... > \mathbf{p}(k)$, with w given; and for $w(1) > w(2) > ... > w(k)$ we have $\mathbf{p}(1) > \mathbf{p}(2) > ... > \mathbf{p}(k)$, with π given.

If the efficiency order among techniques were chosen depending only on s(h) —that is, the physical OE— changes in all technical coefficients would not raise problems in the identification of such a order. Due to its dependency only on the levels of s(h), this would not require hypotheses such as the previous one.

The removal of the hypothesis adopted in the previous Chapters —i.e. the hypothesis that allowed for changes of coefficients only in the process with NPMP— is necessary if we want to take into account in all its extension the phenomenon of technical progress, which obviously cannot be relegated only to one single process.

3.2. Linear technical progress: changes in the labor coefficients

If technical progress involves a reduction in the labor coefficients, two cases can be singled out.

The first case is based on the assumption that there is compensation between reduction in the labor coefficients and increase in the coefficients of necessary consumption embodied into the technical coefficients a_{ij}. In this case the matrix **A**(h) does not change and, consequently, the uniform rate of net product does not change either. The reduction of labor coefficients advantages the level of necessary consumption. In the case in which technique h is in steady state, because of the constraint given by labor availability, this kind of technical progress could enhance further growth. However, we must remember that in our model the labor factor has never been considered scarce.

The other effects are the following. The price-distribution system associated to technique h changes; the maximum rate of growth does not change, but a wage increase occurs for any possible level of the rate of profit due to the fact that labor productivity is increased.

We shall define this progress "linear", because, even though it appears labor saving, it does not modify the structure of the matrix and the standard commodity.

The second case is based on the assumption that the coefficients of necessary consumption are constant. It follows a reduction in the coefficients of matrix **A**(h) and an increase in the uniform rate of net product. This is a linear-structural type of progress: it involves an increase in labor productivity and in the efficiency of the technical matrix. Nothing can be said, instead, about the effects on total labor, until we first establish if there is growth in the produced quantities. What is certain is the change in the price-distribution system with an increase of both the maximum rate of profit and the unit wage.

3.3. Natural technical progress: changes in the coefficients and in the quantities of NPMP

The terminology, "natural" technical progress, stems from the fact that this form of progress deals with NPMP, that is with an entity that origins from "natural" resources. It is possible to distinguish between extensive and intensive technical progress.

In case of extensive technical progress the availability of NPMP of type h increases, that is, T(h) changes. Even with constant **A**(h) and **l**(h), the production of the process utilizing NPMP of type h may grow, therefore raising the production level of the whole technique **A**(h).

The extensive technical progress does not affect the uniform rate of growth of **A**(h). However, if technique h is in steady state because of the constraint given by the availability of NPMP, then an extensive technical progress will produce further accumulation of the net product by means of technique h. This has general consequences on both the dynamics of the whole economic system and on total rents of NPMP of type h, but with one exception. If technique h is the least efficient active technique according to the price-distribution order, the unit rent of type h NPMP will be null, and so will be total rents.

The natural technical progress can also be intensive. Its feature is the reduction of the coefficient $\tau_1(h)$, which allows for an increase of the production of process h. We define intensive this form of technical progress because it involves, given **A**(h) and **l**(h), an increase in both means of production and labor per unit of NPMP.

Intensive technical progress does not change the uniform rate of net product associated to **A**(h), but if technique h is in steady state because of the NPMP constraint, this type of technical progress may enhance further growth.

Intensive technical progress implies an increase in rent per unit of NPMP of type h, if, according to the price-distribution order, h is not the least efficient active technique.

To sum up, both intensive and extensive natural technical progress allow for production expansion of the technique **A**(h) to which they refer. If technique **A**(h) is the least efficient, there are no effects on the price-distribution system. If it is not the least efficient, rents are certainly affected, while prices and the endogenous distributive are affected only in case technical progress leads to the deactivation of the last technique in activity.

4. Potential and actual, absolute and relative technical progress

The previous cases of technical progress can be reclassified from a different point of view with our terminology.

Technical progress is absolute if the new technique —that is changed as a result of changes in the coefficients of the matrix **A**(h), a reduction of the vector **l**(h) or the coefficient $\tau_1(h)$, or the greater availability of NPMP— becomes more efficient of all those already existing, either in activity or not in activity.

In case of absolute technical progress, the technique that embodies the progress —if it was not already— becomes active and this might lead to a temporary deactivation of one or more out of the least efficient techniques.

Technical progress is relative if it allows a technique to be more efficient than at least one already active technique. Also in this case the use of the technique that embodies this kind of technical progress could imply the deactivation of one or more out of the least efficient techniques.

Technical progress is actual if its benefits can be immediately perceived, that is, if it brings about an increase in the present productions and net products.

Technical progress is potential if its benefits will come about only at some future date. For example, this could occur when the system reaches those production levels in which the technique would have entered in a steady state, or when the production levels are such as to require the introduction of the technique embodying the progress.

5. Relationships between technical and technological progress

In many cases an invention-innovation which increases the efficiency of a single technique also increases the efficiency of the compound technology. However, we already know that the efficiency of one technology does not depend exclusively on the efficiency of its single techniques; it also depends on the structural compatibility among the techniques. Therefore an increase in the efficiency of a technique does not always imply technological progress. Difficulties could be raised from the impossibility of accumulating a greater net product due to the weakening of the structural compatibility among techniques activated through time.

Conversely, technological progress does not always require an increase in the efficiency of the single techniques, as expressed by an increase in the uniform rate of net product. In fact, the greater efficiency of the compound technology could be the result of higher accumulation of net products, due to a greater structural compatibility among techniques.

In the following we take into account these three cases:

- the case of technical progress generating technological progress;
- the case of technical progress without technological progress ;
- the case of technological progress without technical progress.

We start to analyze the effects of the technological change on the accumulation and growth of the economic system. After we shall consider the effects on income distribution.

6. Natural and linear technical progress, and technological progress

At first, we take into consideration natural and linear technical progress, and the effects on technological progress. Concerning the technique [**A**(h), **l**(h), τ_1(h), T(h)] affected by the progress we have that the uniform rate of net product and growth as well as the production structure do not change. Concerning the compound technology that comprises the technique, the residuals do not change, except for the cases we deal with shortly.

If natural technical progress affects an active technique stuck in the steady state, let us call it **A**(h^*–i), this turns the technique back to conditions that allow for growth with consequences for all the techniques activated after **A**(h^*–i). Therefore, in this case there are evident effects on the compound technology. Undoubtedly, we have a case of technological progress because the techniques activated after **A**(h^*–i) were less efficient than the former and became active only because — given the scarcity constraint of NPMP of type h^*–i — technique **A**(h^*–i) was in steady state. The introduction of technical progress makes technique **A**(h^*–i) expanding once again. This decreases the weight of the least efficient techniques, thus generating technological progress. In such a case, technical and technological progress are actual.

If natural technical progress concerns an active technique but not stuck yet in the steady state, it turns into technological progress the moment in which that technique would have reached the steady state.

If natural technical progress invests a technique not yet active, we have a potential technical progress that at some point into the future will become technological progress.

Linear technical progress has different effects according to which OE is utilized. If the system follows the dynamic physical OE there are no consequences for the dynamics (given the assumption that labor is not a scarce factor), while it affects the price-distribution system. Obviously, for any given production, the quantity of labor employed by the technique that benefited from the progress is reduced and an increase in the labor productivity takes place. This is the reason why it is possible to speak of technical and technological progress.

Instead, if the system utilizes a price-distribution OE different from the dynamic physical one, then linear technical progress may produce effects leading eventually to the deactivation and substitution of the present techniques, and to changes in their activation place list. Therefore, the effects on the growth of the economic system are quite unpredictable.

If technical progress is linear-structural, we need to qualify further our analysis with additional propositions on the structure of the system, as we shall see in the next section.

7. Structural technical progress with and without technological progress

We now consider the structural technical progress. It consists of a reduction of the matrix coefficients without implying *ipso facto* an increase in the efficiency of the compound technology because of problems of compatibility among the productive structures of the techniques activated through time. Technical progress can distort the structures of the techniques, thus determining the production of larger residuals that could nullify the positive effects of the progress.

In order to determine whether a reduction of the coefficients of a technical matrix involves technological progress, we need to verify if this reduction implies or not implies for that particular technology that embodies the technique an increase in productions, net products, and their respective rates of growth.

For the sake of simplicity, we refer to the case in which the technology is composed by only two techniques: [**A**(1); **A**(2)]. The first technique utilizes NPMP of type 1, and the second technique NPMP of type 2. Then, we consider how productions, net products, and the growth rates of each commodity reacts to changes of the uniform rate of net product of technique **A**(2), that is, after the introduction of a structural technical progress.

Concerning the commodity for which the net product can be entirely accumulated, an increase in s(2) undoubtedly involves an increase in production, net product and rates of growth. But for some of the other commodities the presence of increased residuals could compensate for the greater efficiency due to the higher internal rate of growth of **A**(2).

Concerning the commodities with residuals, from [6.13] we obtain

$$[12.1] \qquad \frac{\partial q_i(1,2;t_2)}{\partial s(2)} = [\mathbf{e}_i'\mathbf{n}(1;\overline{t_1}) - \mathbf{e}_i'\mathbf{r}(1,2;\overline{t_1}+1)]\frac{\partial \sum_{t=1}^{t_2-\overline{t_1}}[1+s(2)]^t}{\partial s(2)} + \\ - \frac{\partial \mathbf{e}_i'\mathbf{r}(1,2;\overline{t_1}+1)}{\partial s(2)} \sum_{t=1}^{t_2-\overline{t_1}}[1+s(2)]^t .$$

The first term on the right-hand side of the equation is positive. The second is either null or positive, if the increase of s(2) does not involve an increase of residuals. If there is a growth of residuals for one commodity, the effect on production can be positive or negative depending on whether such an increase is compensated by an increase in efficiency. For this reason the sign of [12.1] can vary from commodity to commodity.

Concerning the production of the commodity without residuals, from [6.14] it follows

$$[12.2] \qquad \frac{\partial q_{i*}(1,2;t_2)}{\partial s(2)} = n_{i*}(1;\overline{t_1})\frac{\partial \sum_{t=1}^{t_2-\overline{t_1}}[1+s(2)]^t}{\partial s(2)} > 0.$$

Let us now consider the effect of changes in s(2) on the growth rate of production. The commodities with residuals show from [6.17] and after some passages

[12.3] $$\frac{\partial\beta_i(1,2;t_2)}{\partial s(2)} > 0 \quad \text{if} \quad \frac{\partial \mathbf{e}_i'\mathbf{r}(1,2;\bar{t}_1+1)}{\partial s(2)} \leq 0.$$

In the opposite case, the sign of [12.3] can be either positive or negative and it can be different from commodity to commodity. Hence, the properties are the same of those put forward for [12.1]. The diversity between [12.1] and [12.3] nevertheless is a source of possible different signs for the same commodity.

For the commodity without residuals, we obtain after some elaborations

[12.4] $$\frac{\partial\beta_{i*}(1,2;t_2)}{\partial s(2)} > 0,$$

Finally, we take into consideration the dynamic behavior of equations [12.1] and [12.3]

Beyond a certain period of time —that can be also different— [12.1] and [12.3] become certainly positive. The reason behind this phenomenon is the same: the weight of the residuals, which are constant, compared to the total means of production, gradually decreases, whereas the weight of the uniform rate of net product increases.

Let us now take into consideration the changes of the net product. From [6.15] it follows

[12.5] $$\frac{\partial n_i(1,2;t_2)}{\partial s(2)} = [\mathbf{e}_i'\mathbf{n}(1;\bar{t}_1) - \mathbf{e}_i'\mathbf{r}(1,2;\bar{t}_1+1)](t_2-\bar{t}_1)[1+s(2)]^{t_2-\bar{t}_1-1} + \\ - \frac{\partial \mathbf{e}_i'\mathbf{r}(1,2;\bar{t}_1+1)}{\partial s(2)}[(1+s(2))^{t_2-\bar{t}_1}-1].$$

The sign of equation [12.5] can be positive or negative depending on the kind of changes in the residuals. Here, one can resume the same remarks put forward in the case of [12.1].

The commodity without residuals, in turn, shows

[12.6] $$\frac{\partial n_{i*}(1,2;t_2)}{\partial s(2)} = n_{i*}(1;\bar{t}_1)(t_2-\bar{t}_1)[(1+s(2))]^{t_2-\bar{t}_1-1} > 0.$$

We shall now consider the effect of changes in s(2) on growth rates of the net product. The commodity with residuals will have from [6.27] and after some transformations

[12.7] $$\frac{\partial\mu_i(1,2;t_2)}{\partial s(2)} > 0 \quad \text{if} \quad \frac{\partial \mathbf{e}_i'\mathbf{r}(1,2;\bar{t}_1+1)}{s(2)} \leq 0,$$

The opposite case the sign of [12.7] is left undetermined, due to its variations from commodity to commodity and over time.

It is once again useful to stress that the differences among [12.1], [12.3], [12.5] and [12.7] can be a source of different signs for the same commodity.

Concerning the commodity without residuals, from [6.28] it follows

$$\frac{\partial \mu_{i*}(1,2;t_2)}{\partial s(2)} = 1, \quad [12.8]$$

Taking into account the whole time horizon, beyond a certain period of time, which can be different for the two equations, both [12.5] and [12.7] with some mathematical passages show a positive sign.

The previous analysis identifies some cases in which technical progress, as intended by the increase in the uniform rate of growth, also increases the efficiency of the compound technology.

We obtain technical progress and technological progress if the increase in the growth rate does not in turn increase the residuals. Indeed, in this case, [12.1], [12.3], [12.5], and [12.7] are surely positive.

An increase in the uniform rate of growth of a technique undoubtedly brings about an increase in production, net product, and rate of growth of the commodity whose net product can be entirely accumulated. But for the other commodities, the residuals may contrast the greater efficiency due to the higher internal rate of growth of each technique. If the increase in the uniform rate of net product does not bring about an increase in residual, then production, net product, and growth rates of this commodity will increase. Otherwise, if the residual of a commodity increases, then production, net product, and rates of growth may diminish or increase depending on which of the two contrasting effects —respectively increased efficiency or increased residuals— will prevail.

To sum up this point, an increase in the uniform rate of net product of a technique raises the efficiency of the compound technology if residuals do not increase. In this case, the structural technical progress generates technological progress. If the increase of the uniform rate of net product of a technique brings about increased residuals, the relationship between technical and technological progress is not clearly stated.

In the long run (t tending to infinity) the technology including the technique whose internal rate of growth is increased, becomes more efficient, because productions and net products increase and the growth rates do the same since they tend to s(2). This can be seen from [12.1], [12.3], [12.5], and [12.7] that become undoubtedly positive after a certain period of time.

However, there exists a temporal interval in which the structure of the new technology involves an increase in residuals for some commodities, and thus a smaller efficiency, that is, a smaller accumulation of these commodities.

If the availability of the NPMP utilized by the technique incorporating technical progress is sufficient to allow for an increase in productions, net products, and growth rates, namely, to allow [12.1], [12.3], [12.5] and [12.7] to be positive, the technical progress will cause, after some time, an increase in productions, net products and growth rates.

More difficult is to assess if this progress increases also the efficiency of the compound technology. For this, it is necessary to carry out inter-temporal comparisons, in order to ascertain whether the increase in production and net product that will occur in the future compensate for the initial smaller productions and net products of some commodities.

If the availability of NPMP that is employed by the technique incorporating the technical progress is insufficient to make [12.1], [12.3], [12.5], and [12.7] positive, then, the conclusion of whether technological progress has occurred or not, can be achieved by comparing the drop of productions and net products of some commodities with the increase of the others.

8. A proxy for assessing the interrelationship between technical and technological progress

Did technical progress generate technological progress? One way to gain an answer is that of referring to a proxy that allows us to make comparisons through time and between different commodities —in particular those commodities that change in opposite directions their productions and net products.

Such a proxy could be the inter-temporal average rate of value added: that is, the rate that equalizes the present value of the means of production and the present value of the productions obtained with maximum accumulation with the compound technology.

In Chapter VIII we observed that the inter-temporal average rate of value added is a good proxy for the dynamic efficiency of a compound technology. Therefore we may argue that technical progress, which consists of an increase in the internal rate of growth of a technique, generates technological progress if it brings about an increase in the inter-temporal average rate of value added of the compound technology, despite possible increase of residuals for some commodities.

Vice versa, technical progress does not generate technological progress if there is no increase in the inter-temporal average rate of value added of the compound technology. In other words, there is no technical progress if the increase of residuals overtakes the advantages given by the increase in the uniform rate of net product.

9. Technological progress without technical progress

We already know that technological progress may take place even if the efficiency of single techniques do not increase. This is the case when the invention-innovation affects the flexibility of the coefficients in such a way to eliminate the residuals without modifying the internal rates of growth of the techniques. The outcome of these changes is surely an increase of productions, net products and rates of growth of the compound technology. We shall define this "technological progress residual-absorbing".

In order to show that a reduction of residuals increases the efficiency of a technology we refer, for the sake of simplicity, to a technology composed of only two techniques. Starting with this technology, we consider how production, net product and growth rate change after a change of the residual.

Concerning production, we obtain

[12.9]
$$\frac{\partial \mathbf{e}_i'\mathbf{q}(1,2;t_2)}{\partial \mathbf{e}_i'\mathbf{r}(1,2;\overline{t}_1+1)}=$$

$$=\frac{\partial}{\partial \mathbf{e}_i'\mathbf{r}(1,2;\overline{t}_1+1)}\{\mathbf{e}_i'\mathbf{q}(1;\overline{t}_1)+[\mathbf{e}_i'\mathbf{n}(1;\overline{t}_1)-\mathbf{e}_i'\mathbf{r}(1,2;\overline{t}_1+1)]\sum_{t=1}^{t_2-\overline{t}_1}[1+s(2)]^t\}=$$

$$=-[1+s(2)]\frac{[1+s(2)]^{t_2-\overline{t}_1}-1}{s(2)}<0.$$

and for the net product

[12.10]
$$\frac{\partial \mathbf{e}_i'\mathbf{n}(1,2;t_2)}{\partial \mathbf{e}_i'\mathbf{r}(1,2;\overline{t}_1+1)}=$$

$$=\frac{\partial\{\mathbf{e}_i's(1)\mathbf{A}(1)\mathbf{q}(1;\overline{t}_1)+s(2)\mathbf{e}_i'[\mathbf{n}(1;\overline{t}_1)-\mathbf{r}(1,2;\overline{t}_1+1)]\sum_{t=0}^{t_2-\overline{t}_1-1}[1+s(2)]^t\}}{\partial[\mathbf{e}_i'\mathbf{r}(1,2;\overline{t}_1+1)]}=$$

$$=-\{[1+s(2)]^{t_2-\overline{t}_1}-1\}<0.$$

By taking into account the growth rates of productions and net products respectively, it is possible to show

[12.11]
$$\frac{\partial \beta_i(1,2;t_2)}{\partial \mathbf{e}_i'\mathbf{r}(1,2;\overline{t}_1+1)}<0;$$

[12.12]
$$\frac{\partial \mu_i(1,2;t_2)}{\partial \mathbf{e}_i'\mathbf{r}(1,2;\overline{t}_1+1)}<0.$$

From the above relations we note that production, net product of a commodity, and the growth rates of production and net product change in the opposite direction compared to the residual of that commodity. If a reduction of residuals of one or more commodities takes place, then an increase in the technology efficiency occurs, even if the internal rates of growth of its single techniques are still the same. To be precise, the more the decrease of residuals, the greater the technological progress.

If the greater flexibility of the technical coefficients involve both positive and negative changes in the residuals, then we have the following situation. An increase in production, net product and growth rates of commodities whose residual decreases, and a drop in production, net product, and growth rates of commodities whose residual increases.

To verify whether in this case technological progress takes place, we need to perform a comparison between the increases of production and net product of some commodities with the decreases of others.

Once again, therefore, it is useful to consider the inter-temporal average rate of value added that in our setting synthesizes the results of the technological progress.

10. Conclusions

The analysis developed in this Chapter has shown that this theoretical framework allows us to identify many forms of technical and technological progress and their interrelationships; aspects that cannot be always analyzed within the traditional linear production models.

Technical and technological progress have consequences on both the physical system and the price-distribution system. The analysis has been developed by taking into account only the effects of technical and technological progress on the physical system, or better, on the capacity of accumulation and growth. In some cases, though, the information of the physical magnitudes is not sufficient to assess the capacity of accumulation. In fact, in dealing with the different forms of technical progress we have also mentioned the effects on the price-distribution system. However, it is important to deepen the analysis of the consequences of technical and technological progress on income distribution and, in particular, to assess whether, and in which cases, this is convenient for the profit-maker (or technology-maker) operator. That is to say for those operators who drive the accumulation process and decide the choice of techniques.

Chapter XIII – Technical and technological progress, rent, and income distribution

1. Introduction

This Chapter aims to analyze how technological change modifies prices and income distribution, and it also points out further categories of rent related to different types of technical and technological progress.

We already know from the previous Chapters that the theoretical framework of compound technologies let us identify the price-distribution system associated to each technique. More precisely, it let us determine the relative prices and one distributive variable – either wage or profit rate – given the other exogenously and assuming that the NPMP employed by this technique does not generate rent. In the whole economic system exists only one price-distribution system —that associated to the least efficient technique according to the static price-distribution order, which in turn makes all the other active NPMP processes for non-negative rents.

Technical and technological progress may affect the distribution of income and the level of rents throughout the modifications of the price-distribution system, the rent system, or a combination of the two. Let us see how.

2. Technological progress and income distribution

There are four basic cases that should be considered:

i) the case in which progress does not affect the least efficient active technique and the other techniques involved in the progress do not eliminate it either;

ii) the case in which progress does not affect the least efficient active technique, but the other improved techniques are able to substitute it completely;

iii) the case in which the progress affects the least efficient active technique, but the progress is insufficient to change its position;

iv) the case in which the progress affects the least efficient active technique and the increased efficiency moves it upwards from the bottom position.

In the first case, the technical and technological progress do not concern the last active technique, and because it remains the least efficient one, the rent associated to it is still zero. Therefore, the price-distribution system for the whole economic system does not change, that is, prices and wage-profit relationships do remain identical to the past. Instead, the rent system changes, with an increase of rents for all the techniques affected by the progress. This derives from the fact that the gap between improved techniques and the latter technique is widened.

In the second case, the last active technique not only do not receive any positive effect from the progress, but it is also dismissed from the activity by the other improved techniques. In this case the price-distribution system for the whole economic system changes. Rents also change, following the changes of the relative efficiency of the processes, and thus they are difficult to predict.

In the third case, technical progress also affects the technique with zero rent, but not in such a way to change its relative position. In this case, the price-distribution system for the whole economic system changes only if the price-distribution system of the least efficient technique changes. This takes place when technical progress is either linear or structural —an outcome that will affect also the rent system. However, if the price-distribution system of the least efficient active technique does not change (for example in the cases of extensive or intensive natural technical progress), neither the price-distribution system of the whole economic system nor the rent system will be modified.

In the fourth case, the least efficient active technique is affected by technical progress in such a way that it loses its status of "the least efficient". Then, both the price-distribution system and the rent system change.

3. Types of technical progress and consequences on the price-distribution system

The previous remarks can be re-stated with reference to the various cases of technical progress: namely, structural, linear, and natural.

Let us begin with the first case: if the structural technical progress concerns one or more techniques, excluding the least efficient active one that remains unaffected, then only the rent system will change.

If the structural technical progress involves the substitution of the last active technique, then both price-distribution system and rent system will be modified.

Concerning the consequences of a linear technical progress, we have the following scenarios. If this progress concerns one or more active techniques, except the least efficient one, only the rents system will change.

If the linear technical progress involves the substitution of the last active technique, both price-distribution system and rent system will be affected.

As far as natural technical progress is concerned, if it invests one or more active techniques, without implying the substitution of the least efficient one, only the rent system will change.

If the above technical progress, however, determines also the substitution of the least efficient active technique, both price-distribution system and rent system will be altered.

Still, if the same type of technical progress involves the least efficient active technique but without removing it from the last position, then there will be no effects on both price-distribution and rent system.

In short, changes in the price-distribution system and in the rent system take place always when the last active technique changes. Furthermore the rent system changes also when the least efficient technique does not move, but the efficiency of the other techniques increases.

There are therefore several possible scenarios that result from these many combinations. Among these scenarios, we are mainly interested in clarifying some features of the natural technical progress that, in many respects, may be considered the typical kind of progress for a model based on natural resources and rents as it is ours.

In order to introduce the complexity of the different cases, let us compare at first the different consequences of the linear and/or structural progress and the natural technical progress. We consider a technique that is not in activity denoted by **A**(h*+1), and assume that this technique benefits from a linear and/or structural technical progress. If this progress involves a sufficient increase of s(h*+1) and/or an improvement of its wage-profit frontier, then **A**(h*+1) can change its ranking position in the efficiency order and be activated.

This does not occur, instead, in the case of natural technical progress, namely, in the case of either a reduction of τ_1(h*+1), or an increase of T(h*+1).

Let us assume that **A**(h*–i) is an active technique and that it does not hold the last position in the efficiency order. In other words it "gains" some rent. The effects of a reduction of τ_1(h*–i) and/or an increase of T(h*–i) may be different. Natural technical progress advantages the total rent of **A**(h*–i), unless this progress brings out of activity all the techniques that occupy lower positions in the efficiency order. If this occurred, **A**(h*–i), which benefited from technical progress, would become the last active technique. Hence, the rent on **A**(h*–i) would vanish, and both the price-distribution system and the rent system would change. Technical progress would therefore disadvantage the NPMP of type (h*–i), since it loses its rent, but it would advantage the whole economic system, since there is an overall increase of efficiency.

4. Technical, technological progress and operators' behavior

In dealing with the dynamics of income distribution in Chapters X and XI, we closely scrutinized the social operators' behavior. Only to recall our vocabulary, we named technology-maker operators those who earn profits, labor operators those who earn wages, and resource-owner operators those who earn rents.

We saw that during the process of growth, the interest of the different operators can either coincide or clash. This uneven swinging of interests occur also as the result of the introduction of technical or technological progress. Our aim is therefore to inquiry what are the categories that take advantage from the different forms of technical and technological progress and whether the potential losers can exert an opposition such as to contrast or prevent the actual implementation of the technological changes.

Let us now take into account the main stylized cases.

5. Profit rate and quasi-rent in the case of one active technique and structural technical progress

Let us assume that **A**(1) is the only active technique and hence there is no rent. What will be the effect of a structural technical progress that reduces the coefficients of the process employing NPMP? We will certainly have an increase of prices because the efficiency of that process whose commodity is chosen as *numeraire* increases. Given exogenously the unit wage, the profit rate will grow because of technical progress.

Denoting with the index (o) and (n) the situation respectively before and after the introduction of the technical progress, the price-distribution system changes as follow

[13.1] $$[1+\pi(o)]\,\mathbf{A}(1o)'\mathbf{p}(o)+\mathbf{l}\overline{w}=\mathbf{p}(o),$$

$$[1+\pi(n)]\,\mathbf{A}(1n)'\mathbf{p}(n)+\mathbf{l}\overline{w}=\mathbf{p}(n),$$

Since the price of the first commodity remains unchanged, for it is chosen as *numeraire*, this and equations [13.1] lead us to the following relation

$$1=\mathbf{e}_1'\mathbf{p}(o)=\mathbf{e}_1'\{\mathbf{I}-[1+\pi(o)]\,\mathbf{A}(1o)\}^{-1}\,\mathbf{l}\overline{w}=$$

$$=\mathbf{e}_1'\mathbf{p}(n)=\mathbf{e}_1'\{\mathbf{I}-[1+\pi(n)]\,\mathbf{A}(1n)\}^{-1}\,\mathbf{l}\overline{w}.$$

By comparing the third and fifth term of the equality, and since $\mathbf{A}(1o)\geq\mathbf{A}(1n)$, because of technical progress in the sector employing NPMP, the result is

$$\pi(n)>\pi(o),$$

that is to say, an increase of the rate of profit.

An interesting question to ask is whether technical progress, by involving an increase in efficiency, generates also a "spurious" rent given by

[13.2] $$r(1n)=\{[a_{11}(o)-a_{11}(n)]p_1(o)+[\mathbf{a}_{j1}(o)-\mathbf{a}_{j1}(n)]'\,\mathbf{p}_j(o)\}[1+\pi(o)],$$

which is obtained by applying for both techniques the prices, profit rate, and unit wage of the least efficient technique **A**(1o), and making the difference between the price-distribution equations of the process 1 with respectively techniques o and n.

The above equation is not the standard formulation usually utilized with reference to rents and furthermore the variable r(1n) is not referred here to units of NPMP, as it was done up till now with rent, but it rather refers to units of commodity 1 produced. Yet, these changes allow us to answer the question by distinguishing two cases.

If both techniques are activated, then [13.2] defines a quasi-rent associated to the most efficient technique **A**(1n). The assumption that both techniques are in activity may be explained as a transition process —the move from **A**(1o) to **A**(1n), requires time and until it is not completed it generates a quasi-rent. In this case, NPMP of type 1 has to be utilized simultaneously by both techniques, thus raising constraints on their activity level.

Instead, if the substitution of **A**(1n) for **A**(1o) is instantaneous, then there is an increase of the rate of profit, given by $\pi(n) - \pi(o)$. In this second case, the result of [13.2] cannot be defined as rent of any sort —neither quasi- nor spurious rent— because it does compare two techniques that are not simultaneously in activity.

6. Rent in the case of many active techniques and linear and structural technical progress in the process with NPMP

Let us assume that the technique invested by technical progress is active, and it is not the least efficient. Furthermore, let us assume that the active techniques differ only for the process utilizing NPMP. We shall investigate the effects of linear and structural technical progress.

Before the introduction of technical progress, the rent per unit of NPMP associated to **A**(h*–i) is equal to

$$[13.3] \qquad \rho(h^*-i;h^*) = \frac{1}{\tau_1(h^*-i)}\{[1-(1+\pi(h^*))a_{11}(h^*-i)]p_1(h^*)+ \\ -(1+\pi(h^*))\mathbf{a}_{j1}(h^*-i)'\mathbf{p}_j(h^*)]-l_1(h^*-i)\,w(h^*)\}.$$

Denoting with (o) the variables before technical progress, the rent per unit of commodity 1 produced with technique **A**(h*–i, o) is given by

$$[13.4] \quad \tau_1(h^*-i;o)\rho(h^*-i,o;h^*) = [1-(1+\pi(h^*))a_{11}(h^*-i,o)]\,p_1(h^*)+ \\ -(1+\pi(h^*))\mathbf{a}_{j1}(h^*-i,o)'\mathbf{p}_j(h^*)-l_1(h^*-i,o)\,w(h^*).$$

Now let us assume a structural technical progress, denoted by the growth of s(h*–i) which is the result of the fall of either a_{11}(h*–i) or $\mathbf{a}_{j1}$(h*–i) or both, that is, the fall of one or more technical coefficients of the process utilizing a NPMP. Because we assume that the last active technique does not change, prices, unit wage, and profit rate do not change either.

We can see from [13.4] that the effect of this progress is to increase the rent of **A**(h*–i), which is the only technique invested by the progress. Therefore, we reckon that this is a case of rent from technical progress.

The problem is now to find the beneficiaries of this rent. We shall remember that the technology-maker operator will introduce technical progress only if he or she can gain some advantages from it. Therefore, we must distinguish two components in the rents associated to technique [$\mathbf{A}$(h*–i); $\mathbf{l}$(h*–i); τ_1(h*–i); T(h*–i)]: the first is due to the use of (h*–i) NPMP and goes to the owner of such a resource; the second is due to the introduction of technical progress.

In order to identify these two components it is useful to point out that the rent due to the use of NPMP is the "old" rent, or, in other words, the existing rent before the introduction of the technical progress described in equation [13.4]. The rent due to technical progress per unit of commodity 1 is given by the difference between the new rent and [13.4], where the new rent per unit of commodity 1, (r(h*–i,n;h*)), is equal to

$$[13.5] \qquad r(h^*-i,n;h^*) = [1-(1+\pi(h^*))a_{11}(h^*-i,n)]\, p_1(h^*) +$$

$$-(1+\pi(h^*))\mathbf{a}_{j1}(h^*-i,n)'\mathbf{p}_j(h^*) - l_1(h^*-i,n)\, w(h^*),$$

where n denotes the new technique.

In the case of structural technical progress, given that it only affects a_{11} and $\mathbf{a}_{j1}$, we have $\tau_1(h^*-i, o) = \tau_1(h^*-i, n) = \tau_1(h^*-i)$, and $l_1(h^*-i, o) = l_1(h^*-i, n) = l_1(h^*-i)$; the new rent is thus

$$[13.6] \qquad r(h^*-i,n;h^*) = [1-(1+\pi(h^*))a_{11}(h^*-i,n)]\, p_1(h^*) +$$

$$-(1+\pi(h^*))\mathbf{a}_{j1}(h^*-i,n)'\mathbf{p}_j(h^*) - l_1(h^*-i)\, w(h^*),$$

The rent per unit of commodity 1, due to a structural technical progress (r_{stp}(h*–i; h*)), is given by the difference between [13.6] and [13.4], as follows

$$[13.7] \qquad r_{stp}(h^*-i;h^*) = r(h^*-i,n;h^*) - \tau_1(h^*-i)\, \rho(h^*-i,o;h^*) =$$

$$= \{[a_{11}(h^*-i,o) - a_{11}(h^*-i,n)]\, p_1(h^*) +$$

$$+ [\mathbf{a}_{j1}(h^*-i,o) - \mathbf{a}_{j1}(h^*-i,n)]'\ \mathbf{p}_j(h^*)\}\ [1+\pi(h^*)].$$

Let us now take into consideration the effects of linear technical progress, carried out by means of a reduction of l_1(h*–i). In this case, from [13.5] it follows that the new rent per unit of commodity 1 is equal to

$$r(h^*-i,n;h^*) = [1-(1+\pi(h^*))\, a_{11}(h^*-i)]\, p_1(h^*) +$$

$$-(1+\pi(h^*))\mathbf{a}_{j1}(h^*-i)'\mathbf{p}_j(h^*) - l_1(h^*-i,n)\, w(h^*).$$

The rent due to the linear technical progress per unit of commodity 1 (r_{ltp}(h*–i; h*)) is therefore

$$[13.8] \qquad r_{ltp}(h^*-i;h^*) = r(h^*-i,n;h^*) - \tau_1(h^*-i)\, \rho(h^*-i,o;h^*) =$$

$$= [l_1(h^*-i,o) - l_1(h^*-i,n)]w(h^*).$$

The preceding analysis has shown that both structural and linear technical progress involve an increase of rent per product unit, and hence also of the total rent of the new technique $\mathbf{A}$(h*–1,n). Obviously, the technology-maker operator will decide to introduce these types of technical progress only if there exists the opportunity of gaining additional rent.

7. Rent in the case of many active techniques and natural technical progress

Let us now consider the case of natural technical progress. If this progress is intensive and, therefore, only modifies the coefficient $\tau_1(h^*-i)$, the new rent per unit of commodity 1 is given by

$$[13.9]\quad \tau_1(h^*-i,n)\,\rho(h^*-i,n;h^*) = [1-(1+\pi(h^*))\,a_{11}(h^*-i)]\,p_1(h^*) + $$
$$- (1+\pi(h^*))\mathbf{a}_{j1}(h^*-i)'\mathbf{p}_j(h^*) - l_1(h^*-i)\,w(h^*).$$

To determine the rent per product unit due to intensive natural technical progress, we must subtract the old rent from the new one. From [13.9] and [13.4] it follows

$$[13.10]\quad r_{ntp}(h^*-i;h^*) = \tau_1(h^*-i,n)\,\rho(h^*-i,n;h^*) - \tau_1(h^*-i,o)\,\rho(h^*-i,o;h^*) = 0$$

The relation shows that intensive natural technical progress does not change the rent per product unit. This progress involves an increase in the rent per unit of NPMP employed. Indeed, we have

$$[13.11]\qquad \rho(h^*-i,n;h^*) - \rho(h^*-i,o;h^*) =$$
$$= \{[1-(1+\pi(h^*))\,a_{11}(h^*-i)]\,\mathbf{p}_1(h^*) - (1+\pi(h^*))\mathbf{a}_{j1}(h^*-i)'\,\mathbf{p}_j(h^*)] +$$
$$- l_1(h^*-i)w(h^*)\}\left\{\frac{1}{\tau_1(h^*-i,n)} - \frac{1}{\tau_1(h^*-i,o)}\right\}.$$

As [13.10] shows, the increase of the rent per unit of NPMP employed does not determine an increase in the rent per product unit, since the intensive natural technical progress reduces the coefficient of utilization of NPMP. However, the reduction of $\tau_1(h^*-i)$ allows for an increase in the production of commodity 1 obtainable with technique $\mathbf{A}(h^*-i)$. The advantage of intensive natural technical progress lies hence in this increase of production.

Before this progress takes place, the total rent associated to technique $\mathbf{A}(h^*-i)$, —a technique in its steady state since it is not the least efficient active technique— or, in other words, the total rent associated to the maximum quantity obtainable from this technique is given by

$$[13.12]\qquad R(h^*-i,o) = \tau_1(h^*-i,o)\rho(h^*-i,o;h^*)\bar{q}_1(h^*-i,o).$$

After the introduction of the intensive natural technical progress, this rent becomes

$$[13.13]\qquad R(h^*-i,n) = \tau_1(h^*-i,n)\rho(h^*-i,n;h^*)\bar{q}_1(h^*-i,n).$$

Due to the constraint imposed by the availability of NPMP of type h on the maximum achievable production of commodity 1, before and after the technical progress we have respectively

[13.14] $$\tau_1(h*-i,o)\bar{q}_1(h*-i,o) = T(h)$$

and

$$\tau_1(h*-i,n)\bar{q}_1(h*-i,n) = T(h),$$

from which it follows that

[13.15] $$\bar{q}_1(h*-i,n) = \bar{q}_1(h*-i,o)\frac{\tau_1(h*-i,o)}{\tau_1(h*-i,n)}.$$

The change of total rent due to the intensive natural technical progress is therefore given by

[13.16] $$R(h*-i,n) - R(h*-i,o) = [\rho(h*-i,n;h^*) - \rho(h*-i,o;h^*)]T(h).$$

In case of extensive natural technical progress, the rent per unit of NPMP and the rent per product unit do not change. In this as the previous cases, however, the total rent of technique **A**(h*–i) changes, thanks to a greater availability of NPMP.

The maximum total rent of **A**(h*–i) before this progress is

[13.17] $$R(h*-i,o) = \tau_1(h*-i)\rho(h*-i;h^*)\bar{q}_1(h*-i,o);$$

after the introduction of an extensive natural technical progress this rent becomes

$$R(h*-i,n) = \tau_1(h*-i)\rho(h*-i;h^*)\bar{q}_1(h*-i,n).$$

Recalling the following relationship

[13.18] $$\bar{q}_1(h*-i,o) = \frac{T(h,o)}{\tau_1(h*-i)}$$

and

$$\bar{q}_1(h*-i,n) = \frac{T(h,n)}{\tau_1(h*-i)}$$

and, as a consequence of the extensive technical progress,

$$T(h,o) < T(h,n),$$

the change of total rent due to the extensive natural technical progress is given by

[13.19] $$R(h*-i,n) - R(h*-i,o) = \rho(h*-i;h^*)[T(h,n) - T(h,o)].$$

To sum up, the natural technical progress does not involve an increase of the rent per unit of product. However, in reducing the coefficient of utilization of NPMP and/or increasing the availability of NPMP, this technical progress allows for an increase of total rent obtainable by means of that technique with NPMP that is invested by the change. The analysis, therefore, let us conclude with confidence that the benefits of this progress go only to the owner of the NPMP.

8. Technical progress in all processes of a technique

Let us now examine the case of technical progress still concerned with technique **A**(h*–i), but in such a way that it affects the technical coefficients of all processes, and not only that one utilizing NPMP. This is a much more realistic case than the case analyzed previously where changes involved only one specific process.

Prices, unit wage, and profit rate do not change, because we assume that technical progress does not affect the last active technique.

In the foregoing analysis technical progress had the effect of increasing the rent of only the process with NPMP, the only one for which we assumed the possibility of a decrease in the coefficients a_{11}, $\mathbf{a}_{j1}$, l_1, τ_1.

In the present case, the whole technique **A**(h*–i) improves, and thus all its processes can gain a rent due to the different efficiency compared to technique **A**(h*) that is responsible for the determination of prices and the endogenous distributive variable.

Let us focus our considerations on the rent deriving from technical progress per unit of commodity. Natural technical progress does not change this rent; even though for an intensive natural progress we have

$$\tau_1(h^*-i, n) < \tau_1(h^*-i, o), \qquad [13.20]$$

to which it follows an increase of rent per unit of NPMP, as it is shown in [13.3], we get

$$\tau_1(h^*-i, n)\rho(h^*-i, n; h^*) = \tau_1(h^*-i, o)\rho(h^*-i, o; h^*), \qquad [13.21]$$

since the increase of rent per unit of NPMP is counterbalanced by the decrease of τ_1(h*–i). Therefore, we have

$$r(h^*-i; h^*) = \tau_1(h^*-i, n)\rho(h^*-i, n; h^*) = \tau_1(h^*-i, o)\rho(h^*-i, o; h^*),$$

where r(h*–i;h*) indicates the rent caused by the utilization of NPMP per unit of commodity 1.

9. Rent from technological scarcity and technological progress: a simplified case

In case there are only two techniques, **A**(1) and **A**(2), and two commodities, the rent from structural or linear technical progress is determined by the following equations, assuming that technical progress occurs in **A**(1), which then becomes **A**(1n)

$$[a_{11}(1n)p_1(2) + a_{21}(1n)p_2(2)][1+\pi(2)] + l_1(1n)w(2) + \\ + r(1n;2) + r_{1tp}(1n;2) = p_1(2), \qquad [13.22]$$

$$[a_{12}(1n)p_1(2) + a_{22}(1n)p_2(2)][1+\pi(2)] + l_2(1n)w(2) + \\ + r_{2tp}(1n;2) = p_2(2),$$

where $r_{itp}(h^*-i;h^*)$ denotes the rent from linear and structural technical progress per unit of i-th commodity.

From [13.22] it follows

[13.23] $$r_{1tp}(1n;2) = p_1(2) - [a_{11}(1n)p_1(2) + a_{21}(1n)p_2(2)]$$
$$[1+\pi(2)] - l_1(1n)w(2) - r(1n;2),$$
$$r_{2tp}(1n;2) = p_2(2) - [a_{12}(1n)p_1(2) + a_{22}(1n)p_2(2)][1+\pi(2)] - l_2(1n)w(2).$$

The variable r(1n;2) represents the rent per unit of commodity 1 derived from the utilization of NPMP, and it has already been calculated. The variables $r_{1tp}(1n;2)$ and $r_{2tp}(1n;2)$ represent the rent per unit of respectively commodity 1 and 2 generated by the linear and/or structural technical progress in the two processes — i.e. process 1 for the former and process 2 for the latter.

Given exogenously w, the price-distribution system associated to **A**(2) determines **p**(2) and π(2). Therefore from [13.23], we may find out the rent arisen from linear or structural technical progress in the two production processes of technique **A**(1n).

A reasonable doubt comes from the use of our terminology. Can we justify the name of rent given to $r_{1tp}(1n;2)$ and $r_{2tp}(1n;2)$? The answer, in our opinion, is positive because the necessary condition for the existence of these rents is the scarcity of NPMP of type 1. Without this scarcity, technique **A**(2) would not be employed and hence there would be no rent. When the processes that do not make use of NPMP are identical for all techniques, the category of rent will benefit only that process which directly utilizes NPMP. However, the scarcity of NPMP has an effect also on those processes that do not directly utilize NPMP because the technical progress makes them more efficient than the parallel processes of the least efficient active technique.

In conclusion, we can distinguish two types of rent according to the following definitions: r(1;2) is a form of rent from technological scarcity because it is determined from the scarcity of NPMP of type 1 even if a greater efficiency is expected from the process utilizing this NPMP in technique **A**(1) than the corresponding process in technique **A**(2); $r_{1tp}(1n;2)$ and $r_{2tp}(1n;2)$ are rents from technical or technological progress, even though we assume some scarcity of NPMP of type 1.

If natural technical progress were able to eliminate the technological scarcity of NPMP of type 1, the rent from technological scarcity and consequently the rent from technological progress would not exist.

10. Rent from technological scarcity and technological progress: the general case

Let us now take into account a more general case in which the active techniques are h*, each producing m+1 commodities. Technique **A**(h*–i), which is affected by technical progress as it is not the last one in activity, shows a maximum of m+1 rents —some of them obviously could have null values.

These rents are determined by the following system

[13.24] $$[1+\pi(h^*)]\,\mathbf{A}(h^*-i,\,n)'\mathbf{p}\,(h^*) + \mathbf{l}(h^*-i,\,n)w(h^*) + \\ + \mathbf{r}(h^*-i;\,h^*) + \mathbf{r}_{tp}(h^*-i;\,h^*) = \mathbf{p}(h^*),$$

where $\mathbf{r}(h^*-i;h^*)$ is the vector of the rents due to the technological scarcity of NPMP of type h^*-i. These rents are relative to that process which utilizes NPMP, that is, to process 1. The first element of vector $\mathbf{r}(h^*-i;h^*)$ is the rent from technological scarcity per unit of commodity 1. This quantity remains unchanged by the technical progress, and can be determined from [13.4]. The other m elements of the vector are null, because the other m processes do not utilize NPMP. Therefore, we have

[13.25] $$\mathbf{r}(h^*-i;h^*) = \begin{bmatrix} r(h^*-1;h^*) \\ 0 \\ \cdot \\ \cdot \\ \cdot \\ 0 \end{bmatrix}.$$

In turn, $\mathbf{r}_{tp}(h^*-i;h^*)$ is the vector of rents due to structural or linear technical progress —rents that can occur in each production process. Therefore, we have

$$r_{tp}(h^*-i;h^*) = \begin{bmatrix} r_{1tp}(h^*-i;h^*) \\ r_{2tp}(h^*-i;h^*) \\ \cdot \\ \cdot \\ \cdot \\ r_{m+1tp}(h^*-i;h^*) \end{bmatrix}.$$

The rents deriving from linear or structural technical progress which take place as a result of the decrease of the coefficients in $\mathbf{A}(h^*-i)$ or in $\mathbf{l}(h^*-i)$ can be determined by means of system [13.24] in the following way

$$\mathbf{r}_{tp}(h^*-i;h^*) = \{[\mathbf{I} - [1+\pi(h^*)]\mathbf{A}(h^*-i,n)'\}\mathbf{p}(h^*) + \\ -\mathbf{l}(h^*-i,n)w(h^*) - \mathbf{r}(h^*-i;h^*),$$

where $\mathbf{p}(h^*)$, $\pi(h^*)$, $w(h^*)$, and $\mathbf{r}(h^*-i;h^*)$ remain unchanged, because they are determined by the least efficient technique in activity which is kept, *ex hyphotesi*, constant.

11. Conclusions

Even though the analysis of this Chapter was focused on few selected cases, new types of rent deriving from technological progress have clearly emerged. In fact, we have analyzed the consequences of different types of technical progress both on rent per product unit and on total rent.

It is commonly held that technological progress makes the role of natural resources and primary commodity of secondary importance. As it has been shown in the previous analysis, our point of view is quite different. In our opinion, technological progress is the mean by which absolute scarcities become relative scarcities. In so doing, we confirm the fundamental role played by technological progress in the weakening of scarcity constraints on growth. However, we also pointed out that the concept of scarcity relative to NPMP is quite complex. The elementary idea is that relative scarcity implies a slowdown in economic growth, up to the steady state. From then on, absolute scarcity takes place. Relative scarcity is thus a pre-condition of absolute scarcity.

From our viewpoint, the degree of relative scarcity, which takes place when at least two techniques are in activity, continues to change under the pressure of technical and technological progress. Thus, natural resources can be interpreted as scarcities that become relative thanks to the presence of technical progress. It is because of this link that natural scarcities are in our framework also technological scarcities, namely an increase of technological progress (i.e. a relaxation of technological scarcity) will also signify a decrease of the scarcity of natural resources. In turn, rent, in its different forms, is the mirror of technological scarcity in the price-distribution domain. This study has taken into account several types of rent or quasi-rent, and analyzed their relations with profits and wages. In particular this Chapter has shown how the scarcity of NPMP is a necessary condition to develop from technological or technical progress some form of rents also among processes that do not directly utilize NPMP.

Technological scarcity is, however, a broader category than that of natural resources. It involves all those processes, techniques, or technologies that show scale constraints for the scarcity of one factor, or for any other binding constraint involving the simultaneous activity of two techniques with different degrees of efficiency. We can therefore reinterpret some of the previous analysis from a different perspective. Namely, we can assimilate the NPMP which causes in a technique the raise of rent to a broader category that encompasses any other factor constraint including even the entrepreneurial-organizational factor —the less natural among all the factors of production.

Obviously, to develop this re-interpretation would require further analysis, which lies outside the scope of the present volume.

Chapter XIV – Conclusions and further lines of research

1. Synthesis of results

This volume attempted to achieve several objectives and we believe it did. Its starting point was historical-theoretical. We were convinced that the issues on natural resources, technologies and rent did not receive the attention in the economic thought that they deserve. Indeed, we showed how economic theory swung back and forth around them through time. Recently these themes were considered far less relevant than those —certainly central but not exhaustive— that explained economic growth exclusively in terms of produced means of production.

In particular, economic theory in its uniperiodal or static and dynamic multi-sectoral versions, —with few exceptions— underestimated or did not perceive the evidence emerging from economic history and the current situation in which natural resources played and continue to play a significant role. This empirical relevance is not discounted even in those economic systems —such as the developed economies—where growth is dominated by capital accumulation and technological change.

Furthermore, modern economic theory did not perceive the category of rent in all its significance. Rent as an income category can be representative of a wide variety of scarcities which may be easily related to technological change and progress. Though new, these categories can be theoretically handled in a fashion similar to that applied to natural resources.

By and large our analysis attempts precisely this. We started by referring to the old categories of scarce resources and rent that the Classical School linked to the "land" factor. Then we dealt with the problem of whether and how it is possible to make these original categories evolve towards a more general class of concepts concerned with technology that would generate both technological scarcity and technological rent.

Without obviously pretending to offer a simplified re-exposition of our analysis —an almost impossible task given the heavy analytic apparatus— we summarize here several lines of our work which, though do not follow the order of the Chapters, aim to show the most significant problems we faced in this volume.

The first problem is that of building a multi-sectoral model with scarce resources, which we also called non-produced or non-reproduced means of production: an input in the production of basic commodities or primary commodities. The presence of scarce resources gives rise to scale constraints that require, as production grows, the activation of numerous processes that use different qualities of non-produced means of production to obtain the same primary commodity. This affects the outcomes of both the price-distribution system and the physical-quantity system and makes the two systems also causally interconnected. That is the solutions of the price-distribution system influence the solutions of the physical-quantity system and, in turn, the latter affects some variables of the former. Therefore, the independence of the two systems, as typical of the linear production models, is lost.

The second problem concerns the efficiency order of the processes that use non-produced means of production to produce the same primary commodity. We identified the orders of efficiency of the following classes: physical-quantity OE; static price-distribution OE; dynamic-physical OE; dynamic-values OE; and dynamic price-distribution OE. According to the different conditions of production growth and accumulation, each of these efficiency orders, in turn, becomes crucial in deciding the activation sequence of processes with non-produced means of production.

The third problem concerns the determination of prices and distribution of income. We studied this issue in a static and comparative static setting and we analyzed how changes in the activity level will affect such determinations. Compared to the usual linear models of production and distribution what emerged here is a set of important new features concerning in particular the role of rent and the rentability order among processes with non-produced means of production. We showed that at any given efficiency order, the rentability order among such processes could change with the increase of activity levels. These aspects are equally important with reference to changes of the exogenous distributive variable. Such changes may modify the order of price-distribution efficiency and they may involve the activation of processes previously out of use or, vice versa, make no longer viable previous active processes. In synthesis, the presence of natural resources and non-produced means of production profoundly modifies the relations between wages and profits because of rent. Furthermore, it influences the kind of impact that changes in the level of activity or in the exogenous distributive variable —either unit wage, or profit rate— have on the system.

The fourth problem concerns the changes faced by technology in the presence of natural resources and non-produced means of production. In order to investigate these problems in a static and dynamic context, we developed two alternative models: one shaped by global technologies, and the other shaped by composed technologies.

In the model of global technologies, the technological matrix contains many processes producing the same primary commodity through the utilization of splitting coefficients. They allow us to identify a rate of net product connected to the technology and to analyze the effects of variations in the activity level. This is an original theoretical framework, that significantly modifies the well-known technological matrices of the linear production models. In our study it is used to make a comparative static analysis.

In the model of composed technologies there exists a multiplicity of techniques each one characterized by either a natural resource or a non-produced means of production. Any single technique differs from the others but they are then composed in the processes of accumulation and growth. The result is a non-proportional dynamic process since the different structure of the technical matrices generates residuals of production that cannot be accumulated. This calls for a complex analysis of the orders of efficiency among techniques (dynamic physical

OE; dynamic-values OE; dynamic price-distribution OE) and, therefore, also of their sequence of activation in the accumulation and growth process.

The fifth problem concerns the features of the dynamic process. The traditional result that the constant rate of maximum growth equals the uniform rate of net product —which is also the rate of accumulation— is no longer feasible with the presence of non-produced means of production. In its place, several different alternative dynamic paths emerge which depend on the time horizon, the residuals that cannot be accumulated, the net products, their order, and the uneven rates of growth of the individual techniques. The possible cases were too many to make an analytical solution possible. Therefore, we developed some numerical simulations. The analysis of these different cases led to identify two orders of dynamic efficiency: one dynamic-physical which is based on the uniform rates of the net product held by the different techniques and their structural compatibility; and one dynamic-values which is based on the average inter-temporal rate of value added that allows to rank the different techniques when the existence of different residuals and time horizons prevents the determination of the dynamic-physical order of efficiency.

In such a framework we dealt also with the question of establishing whether the dynamic efficiency order of maximum growth and the price-distribution efficiency order were compatible. The question is important because the profit earners —or in other words the operator who guides the accumulation and chooses the techniques—act according to the results of the price-distribution efficiency order. The conclusion we achieve is positive: there exists a dynamic price-distribution efficiency order that is capable of determining a choice of technologies corresponding to the maximum rate of growth.

The sixth problem concerns the analysis of the effects of accumulation and growth on the distribution of income among wages, profits, and rents —both in terms of individual units, aggregate magnitudes and relative shares.

Some interesting scenarios emerged from this study of either collusion or conflict of interest among the operators who control the different factors of production and, respectively, earn wages, profits, and rents.

In particular, our analysis —limited to the case of maximum accumulation— investigated the effects of growth on these various categories of income earners. Concerning worker, after having fixed the unit wage exogenously in terms of commodity 1, we gained the following results. Because the wage is linked to commodity 1, workers are safeguarded with a wage-indexation that keeps up with the dynamics of that commodity. However, because the production process of commodity 1 becomes increasingly less efficient, we observed that workers, though they benefit in terms of real wage and level of employment, might lose something in terms of distributive shares.

When the entire accumulation of net products is impossible to achieve, the consequences could affect workers and not profit earners who may find their income share increased over the total value added. This position of advantage of the profit earners may occur despite the fact that the process of growth, with the loss of efficiency in the *numeraire* sector, continues to transfer purchasing power to rent earners.

The outcome of this analysis confirms the central importance of the physical-technological system —with all its scarcity-based features— in shaping the distribution of income. The most important innovative aspect concerns rents, which profoundly modifies the distribution process, disclosing the complex web of interests of the different social categories during the process of accumulation.

The seventh problem concerns technical and technological progress. The existence of non-produced means of production gives rise to several complex categories of technical progress —structural, natural, linear, absolute, and relative technical progress. They are complex categories because in a model characterized by compound technologies, a technical progress can be classified only by referring to several variables. In turn the key distinction between progress of one technique and progress of the technology was made to assess the interrelations of these two phenomena. We also saw how differently they affect the economic system in its capacity of accumulation and growth and in its capacity to relax the constraint of the non-produced means of production.

Technical and technological progress, furthermore, generate changes in the prices and income distribution. Here, we identify clearly some new types of rent connected to the various types of progress. We also evaluate the interest that the single social categories have in favoring, hindering or retarding the introduction of the various type of progress.

What ultimately emerges from this model is that scarce resources, scarce technologies and the technological rents associated to them, play a crucial role in a vast range of phenomena such as production, distribution, accumulation, growth, choice of techniques, and technological progress. The well-established results of those multi-sectoral models of production that neglect scarce resources and non-produced production means, in our new framework, may be rejected in some cases and widely modified in others.

2. Ongoing extensions: *numeraire*, re-integration, and the environment

Our analysis is by no means complete and its numerous limitations are easily recognizable. The first one is the "partiality" of the model so heavily focussed on scarce resources, non-produced production means, techniques, technologies and rent. As we reminded in the introductory Chapter, the principal aim of a theoretical analysis, however, is not that of being a complete or a wide representation of reality: this can be achieved through descriptive or stylized studies that remain central for economics.

Neither was our ambition to formulate a new "general model", something which would be entirely wishful, given that economic theory has centuries of history and elaboration and that it is very difficult to introduce innovations of general character to such a sizeable body of knowledge. In fact, the evaluation of a theoretical contribution is always based on the trade off between rigor on one hand and realism on the other; we are conscious that frequently what one gains in rigor, one loses in realism.

At the end of a theoretical analysis, however, we would like to suggest some main lines of further development that can be pursued without loosing much coherence with the initial model and research questions. In particular, we shall put forward several lines of development that are already at an advanced stage of elaboration —or even at a conclusive stage. They are not developed here since the analysis of the previous Chapters is sufficiently complex to exhaust the whole volume.

These lines of research refer to the numeraire, the reintegration of natural resources, and the environment. Among these developments, that of the numeraire is quite complex and open to several options, yet it is not a necessary extension, whereas the lines of development concerning the environment and reintegration of resources are almost an obvious further step of the model. Let us briefly look at them.

2.1 *Numeraire*

In the previous analysis we chose as numeraire, the primary commodity directly produced with the scarce resource, for example, "corn". This choice has its advantages —as already shown— in the determination of the orders of efficiency and rentability of processes with scarce resources and non-produced means of production.

An alternative line of analysis would be that of introducing as numeraire a primary commodity with very different characteristics: gold.

This choice may seem unusual to those who forget economic history and the history of economic thought —subjects that instead we persist to consider crucial for economics. Gold was, except some intervals, for almost 250 years, the numeraire of the international monetary system and many national economies too —precisely from around 1717 until 1971, when the gold-dollar standard came to an end and the dollar was no longer convertible in gold (Quadrio Curzio 1982; 1985b; 1989; 1996a).

Concerning the history of economic thought, one needs only to refer back to David Ricardo, who wrote:

> "If equal quantities of labour, with equal quantities of fixed capital, could at all times obtain, from that mine which paid no rent, equal quantities of gold, gold would be as nearly an invariable measure of values, as we could in the nature of things possess. The quantity indeed would enlarge with the demand, but its value would be invariable, and it would be eminently well calculated to measure the varying value of all other things." (Ricardo, 1817, p. 87)

We know that Ricardo's perspective in dealing with gold as the perfect numeraire clashed with theoretical considerations. Nowadays we may also add that its failure is based on natural obsolescence, given the dominance of fiduciary money, global finance circulation and atypical and derivative financial instruments.

However, this is not a sufficient reason to abandon in economic theory the issue of gold in those models —as it is in a pure form ours— based on production and distribution. In the discussions of economic policy, every now and then, the problem of gold and of the physical numeraire returns to the surface. Furthermore, central banks and the international monetary organizations continue to hold gold as reserve of last instance (Quadrio Curzio 1982; 1985b; 1989; 1996a).

Introducing gold as the numeraire, would be interesting for several reasons. It is mainly a non-basic, produced commodity which utilizes for its own production, either directly or indirectly, other commodities of the economic system.

The production of gold could be represented in a sub-system with different processes, each of which producing gold with different efficiencies, so that rents can be created also in the production of gold. The least efficient process would have zero rent and the price of gold established in such a process would become the numeraire of the price system.

These somewhat self-references to Quadrio Curzio's studies on gold show that for years one of the author of this book considered the problems of the gold-numeraire. The main perils rise from the fact that though gold is itself produced (with scarcity), it is also a non-basic commodity which production cost is highly dependent on distribution and techniques.

If the adoption of this numeraire were made, the previous analysis of price, distribution, and production would have been profoundly different.

2.2. Reintegration of natural resources

In our model natural resources have an infinite duration and do not need reintegration. This is obviously a simplifying assumption that should be hopefully removed. Dropping the above assumption implies that one part of means of production, circulating capital, and labor should be employed to reintegrate natural resources. Analytically, this can be considered in various ways.

The first option is that of increasing the technical coefficients of those processes producing the primary commodity. This supposes the reintegration within such processes and imputes an adjustment of the technical coefficients simply in accounting terms. The result would be of reducing the rate of net product of each technique —an outcome that would reverse its effects on both prices and distributive variables. In particular, the effects on rent will depend on how much the reintegration costs fall upon the owners of the natural resources and rent earners—a typical problem that requires economic-institutional evaluations.

The second option is that of isolating a specific production process for natural resources and monitoring the dynamics of the stock of resources with its variations through time. Their (partial or total) reintegration requires that a part of the net product is diverted towards this end and such a repositioning will inevitably affect distribution, accumulation, and growth.

Finally, when scarce resources are produced means of production which are currently in use but no longer reproduced, there is no reintegration problem — these resources will slowly peter out until they disappear from the economic system. Such a phenomenon does not necessarily imply a reduction of the scale of production of the economic system. It is reasonable, in fact, to suppose that new waves of these type of means of production will become available. These different possibilities will also affect rents and distribution, as well accumulation and dynamic process, *vis a vis* with what occurs to the technical progress.

An important difference is therefore determined between natural resources and produced, but not reproduced, means of production: the former must be reintegrated, whereas the latter must be substituted.

2.3. The environment

As already noted in Chapter I, the environment is nowadays one of the most important issues, and jointly with the problem of natural resources, gives rise to broader concerns than those simply related to natural scarcities.

The boundary line between environment and natural resources is often extremely difficult to draw. From an economic standpoint whereas natural resources are always imputed with a price since the primary commodities made from them are costly inputs of production, the environmental resources have rarely obtained the same treatment. For a long time the economic operators —both public and private— considered environmental resources as free goods. Consequently, economic analysis has for long time neglected the issue.

Recently things have started to change with the steady rise of economic theories, models, and applications concerned with environmental problems. The size of this literature is such as to constitute already a separate discipline, so that economic analysis is now placed side by side with natural sciences and technology in dealing with the environmental puzzles.

In our model the issues of environmental resources can be analyzed from the standpoint of the traditional two categories: price-distribution and physical-quantity system.

With respect to the former, price determination depends on both taxation, the conditions of environmental preservation, and the restoration of environmental resources. These conditions also affect income distribution, with the formation of environmental rents due to the different environmental impact of the production processes. If environmental taxes are included into production costs and transferred on prices, then those processes less environmental intensive can either lower prices, and drive the owners of processes more environmental intensive out of production; or, conversely, equalize the price at the higher level and earn a rent for their greater environmental efficiency.

With respect to the latter category —the physical-quantity system— and its dynamics, the existence of environmental resources generates scale constraints to economic growth and forces changes in the choice of techniques, with general consequences for the whole economic dynamics.

From both quantity constraints and opportunities of environmental rents the economy derives incentives to promote environmental innovations in the attempt of reducing costs and relaxing planetary scarcity. Since, however, the environmental resources are rarely privately owned, the scarcity is usually perceived at aggregate level rather than at individual level of production or consumption. This stresses the central role of the legal and institutional factors since they can ultimately set the limits of the environmental exploitation.

In conclusion: the previous model can be modified in such a way as to take into account environmental resources alongside natural resources and to consider environmental rents alongside natural rents; both being categories of technological rents. At this regard, our elaborations have reached an interesting stage of development.

The environmental issue can also be introduced into the model in a different way that —curiously enough— links to the notion of accumulated residuals but in an entirely new and peculiar form: that of wastes. It is well-known that all processes of growth, production, and consumption bring about an increasing volume of wastes that can neither be accumulated nor consumed. Yet, they represent social and private costs for either their degradation of the environment or for their disposal. The choice of techniques that minimize wastes and promote processes of disposal becomes therefore advisable. All this has clear consequences on the dynamics of the economic system, prices, and distribution (Quadrio Curzio, Prosperetti, and Zoboli 1994a; 1994b). Since we are quite confident that the problem of wastes will eventually affect the overall dynamics of the economic system, we are aiming to enrich the model also with the introduction of this aspect.

To sum up, the reintegration of natural resources and the conservation of environmental resources lead us to a general consideration that was already advanced in Chapter I. Namely, the wealth of the nation cannot be exclusively equated to the level of national income, but should include many other factors, among which the natural-environmental resources hold a crucial importance.

3. The range and complexity of a "complete" theory of economic dynamics

In conclusion of our analysis we shall make two final remarks. On the one hand we suggest some additional extensions of our analysis; on the other hand, we recall some studies of economic dynamics just to remind us the vast range and complexity of this field, and the absence of a complete analysis of economic dynamics.

The first remark concerns further possible extensions. Apart from those already listed, the model could be generalized to include other issues, such as fixed capital, demand, and international economic relations. These are extensions that would broaden the scope of the model, but not its originality that —as it has been frequently expressed— we focused on scarce resources, technological rents, and technological scarcities.

Let us consider fixed capital. Our model assumes implicitly the existence of a stock of fixed capital that does not create constraints to growth, and does not absorb net product either.

Now, the model can be modified by following the tradition —which is, however, less uniform than what appears at first look— of multi-sectoral models with fixed capital *à la* von Neumann-Leontief-Sraffa and Pasinetti, or by seeking to introduce fixed capital, in a way formally similar to stocks of non-produced means of production.

The latter solution may seem paradoxical as fixed capital is indeed produced, reproduced, and increases through time. Yet, fixed capital exists with different qualities and its stock cannot be increased in the short period in remarkable dimensions if compared to that already in existence. Consequently, it can generate temporary constraints to the scale of production, it can generate rents (or quasi-rents), and it raises requirements in terms of net product for its replacement and growth.

Concerning another possible extension on demand side, we call attention to the fact that in our model the overall demand was linked to accumulation and growth, while consumption demand has been treated always in terms of fixed coefficients.

The simplification can be removed without shadowing the main concern of the model, i.e. the accumulation process. We suggest two possible ways. The first is by connecting economic growth with changes of the consumption coefficients; the second is by introducing explicit laws of the evolution of consumption demand, as other scholars did.

The analysis of how tastes, prices and disposable income affect the level of consumption demand is outside the domain of the present theoretical framework. What our model is interested on are the effects that different hypotheses of consumption have on growth, or, vice versa, the effects created on consumption by different hypotheses of growth. The introduction of this analysis would have far-reaching consequences also for the residuals of accumulation. In other words, dynamic paths of consumption affect the accumulation process and the degree of reintegration of natural and environmental resources. Conversely, different paths of accumulation and reintegration of natural and environmental resources affect the opportunities of consumption. Though these extensions can be framed in our model, the consumption pattern must eventually be treated with radical simplifications to capture only the essential features of mutual dependence with the long-term dynamics.

About international economic relations there are many different ways of introducing this dimension in a model geared around technology.

In the past Chapters we argued at length how the technological rigidities prevent the elimination of the residuals of accumulation. There exists, therefore, a first immediate way of taking international trade into account, namely its connection with the problem of residuals.

International trade makes easier to change net products according to the technological structure of the economy: exports can be used for selling the residuals that cannot be internally accumulated and imports for acquiring those commodities that can be indeed accumulated.

In other words, the degree of openness of a country affects the physical-quantity system. But important changes involve also the price-distribution system. For example one crucial analytical problem would be the determination of prices, as well as surpluses and deficits of trade balances in an international context. Undoubtedly, the transformation of our model of production into an "open" model would be subjected to interesting modifications with the emergence of novel categories of rents from international trade.

Obviously, there exist other more general frameworks to introduce the role of international economic relations, as probably a rapid review of the literature in the field may suggest. But let us move on with the other consideration.

The second remark we would like to make in this final Chapter deals with the range and complexity of problems concerning economic dynamics, growth, and development. It is such a big issue that not even an entire volume would suffice to capture the boundless literature on this topic. One must be completely conscious of this, and as a proof of our limited scope we refer to only four of the most important Italian economists of the post-World War II: Giorgio Fuà, Siro Lombardini, Luigi Pasinetti, and Paolo Sylos Labini. In complementary —though very different— ways, they have devoted a lot of their work to the problems of economic growth. In our opinion their contributions show a peculiar line of research of the Italian School of political economy, which has international relevance precisely with issues concerning growth and development. It is, thus, worth mentioning very briefly their contributions in order to underline our awareness on the partial character of the present work.

Fuà (1993) points out that it has become common practice to refer to levels of per capita income and their rate of growth in order to judge whether and to what extent countries are advancing along the road of "progress". Usually, however, these statistics are charged with meanings that they do not actually possess, and this imposes a careful "discernment" in their evaluation. This is exactly what Fuà does. He starts with an accurate analysis of figures about growth for a great number of countries and a long period of time. Then he moves to two important issues. Firstly, the connections but also the divergence between economic growth —as expressed by the growth of income, and, hence, by the quantity of goods— and the level of welfare; and secondly, the difficulties of obtaining in the advanced economies satisfactory measurement of growth by using the traditional statistics. These statistics, in fact, are mainly concerned with physical commodities and do not capture adequately the merchandised innovations, the tertiary sector's output. In this fascinating analysis Fuà concludes that

> "... in the rich countries [...] we must shift our attention away from the traditional theme of the quantity of goods produced to others that can no longer be regarded of secondary importance for the public good. Consider, for example [...] the satisfaction or the non satisfaction that work brings to those who engage in it". (Fuà, 1993, p. 107).

Lombardini (1996) reminds us that "the" model of economic growth does not exist. Those models that analyze the problems of economic growth and development can only offer instruments that our critical reasoning must use in a context of social and institutional understanding. Only the combination of these two different dimensions of knowledge allows us to draw actual explanations of the processes at stake in each country. Lombardini also reminds us that the mathematical complexity of these models always risk to transform theory in a pure formal exercise. Lombardini then develops his analysis along two extremely original lines: one, stemming from the Solow model of growth, investigates the effects of technical progress as a consequence of the consumer and firm optimization; another, based on a Schumpeterian framework, explains problems of innovation and social selection in order to determine their contribution to growth.

In conclusion of his historical survey of the theories and the models of growth, Lombardini asks if there exists "the true" theory of growth. His answer is negative. Theory always takes a specific definition of economic system and chooses a select set of tools and methods for its analysis. But all definitions are partial and each tool or method can clarify some specific aspects of an economic system, leaving aside others.

Pasinetti (1993) perceives two mechanisms as basis of the long-term dynamics of the industrialized economies: capital accumulation and technical progress. Usually the prevalence was given to the first element. Pasinetti, instead, takes up an opposite view by assigning the central role to technical progress and linking this to the process of "human learning". Structural economic dynamics is thus represented in an economy of "pure labor" by still using the traditional variables, but with further emphasizes on the processes of social and institutional learning, the diffusion of information and know-how. Pasinetti concludes his original analysis as follows:

> "The immaterial technical knowledge (on which the 'new' type of wealth is based) can be transferred from one individual to other individuals – in principle, to all

other individuals – without being lost by those who originally had it. Its nature is no longer exclusively individualistic.

Furthermore, the productivity of the single individuals, which springs from it, does increase because of the improvement of individual knowledge (communicable to others), but also presupposes to be inserted into a whole framework which relies, so to speak, on a "social' organisation." (Pasinetti, 1993, p. 175)

Sylos Labini (1992) shows how economic theory is currently too much focussed on static analysis, and too little on dynamic analysis. Yet, the latter should be deserved a far greater relevance given the transformations that are undergoing in technology, organization, and institutions. Sylos Labini reminds us of the importance in economic dynamics of the Classical and Schumpeterian methodological framework. After having pointed out that this framework is based on the interaction that links dynamic theory to the historical analysis founded upon the notion of path dependence, he calls attention to the central problem that should invest every economist: that of being analytically rigorous in judging reality, but also capable of understanding facts.

With these methodological assumptions, Sylos Labini analyzes prices behavior in different market conditions, with particular originality in the case of oligopoly. His contribution deals also with the behavior of large firms, cyclical development and its applications to the Italian case, income distribution, and inflation.

Sylos Labini's entire analysis shows that economic dynamics depends on complex interactions of firms, innovations, and the behavior of large social categories, such as wage and profit earners, and government. Basically, he accomplishes an important merging between micro and macroeconomic aspects of economic dynamics.

These four references reinforce our awareness of the partial character of our work. However, they also reinforce the idea that partial contributions may be useful when they are placed in broader frameworks of economic analysis.

The framework that we have chosen is that of multi-sectoral dynamics, focused on production and distribution problems. On this basis, the model can be further developed in many directions. To remain coherent, however, with its original purposes, these potential developments must be conceived in the light of the trilogy scarce resources, technologies, and rent.

APPENDIX A - Techniques and technologies analyzed in the numerical examples (Chapters VII, VIII, IX, X, XI)

Matrices of technical coefficients

In this section the matrices of the technical coefficients are reproduced. For each matrix the uniform rate of the net product and the production structure compatible with growth for this uniform rate is shown. Moreover for each technique using NPMP of type 2 is indicated the vector of residuals generated when this technique is activated within the technology which includes **A**(1) and afterwards.

$$\mathbf{A}(1) = \begin{bmatrix} 0.3 & 0.2 & 0.1 \\ 0.05 & 0.3 & 0.05 \\ 0.5 & 0.4 & 0.25 \end{bmatrix},$$

$s(1) = 2/3$; $\mathbf{q}(1) = [q_1, 0.5q_1, 2q_1]$;

$$\mathbf{A}(2a) = \begin{bmatrix} 0.5 & 0.2 & 0.1 \\ 0.45 & 0.3 & 0.05 \\ 0.15 & 0.4 & 0.25 \end{bmatrix},$$

$s(2a) = 0.25$; $\mathbf{q}(2a) = [q_1, q_1, q_1]$;

$\mathbf{r}(1, 2a; t) = [2, 0, 6]$;

$$\mathbf{A}(2b) = \begin{bmatrix} 0.5 & 0.2 & 0.1 \\ 0.33 & 0.3 & 0.05 \\ 0.45 & 0.4 & 0.25 \end{bmatrix},$$

$s(2b) = 0.25$; $\mathbf{q}(2b) = [q_1, 0.8q_1, 1.4q_1]$;

$\mathbf{r}(1, 2b; t) = [1.5, 0, 4.5]$;

$$\mathbf{A}(2c) = \begin{bmatrix} 0.5 & 0.2 & 0.1 \\ 0.15 & 0.3 & 0.05 \\ 0.9 & 0.4 & 0.25 \end{bmatrix},$$

s(2c) = 0.25; $\mathbf{q}(2c) = [q_1, 0.5\, q_1, 2q_1]$;

$\mathbf{r}(1, 2c; t) = [0, 0, 0]$;

$$\mathbf{A}(2d) = \begin{bmatrix} 0.1 & 0.2 & 0.1 \\ 0.85 & 0.3 & 0.05 \\ 0.85 & 0.4 & 0.25 \end{bmatrix},$$

s(2d) = 0.25; $\mathbf{q}(2d) = [q_1, 2q_1, 3q_1]$;

$\mathbf{r}(1, 2d; t) = [3, 0, 5]$;

$$\mathbf{A}(2e) = \begin{bmatrix} 0.1 & 0.2 & 0.1 \\ 0.25 & 0.3 & 0.05 \\ 2.35 & 0.4 & 0.25 \end{bmatrix},$$

s(2e) = 0.25; $\mathbf{q}(2e) = [q_1, q_1, 5q_1]$;

$\mathbf{r}(1, 2e; t) = [2.4, 0.4, 0]$;

$$\mathbf{A}(2f) = \begin{bmatrix} \frac{181}{310} & 0.2 & 0.1 \\ 0.15 & 0.3 & 0.05 \\ 0.9 & 0.4 & 0.25 \end{bmatrix},$$

$$s(2f) = \frac{3}{17}; \mathbf{q}(2f) = \left[q_1, \frac{27}{62} q_1, \frac{111}{62} q_1 \right];$$

$\mathbf{r}(1, 2f; t) = [0, 0.26, 0.84]$;

$$\mathbf{A}(2g) = \begin{bmatrix} 0.37 & 0.2 & 0.1 \\ 0.0625 & 0.3 & 0.05 \\ 0.58 & 0.4 & 0.25 \end{bmatrix},$$

s(2g) =7/13; $\mathbf{q}(2g) = [q_1, 0.45q_1, 1.9q_1]$;

$\mathbf{r}(1, 2g; t) = [0, 0.2, 0.4]$;

$$\mathbf{A}(2i) = \begin{bmatrix} 0.4 & 0.2 & 0.1 \\ 1.3 & 0.3 & 0.05 \\ 0.7 & 0.4 & 0.25 \end{bmatrix},$$

$s(2i) = 1$; $\mathbf{q}(2i) = [q_1, 2q_1, 2q_1]$;

$\mathbf{r}(1, 2i; t) = [3, 0, 6]$;

$$\mathbf{A}(2l) = \begin{bmatrix} \frac{333}{820} & 0.2 & 0.1 \\ 0.15 & 0.3 & 0.05 \\ 0.9 & 0.4 & 0.25 \end{bmatrix},$$

$$s(2l) = \frac{1}{3}; \mathbf{q}(2l) = \left[q_1, \frac{24}{41} q_1, \frac{93}{41} q_1 \right];$$

$\mathbf{r}(1, 2l; t) = [0.58, 0, 0.25]$;

$$\mathbf{A}(2m) = \begin{bmatrix} \frac{19}{64} & 0.2 & 0.1 \\ 0.15 & 0.3 & 0.05 \\ 0.9 & 0.4 & 0.25 \end{bmatrix},$$

$$s(2m) = \frac{3}{7}; \mathbf{q}(2m) = \left[q_1, \frac{45}{64} q_1, \frac{21}{8} q_1 \right];$$

$\mathbf{r}(1, 2m; t) = [1.16, 0, 0.53]$;

$$\mathbf{A}(2n) = \begin{bmatrix} 0.43 & 0.2 & 0.1 \\ 0.587 & 0.3 & 0.05 \\ 0.02 & 0.4 & 0.25 \end{bmatrix},$$

$s(2n) = 21/79$; $\mathbf{q}(2n) = [q_1, 1.3q_1, q_1]$;

$\mathbf{r}(1, 2n; t) = [2.46, 0, 2.46]$;

$$\mathbf{A}(2o) = \begin{bmatrix} 0.09 & 0.2 & 0.1 \\ 0.68 & 0.3 & 0.05 \\ 0.08 & 0.4 & 0.25 \end{bmatrix},$$

s(2o) =31/69; $\mathbf{q}(2o) = [q_1, 2q_1, 2q_1]$;

$\mathbf{r}(1, 2o; t) = [4.5, 0, 9]$;

$$\mathbf{A}(3) = \begin{bmatrix} \frac{314}{620} & 0.2 & 0.1 \\ \frac{19}{124} & 0.3 & 0.05 \\ \frac{566}{620} & 0.4 & 0.25 \end{bmatrix},$$

s(3) =0.24; $\mathbf{q}(3) = [q_1, 0.5q_1, 2q_1]$;

$\mathbf{r}(2c,3; t) = [0, 0, 0]$.

List of notations

Frequently used acronyms

PCC1– primary commodity or commodity 1;
NPMP – non-produced means of production;
OE – order of efficiency;
OR – order of rentability.

Production processes, production techniques, technologies

$[\mathbf{a}_1(h)'; l_1(h); \tau_1(h)]$ – production process of PCC1 using NPMP of type h;

$[\mathbf{a}_1'; l_j]$ – production process of commodity j;

$\mathbf{A}(h) = [\mathbf{a}_1(h); \mathbf{a}_2; \ldots; \mathbf{a}_{m+1}]$ and $\mathbf{l}'(h) = [l_1(h), l_2, \ldots, l_{m+1}]$ – representation of the production technique that uses NPMP of type h;

$\mathbf{A}_\alpha(1,2)$ and $\mathbf{l}(1,2)' = [l_1(1), l_1(2), l_2, \ldots, l_{m+1}]$ – representation of the global technology of the economic system when two processes with NPMP are used jointly with other m processes;

$\mathbf{A}_\alpha(1, \ldots, k)$ and $\mathbf{l}(1, \ldots, k)$ – representation of the global technology of the economic system when k processes with NPMP are used jointly with other m processes;

$[\mathbf{A}(h); \mathbf{A}(h+1); \ldots]$ – representation of a technology composed of techniques using NPMP of different types;

Technical coefficients (matrices, vectors, scalars) and related variables

$\mathbf{I}$ – identity matrix;

$\mathbf{A}(h) = [\mathbf{a}_1(h); \mathbf{a}_2; \ldots, \mathbf{a}_{m+1}]$ – matrix of the technical coefficients with a process employing NPMP of type h;

$\lambda(h)$ – eigenvalue of $\mathbf{A}(h)$;

$s(h)$ – uniform rate of net product of the technique $\mathbf{A}(h)$;

$\mathbf{a}_i(h) = [a_{11}(h), \ldots, a_{m+1,1}(h)]$ – vector of coefficients of the m+1 commodities necessary in order to produce a unit of PCC1;

$\mathbf{a}_j = [a_{1j}, \ldots, a_{m+1,j}]$ – vector of coefficients of the m+1 commodities necessary in order to produce a unit of commodity j;

$\mathbf{l}(h)' = [l_1(h), \ldots, l_{m+1}]$ – vector of labor coefficients;

$\tau_1(h)$ – technical coefficient of NPMP of type h;

$\mathbf{A}_\alpha(1,2)$ – matrix representing the global technology of the economic system when two processes with NPMP are used;

$s_\alpha(1,2)$ – uniform rate of growth of technology $\mathbf{A}_\alpha(1,2)$;

$\mathbf{l}(1,2)' = [l_1(1), l_1(2), l_2, \ldots, l_{m+1}]$ – vector of the labor technical coefficients associated to $\mathbf{A}_\alpha(1,2)$;

$\mathbf{A}_\alpha(1, \ldots, k)$ – matrix representing the global technology of the economic system when k processes with NPMP are used jointly with other m processes;

$s_\alpha(1, \ldots, k)$ – uniform rate of growth of technology $\mathbf{A}_\alpha(1, \ldots, k)$;

$\mathbf{l}(1, \ldots, k)$ – vector of the labor technical coefficients of $\mathbf{A}_\alpha(1, \ldots, k)$;

$\mathbf{A}_\alpha^*(k-1, k)$ – matrix of order m+2 that, with some aggregations, describes the global technology;

$\mathbf{A}_{ij}$ – sub-matrix composed of the last m rows and columns of the matrix $\mathbf{A}_\alpha^*(k-1, k)$;

$\alpha_{1j}(h)$ – splitting coefficient identifying the measure in which the process employing NPMP of type k supplies the PCC1 to each other process of the economic system;

$\alpha_1(k)' = [\alpha_{12}(k), \alpha_{13}(k), \ldots, \alpha_{1,m+1}(k)]$;

$$\alpha_{1j}^*(k-1) = \sum_{v=1}^{k-1} \alpha_{ij}(v),\ j = 2, \ldots, m+1;$$

$\alpha_1^*(k-1)' = [\alpha_{12}^*(k-1), \ldots, \alpha_{1,m+1}^*(k-1)]$;

$\gamma(v)$ – ratio between the maximum quantity of commodity 1 produced by the process v and the quantity of commodity 1 produced by the first k–1 processes activated at the maximum level of production;

$$a_{i1}^*(k-1) = \sum_{v=1}^{k-1} a_{i1}(v)\gamma(v),\ i = 1, \ldots, m+1;$$

$\mathbf{a}_1^*(k-1) = [a_{21}^*(k-1), \ldots, a_{m+1,1}^*(k-1)]$;

$$l_1^*(k-1) = \sum_{v=1}^{k-1} l_1(v)\gamma(v);$$

$\mathbf{l}_\alpha^*(k-1,k)' = [\mathbf{l}_1^*(k-1), l_1(k), l_2, \ldots, l_{m+1}]$;

$\mathbf{a}_1(k)' = [a_{21}(k), a_{31}(k), \ldots, a_{m+1,1}(k)]$;

$\mathbf{a}_{ji} = [a_{21}, \ldots, a_{m+1,1}]$;

$\mathbf{c}_{1i}(h^*)$ – vector of cofactors of the first row of the matrix $[\mathbf{I}-(1+\pi)\,\mathbf{A}(h^*)]$;

$\mathbf{c}_{ji}(h^*)$ – vector of cofactors of the j-th row of the matrix $[\mathbf{I}-(1+\pi)\mathbf{A}(h^*)]$.

Quantity and prices

$q_1(h)$ – quantity of commodity 1 produced by the process h, h=1, … , k;

$\bar{q}_1(h)$ – maximum producible quantity of commodity 1 by the process h;

q_j, j=2, …, m+1 – quantity of the producible commodities produced without using the non-produced means of production;

$\mathbf{p}(h)=[p_1(h), \dots, p_{m+1}(h)]$ – vector of prices of technique $\mathbf{A}(h)$;

$\mathbf{q}_\alpha(1,2)= [q_1(1), q_1(2), q_2, \dots, q_{m+1}]$ – vector of the quantity of technology $\mathbf{A}_\alpha(1,2)$;

$\mathbf{q}_\alpha(1, \dots, k)$ – vector of the quantity of technology $\mathbf{A}_\alpha(1, \dots, k)$;

$\mathbf{n}_\alpha(1, \dots, k)$ – vector of the net products of technology $\mathbf{A}_\alpha(1, \dots, k)$;

$\bar{q}^*_1(k-1)$ – quantity of commodity 1 produced by the first k–1 processes activated at the maximum level;

$\mathbf{q}^*_\alpha=[q_1(k), q_2, \dots, q_{m+1}]$ – sub-vector composed of the last m+1 elements of the vector $\mathbf{q}^*_\alpha(k-1, k)$ normalised with respect to the first element which is equal to 1;

$p^*_1(k-1)$ – price of PCC1 produced by the aggregate process k–1;

$\mathbf{p}^*_\alpha = [p^*_1(k-1), p_1(k), p_2, \dots, p_{m+1}]$ – left eigenvector of the matrix $\mathbf{A}^*_\alpha(k-1, k)$;

$\mathbf{q}(h; t)$ – vector of the quantity produced by the technique $\mathbf{A}(h)$ in period t;

$\mathbf{n}(h; t)$ – vector of net products of technique $\mathbf{A}(h)$ in period t;

$\mathbf{m}(h; t)$ – vector of means of production used by the technique $\mathbf{A}(h)$ in period t;

$\mathbf{q}(1, 2; t)$ – vector of total productions of the active sub-systems 1 and 2 in period t;

$\mathbf{n}(1, 2; t)$ – vector of total net products of the active subsystems 1 and 2 in period t;

$\mathbf{m}(1, 2; t)$ – vector of means of production used by the active sub-systems 1 and 2 in period t;

$\mathbf{r}(1,2; t)$ – vector of residuals generated when the technique using NPMP of type 2 is activated.

Distributive variables: wages, profits, and rents

$\pi(h)$ – rate of profit;

$w(h)$ – unit wage;

$\rho(h; h^*)$ – rent per unit of NPMP of type h when h^* is the least efficient process;

$r(h; h^*)$ – rent per unit of commodity 1 produced employing NPMP of type h when h^* is the least efficient process;

$r_{stp}(h^*-i; h^*)$ – rent per unit of commodity 1 due to structural technical progress;

$r_{ltp}(h^*-i; h^*)$ – rent per unit of commodity 1 due to linear technical progress;

$r_{ntp}(h^*-i; h^*)$ – rent per unit of commodity 1 due to natural technical progress;

$r_{itp}(h^*-i; h^*)$ – rent per unit of the i-th commodity due to structural and/or linear technical progress;

$\mathbf{r}(h^*-i; h^*)$ – vector of rents due to technological scarcity of NPMP of type h^*-i;

$\mathbf{r}_{tp}(h^*-i; h^*)$ – vector of rents due to structural and/or linear technical progress;

$Y(1, \dots, h^*)$ – value added of the economic system when the activity level is such that h^* processes with NPMP are used;

$W(1, \dots, h^*)$ – total wages when the activity level is such that h^* processes with NPMP are used;

$\Pi(1, \dots, h^*)$ – total profits when the activity level is such that h^* processes with NPMP are used;

$R(1,\ldots,h^*) = \sum_{h=1}^{h^*} \rho(h)T(h)$ – total rents when the activity level is such that h^* processes with NPMP are used;

$Y(1;t)$ – value added of the economic system in period t when only technique $\mathbf{A}(1)$ is activated;

$W(1;t)$ – total wages in period t when only technique $\mathbf{A}(1)$ is activated;

$\Pi(1;t)$ – total profits in period t when only technique $\mathbf{A}(1)$ is activated;

$R(1;t)$ – total rents in period t when only technique $\mathbf{A}(1)$ is activated;

$Y(1,2;t)$ – value added of the economic system in period t when technology $[\mathbf{A}(1); \mathbf{A}(2)]$ is activated;

$W(1,2;t)$ – total wages in period t when technology $[\mathbf{A}(1); \mathbf{A}(2)]$ is activated;

$\Pi(1,2;t)$ – total profits in period t when technology $[\mathbf{A}(1); \mathbf{A}(2)]$ is activated;

$R(1,2;t)$ – total rents in period t when technology $[\mathbf{A}(1); \mathbf{A}(2)]$ is activated;

$\omega_w(t)$ – share of wages on value added in period t;

$\omega_\pi(t)$ – share of profits on value added in period t;

$\omega_R(t)$ – share of rents on value added in period t.

Other notations

h^* – the least efficient process;

$\underline{T}(h)$ – availability of NPMP of type h;

$\bar{l}$ – available labor force;

$\bar{t}_h$ – period at the end of which the full employment of T(h) occurs;

$l(h^*)$ – labor employed in the standard system of the sub-system pwπ of type h^*;

i^* – commodity whose net product can be entirely accumulated;

$\mathbf{e}_i' = [0, 0, \ldots, 1(i), \ldots, 0]$ – unit vector; the position of number 1 changes according to index i;

$\beta_i(1,2;t)$ – growth rate of production of commodity i between period t–1 and period t with techniques 1 and 2;

$\mu_i(1,2;t)$ – growth rate of the net product of commodity i between period t–1 and period t with techniques 1 and 2;

$\delta_i(1,2;t)$ – rate of net product of commodity i in period t with techniques 1 and 2;

i – inter-temporal rate of discount;

I – inter-temporal average rate of value added.

References

Abramovitz, M. (1950), *Inventories and Business Cycles*, New York, NBER.

Abramovitz, M. (1952), Economics of growth, in B.F. Haley (ed.), *Survey of Contemporary Economics*, American Economic Association, Homewood, Illinois, Irwin, vol. II.

Abramovitz, M. (1956), Resources and output trends in the United States since 1870, *American Economic Review*, vol. XLVI, pp. 5-23.

Abramovitz, M. (1961), The nature and significance of Kuznets cycles, *Economic Development and Cultural Change*, vol. 9, n. 3.

Alexandratos, N. (1993), Agricoltura mondiale e alimentazione nei Paesi in via di sviluppo: prospettive per la fine del secolo, *Innovazione e Materie Prime*, n. 1, pp. 68-89.

Anderson, J. (1777), *An Inquire into the Nature of the Corn-Laws; With a View to the New Corn-Bill Proposed for Scotland*, Edinburgh.

Antonelli, G. and Quadrio Curzio, A. (1988) (eds.), *The Agro-Technological System towards 2000*, Amsterdam, North Holland.

Bairoch, P. (1969), Agriculture and the Industrial Revolution (1700-1914), in *The Fontana Economic History of Europe*, London, vol. III, n.8.

Cannan, E. (1893), *History of the Theories of Production and Distribution in English Political Economy from 1776 to 1848*, I edition, London, P.S. King and Sons Ltd, III edition, 1917.

Castellino, O. (1990), *Introduzione a Kuznets S.*, in O. Castellino (ed.), *Popolazione, tecnologia, sviluppo,* Bologna, Il Mulino.

Cipolla, C.M. (1966), *Uomini, tecniche, economie*, Milan, Feltrinelli.

Clark, C. (1940), *Conditions of Economic Progress*, London, Macmillan.

Clark, C.W. (1976), *Mathematical Bioeconomics*, New York, John Wiley and Sons.

Clark, C.W. and Munn, R.E. (1986) (eds.) *Sustainable Development of the Biosphere*, Cambridge, Cambridge University Press.

Colombo, U. (1992), Sustainable energy development, in IIASA, *Science and Sustainablility. Selected Papers on IIASA's 20th Anniversary*, Laxenburg.

Dasgupta, P. (1982) *The Control of Resources*, Oxford, Basic Blackwell.

Dasgupta, P. and Heal, G.M. (1981), *Economic Theory and Exhaustible Resources*, Cambridge, Cambridge University Press.

Deane, P. (1967), *The First Industrial Revolution*, Cambridge, Cambridge University Press.

Domar, E. (1946), Capital expansion, rate of growth and employment, *Econometrica*, vol. 14, pp. 137-147.

Duchin, F. and Lange, G.M. (1994), *The Future of the Environment. Ecological Economics and Technological Change*, Oxford, Oxford University Press.

Faliva, M. (1975), Alcune formule di derivazione in termini matriciali, *Statistica*, n.35, pp. 329-340.

Fetter, F.A. (1932), Rent, in *Encyclopedia of the Social Sciences*, New York, The Macmillan Company, vol. XIII.

Fisher, A.C. (1981), *Resources and Environmental Economics*, Cambridge, Cambridge University Press.

Forester, T. (1988), *The Materials Revolution*, Oxford, Basic Blackwell.

Forrester, J. (1971), *World Dynamics*. Cambridge, Massachusetts, MIT Press.

Fortis, M. (1981), Modelli globali e scenari di sviluppo mondiale, *Energia*, n.2, pp. 32-57.

Fortis, M. (1994), *Competizione tecnologica e sviluppo industriale. Fasi dell'economia mondiale dal 1850 al 1990*, Bologna, Il Mulino.

Fuà, G. (1980), *Problemi dello sviluppo tardivo in Europa. Rapporto su sei paesi appartenenti all'OCSE*, Bologna, Il Mulino.

Fuà, G. (1992), *Lo sviluppo economico in Italia*, IV edition, Milan, Angeli.

Fuà, G. (1993), *Crescita economica. Le insidie delle cifre*, Bologna, Il Mulino.

Fuà, G. (1986) (ed.) *Conseguenze economiche dell'evoluzione demografica*, Bologna, Il Mulino.

Gille, B. (1986), *The History of Techniques*, 2 vols., New York, Gordon and Breach Science Publishers.

Hahn, F.H. and Matthews, R.C.O. (1965), The theory of economic growth: a survey, in *Surveys of Economic Theory*, American Economic Association-Royal Economic Society, 3 vols., London, Macmillan.

Harrod, R. (1939), An essay in dynamic theory, *Economic Journal*, vol. XLIX, pp. 14-33.

Harrod, R. (1948), *Towards a Dynamic Economics*, London, Macmillan.

Hicks, J. (1965), *Capital and Growth*, Oxford, Clarendon Press.

Hoffman, W. (1931), *Stadien und Typen der Industrialisierung*, English translation: *The Growth of Industrial Economies*, Manchester, Manchester University Press, 1958.

Hotelling, H. (1931), The economics of exhaustible resources, *Journal of Political Economy*, vol. XXXIX, pp. 137-175.

Jevons, W.S. (1865), *The Coal Question*, London.

Kaldor, N. (1955-56), Alternative theories of distribution, *Review of Economic Studies*, n. 2, pp. 83-100.

Kallio, M., Dykstra, D.P. and Binkley, C.S. (1987) (eds.), *The Global Forest Sector: An Analytical Perspective*, Chichester, John Wiley and Sons.

Keynes, J.M. (1936), *The General Theory of Employment Interest and Money*, London, Macmillan.

Kurz, D.H. and Salvadori, N. (1995), *Theory of Production*, Cambridge, Cambridge University Press.

Kuznets, S. (1930), *Secular Movements in Production and Prices: Their Nature and their Bearing upon Cyclical Fluctuations*, Boston, Houghton Mifflin Co.

Kuznets, S. (1955), Toward a theory of economic growth, in *Economic Growth and Structure, Selected Essay*, London, Heinemann Educational Books Ltd, 1965, pp. 1-81.

Kuznets, S. (1965), *Economic Growth and Structure: Selected Essays*, London, Heinemann Educational Books Ltd.

Kuznets, S. (1966), *Modern Economic Growth: Rate, Structure and Spread*, New Haven, Yale Press University Press.

Kuznets, S. (1972), Innovations and adjustment in economic growth, *Swedish Journal of Economics*, vol. 74, n. 4.

Kuznets, S. (1990), *Popolazione, tecnologia, sviluppo*, (ed.) O. Castellino, Bologna, Il Mulino.

Landes, D.S. (1969), *The Unbound Prometheus: Technological Change and Industrial Development in Western Europe from 1750 to the Present*, Cambridge, Cambridge University Press.

Leontief, W. (1941), *The Structure of American Economy, 1919-1929*, Cambridge, Massachusetts, Harvard University Press.

Leontief, W. (1951), *The Structure of the American Economy, 1919-1939*, New York, Oxford University Press.

Leontief, W. (1953a), *Domestic Production and Foreign Trade: Further Theoretical and Empirical Analysis*, also published in W. Leontief, *Input-Output Economics*, New York, Oxford University Press, 1966.

Leontief, W. (1953b), *Studies in the Structure of the American Economy*, New York, Oxford University Press.

Leontief, W., Carter, A.P. and Petri, P. (1977), *The Future of the World Economy*, Oxford, Oxford University Press.

Lombardini, S. (1996), *Growth and Economic Development*, London, Edward Elgar.

Lombardini, S. and Quadrio Curzio, A. (eds.) (1972), *La distribuzione del reddito nella teoria economica*, Milan, Angeli.

Malthus, T.R. (1798), *An Essay on the Principle of Population*, London.

Malthus, T.R. (1814), *Observations on the Effects of the Corn Laws and of a Rise or Fall in the Price of Corn on the Agriculture and General Wealth of the Country*, London, J.Johnson.

Malthus, T.R. (1815a), *An Inquiry into the Nature and Progress of Rent and the Principles by which it is Regulated*, London, J. Murray.

Malthus, T.R. (1815b), *The Grounds of an Opinion on the Policy of Restricting the Importation of Foreign Corn*, London, J. Murray.

Manara, C.F. and Nicola, P.C. (1970), *Elementi di economia matematica*, II edition, Milan, Viscontea.

Marshall, A. (1920), *Principles of Economics*, London, Macmillan, VIII edition.

Meade, J. (1961), *A Neoclassical Theory of Economic Growth*, London, Unwin University Books, II edition 1964.

Meadows, D.H., Meadows, D.L., Randers, J. and Behrens, III W.W. (1972), *The Limits to Growth. The First Report of the Club of Rome Project*, New York, Universe Book.

Meadows, D.H., Meadows, D.L. and Randers, J. (1992), *Beyond the Limits*, Post Mills, VT, Chelsea Green Publishing Company.

Mills, J.S. (1848), *Principles of Political Economy*, 2 vols. London, J.W. Parker.

Mitchell, W. (1913), *Business Cycles*, Berkeley, University of California Press.

Mitchell, W. (1945), *The National Bureau's First Quarter Century*, 25th Annual Report of the National Bureau of Economic Research, New York.

Mokyr, J. (1990), *The Lever of Riches. Technological Creativity and Economic Progress*, Oxford, Oxford University Press.

Parikh, K.S., Fisher, G., Frohberg, K. and Gulbrandsen, O. (1988), *Towards Free Trade in Agriculture*, International Institute for Applied Systems Analysis, Dordrecht, Martinus Nijhorf Publisher.

Pasinetti, L. (1960), A mathematical formulation of the Ricardian system, *Review of Economic Studies*, vol. XXVII, pp. 78-98.

Pasinetti, L. (1975), *Lezioni di teoria della produzione*, I edition, Bologna, Il Mulino, English translation: *Lectures on the Theory of Production*, London, Macmillan, 1977.

Pasinetti, L. (1981), *Structural Change and Economic Growth: A Theoretical Essay on the Dynamics of the Wealth of Nations*, Cambridge, Cambridge University Press.

Pasinetti, L. (1993), *Structural Economic Dynamics. A Theory of Economic Consequences of Human Learning*, Cambridge, Cambridge University Press.

Pearce, D.W. and Turner, R.K. (1990), *Economics of Natural Resources and the Environment*, New York, Harvester Wheatsheaf.

Pellizzari, F. (1985), *La teoria economica delle risorse naturali*, Milan, Angeli.

Petty, W. (1662), A treatise of taxes and contributions, London, in C.H. Hull (ed.), *The Economic Writings of sir William Petty*, Cambridge, Cambridge University Press, 1899.

Quadrio Curzio, A. (1967), *Rendita e distribuzione in un modello economico plurisettoriale*, Milan, Giuffrè.

Quadrio Curzio, A. (1972), La distribuzione del reddito nella teoria economica: un commento, in S. Lombardini and A. Quadrio Curzio (eds.), *La distribuzione del reddito nella teoria economica*, Milan, Angeli, pp. 13-49.

Quadrio Curzio, A. (1975), *Accumulazione del capitale e rendita*, Bologna, Il Mulino.

Quadrio Curzio, A. (1980), Rent, income distribution and orders of efficiency and rentability, in L. Pasinetti (ed.), *Essay on the Theory of Joint Production*, London, Macmillan, pp. 219-240 (Italian edition, Rendita e distribuzione del reddito, ordine di efficienza e di redditività, in L. Pasinetti (1977) (ed.), *Contributi alla teoria della produzione congiunta*, Bologna, Il Mulino, pp. 301-327).

Quadrio Curzio, A. (1982)· (ed.), *The Gold Problem. Economic Perspectives*, Oxford, Oxford University.

Quadrio Curzio, A. (1982), Materie prime: identità di un problema e finalità di un rapporto, *Materie Prime. Rapporto di analisi economiche*, Bologna, Nomisma, year I, n.1, pp. 13-18.

Quadrio Curzio, A. (1983), Alternative explanations: a comment on Grilli, in J.A. Kregel (ed.), *Distribution, Effective Demand and International Economic Relations*, London, Macmillan, pp. 142-152.

Quadrio Curzio, A. (1985a), Risorse naturali, in *Nuova enciclopedia del diritto e dell'economia*, Milan, Garzanti.

Quadrio Curzio, A. (1985b), Dal rifiuto del numerario aureo ai prezzi quasi ufficiali dell'oro, *Rivista Internazionale di Scienze Economiche e Commerciali*, pp. 965-987.

Quadrio Curzio, A. (1986), Technological scarcity: an essay on production and structural change, in M. Baranzini and R. Scazzieri (eds.), *Foundation of Economics – Structure of Inquiry and Economic Theory*, Oxford, Basic Blackwell, pp. 311-338.

Quadrio Curzio, A. (1987a), Land rent, in J. Eatwell, M. Milgate and P. Newman (eds.), *The New Palgrave: A Dictionary of Economics*, London, Macmillan, vol. III, pp. 118-121.

Quadrio Curzio, A. (1987b), Agrosistema: rinnovabilità dei fattori e qualità dell'ambiente, *Materie prime*, year VI, n. 1, pp. 107-108.

Quadrio Curzio, A. (1988), Le scarsità "relative" nella storia della teoria economica e rilevanza attuale, in C.M. Guerci and G. Zanetti (eds.), *Sviluppo economico e vincolo energetico*, Bologna, Il Mulino, pp. 39-53.

Quadrio Curzio, A. (1989) (ed.), *Oro: storia, protagonisti, problemi*, Istituto per l'Enciclopedia della Banca e della Borsa, Roma, Newton Compton Editori.

Quadrio Curzio, A. (1989), Attualità e continuità dei problemi economici dell'oro, in A. Quadrio Curzio (ed.), *Oro: storia, protagonisti, problemi*, Istituto per l'Enciclopedia della Banca e della Borsa, Newton Compton Editori, pp. 23-60.

Quadrio Curzio, A. (1990), *Rent, Distribution, and Economic Structure: A Collection of Essay*, Quaderni Dynamis, 1/90, Milan, IDSE-CNR.

Quadrio Curzio, A. (1992a), Riflessioni su innovazione, ricerca, risorse, *Innovazione e Materie Prime*, n. 1, pp. 9-14.

Quadrio Curzio, A. (1992b), Risorse naturali, in *Enciclopedia dell'Economia*, Milan, Garzanti.

Quadrio Curzio, A. (1993a), Risorse naturali e scarsità, *Innovazione e Materie Prime*, n. 2-3, pp. 103-115.

Quadrio Curzio, A. (1993b), Innovation, resources and world economy: a survey on twelve years of contributions through two Journals, *Innovazione e Materie Prime*, n. 2-3, pp. 5-20.

Quadrio Curzio, A. (1994), La distribuzione della ricchezza e del reddito, in *Enciclopedia delle Scienze Sociali*, Roma, Istituto della Enciclopedia Italiana Treccani.

Quadrio Curzio, A. (1996a), Oro, in *Enciclopedia delle Scienze Sociali*, Roma, Istituto della Enciclopedia Italiana Treccani.

Quadrio Curzio, A. (1996b), Production and efficiency with global technologies (with an appendix of C.F. Manara and M. Faliva) in M. Landesmann and R. Scazzieri (eds.), *Production and Economic Dynamics*, Cambridge, Cambridge University Press (revised english version of A. Quadrio Curzio, C.F. Manara and M. Faliva, 1987).

Quadrio Curzio, A. (1997), Rendita, in *Enciclopedia delle scienze sociali*, Roma, Istituto della Enciclopedia Italiana Treccani.

Quadrio Curzio, A. (1998), Rent, in H.D. Kurz and N. Salvadori (eds.), *Elgar Companion to Classical Economics (ECCE)*, Cheltenham, Edward Elgar.

Quadrio Curzio, A. and Antonelli, G. (1988), Introduction. The development of an agro-technological system between market pulls and structural pushes, in G. Antonelli and A. Quadrio Curzio (eds.), *The Agro-Technological System Towards 2000*, Amsterdam, North-Holland, pp. 1-16.

Quadrio Curzio, A. and Fortis, M. (1985), Dinamica degli impieghi industriali di materie prime: un'analisi comparata tra sei paesi sviluppati, 1963-1982, in T. Cozzi (ed.) *Moneta ed Economia Internazionale*, Cassa di Risparmio di Torino.

Quadrio Curzio, A. and Fortis, M. (1986), Industrial raw materials: a multy-country, multi-commodity analysis, 1971-1983, *Studies in Banking and Finance*, n. 4, pp. 99-107.

Quadrio Curzio, A. and Pellizzari, F. (1981), La teoria economica delle risorse naturali, *Energia*, n.3, pp. 14-29.

Quadrio Curzio, A. and Pellizzari, F. (1991), Structural rigidities and dynamic choice of technology, *Rivista Internazionale di Scienze Economiche e Commerciali*, year XXXVII, pp. 482-517.

Quadrio Curzio, A. and Pellizzari, F. (1998), Extensive and intensive rent, in H.D. Kurz and N. Salvadori (eds.), *Elgar Companion to Classical Economics (ECCE)*, Cheltenham, Edward Elgar.

Quadrio Curzio, A. and Scazzieri, R. (1983), *Sui momenti costitutivi dell'economia politica*, Bologna, Il Mulino.

Quadrio Curzio, A. and Scazzieri, R. (1986), The exchange production duality and the dynamics of economic knowledge, in M. Baranzini and R. Scazzieri (eds.), *Foundations of Economics – Structure of Inquiry and Economic Theory*, Oxford, Basil Blackwell, pp. 377-407.

Quadrio Curzio, A. and Zoboli, R. (1995a) (eds.), *Scienze, economia e tecnologia per l'ambiente*, Milano, Quaderni della Fondazione Cariplo per la Ricerca Scientifica.

Quadrio Curzio, A. and Zoboli, R. (1995b), *Ambiente e dinamica globale*, Bologna, Il Mulino, Collana della Fondazione Cariplo per la Ricerca Scientifica.

Quadrio Curzio, A., Fortis, M. and Zoboli, R. (1991), Technology and natural resources in the growth of the economies, *Innovazione e Materie Prime*, n. 1, pp. 1-16.

Quadrio Curzio, A., Fortis, M. and Zoboli, R. (1994), *Innovation, Resources and Economic Growth*, Berlin-Heidelberg, Springer-Verlag.

Quadrio Curzio, A, Fortis, M. and Zoboli, R. (1994), Innovation, resources and economic growth: changing interactions in the world economy, in A. Quadrio Curzio, M. Fortis and R. Zoboli (eds.), *Innovation, Resources and Economic Growth*, Berlin-Heidelberg, Springer-Verlag, pp. 3-35.

Quadrio Curzio, A., Manara, C.F. and Faliva, M. (1987), Produzione ed efficienza con tecnologie globali, *Economia Politica*, year IV, pp. 11-47.

Quadrio Curzio, A., Prosperetti, L. and Zoboli, R. (1994a), (eds.) *I rifiuti solidi urbani. Prospettive economiche, tecnologiche e ambientali*, Bologna, Il Mulino, Collana della Fondazione Cariplo per la Ricerca Scientifica.

Quadrio Curzio, A., Prosperetti, L. and Zoboli, R. (1994b), *The Management of Municipal Solid Waste in Europe: Economic, Technological and Environmental Perspectives*, Amsterdam, Elsevier Science Publishers.

Quesnay, F. (1758), *Tableau économique*, Berlin, Akademie-Verlag, 1965.

Ray, G. (1983), Il contributo della scienza e della tecnologia all'offerta di materie prime industriali. Part I and II, *Materie Prime*, n.1, pp. 93-99, n.2, pp. 99-110.

Ricardo, D. (1815), *An Essay on the Influence of a Low Price of the Corn on the Profits of Stock*, in P. Sraffa and M. Dobb (eds.), *The Works and Correspondence of David Ricardo*, Cambridge, Cambridge University Press, 1951, vol. IV.

Ricardo, D. (1817), *On the Principles of Political Economy and Taxation*, in P. Sraffa and M. Dobb (eds.), *The Works and Correspondence of David Ricardo*, Cambridge, Cambridge University Press, 1951, vol. I.

Robinson, J.V. (1956), *The Accumulation of Capital*, London, Macmillan.

Roncaglia, A. (1978), *Sraffa and the Theory of Prices*, New York, John Wiley and Sons.

Rosenberg, N. (1982), *Inside the Block Box, Technology and Economics*, Cambridge, Cambridge University Press.

Rosenberg, N. (1994), *Exploring the Black Box. Technology, Economics and History.* Cambridge, Cambridge University Press.

Rostow, W.W. (1960), *The Stages of Economic Growth*, Cambridge, Cambridge University Press.

Samuelson, P.A. (1987), Sraffian economics, in J. Eatwell, M. Milgate and P. Newman (eds.), *The New Palgrave: A Dictionary of Economics*, London, Macmillan, vol. IV, pp. 452-461.

Schumpeter, J.A. (1912), *The Theory of Economic Development*, Leipzig, Dunker & Humblot.

Schumpeter, J.A. (1954), *History of Economic Analysis*, New York, Oxford University Press.

Sen, A. (1970) (ed.), *Growth Economics*, Middlesex, Penguin Books.

Sensini, G. (1912), *La teoria della rendita*, Roma, Libraria.

Shiklomanov, I.A. (1994), World water resources: assessment and prediction, in A. Quadrio Curzio, M. Fortis and R. Zoboli (eds.), *Innovation Resources and Economic Growth*, Berlin Springer-Verlag, pp. 251-275.

Smith, A. (1776), *An Inquiry into the Nature and Causes of Wealth of Nations*, 2 vol, London, critical edition in R.H. Campbell, A.S. Skinner and W.B. Todd (eds.), *The Glasgow Edition of the Works and Correspondence of Adam Smith*, 2 vols., London, 1976.

Solow, R.M. (1956), A contribution to the theory of economic growth, *Quarterly Journal of Economics*, vol. 70, pp. 65-94.

Sraffa, P. (1960), *Production of Commodities by Means of Commodities – Prelude to a Critique of Economic Theory*, Cambridge, Cambridge University Press.

Stigler, J. (1941), *Production and Distribution Theories*, New York, Macmillan.

Sylos Labini, P. (1992), *Elementi di dinamica economica*, Bari, Laterza.

Torrens, R. (1815), *An Essay on the External Corn Trade*, I edition, London, Longman, Hurst, Rees, Orme & Brown, II edition, 1820.

Usher, A.P. (1982), *A History of Mechanical Inventions*, I edition, 1929, New York, Dover Publications Inc.

Valassina, G. (1976), *La teoria della rendita nella storia del pensiero economico*, Milano, Vita e Pensiero.

Von Neumann, J. (1937), *Uber ein ökonomisches Gleichungs-system und eine Verallgemeinerung der Brouwerschen Fixpunksatzews*, in *Ergebnisse eines mathematischen Kolloquiums*, vol. VIII, Vienna, pp. 73-83 (english edition (1945-46), A model of general economic equilibrium, *Review of Economic Studies*, vol. XIII).

West, E. (1815), *Essay on the Application of Capital to Land, with Observations Showing the Impolicy of Any Great Restriction of the Importation of Corn, and that the Bounty of 1668 did not lower the Price of it* (reprinted in (1903), *A Reprint of Economic Tracts*, Baltimore, John Hopkins Press).

Wicksteed, P.H. (1894), *An Essay on the Co-ordination of the Laws of Distributions*, London, Macmillan.

Wolman, M.G. and Fournier, F.G.A. (1987) (eds.), *Land Transformation in Agriculture*, Chichester, John Wiley and Sons.

World Bank (1992), *World Development Report. Development and the Environment*, New York, Oxford University Press.

World Bank (1995), *World Bank Atlas*, Washington D.C., World Bank.

Zoboli, R. (1994), The economic impact of forest decline in Europe, in A. Quadrio Curzio, M. Fortis and R. Zoboli (eds.), *Innovation Resources and Economic Growth*, Berlin, Springer-Verlag, pp. 221-250.

Druck: Strauss Offsetdruck, Mörlenbach
Verarbeitung: Schäffer, Grünstadt

GPSR Compliance

The European Union's (EU) General Product Safety Regulation (GPSR) is a set of rules that requires consumer products to be safe and our obligations to ensure this.

If you have any concerns about our products, you can contact us on ProductSafety@springernature.com

In case Publisher is established outside the EU, the EU authorized representative is:

Springer Nature Customer Service Center GmbH
Europaplatz 3
69115 Heidelberg, Germany

Batch number: 10704039

Printed by Printforce, the Netherlands